A HANDBOOK FOR THE STUDY OF HUMAN COMMUNICATION:
Methods and Instruments for Observing, Measuring, and Assessing Communication Processes

COMMUNICATION AND INFORMATION SCIENCE

Edited by
BRENDA DERVIN
The Ohio State University

Recent Titles:

Susanna Barber • News Cameras in Courtrooms
Jorg Becker, Goran Hedebro & Leena Paldan • Communication and Domination
Lee Becker, Jeffrey Fruit, & Susan Caudill • The Training and Hiring of Journalist
Herbert Dordick, Helen Bradley, & Burt Nanus • The Emerging Network Marketplace Revised Edition
Sara Douglas • Labor's New Voice: Unions and the Mass Media
William Dutton & Kenneth Kraemer • Modeling as Negotiating
Fred Fejes • Imperialism, Media, and the Good Neighbor
Glen Fisher • American Communication in a Global Society Revised Edition
Howard Frederick • Cuban-American Radio Wars
Gladys Ganley & Oswald Ganley • Global Political Fallout: The VCRs First Decade 1976–1985
Gerald Goldhaber & George Barnett • The Handbook of Organizational Communication
W. J. Howell, Jr. • World Broadcasting in the Age of the Satellite
Heather Hudson • When Telephones Reach the Village
Meheroo Jussawalla, Donald L. Lamberton & Neil D. Karunaratne • Information Economics in the Asian Pacific
James Larson • Television's Window on the World
John Lawrence • The Electronic Scholar
Thomas Lindlof • Natural Audiences
Kenneth Mackenzie • Organizational Design
Armand Mattelart and Hector Schmucler • Communication and Information Technologies
Kaarle Nordenstreng • The Mass Media Declaration of UNESCO
David Paletz • Political Communication Research
Everett Rogers & Francis Balle • The Media Revolution in America and in Western Europe
Jorge Reina Schement & Leah Lievrouw • Competing Visions, Social Realities: Social Aspects of the Information Society
Herbert Schiller • Information and the Crisis Economy
Jorge Schnitman • Film Industries in Latin America
Jennifer Daryl Slack • Communication Technologies and Society
Jennifer Daryl Slack & Fred Fejes • The Ideology of the Information Age
Keith Stamm • Newspaper Use and Community Ties
Charles H. Tardy • A Handbook for the Study of Human Communication
Robert Taylor • Value-Added Processes in Information Systems
Sari Thomas • Studies in Mass Media and Technology, Volumes 1–3
Lea Stewart & Stella Ting-Toomey • Communication, Gender, and Sex Roles in Diverse Interaction Contexts
Tran Van Dinh • Communication and Diplomacy
Tran Van Dinh • Independence, Liberation, Revolution
Barry Truax • Acoustic Communication
Georgette Wang and Wimal Dissanayake • Continuity and Change in Communication Systems
Frank Webster & Kevin Robins • Information Technology: A Luddite Analysis
Carol Weinhaus & Anthony G. Oettinger • Behind the Telephone Debates

A HANDBOOK FOR THE STUDY OF HUMAN COMMUNICATION:
Methods and Instruments for Observing, Measuring, and Assessing Communication Processes

edited by
Charles H. Tardy

Ablex Publishing Corporation
Norwood, N.J. 07648

Printed in the United States of America

Library of Congress Cataloging-in-Publication Data

A Handbook for the study of human communication.
    (Communication and information science)
    Bibliography: p.
    Includes index.
    1. Communication—Methodology. I. Tardy, Charles H.
    II. Title. III. Series.
P91.H36 1987   001.51'01'8   87–14317
ISBN 0-89391-424-X

Ablex Publishing Corporation
355 Chestnut Street
Norwood, New Jersey 07648

Contents

Table of Chapter Appendices

This book is dedicated to teachers, especially mine. They inspire students to ask the interesting questions.

The Authors

Leslie A. Baxter is Associate Professor and Chair of the Department of Communications at Lewis and Clark College, Portland, Oregon, 97219.

James J. Bradac is Professor in the Communication Studies Program at the University of California at Santa Barbara, Santa Barbara, California, 93106.

Brant R. Burleson is Associate Professor in the Department of Communication at Purdue University, West Lafayette, Indiana, 47907.

Noshir Contractor is Assistant Professor in the Department of Speech Communication at the University of Illinois at Urbana-Champaign.

Dennis S. Gouran is Professor and Chair of the Department of Speech Communication at the Pennsylvania State University, University Park, Pennsylvania, 16802.

John O. Greene is Assistant Professor in the Department of Communication at Purdue University, West Lafayette, Indiana, 47907.

Randy Y. Hirokawa is Assistant Professor in the Department of Communication Studies at the University of Iowa, Iowa City, Iowa, 52242.

Mark R. Leary is Assistant Professor in the Department of Psychology at Wake Forest University, Winston-Salem, North Carolina, 27109.

Peter R. Monge is Professor of Communications at the Annenberg School of Communications, University of Southern California, Los Angeles, California, 90089.

Stuart J. Sigman is Assistant Professor in the Department of Communication at the State University of New York at Buffalo, Buffalo, New York, 14260.

Brian H. Spitzberg is Assistant Professor in the Division of Communication and Public Address at North Texas State University, Denton, Texas, 76203–5266.

Richard L. Street, Jr. is Associate Professor in the Department of Speech Communication at Texas Tech University, Lubbock, Texas, 79409.

Sheila J. Sullivan is a doctoral candidate in the Department of Communication at the State University of New York at Buffalo, Buffalo, New York, 14260.

Charles H. Tardy is Associate Professor in the Department of Speech Communication at the University of Southern Mississippi, Hattiesburg, Mississippi, 39406–5131.

Michael A. Waltman is Assistant Professor in the Department of Communication at the University of Tulsa, Tulsa, Oklahoma, 74104.

Marcley Wendell is a doctoral candidate in the Department of Communication at the State University of New York at Buffalo, Buffalo, New York, 14260.

Preface

This book describes the available options and the rationale for selecting among them for observing, measuring, or assessing processes of communication. This approach contrasts radically to that in many preceding volumes which explain the applicability of general types of quantitative research, for example, content analysis, laboratory experiments, and statistical analysis to the study of communication. Our approach focuses on the methodological problems and solutions unique to the study of communication.

We do not, however, intend to provide a "cookbook" for research. Decisions as to which strategies to utilize ultimately rest with the person conducting research. This volume does not attempt to replace the investigator's prerogative with dictum. Rather, it provides the reader with an outline of the problems and/or alternatives that face the researcher.

Though all the chapters share certain common goals, each reflects unique concerns dictated by the state of research in its respective content area. While instruments may be of primary concern in one chapter they may be absent in another. While one chapter makes specific recommendations for a measurement strategy, another concludes that current alternatives are problematic and new ones need to be devised. The authors assess the state of the art on methods utilized in a particular research area and render appropriate conclusions and judgments.

A brief summary of the 15 chapters best illustrates the methodological philosophy of this volume. Burleson and Waltman's (Chapter 1) discussion of cognitive complexity focuses on a single measure: the Role Category Questionnaire. The authors convincingly demonstrate its superiority and provide valuable insight into its use. Greene (Chapter 2) reviews the "possibilities and pratfalls" for studying cognitive processes related to communication. Because his is an infinitely broader topic, the discussion is limited to more general methodological considerations. Readers are directed to other sources for additional information about specific techniques and strategies. In a sense, the chapter functions as a map to direct investigators through a maze of problems associated with the study of cognitive processes. Spitzberg (Chapter 3) undertakes an exhaustive survey of instruments used to assess communication competence. Space limitations prohibit the inclusion of additional information about the more than 100 instruments identified. Monge and Contractor (Chapter 4) describe the types of communication variables used in network studies. Procedures for measuring these variables, as well as methods of acquiring network data, are discussed. The authors also address the important and controversial issue of the validity of self-report network data. Street (Chapter 5) provides a rationale for the behavioral observation of communication style. He reviews problems faced by investigators, makes recommendations for minimizing them, and provides data to illustrate his conclusions. Methods of discourse analysis for the study of conversational structure are reviewed by Sigman, Sullivan, and Wendell (Chapter 6). Data acquisition, transcription procedures, units of analysis, and informant data are among the topics covered. Their chapter provides coherence to a disparate body of literature. Baxter (Chapter 7) examines instruments used in the study of dyadic personal relationships. She identifies a wide range of useful measures for describing and evaluating significant interpersonal relationships. Hirokawa (Chapter 8) examines the use of interaction analysis to study groups and discusses the method's appropriateness as well as specific concerns for undertaking interaction analysis. Many of the ideas about interaction analysis are relevant to its use in contexts other than the small group. Gouran (Chapter 9) reviews measures of group decision-making outcomes and concludes that prior concepts of correctness, quality, utility, and acceptability are deficient. He offers appropriateness as a more useful concept and provides suggestions for its operationalization. In a chapter on interpersonal evaluations, I assess (Chapter 10) scales for the measurement of attraction and trust. Though not the only evaluative aspects of relationships, these two topics are of perennial interest to a wide variety of researchers. I also discuss systems for coding interpersonal interaction (Chapter 11). Unlike the chapter by Hirokawa, the only aspect of interaction analysis considered here is the choice of alternative coding schemes. The discussion will aid researchers in identifying and selecting among procedures developed to categorize observed interaction. Bradac (Chapter 12) discusses methodological problems for the study of language. He addresses accent, rate, intensity, immediacy, powerful and powerless styles, and lexical diversity. I examine (Chapter 13) the procedures used to operationalize self-disclosure. In addition to reviewing instruments designed for various purposes, this chapter discusses the experimental manipulation of self-disclosure. The review of social support measures (Chapter 14) first delineates aspects of the concept. An earlier version of this article appeared in the *American Journal of Community Psychology*. Several important changes were necessitated by the rapid accumulation of research on this topic. Leary (Chapter 15) discusses the measurement of anxiety, as associated with communication in the interpersonal context. He examines scales designed to measure communication apprehension, shyness, and other related concepts.

The research philosophy implicit in these chapters is the book's strength and weakness. The empirical and quantitative orientation of the chapters reflects a useful approach to research. Though qualitative methods of studying communication are extremely important, a single volume cannot provide a comprehensive treatment of all perspectives. Nor is the purpose of this volume to convince others of the utility of this type of research. Rather, we hope to facilitate the conduct of research by scholars with similar interests.

The selection of the communication processes to be included in this book posed problems. The opportunity to select the topics which I thought were most important to the study of interpersonal communication, broadly defined, was challenging and humbling. I endeavored to include discussions of issues which were timeless but not trite; timely but not trendy. The volume should not be historically pedantic, on the one hand, or irrelevant by the time of publication, on the other. Pragmatic considerations also influenced my decisions. The topic selection should appeal to a broad audience. Some topics were not included because they could not be treated adequately in the available space or because of existing comparable discussions. As editor I assume all responsibility for errors of omission and comission.

Many people helped make this volume possible. I thank the contributing authors for sharing my vision and committing their time and energy to seeing it materialize. Melvin Voigt and Ablex Publishers have been patient and supportive. I am especially grateful to the authors and publishers who allowed us to reprint their instruments. The University of Southern Mississippi assisted my work by providing a summer research grant, teaching load reductions, and allowing a one-semester sabbatical. Richard L. Conville provided encouragement at the right times. Lawrence A. Hosman's comments were always useful. A special thanks goes to my wife Chris for her endearing support.

Charles H. Tardy

CHAPTER 1

Cognitive Complexity: Using The Role Category Questionnaire Measure

Brant R. Burleson and Michael S. Waltman

Research concerned with stable individual differences in social-cognitive ability has often utilized the concept of *cognitive complexity*. In general, the term indexes the degree of differentiation, articulation, and integration within a cognitive system. That is, a cognitive system composed of a comparatively large number of finely articulated, well integrated elements is regarded as relatively complex. Although most discussions of cognitive complexity make some reference to the notions of differentiation, abstractness, articulation, and integration, several quite distinct conceptualizations and operationalizations of the cognitive complexity construct have appeared in the literature (see the reviews by Goldstein & Blackman, 1978; Miller & Wilson, 1979; D. O'Keefe & Sypher, 1981; Streufert & Streufert, 1978). Moreover, different measures of cognitive complexity have often been found either uncorrelated or only weakly correlated—findings indicating that the various measures of cognitive complexity are not all assessing the same thing (e.g., see D. O'Keefe & Sypher, 1981, pp. 75–76).

This chapter focuses on only one approach to the study of cognitive complexity, an approach introduced by Walter H. Crockett (1965). There are two reasons for this limited focus. First, virtually all cognitive complexity research appearing in the human communication literature has made use of Crockett's conceptualization and operationalization of this variable. This research has stemmed largely from the theoretical perspective of *constructivism* (see Delia, O'Keefe, & O'Keefe 1982)—a perspective which has subsumed Crockett's analysis of cognitive complexity within more general analyses of social cognition and sophisticated interpersonal functioning. Second, a recent

1

review (D. O'Keefe & Sypher, 1981) comparing a number of different cognitive complexity measures along several criteria concluded that only Crockett's approach to the assessment of cognitive complexity satisfied "all the criteria for an adequate complexity measure" (p. 85). In other words, of the most commonly employed measures of cognitive complexity, Crockett's measure appears to be the most reliable and the most valid.

Theoretical Foundations of the Cognitive Complexity Construct

This section presents a brief overview of the theoretical framework underlying the constructivist approach to the measurement of cognitive complexity.[1] More detailed presentations are available in several sources (e.g., Crockett, 1965; Delia, 1976; Delia et al., 1982; B. O'Keefe & Delia, 1982).

Crockett's (1965) original analysis of cognitive complexity is based on a fusion of the personal construct psychology of Kelly (1955) and the structural-development theory of Werner (1957). From Kelly, Crockett drew the basic unit of cognitive structure: the personal construct. Kelly assumed that features of the world are never apprehended directly, but rather are always apprehended through the mediation of the psychological structures termed "personal constructs." Personal constructs are "transparent templates" or bipolar dimensions which a person "creates and then attempts to fit over the realities of which the world is composed" (Kelly, 1955, p. 9). As such, personal constructs constitute the basic cognitive structures through which persons interpret, anticipate, evaluate, and understand aspects of the world.

Kelly (1955) argued that each construct has a specific focus and range of convenience. That is, for each construct, some events fall within the specific focus of the construct, other events fall outside this focus but are still capable of being understood through the mediation of the construct, while still other events fall outside the range of the construct and thus are irrelevant to it. In addition, Kelly maintained that constructs having a similar range of convenience (i.e., applying to roughly the same domain of phenomena) are organized

---

[1] The theoretical analysis of cognitive complexity presented here is based on the "original" analysis of this construct detailed in such sources as Crockett (1965) and Delia (1976). More recent theoretical analyses of the cognitive complexity construct are discussed briefly in the concluding section of this chapter and in detail by B. O'Keefe (1984) and B. O'Keefe and Delia (1982).

within specific subsystems. Constructs are organized hierarachically, such that some elements in the subsystem subsume or imply other elements. Thus, for example, constructs whose range and/or focus of convenience include the thoughts, behaviors, characteristics, and qualities of other people form a subsystem of *interpersonal constructs.*

Werner's structural-developmental theory provided Crockett a way of dealing with systematic differences in the structure of individuals' personal constructs. According to Werner, all things said to "develop" do so in accord with the *Orthogenetic Principle:* "Wherever development occurs, it proceeds from a state of relative globality and lack of differentiation to states of increasing differentiation, articulation, and hierarchic integration" (Werner, 1957, p. 126). Applied to personal constructs, Werner's Orthogenetic Principle suggests that over the course of childhood and adolescence, persons will develop more dif-ferentiated (i.e., numerically larger) construct systems, more articu-lated systems (i.e., systems composed of more refined and abstract elements), and more integrated (i.e., organized) systems. This general prediction has been supported by substantial empirical research: nu-merous studies have found that children's construct systems become increasingly differentiated, increasingly abstract, and increasingly or-ganized (Burleson, 1984a; Delia, Kline, & Burleson, 1979; Scarlett, Press, & Crockett, 1971).

For both Kelly and Werner, development is seen to occur in specific domains of activity and involvement. The degree of elaboration within any subsystem of constructs is a function of a person's experience, involvement, and activity with the domain of events for which a particular subsystem of constructs is developed. Thus, it is quite possible for an individual to possess a highly developed subsystem of *interpersonal* constructs while simultaneously possessing relatively un-developed subsystems of constructs for other phenomenal domains (e.g., furniture, automobiles). Consistent with Werner's conception of development, a highly developed system of interpersonal constructs contains (a) a relatively large number of elements (i.e., high differ-entiation), (b) elements that focus on the psychological, motivational, and dispositional qualities of others rather than the physical appear-ance, specific behaviors, and demographic characteristics of others (i.e., abstract rather than concrete elements), and (c) elements exhib-iting relatively extensive organizational bonds with other elements (i.e., integrated elements).

Because development is viewed as proceeding in specific domains of activity and involvement, the constructivist perspective provides a way of addressing systematic individual differences in the structure of the interpersonal construct system. That is, any particular group of individuals (either adults or children of the same age) is likely to contain both some persons with relatively differentiated, abstract, and organized systems of interpersonal constructs and some persons with relatively sparse, concrete, and unorganized systems of interpersonal constructs. The available evidence indicates that relatively stable individual differences in interpersonal construct system development are present in groups of both children (e.g., Delia, Burleson, & Kline, 1979) and adults (e.g., Crockett, 1965; D. O'Keefe, Shepherd, & Streeter, 1982).

From the constructivist point of view (e.g., Crockett, 1965; Delia, 1976), developmentally advanced systems of constructs can be characterized as relatively *complex*. That is, persons with relatively differentiated, abstract, and organized systems of constructs in a particular domain are considered cognitively complex in that domain. Thus, for example, someone with a relatively differentiated, abstract, and organized system of interpersonal constructs would be regarded as having a relatively high level of *interpersonal cognitive complexity*.

As noted above, constructivism views the personal construct as the basic element or scheme underlying the operation of all cognitive processes; thus, interpersonal constructs are viewed as the basic cognitive structures underlying all social perception processes (typical social perception processes include such mental activities as making causal attributions, inferring dispositional qualities from behavior, identifying affective states, forming overall impressions of others, organizing and integrating information about others, evaluating aspects of others' conduct and traits, inferring the perspective or taking the role of others, etc.). Because all social perception processes are viewed as occurring through the application of interpersonal constructs, persons with more complex systems of interpersonal constructs (i.e., higher levels of interpersonal cognitively complexity) should exhibit more advanced social perception skills than persons with less complex interpersonal construct systems. That is, persons with relatively complex systems of interpersonal constructs should be better able than their less complex counterparts to form more organized and integrated impressions of others, recognize relevant dispositional and affective features of others, integrate potentially inconsistent information about others, represent and understand the cognitive, affective, and motivational features of others' perspectives, and so forth. Moreover, because many of these social perception processes play important roles in a variety of communication processes (e.g., message production, message interpretation, structuring conversational interactions), individuals with relatively high levels of interpersonal cognitive complexity should exhibit more sophisticated communicative functioning than less complex individuals. In short, the constructivist perspective maintains that interpersonal cognitive complexity is an important determinant of both advanced social-cognitive functioning and advanced communicative functioning.

Assessing Cognitive Complexity Through the RCQ

Crockett's (1965) analysis led him to formulate the Role Category Questionnaire (RCQ) as a tool through which interpersonal cognitive complexity could be assessed. All forms of the RCQ require subjects to describe several persons, typically peers, known to them. These interpersonal impressions can then be scored for several different features, including degree of differentiation, the abstractness of the constructs appearing in the impression, and the degree of impression organization.

Eliciting Interpersonal Impressions

The RCQ is a "free-response" task. Subjects are simply told to describe a set of peers, and few constraints are put on these descriptions.

  Current standard procedures for eliciting interpersonal impressions. Considerable research experience with the RCQ has indicated that reliable estimates of construct system properties can be obtained from as few as two interpersonal impressions. Consequently, current standard procedures for the RCQ include having subjects describe, in writing, two persons well known to them: a liked peer and a disliked peer. Each peer is described for approximately five minutes. The two-role version of the RCQ is administered through a three-page questionnaire (see Appendix 1). Total time for administration of the two-role version of the RCQ is approximately 15 minutes.

  Common variations in the structure and administration of the RCQ. Characteristics of the subject sample, theoretical concerns, or logistical matters may require departures from the standard procedures. A common variation on standard RCQ procedures for eliciting interpersonal impressions is the oral administration of the RCQ. In such cases, subjects are orally told the purpose of the task, asked to name or give some identifying symbol for the figures to be described, and then to describe each figure orally. Prompts (e.g., "Is there anything else you can tell me about the kind of person Mary is?") are frequently employed to ensure the maximum description is elicited of each figure. The oral impressions produced by subjects are typically tape recorded and these recordings are then transcribed and coded. The oral elic-

itation of interpersonal impressions is considerably more labor intensive than is the written procedure; Subjects must be processed individually rather than in groups and transcripts must be prepared before
coding can begin. In spite of the extra work, however, the orally
administered RCQ is clearly the method of choice when working with
certain populations (e.g., young children, persons unfamiliar with
writing tasks, persons with developmental or physical disabilities).
Orally administered versions of the RCQ have been successfully employed with both children (e.g., Burleson, 1984a; Delia, Kline, &
Burleson, 1979) and adults (e.g., Applegate, Burke, Burleson, Delia,
& Kline, 1985), and should be used when it is suspected that task-
demands of the written RCQ would attenuate the quality or length
of subjects' interpersonal impressions.

A second variation is to have more than two figures described
when it is believed that greater "test length" will result in more
reliable measurements of construct system properties (e.g., Burleson,
1984a).

A final variation is not to enforce the precise amount of time
subjects are given to write their descriptions of each figure. Subjects
are normally instructed to "spend only about five minutes" describing
each figure (see Appendix 1). D. O'Keefe et al. (1982) had subjects
complete both strictly timed and untimed versions of the RCQ. They
found that although subjects produced more differentiated impressions
(i.e., impressions containing a larger number of interpersonal constructs) in the untimed condition, there was a high correlation between
the number of constructs produced in the two conditions ($r = .84$).
Since the absolute, as opposed to relative, number of constructs
appearing in impressions is rarely of concern, their results suggest
that there is little practical difference in the timed and untimed
versions of the RCQ.

For the sake of consistency, researchers should probably employ
the standard version of the RCQ whenever practical. However, minor
variations in administration procedures appear not to affect the results
typically obtained. Moreover, some variations in the standard procedures may be mandated by characteristics of the subject sample
(e.g., the use of oral procedures when working with young children).

Coding Interpersonal Impressions

The descriptions or impressions of persons known to the subject in
RCQs must be analyzed and coded to yield measures of construct
system properties.

Differentiation coding. Regardless of the specific aspect of construct system development ultimately scored, coding work must begin with the identification of the individual constructs contained in subjects' interpersonal impressions. In coding impressions, interpersonal constructs are operationally defined as any characteristic, quality, trait, motivation, belief, habit, mannerism, or behavior attributed by the subject to the described person. Crockett, Press, Delia, and Kenney (1974) detail specific procedures and rules to be followed in identifying and counting the constructs in an impression (see Appendix 2).

As Crockett et al. (1974, p. 2) note, differentiation refers to "the number of parts of the whole." Thus, when only the number of constructs contained in the elicited impressions is coded, the resulting score is most properly regarded as an index of *interpersonal construct differentiation*. In scoring impressions for degree of differentiation, constructs pertaining to others' physical characteristics, appearance, demographic characteristics, and social roles are not usually scored (see Rule 5 in Appendix 2). Under some circumstances, however, such constructs may be included in differentiation codings. For example, the interpersonal impressions of children and some adolescents are often dominated by constructs pertaining to the appearance, roles, and specific behavior of others. Because children typically construe others along such dimensions, it would be inappropriate (and invalid) to exclude such constructs from differentiation codings.

Although procedures are also available for coding the abstractness and organization of interpersonal constructs (see below), differentiation scores frequently have been found moderately to highly associated with abstractness and organization scores derived from the RCQ (see the review by D. O'Keefe & Sypher, 1981). Consequently, the differentiation score obtained from the RCQ has been regarded as a good, overall index of interpersonal cognitive complexity. It has also been found, however, that construct abstractness or organization is a theoretically more appropriate index of construct system development than differentiation under some circumstances (e.g., Delia et al., 1979; B. O'Keefe & Delia, 1979). Thus, the specific measure of construct system development used in a particular study has (and should be) a function of the particular issues addressed by that study.

The RCQ is assumed to sample, rather than exhaustively tap, the interpersonal construct system. Thus, the constructs elicited by the RCQ are assumed to constitute a representative sample of the total number of interpersonal constructs an individual has available.[2] It has

---

[2] The notion that the RCQ obtains representative samples of persons' interpersonal constructs has been subject to considerable criticism recently; see the concluding section of this chapter for versions of these critiques.

further been assumed that individuals with a larger number of interpersonal constructs available will express a greater number of constructs when responding to the RCQ; this latter assumption, is, of course, consistent with the notion that cognitively complex individuals have more differentiated systems of interpersonal constructs than relatively noncomplex individuals.

Abstractness coding. Several similar systems have been developed for coding the *abstractness* of interpersonal constructs, the extent to which constructs pertain to such psychological characteristics as traits, motives, and dispositions. Typically, each construct identified in differentiation codings has been scored within a hierarchically ordered set of categories for its degree of abstractness. For example, Delia, Clark, and Switzer (1974) scored constructs elicited by the RCQ within one of five hierarchically ordered categories: (a) physical descriptions, (b) role constructs, including name, age, and sex, (c) descriptions of the other's general behaviors or specific actions, (d) reports of specific or general beliefs and attitudes, and (e) abstract dispositional and personality constructs (see also Applegate, 1980a; Burleson, 1984a). The general principle underlying this and related hierarchies for scoring abstractness is that understanding others in relatively abstract terms represents a more advanced mode of psychological functioning; abstract construals of others provide a better basis for understanding and anticipating the actions of others than do concrete construals. This assumption is supported by the well-documented developmental shift from reliance on relatively concrete constructs to relatively abstract constructs (e.g., Barenboim, 1981; Scarlett et al., 1971).

Since the coding systems discussed above pertain to the scoring of individual constructs for degree of abstractness, some algorithm must be employed to represent the abstractness of the construct system as a whole. Several different algorithms have been employed, including the frequency of abstract constructs, the proportion of abstract constructs, a total abstractness score, and a mean construct abstractness score. Use of the frequency and proportional algorithms requires dichotomizing constructs into either "concrete" or "abstract" elements; although somewhat crude, such indices may prove useful, especially when large differences in abstractness can be anticipated (as in developmental research; see Delia, Kline, & Burleson, 1979). The total abstractness score (formed simply by summing the abstractness scores awarded each separate construct) is problematic in that it tends to confound the dimension of abstractness with the dimension of differentiation. Preferable to the total abstractness score is the *mean* construct abstractness score (formed by dividing the total abstractness score by the differentiation score). The mean construct

abstractness index has the advantage of being conceptually independent (though not statistically independent) of construct differentiation or "cognitive complexity" scores.

Organization coding. Organization or integration pertains to the
extent to which constructs are systematically related to one another.
Two systems have been developed for coding construct system organization, each system scoring impressions for the extent to which variability in the behaviors and/or actions of others is represented and
reconciled through the use of superordinate constructs. Due to their
complexity and relatively infrequent use, the systems for coding construct system organization are not discussed here; however, Crockett
et al. (1974) provide detailed discussions of the nature and use of
these systems.

Training Coders and Assessing Intercoder Reliability

Reasonably bright persons can be trained to reliably code RCQ impressions for differentiation and abstractness in a relatively short period
of time. Coding impressions for differentiation is easiest, and novices
can be trained, usually in less than two hours. Training novices to
code for abstractness will generally require an additional two hours.
Coding impressions for degree of organization is much more difficult
and may require 10 to 12 hours.

In training novices to code impressions for differentiation, a six-
step process has proved useful. First, the novice is told to read through
approximately five sets of RCQ impressions to give him or her a
"feel" for the data. Next, the novice is introduced to relevant parts
of the Crockett et al. (1974) coding manual, told to read these portions
of the manual carefully, and ask questions. Third, the trainer (an
experienced coder) models the coding of several impressions, illustrating and exemplifying the coding rules discussed in the coding
manual—an especially effective training technique. Fourth, the trainer
and novice should jointly work through a sample of 20 to 30 sets of
impressions, discussing problems, the application of coding rules, and
difficult cases. Fifth, the novice should engage in a "coding rehearsal,"
scoring about 20 sets of impressions. These codings should then be
reviewed by the trainer with feedback to the novice about any adjustments required. The novice should then be ready to code impressions for differentiation independently, followed by a formal assessment of interrater reliability employing at least 25 sets of impressions
(or 20% of the total number of impressions). The steps can then be
repeated to train the novice in coding for abstractness.

With this training procedure, very high levels of interrater reliability can be obtained. Reliabilities exceeding .90 for both differentiation and abstractness codings are common, and those below .85 are relatively rare. Researchers outside of the constructivist framework and not trained by "expert" coders have also obtained high interrater reliabilities; for example, Beatty and Payne (1985) report interrater reliabilities of .88, .86, and .87 for differentiation codings. The relatively high interrater reliabilities obtained by researchers such as Beatty and Payne suggest that training in coding procedures by an "expert" is not needed to attain acceptable levels of coding reliability; apparently, Crockett et al.'s (1974) coding manual provides sufficient information to ensure reliable coding.

Reliability and Validity of RCQ Assessments of Cognitive Complexity

In their review comparing the validity of different cognitive complexity measures, D. O'Keefe and Sypher (1981) identified five criteria along which measures of complexity could be evaluated. First, a complexity measure should yield a temporally stable assessment of cognitive complexity in adult populations; that is, a complexity measure should exhibit an acceptable level of test-retest reliability. Second, a measure of cognitive complexity should be positively associated with chronological age across childhood and adolescence. Third, a measure of cognitive complexity should be positively associated with other indices of social-cognitive ability. Fourth, since cognitive complexity is presumed to underlie advanced communicative functioning, a measure of complexity should be positively associated with theoretically relevant communicative behaviors. Fifth, since cognitive complexity is conceived as conceptually distinct from general intellectual and verbal factors (e.g., verbal intelligence, fluency, IQ), measures of complexity should exhibit independence from such variables. In addition, since cognitive complexity is viewed as conceptually distinct from standard personality dispositions and traits (e.g., control orientations, emotional empathy), measures of complexity should exhibit independence from assessments of these traits. It should be noted that the criteria articulated by D. O'Keefe and Sypher reflect the traditional concerns of reliability, convergent validity, and discriminant validity.

Reliability

The dimensions of construct system structure discussed in this chapter (i.e., differentiation, abstractness, and organization) presumably constitute stable, individual-difference variables. Thus, measurements of construct system structure obtained through the RCQ should exhibit acceptable levels of test-retest reliability in adult populations. Crockett (1965), utilizing the original eight-role version of the RCQ, reported a four-month test-retest reliability of .95 for differentiation scorings. D. O'Keefe et al. (1982) reported test-retest reliabilities of .84 and .86 for differentiation scores over a four-week period based on two different versions of the standard, two-role RCQ. Thus, it appears that measures of construct system differentiation derived from the RCQ exhibit adequate temporal stability. No evidence has been published pertaining to the test-retest reliability of construct system abstractness and organization scores derived from the RCQ; however, since differentiation, abstractness, and organization scores from the RCQ are normally moderately to highly intercorrelated (see D. O' Keefe & Sypher, 1981), it is likely that assessments of abstractness and organization obtained from the RCQ also exhibit acceptable levels of temporal stability.

Since the most commonly employed version of the RCQ has subjects describe only two figures (a liked peer and a disliked peer), the RCQ is not a true "multi-item" test. Nonetheless, there is some evidence that the two descriptions of peers elicited by the RCQ provide an internally consistent measure of construct differentiation. Published correlations between the number of interpersonal constructs contained in subjects' impressions of liked and disliked peers have included .43 (Burleson, Applegate, & Neuwirth, 1981), .64 (Beatty & Payne, 1985), and .67 (Beatty & Payne, 1984); these correlations translate to internal consistency coefficients (i.e., Cronbach's *alphas*) of .60, .78, and .80. In an unpublished study, Delia, Kline, Burleson, Clark, Applegate, and Burke (1980) administered a four-role version of the RCQ. Internal consistencies (*alpha* coefficients) for these "four-item" measures were .84 for differentiation, .78 for abstractness, and .67 for organization.

As D. O'Keefe and Sypher (1981, p. 77) indicate, since cognitive complexity is viewed as an individual-difference variable, "variability in scores on the instrument should be largely attributable to respondents (i.e., the individuals whose 'individual differences' are putatively being assessed) rather than to, e.g., variations in test forms or conditions." The one study focusing on this issue (Horsfall, 1969) found that most of the variance in the RCQ measure of differentiation was, in fact, attributable to respondents, whereas most of the variance in another popular measure of cognitive complexity (Tripodi & Bieri, 1963) was attributable to the valence of the role figures being rated.

Thus, it appears that the RCQ constitutes a true, individual-difference measure.

Association with Chronological Age

Since the constructivist analysis of cognitive complexity is grounded in Werner's (1957) structural-developmental theory, it is anticipated that, with development, systems of interpersonal constructs will become progressively more differentiated, abstract, and organized. Methodologically, this means that valid measures of construct system properties should be positively associated with chronological age across the span of childhood and adolescence. Numerous cross-sectional and longitudinal studies undertaken by constructivist researchers (e.g., Burleson, 1984a; Clark & Delia, 1977; Delia, Burleson, & Kline, 1979; Delia, Kline, & Burleson, 1979; Scarlett et al., 1971) have found that measures of construct system differentiation, abstractness, and/or organization obtained from the RCQ are positively associated with chronological age. Significantly, these findings have been widely replicated by other researchers (e.g., Barenboim, 1977, 1981; Barratt, 1977; Bigner, 1974; Biskin & Crano, 1977; Livesley & Bromley, 1973; Peevers & Secord, 1973; Wegner, 1977) who have employed methods similar to the RCQ to elicit interpersonal impressions from children and adolescents. However, it is important to note that not all measures of cognitive complexity reliably exhibit the expected association with age; for example, several researchers (e.g., Barenboim, 1977; Barratt, 1977; see the review by D. O'Keefe & Sypher, 1981) have found Bieri's "grid" measure of cognitive complexity (Tripodi & Bieri, 1963) unassociated with chronological age during childhood and adolescence. Indeed, only measures of cognitive complexity based on Crockett's RCQ appear reliably associated with age across the span of childhood and adolescence.

Association with Social Perception Skills and Social-Cognitive Abilities

Within the constructivist framework, interpersonal constructs are viewed as the basic cognitive structures underlying a wide array of social perception processes. Since all social perception processes are viewed as occurring through the application of interpersonal constructs, persons with more developed systems of constructs (i.e., more differentiated, abstract, and organized systems of constructs) should exhibit more advanced social perception skills and social-cognitive processes, such as impression organization, information integration, social evaluation, and social perspective taking.

Impression organization. The nature of others is not immediately given in behavior; consequently, in forming impressions of others, perceivers must make inferences about the characteristics and qualities of others from observed behavior, infer other qualities from behaviorally-based inferences, and organize these inferences into a relatively complete and satisfying "picture" of the other. Highly organized impressions of others provide perceivers with a more comprehensive, flexible, and stable understanding of others. In contrast, poorly organized impressions provide a less complete account of the other's characteristics, are more labile, and are less stable. Several studies have found that interpersonal construct differentiation, as assessed by the RCQ, is positively associated with the degree of organization exhibited in naturally formed impressions (e.g., Delia, Clark, & Switzer, 1974; Delia & Murphy, 1983; B. O'Keefe, 1984). Moreover, some research (e.g., Delia et al., 1974) indicates that RCQ-assessed construct differentiation is associated with the formation of more dispositionally and motivationally-oriented impressions—qualities that presumably aid the perceiver in anticipating and understanding the other's behavior across an array of situations. Thus, measures of cognitive complexity based on the RCQ are good predictors of the level of organization attained in naturally formed impressions.

Information integration. Considerable research also indicates that construct differentiation, as assessed by the RCQ, is a good predictor of the ability to recognize, reconcile, and integrate potentially inconsistent information about others. Regardless of the mode in which inconsistent information has been presented to subjects, persons with highly differentiated systems of interpersonal constructs (as assessed by the RCQ) have been found better able than their less differentiated counterparts to reconcile and integrate information about others (e.g., Crockett, Gonyea, & Delia, 1970; Delia, 1972; Delia, Gonyea, & Crockett, 1971; Mayo & Crockett, 1964; Meltzer, Crockett, & Rosenkrantz, 1966; Nidorf & Crockett, 1965; B. O'Keefe, Delia, & O'Keefe, 1977; Rosenbach, Crockett, & Wapner, 1973; Rosenkrantz & Crockett, 1965). Several factors have been found to attenuate the ability of cognitively complex individuals to integrate inconsistent information (e.g., emotional involvement, instructional sets, perceived similarity to the target); in particular, the induction of an *evaluative* set on the part of perceivers has been found to attenuate the effects of cognitive complexity with respect to information integration (e.g., see Crockett, Mahood, & Press, 1975; Press, Crockett & Delia, 1975).

Social evaluation and reliance on evaluative consistency principles. As noted, the experimental induction of an evaluative set has been found to reduce the extent to which high complexity perceivers integrate inconsistent information about others. This finding suggests that, under most normal conditions, cognitively complex perceivers are less reliant on evaluative consistency principles in processing information and less dominated by global evaluations in making judgments and reaching decisions. More specifically, D. O'Keefe (1980) has suggested that global evaluation (e.g., like/dislike, good/bad) constitutes *one* dimension of judgment all perceivers have available for cognizing features of the world or constructing plans of action, but that because cognitively complex perceivers have many more dimensions of judgment available to them than less complex perceivers, they should be less reliant on and dominated by the dimension of evaluation. Several studies (Delia & Crockett, 1973; Delia, Crockett, & Gonyea, 1970; Press, Crockett, & Rosenkrantz, 1969) have found that cognitively complex persons (as determined by the RCQ) exhibit less reliance on evaluatively-based schemes (i.e., balance schemes) in learning patterns of social relationships than noncomplex persons. In a somewhat related vein, D. O'Keefe and Brady (1980) found that cognitively complex perceivers were less likely than noncomplex perceivers to exhibit attitude polarization after brief periods of thought.

RCQ assessments of interpersonal cognitive complexity have also been found related to the strength of the attitude-behavior relationship. D. O'Keefe and Delia (1981) reasoned that because cognitively complex persons should be less dominated by global evaluation in making decisions, high complexity individuals should exhibit less attitude-behavior consistency than low complexity persons. As expected, these researchers found that individuals with highly differentiated systems of interpersonal constructs displayed less consistency in their attitudes and behavioral intentions than did persons with less differentiated construct systems; somewhat similar findings have been reported in two other investigations (Delancey & Swanson, 1981; D. O'Keefe & Shepherd, 1982). Recently, however Babrow and O'Keefe (1984) found that RCQ-assessed complexity in a noninterpersonal domain (college classes) had no effect on the strength of the attitude-behavior relation in that domain. Thus, it is possible that cognitive complexity may have a moderating effect on the attitude-behavior relationship only in the interpersonal domain. In any event, existing research clearly indicates that assessments of interpersonal cognitive complexity obtained through the RCQ are appropriately related to less reliance on global evaluation and evaluative consistency principles.

Social perspective-taking ability. Role-taking or social perspective-taking ability, the capacity to infer and represent the cognitions and feelings of another, has frequently been regarded as a major social-cognitive ability underlying competent and effective communication (Mead, 1934; Piaget, 1926; see the review by Burleson, 1984b). Individual differences in interpersonal construct system development, as assessed by the RCQ, have been found associated with perspective-taking ability in samples of both adults and children. For example, several studies (e.g., Beatty & Payne, 1984; Hale & Delia, 1976; Losee, 1976; Sarver, 1976) have found construct system differentiation scores derived from RCQ positively associated with adults' performance on Hale and Delia's (1976) Social Perspectives Task (SPT). Construct differentiation, however, was found by H. Sypher and O'Keefe (1980) to be only marginally associated with adults' performance on a perspective-taking measure developed by Pelias (1984). Children's performances on the SPT and Rothenberg's (1970) affective role-taking measure have also been found positively associated with both construct system differentiation and abstractness even when controling for the potentially confounding effect of age (Burleson, 1982a; Clark & Delia, 1977; Sarver, 1976). Quite clearly, individual differences in construct system development, as assessed by the RCQ, are related to varied measures of perspective-taking ability.

Association with Advanced Communicative Functioning

A central area of inquiry for constructivist researchers has focused on the contributions of the interpersonal construct system to sophisticated modes of communicative functioning (see the reviews by Burleson, in press; Clark & Delia, 1979; Delia & O'Keefe, 1979; Delia et al., 1982; B. O'Keefe & Delia, 1982; D. O'Keefe & Sypher, 1981). The present section considers relationships between RCQ-based measures of cognitive complexity and five communication variables: (a) message production, (b) communicative effectiveness, (c) message interpretation, (d) the structuring of interactions, and (e) the content of interactions.

Message production. Perhaps the largest single body of constructivist research has focused on the relationship between developed systems of interpersonal constructs and the production of *person-centered* messages. Briefly, person-centered messages are those which reflect awareness of and adaptation to the subjective, affective, and relational aspects of communicative contexts. Perhaps the most distinctive feature of constructivist studies of message production is the use of hierarchically-ordered coding systems to score the person-centeredness of messages (see Clark & Delia, 1979; also: Applegate, 1980a, 1982a; Applegate, et al., 1985; Burke & Clark, 1982; Burleson, 1980, 1982b; Clark &

Delia, 1976; Kline & Ceropski, 1984; B. O'Keefe & Delia, 1979; Rowan, 1985; Samter & Ely, 1985).

A large number of studies have found measures of construct system differentiation and/or abstractness positively associated with varied indices of person-centered message production (e.g., Applegate, 1980b, 1982b; Burleson, 1983, 1984a; Clark & Delia, 1977; Delia & Clark, 1977; Delia, Kline, & Burleson, 1979; Hale, 1980, 1982; B. O'Keefe & Delia, 1979; Rowan, 1985; Samter & Burleson, 1984; Shepherd & O'Keefe, 1984a; H. Sypher, Witt, & Sypher, 1986). Although not all studies have found the expected relationship between measures of person-centered message production and RCQ-based indices of construct system development (e.g., Losee, 1976; Ritter, 1979), the great majority of studies have found the anticipated relationship. Indeed, the consistency and generality of the relationship between construct system development and person-centered communication is quite impressive, having been found to hold across: (a) diverse subject populations (children, adolescents, college students, mothers of young children, teachers, daycare workers, nurses, medical students, residence hall counselors, and police officers), (b) different instrumental goals pursued by speakers (persuading, comforting, regulating or disciplining, informing, and managing conflicts), (c) different subsidiary objectives pursued by speakers (identity management, face protection, relationship enhancement), (d) different measures of construct system development (differentiation, abstractness), (e) different aspects of communicative behavior (quality of messages, quality of message rationales, number of messages, variety of messages), (f) differences in the media or modality used to assess both construct system development and communicative behavior (oral modality, written modality), (g) different means used to elicit communicative behavior (hypothetical situations, experimentally structured situations, real world situations), and (h) the statistical control of numerous potentially confounding factors (age, sex, social class, verbal and intellectual abilities, personality and motivational orientations). (For detailed reviews, see Burleson, in press; D. O'Keefe & Sypher, 1981.)

Communication effectiveness. Several studies indicate that the messages typically employed by persons scoring highly on the RCQ are more effective at attaining their intended instrumental goal and produce more desirable short- and long-term outcomes (Burleson, 1985, 1986; Burleson & Fennelly, 1981; Burleson & Samter, 1985a,b; Burleson & Waltman, 1986; Samter, Burleson, & Basden, 1986a,b; Shepherd & O'Keefe, 1984b, 1985). Other research indicates that there are connections of a more direct nature between interpersonal construct system development and communication effectiveness. For example,

Burleson and Waltman (1986) found that children with highly differentiated construct systems (as assessed by the RCQ) were perceived by both peers and teachers as providing social support more often to other children experiencing problems. Research conducted in organizational contexts indicates that successful performance in the organization (as assessed by indices such as promotions, job level, and supervisor evaluations) is positively associated with RCQ-assessments of cognitive complexity (Husband, 1981; B. Sypher, Sypher, & Leichty, 1983; B. Sypher & Zorn, 1986).

Message interpretation, structuring interactions, and the content of interactions. Concern with the effects of cognitive complexity on message interpretation, the structuring of interactions, and the content of interactions has emerged only quite recently; consequently, comparatively little research has been conducted on these topics. However, the available evidence pertaining to these topics provides additional support for the validity of RCQ assessments of cognitive complexity.

With respect to message interpretation, Samter et al. (1986b) found that high-complexity perceivers formed more differentiated impressions of a message source when that source employed relatively sophisticated comforting messages, whereas the impressions of the message source formed by low-complexity perceivers did not vary as a function of message sophistication; these results were interpreted as indicating that high-complexity perceivers better recognize and appreciate sophisticated forms of communicative behavior than do low-complexity perceivers. Somewhat similar results are reported by Burleson and Samter (in press) and Shepherd and O'Keefe (1984a).

A few studies have begun to examine the effects of cognitive complexity on structuring of conversational interactions. For example, Ellis, Hamilton, and Aho (1983) found a marginally significant effect for construct system differentiation on the ability to reconstruct the opening sequence of a scrambled conversation. Samter and Burleson's (1984) results suggest that cognitively complex persons are more likely than their noncomplex counterparts to define and structure interactions spontaneously so as to accommodate the needs and interests of others. Daly, Bell, Glenn, and Lawrence (1985) found the RCQ measure of interpersonal cognitive complexity significantly associated with the use of verbal back channels during an intial "get acquainted" conversation; verbal back channels have often been conceptualized as devices for controlling the conversational floor (see Duncan & Fiske, 1977). Daly et al. also found the RCQ measure of interpersonal cognitive complexity positively associated with a measure tapping the complexity of representations of conversations.

Finally, the results of studies examining the effect of cognitive complexity on the content of interaction suggest that cognitively complex individuals spend, when interactional constraints permit, relatively more time talking about the personal qualities of themselves and others, their relationships with others, and their relationship with their partner (Delia, 1974; Delia, Clark, & Switzer, 1979; Delia & Murphy, 1983).

Discriminant Validity of the RCQ: Independence from General Intellectual, Verbal, and Personality Orientations

Independence from general intellectual and verbal traits. Because the RCQ is a free-response task in which persons must verbally express (either orally or in writing) their impressions of others, concern has quite naturally been expressed about the extent to which assessments of cognitive complexity derived from the RCQ may be confounded by factors such as verbal ability, intelligence, and writing skills (e.g., Miller & Wilson, 1979). These concerns have been addressed in a number of studies, with results indicating that RCQ assessments of cognitive complexity are generally unrelated to independent assessments of such variables as verbal intelligence, verbal fluency, general intelligence, and academic achievement (Applegate et al., 1985; Burleson et al., 1981; Burleson & Waltman, 1986; Crockett, 1965; Delia & Crockett, 1973; Hale, 1980; Press et al., 1969; Rowan, 1985; Scarlett et al., 1971; H. Sypher & Applegate, 1982). In addition, assessments of cognitive complexity obtained from written responses to the RCQ have been found unassociated with such factors as writing speed (Burleson et al., 1981) and narrative writing skill (Burleson & Rowan, 1985). Only among young children have significant associations been found between assessments of cognitive complexity and general intellectual and verbal factors (see Burleson et al., 1981; Scarlett et al., 1971); however, the available evidence indicates that these significant associations represent a fusion among cognitive and social-cognitive abilities in young children—a fusion that fades by middle childhood (see Biskin & Crano, 1977; Scarlett et al., 1971).

Recently, however, some researchers (Beatty & Payne, 1984, 1985; Powers, Jordan, & Street, 1979) have alleged that RCQ assessments of cognitive complexity are seriously confounded by a variable termed "loquacity." Although no theoretical analysis of the loquacity construct has been presented, loquacity has been operationally defined as the number of words written in response to the RCQ. Given this operational definition of loquacity, it is not surprising that significant associations between loquacity (the number of words appearing in interpersonal impressions) and cognitive complexity (the number of interpersonal constructs appearing in these same impressions) have frequently been reported (e.g., Beatty & Payne, 1984, 1985; Burleson et al., 1981; Powers et al., 1979). This correlation is not surprising for the simple reason that *persons must use words to express constructs;* consequently, persons who express more constructs in responding to the RCQ will quite naturally tend to use more words. This means that the operationalization of loquacity employed by researchers such as Beatty and Payne and Powers et al. is conceptually confounded with cognitive complexity (for a detailed statement of this argument, see Burleson, Waltman, & Samter, in press). Moreover, assessments of loquacity that are conceptually independent from cognitive complexity (e.g., the *average* number of words used to express a construct, the number of words spoken in an informal conversation, the number of turns taken in a conversation, the average length of a conversational turn) have generally been found unrelated to both cognitive complexity and frequent social-cognitive and communicative correlates of cognitive complexity (Burleson et al., 1981; Burleson et al., in press; Daly et al., 1985). There is, then, little reason for supposing that RCQ assessments of cognitive complexity are confounded by loquacity or other general verbal traits.

Independence from general personality traits. The developmental level of interpersonal construct system (i.e., level of cognitive complexity) is viewed as conceptually distinct from most general personality traits and orientations. Consistent with this requirement, RCQ assessments of cognitive complexity have been found weakly and generally nonsignificantly associated with a number of common personality traits, including: emotional empathy (Burleson, 1983; Burleson & Samter, 1985b; Burleson & Waltman, 1986; Kline & Ceropski, 1984; Samter, 1983), locus of control (Borden, 1979; Burleson & Samter, 1985b; Rowan, 1985; Samter, 1983), intolerance for ambiguity (H. Sypher & Applegate, 1982), values orientations (Borden, 1979), communication apprehension (Burleson & Samter, 1985b; Samter, 1983), and dispositional empathy (Borden, 1979). One study (Delia & O'Keefe, 1976) found cognitive complexity negatively correlated at weak to moderate levels with Machiavellianism, but two other studies (Borden, 1979; H. Sypher, Nightingale, Vielhaber, & Sypher, 1981) detected no significant association between cognitive complexity and Machiavellianism. B. Sypher, Sypher, and Leichty (1983) found complexity weakly associated with the extraversion subscale of Snyder's (1974) self-monitoring scale, but unassociated with the acting and other-directed subscales of this instrument. Finally, two studies (Beatty & Payne, 1985; Rowan, 1985) found cognitive complexity weakly, but significantly, negatively related to writing apprehension; this latter finding is perhaps not too surprising since in both studies cognitive complexity was assessed through the written version of the RCQ.

The low and generally nonsignificant relationships between RCQ-assessed cognitive complexity and many personality traits suggest that the reported relationships between cognitive complexity and, for example, the production of sophisticated messages, are not meaningfully confounded by various personality traits. Indeed, Samter and Burleson (1984) partialled out the effects of emotional empathy, locus of control, and two aspects of communication apprehension from the relationship between cognitive complexity and sensitive comforting behavior; the resulting fourth-order partial correlation of .31 was barely smaller than the zero-order correlation of .33. In sum, it appears that RCQ assessments of cognitive complexity are essentially independent from numerous personality traits and, further, that personality traits generally do not confound reported relationships between cognitive complexity and advanced modes of social-cognitive and communicative functioning.

Conclusion

The evidence reviewed in this chapter indicates that Crockett's RCQ provides reliable and valid assessments of interpersonal cognitive complexity. In spite of the strong evidence, there recently has been increased speculation regarding just what the RCQ actually measures and how this instrument manages to measure whatever it does measure (see B. O'Keefe, 1984). More specifically, questions have been raised about (a) the precise features of the interpersonal construct system tapped by the RCQ, and (b) the nature of the social-cognitive processes contributing to the production of the interpersonal impressions elicited by the RCQ.

Initially, it was proposed that the interpersonal impressions elicited by the RCQ contained representative samples of individuals' interpersonal constructs; thus, it was assumed that the degree of differentiation, abstractness, and organization contained in the impressions elicited by the RCQ reflected the degree of differentiation, abstractness, and organization in the interpersonal construct system as a whole (see Crockett, 1965). Recently, however, B. O'Keefe & Delia (1982) have argued that this original interpretation of RCQ scores is probably flawed since it reflects an overly assimilative view of the impression formation process. These theorists offer two alternative interpretations for what the RCQ may tap: (a) *abstract differentiation* (the number of dispositional constructs an individual has available for interpreting behavior), and (b) differences in the organization of beliefs about others. The abstract differentiation interpretation of RCQ scores is based on the notions that the instructions for the RCQ create a set to describe others in abstract terms, standard scoring procedures for the RCQ typically exclude many concrete constructs from differentiation codings, and that differentiation and abstractness scores based on the RCQ have frequently been found moderately to highly intercorrelated. Viewing the RCQ as tapping differences in the organization of beliefs about others is premised on the assumptions that "all perceivers have the same numbers and types of constructs, but perceivers differ in the degree to which their beliefs about others are organized into stable general impressions by higher-order schemas" (B. O'Keefe & Delia, 1982, p. 64). Presumably, persons with more highly organized sets of interpersonal beliefs could more easily and readily retrieve these beliefs, and thus would produce more differentiated impressions in response to tasks such as the RCQ. Although both of these alternative interpretations for RCQ scores are theoretically interesting, it is not clear how either alternative overcomes the "assimilative" bias supposedly undermining the original interpretation of RCQ scores, since both abstract construing and belief organization represent processes occurring within the perceiver that are not necessarily influenced by characteristics of the perceived or the context.

B. O'Keefe (1984) has suggested a third possible interpretation of the RCQ. She maintains that intepersonal constructs may be organized into several relatively distinct subsystems, each subsystem of interpersonal constructs having a particular domain of relevance. O'Keefe proposes that all persons have a subsystem of "core constructs"— constructs which are "primarily functional for making decisions about relationships and, in particular, whether to pursue or avoid a close relationship with a target" (1984, p. 283). Constructs within this "core" generally pertain to "evaluations of the target's general quality as a person, assessments of moral character, and dispositions that are relevant to neither interpersonal demeanor nor practical tasks" (p. 283). She suggests that the RCQ, rather than tapping indices, such as differentiation within the entire system of interpersonal constructs, only assesses differentiation within the subsystem of "core" interpersonal constructs.

Each of these three alternative interpretations of what the RCQ taps is intriguing, and each of these alternatives has some empirical evidence supporting it (see B. O'Keefe & Delia, 1982; B. O'Keefe, 1984). However, none has sufficient empirical support to warrant its endorsement and the rejection of the alternatives. Indeed, none of the three interpretations suggested by B. O'Keefe and Delia can easily account for the findings of some empirical studies, especially those conducted in developmental contexts. For example, both the "abstract differentiation" account and the "core construct" account maintain that the RCQ taps a specific sub-domain of interpersonal constructs (either abstract, dispositional constructs or core, relationship-centered constructs). Yet, research conducted in developmental contexts has frequently found (a) that the construct systems of children and adolescents are often dominated by relatively concrete constructs (i.e., constructs pertaining to physical appearance, social roles, and specific behaviors), and (b) that *total* interpersonal construct differentiation, rather than abstract differentiation, has often been the *best* predictor of social-cognitive and communicative abilities in samples of children and adolescents (e.g., Burleson, 1982a, 1984a; Delia, Kline, & Burleson, 1979). These findings suggest that, at least for children and adolescents, the RCQ may tap total interpersonal construct differentiation rather than degree of differentiation within some subset of interpersonal constructs; if this interpretation is valid for children and adolescents, there is no reason to suppose it might not also be valid for adults. The "belief organization" interpretation of RCQ scores may also be seriously undermined by the findings of some developmental research. As noted above, the belief organization interpretation assumes that all persons have essentially the same number of interpersonal constructs available, but that there are individual differences in the organization, and hence retrievability, of beliefs about others. Unfortunately, the assumption that all perceivers have basically the same number of interpersonal constructs available is quite inconsistent with the extensively replicated finding that the interpersonal construct system becomes progressively more differentiated during the course of childhood and adolescence.

In short, the findings of developmental studies raise important questions about the adequacy of the three alternative interpretations of RCQ scores. Indeed, the findings of developmental studies appear most consistent with the original interpretation of the RCQ as tapping the degree of total differentiation within the interpersonal construct system; of course, as noted above, this original interpretation is problematic on other grounds. At present, then, none of the four available interpretations for what RCQ scores represent is completely adequate.

A second issue of concern has to do with the processes underlying the production of the interpersonal impressions elicited by the RCQ. Crockett's (1965) original account maintained that persons producing more differentiated impressions in response to the RCQ had a larger number of constructs *available* in their interpersonal construct systems than persons producing less differentiated impressions. This view is consistent with the notion that the RCQ taps the level of differentiation within the interpersonal construct system as a whole. More recently it has been proposed that persons scoring highly on the RCQ might not have a larger number of interpersonal constructs available to them, but rather can more easily *access* their interpersonal constructs (see B. O'Keefe & Delia, 1982; H. Sypher & Applegate, 1984). A third possibility is that persons scoring highly on the RCQ may have both more constructs available to them and be able to access those constructs with greater ease. As yet, there is no empirical evidence indicating that any one of these three possibilities is superior to the other. Encouragingly, however, focus on such issues as construct availability versus construct accessibility represent efforts to integrate traditional constructivist analyses of social cognition within the more general analyses of cognitive functioning gaining currency in the field of psychology (see H. Sypher & Applegate, 1984).

Increased theoretical and empirical interest in just what the RCQ measures and how it manages to measure what it does measure are not reasons for despair, but rather indicate a healthy, ongoing interest in the precise character of important social-cognitive processes and how these processes contribute to communicative functioning. The development and use of the RCQ in research on social cognition and communication has led to significant advances in our knowledge in such areas as communicative development, functional communication skills, social perception, and effective interpersonal behavior. Refinements in the interpretation of the scores generated by the RCQ can be expected to further enhance our understanding of these and related topics.

APPENDIX 1

The Two-Role Version of the RCQ

Age _____ I.D.# _____ Class Time _____ Sex _____

Our interest in this questionnaire is to learn how people describe others whom they know. Our concern here is with the habits, mannerisms—in general, with the personal characteristics, rather than the physical traits—which characterize a number of different people.

In order to make sure that you are describing real people, we have set down a list of two different categories of people. In the blank space beside each category below, please write the initials, nicknames, or some other identifying symbol for a person of your acquaintance who fits into that category. Be sure to use a different person for each category.

1.   A person your own age whom you like. _____
2.   A person your own age whom you dislike. _____

Spend a few moments looking over this list, mentally comparing and contrasting the people you have in mind for each category. Think of their habits, their beliefs, their mannerisms, their relations to others, any characteristics they have which you might use to describe them to other people.

If you have any questions about the kinds of characteristics we are interested in, please ask them.

Please look back to the first sheet and place the symbol you have used to designate the person in category 1 here _____.

Now describe this person as fully as you can. Write down as many defining characteristics as you can. Do not simply put down those characteristics that distinguish him/her from others on your list, but include any characteristics that he/she shares with others as well as characteristics that are unique to him/her. Pay particular attention to his/her habits, beliefs, ways of treating others, mannerisms, and similar attributes. Remember, describe him/her as completely as you can, so that a stranger might be able to determine the kind of person he/she is from your description. Use the back of this page if necessary. *Please spend only about five (5) minutes describing him/her.*

This person is:

_____

_____

_____

_____

_____

_____

Please look back to the first sheet and place the symbol you have used to designate the person in category 2 here _____.

Now describe this person as fully as you can. Write down as many defining characteristics as you can. Do not simply put down those characteristics that distinguish him/her from others on your list, but include any characteristics that he/she shares with others as well as characteristics that are unique to him/her. Pay particular attention to his/her habits, beliefs, ways of treating others, mannerisms, and similar attributes. Remember, describe him/her as completely as you can, so that a stranger might be able to determine the kind of person he/she is from your description. Use the back of this page if necessary. _Please spend only about five (5) minutes describing him/her._

This person is:

_____

_____

_____

_____

_____

APPENDIX 2

Scoring Rules for Differentiation Codings (From Crockett et al., 1974)

Scoring the degree of differentiation of the impression involves identifying, recording, and counting the number of elements that an impression includes. The decision as to which elements of an impression are to be scored as constructs is sometimes difficult to make. To reduce the ambiguity in scoring procedures, a set of rules have been developed which clarify the application of the general principles just discussed.

Rule 1. (a) Whenever it is debatable whether a phrase should be scored as one construct or several constructs, or (b) when two nearly synonymous but not identical qualities are mentioned in an impression, the subject should be given the benefit of the doubt and multiple constructs should be scored instead of just one. Further specifications of this rule are provided in Rules 2 through 4.

Rule 2. When the subject uses an adverbial or adjectival qualifier which, as used, appears to be an intrinsic part of the noun it modifies, contrary to Rule 1, the two words are to be scored as one construct.

In such instances, it is presumed that the qualifier refers to the degree to which the attribute is held, or to one manner in which it appears, rather than to a qualitatively different attribute. Thus, the phrase "unreasonably selfish" is scored as one construct, not as both "unreasonable" and "selfish" because the word "unreasonably" refers more to the degree of selfishness than to a distinct quality of unreasonableness.

Rule 3. Identical, repeated words or phrases are scored only once. Words which are very similar in meaning but which are not identical are scored twice.

Thus, if a subject describes the other person as "domineering, assertive, and aggressive," all three are scored as constructs. Similarly, if the other person is described as a "hard and thorough worker," two constructs are scored on the assumption that the subject is reporting both a hard worker and a thorough worker and that the two adjectives describe somewhat different aspects of the other person. On the other hand, if a person is described as "helpful" twice in the same question—even if it is phrased as "very helpful" the second time—only one construct should be scored.

Rule 4. Idiomatic constructions which run to several words are usually scored as one construct.

Thus, the statement "John is a big, fat slob" is scored as only one construct because it is conventionally used as a single unit.

Rule 5. Only qualities which are relevant to the task the subject has been set should be scored as constructs.

In most of our studies only aspects of the other person's personality or his stimulus value for his associates have been scored as constructs owing to the nature of the task that was set for the subject. Physical traits, information about the other person's social role, his age, or the like usually are not scored. Sometimes this restriction must be liberalized, however. For example, Noymer (1965) conducted an experiment in which subjects formed impressions from pictures which were presented at gradually increasing shutter speeds. It was expected that the content of subjects' impressions would shift, with increased exposure, from descriptions of the other person's appearance and dress to inferences about his internal, dispositional qualities. In this case, carrying out the critical comparisons in the experiment required the scoring of both dispositional and external qualities in subjects' descriptions.

Rule 6. General statements about what people should do about the nature of mankind or about the subject's own feelings are not scored as constructs unless they are specifically tied to characteristics of the person who is being described.

For example, statements like "People should be humble," "No one likes people who are selfish," "Nobody is perfect," or "I would like him as a roommate" (as opposed to "He would make a good roommate") say nothing about the person under consideration, however much they may say about the criteria the subject has used in evaluating the person.

References

Applegate, J.L. (1980a). Adaptive communication in educational contexts: A study of teachers' communicative strategies. *Communication Education,* 29, 158–170.

Applegate, J.L. (1980b). Person- and position-centered communication in a day-care center. In N.K. Denzin (Ed.), *Studies in symbolic interaction* (Vol. 3, pp. 59–96). Greenwich, CT: JAI Press.

Applegate, J.L. (1982a, February). *Construct system development and identity-management skills in persuasive contexts.* Paper presented at the Western Speech Communication Association convention, Denver.

Applegate, J.L. (1982b). The impact of construct system development on communication and impression formation in persuasive contexts. *Communication Monographs,* 49, 277–289.

Applegate, J.L., Burke, J.A., Burleson, B.R., Delia, J.G., & Kline, S.L. (1985). Reflection-enhancing parental communication. In I.E. Sigel (Ed.), *Parental belief systems: The psychological consequences for children* (pp. 107–142). Hillsdale, NJ: Erlbaum.

Babrow, A.S., & O'Keefe, D.J. (1984). Construct differentiation as a moderator of attitude-behavior consistency: A failure to confirm. *Central States Speech Journal, 35,* 160–165.

Barenboim, C. (1977). Developmental changes in the interpersonal cognitive system from middle childhood to adolescence. *Child Development, 48,* 1467–1471.

Barenboim, C. (1981). The development of person perception in childhood and adolescence: From behavioral comparisons to psychological constructs to psychological comparisons. *Child Development, 52,* 129–144.

Barratt, B.B. (1977). The development of peer perception systems in childhood and early adolescence. *Social Behavior and Personality, 5,* 351–360.

Beatty, M.J., & Payne, S.K. (1984). Loquacity and quantity of constructs as predictors of social perspective-taking. *Communication Quarterly, 32,* 207–210.

Beatty, M.J., & Payne, S.K. (1985). Is construct differentiation loquacity? A motivational perspective. *Human Communication Research, 11,* 605–612.

Bigner, J.J. (1974). A Wernerian developmental analysis of children's descriptions of siblings. *Child Development, 45,* 317–323.

Biskin, D.S., & Crano, W. (1977). Structural organization of impressions derived from inconsistent information: A developmental study. *Genetic Psychology Monographs, 95,* 331–348.

Borden, A.W. (1979). *An investigation of the relationships among indices of social cognition, motivation, and communicative performance.* Unpublished doctoral dissertation, University of Illinois at Urbana-Champaign.

Burke, J.A., & Clark, R.A. (1982). An assessment of methodological options for investigating the development of persuasive skills across childhood. *Central States Speech Journal, 33,* 437–445.

Burleson, B.R. (1980). The development of interpersonal reasoning: An analysis of message strategy justifications. *Journal of the American Forensic Association, 17,* 102–110.

Burleson, B.R. (1982a). The affective perspective-taking process: A test of Turiel's role-taking model. In M. Burgoon (Ed.), *Communication Yearbook* (Vol. 6, pp. 473–488). Beverly Hills, CA: Sage.

Burleson, B.R. (1982b). The development of comforting communication skills in childhood and adolescence. *Child Development, 53,* 1578–1588.

Burleson, B.R. (1983). Social cognition, empathic motivation, and adults' comforting strategies. *Human Communication Research, 10,* 295–304.

Burleson, B.R. (1984a). Age, social-cognitive development, and the use of comforting strategies. *Communication Monographs, 51,* 140–153.

Burleson, B.R. (1984b). Role-taking and communication skills in childhood: Why they *aren't* related and what can be done about it. *Western Journal of Speech Communication, 48,* 155–170.

Burleson, B.R. (1985, April). *Communicative correlates of peer acceptance in childhood.* Paper presented at the biennial meeting of the Society for Research in Child Development, Toronto.

Burleson, B.R. (1986). Communication skills and childhood peer relationships: An overview. In M.L. McLaughlin (Ed.), *Communication Yearbook* (Vol. 9, pp. 143–180). Beverly Hills, CA: Sage.

Burleson, B.R. (in press). Cognitive complexity and person-centered communication: A review of methods, findings, and explanations. In J.C. McCroskey & J.A. Daly (Eds.), *Personality and interpersonal communication.* Beverly Hills, CA: Sage.

Burleson, B.R., Applegate, J.L., & Neuwirth, C.M. (1981). Is cognitive complexity loquacity? A reply to Powers, Jordan, and Street. *Human Communication Research, 7,* 212–225.

Burleson, B.R., & Fennelly, D.A. (1981). The effects of persuasive appeal form and cognitive complexity on children's sharing behavior. *Child Study Journal, 11,* 75–90.

Burleson, B.R., & Rowan, K.E. (1985). Are social-cognitive ability and narrative writing skill related? *Written Communication, 2,* 25–43.

Burleson, B.R., & Samter, W. (1985a). Consistencies in theoretical and naive evaluations of comforting messages. *Communication Monographs, 52,* 103–123.

Burleson, B.R., & Samter, W. (1985b). Individual differences in the perception of comforting messages: An exploratory investigation. *Central States Speech Journal, 36,* 39–50.

Burleson, B.R., Waltman, M.S., & Samter, W. (in press). More evidence that cognitive complexity is not loquacity: A reply to Beatty and Payne. *Communication Quarterly.*

Burleson, B.R., & Waltman, P.A. (1986, May). *Social cognitive and communicative characteristics of popular, rejected and supportive preadolescents.* Paper presented at the annual convention of the International Communication Association, Chicago.

Clark, R.A., & Delia, J.G. (1976). The development of functional persuasive skills in childhood and early adolescence. *Child Development, 47,* 1008–1014.

Clark, R.A., & Delia, J.G. (1977). Cognitive complexity, social perspective-taking, and functional persuasive skills in second-to-ninth-grade children. *Human Communication Research, 3,* 128–134.

Clark, R.A., & Delia, J.G. (1979). *Topoi* and rhetorical competence. *Quarterly Journal of Speech, 65,* 187–206.

Crockett, W.H. (1965). Cognitive complexity and impression formation. In B.A. Maher (Ed.), *Progress in experimental personality research* (Vol. 2, pp. 47–90). New York: Academic.

Crockett, W.H., Gonyea, A.H., & Delia, D.G. (1970). Cognitive complexity and the formation of impressions from abstract qualities or from concrete behaviors. *Proceedings of the 78th Annual Convention of the American Psychological Association, 5,* 375–376.

Crockett, W.H., Mahood, S.M., & Press, A.N. (1975). Impressions of a speaker as a function of set to understand or to evaluate, of cognitive complexity, and of prior attitudes. *Journal of Personality, 43,* 168–178.

Crockett, W.H., Press, A.N., Delia, J.G., & Kenney, C.J. (1974). *The structural analysis of the organization of written impressions.* Unpublished manuscript, Department of Psychology, University of Kansas, Lawrence, KS.

Daly, J.A., Bell, R.A., Glenn, P.J., & Lawrence, S. (1985). Conceptualizing conversational complexity. *Human Communication Research, 12,* 30–53.

DeLancey, C.A., & Swanson, D.L. (1981, May). *Construct differentiation and the relationship of attitudes and behavioral intentions in the political domain.* Paper presented at the International Communication Association convention, Minneapolis.

Delia, J.G. (1972). Dialects and the effects of stereotypes on interpersonal attraction and cognitive processes in impression formation. *Quarterly Journal of Speech, 58,* 285–297.

Delia, J.G. (1974). Attitude toward the disclosure of self-attribution and the complexity of interpersonal constructs. *Speech Monographs, 41,* 119–126.

Delia, J.G. (1976). A constructivist analysis of the concept of credibility. *Quarterly Journal of Speech, 62,* 361–375.

Delia, J.G., Burleson, B.R., & Kline, S.L. (1979, April). *Person-centered parental communication and the development of social-cognitive and communicative abilities.* Paper presented at the annual convention of the Central States Speech Association, St. Louis.

Delia, J.G., & Clark, R.A. (1977). Cognitive complexity, social perception, and the development of listener-adapted communication in six-, eight-, ten-, and twelve-year-old boys. *Communication Monographs, 44,* 326–345.

Delia, J.G., Clark, R.A., & Switzer, D.E. (1974). Cognitive complexity and impression formation in informal social interaction. *Speech Monographs, 41* 299–308.

Delia, J.G., Clark, R.A., & Switzer, D.E. (1979). The content of informal conversations as a function of interactants' interpersonal cognitive complexity. *Communication Monographs, 46,* 274–281.

Delia, J.G., & Crockett, W.H. (1973). Social schemas, cognitive complexity, and the learning of social structures. *Journal of Personality, 41,* 413–429.

Delia, J.A., Crockett, W.H., & Gonyea, A.H. (1970). Cognitive complexity and the effects of schemas on the learning of social structures. *Proceedings of the 78th Annual Convention of the American Psychological Association, 5,* 373–374.

Delia, J.G., Gonyea, A.H., & Crockett, A.H. (1971). The effects of subject-generated and normative constructs upon the formation of impressions. *British Journal of Social and Clinical Psychology, 10,* 301–305.

Delia, J.G., Kline, S.L., & Burleson, B.R. (1979). The development of persuasive communication strategies in kindergarteners through twelfth graders. *Communication Monographs, 46,* 241–256.

Delia, J.G., Kline, S.L., Burleson, B.R., Clark, R.A., Applegate, J.L., & Burke, J.A. (1980). *Social-cognitive and communicative skills of mothers and their children.* Unpublished manuscript, University of Illinois at Urbana-Champaign.

Delia, J.G., & Murphy, M.A. (1983, November). *Roommates' construct differentiation, impressions, and person-centered communication: An analysis of perceiver and target effects.* Paper presented at the annual convention of the Speech Communication Association, Washington, DC.

Delia, J.G., & O'Keefe, B.J. (1976). The interpersonal constructs of Machiavellians. *British Journal of Social and Clinical Psychology, 15,* 435–436.

Delia, J.G., & O'Keefe, B.J. (1979). Constructivism: The development of communication. In E. Wartella (Ed.), *Children communicating* (pp. 157–185). Beverly Hills, CA: Sage.

Delia, J.G., O'Keefe, B.J., & O'Keefe, D.J. (1982). The constructivist approach to communication. In F.E.X. Dance (Ed.), *Human communication theory* (pp. 147–191). New York: Harper & Row.

Duncan, S., & Fiske, D.W. (1977). *Organization of behavior in face-to-face interaction.* Chicago: Aldine.

Ellis, D.G., Hamilton, M., & Aho, L. (1983). Some issues in conversation coherence. *Human Communication Research, 9,* 267–282.

Goldstein, K.M., & Blackman, S. (1978). *Cognitive style: Five approaches and relevant research.* New York: Wiley.

Hale, C.L. (1980). Cognitive complexity-simplicity as a determinant of communicative effectiveness. *Communication Monographs, 47,* 304–311.

Hale, C.L. (1982). An investigation of the relationship between cognitive complexity and listener-adapted communication. *Central States Speech Journal, 33,* 339–344.

Hale, C.L., & Delia, J.G. (1976). Cognitive complexity and social perspective-taking. *Communication Monographs, 43,* 195–203.

Horsfall, R.B. (1969). *A comparison of two cognitive complexity measures.* Unpublished doctoral dissertation, The Johns Hopkins University, Baltimore.

Husband, R.L. (1981). *Leadership: A case study, phenomenology, and social-cognitive correlates.* Unpublished doctoral dissertation, University of Illinois at Urbana-Champaign.

Kelly, G.A. (1955). *The psychology of personal constructs* (2 Vols.). New York: W. W. Norton.

Kline, S.L., & Ceropski, J.M. (1984). Person-centered communication in medical practice. In J.T. Wood & G.M. Phillips (Eds.), *Human decision-making* (pp. 120–141). Carbondale, IL: Southern Illinois University Press.

Livesley, W.J., & Bramley, D.B. (1973). *Person perception in childhood and adolescence.* New York: Wiley.

Losee, G. D. (1976). *An investigation of selected interpersonal and communication variables in marital relationships.* Unpublished doctoral dissertation, University of Illinois at Urbana-Champaign.

Mayo, C.W., & Crockett, W.H. (1964). Cognitive complexity and primacy-recency effects in impression formation. *Journal of Abnormal and Social Psychology, 68,* 335–338.

Mead, G.H. (1934). *Mind, self, and society.* Chicago: University of Chicago Press.

Meltzer, B., Crockett, W.H., & Rosenkrantz, P.S. (1966). Cognitive complexity, value congruity, and the integration of potentially incompatible information in impressions of others. *Journal of Personality and Social Psychology, 4,* 338–343.

Miller, A., & Wilson, P. (1979). Cognitive differentiation and integration: A conceptual analysis. *Genetic Psychology Monographs, 99,* 3–40.

Nidorf, L.J., & Crockett, W.H. (1965). Cognitive complexity and the integration of conflicting information in written impressions. *Journal of Social Psychology, 66,* 165–169.

O'Keefe, B.J. (1984). The evolution of impressions in small working groups: Effects of construct differentiation. In H.E. Sypher & J.L. Applegate (Eds.), *Communication by children and adults: Social cognitive and strategic processes* (pp. 262–291). Beverly Hills, CA: Sage.

O'Keefe, B.J., & Delia, J.G. (1979). Construct comprehensiveness and cognitive complexity as predictors of the number and strategic adaptation of arguments and appeals in a persuasive message. *Communication Monographs, 46,* 231–240.

O'Keefe, B.J., & Delia, J.G. (1982). Impression formation and message production. In M.E. Roloff & C.R. Berger (Eds.), *Social cognition and communication* (pp. 33–72). Beverly Hills, CA: Sage.

O'Keefe, B.J., Delia, J.G., & O'Keefe, D.J. (1977). Construct individuality, cognitive complexity, and the formation and remembering of interpersonal impressions. *Social Behavior and Personality, 5,* 229–240.

O'Keefe, D.J. (1980). The relationship of attitudes and behavior: A constructivist analysis. In D.P. Cushman & R.D. McPhee (Eds.), *The message-attitude-behavior relationship: Theory, methodology, and application.* New York: Academic Press.

O'Keefe, D.J., & Brady, R.M. (1980). Cognitive complexity and the effects of thought on attitude change. *Social Behavior and Personality, 8,* 49–56.

O'Keefe, D.J., & Delia, J.G. (1981). Construct differentiation and the relationship of attitudes and behavioral intentions. *Communication Monographs, 48,* 146–157.

O'Keefe, D.J., & Shepherd, G.J. (1982). Interpersonal construct differentiation, attitudinal confidence, and the attitude-behavior relationship. *Central States Speech Journal, 33,* 416–423.

O'Keefe, D.J., Shepherd, G.J., & Streeter, T. (1982). Role category questionnaire measures of cognitive complexity: Reliability and comparability of alternative forms. *Central States Speech Journal, 33,* 333–338.

O'Keefe, D.J., & Sypher, H.E. (1981). Cognitive complexity measures and the relationship of cognitive complexity to communication: A critical review. *Human Communication Research, 8,* 72–92.

Peevers, B.H., & Secord, P.F. (1973). Developmental changes in the attribution of descriptive concepts to persons. *Journal of Personality and Social Psychology, 27,* 120–138.

Pelias, R.J. (1984). Oral interpretation as a training method for increasing perspective-taking abilities. *Communication Education, 33*, 143–151.

Plaget, J. (1926). *The language and thought of the child.* London: Routledge & Kegan Paul.

Powers, W.A., Jordan, W.J., & Street, R.L. (1979). Language indices in the measurement of cognitive complexity: Is complexity loquacity? *Human Communication Research, 6*, 1, 69–73.

Press, A.N., Crockett, W.H., & Rosenkrantz, P.S. (1969). Cognitive complexity and the learning of balanced and unbalanced social structures. *Journal of Personality, 37*, 541–553.

Press, A.N., Crockett, W.H., & Delia, J.G. (1975). Effects of cognitive complexity and of perceiver's set upon the organization of impressions. *Journal of Personality and Social Psychology, 32*, 865–872.

Ritter, E.M. (1979). Social perspective-taking ability, cognitive complexity, and listener-adapted communication in early and late adolescence. *Communication Monographs, 46*, 40–51.

Rosenbach, D., Crockett, W.H., & Wapner, S. (1973). Developmental level, emotional involvement, and the resolution of inconsistency in impression formation. *Developmental Psychology, 8*, 120–130.

Rosenkrantz, P.S., & Crockett, W.H. (1965). Some factors influencing the assimilation of disparate information in impression formation. *Journal of Personality and Social Psychology, 2*, 397–402.

Rothenberg, B.B. (1970). Children's social sensitivity and the relationship to interpersonal competence, intrapersonal comfort, and intellectual level. *Developmental Psychology, 2*, 335–350.

Rowan, K.E. (1985). *Explanatory writing skills: Theoretical analysis and an empirical investigation of individual differences.* Unpublished doctoral dissertation, Purdue University, West Lafayette, IN.

Samter, W. (1983). *Effects of cognitive and motivational variables on comforting behavior in a quasi-natural context.* Unpublished master's thesis, Purdue University.

Samter, W., & Burleson, B.R. (1984). Cognitive and motivational influences on spontaneous comforting behavior. *Human Communication Research, 11*, 231–260.

Samter, W., Burleson, B.R., & Basden, L. (1986a, April). *Comforting conversations: The effects of strategy type on evaluations of messages and message producers.* Paper presented at the Central States Speech Association Convention, Cincinnati.

Samter, W., Burleson, B.R., & Basden, L. (1986b, May). *Behavioral complexity is in the eye of the beholder: Effects of cognitive complexity and message complexity on impressions of the source of comforting messages.* Paper presented at the annual convention of the International Communication Association, Chicago.

Samter, W., & Ely, T. (1985, April). *Children's conflict management strategies: Assessments of individual and situational differences.* Paper presented at the Central States Speech Association convention, Indianapolis.

Sarver, J.L. (1976). *An exploratory study of the antecedents of individual differences in second- and seventh-graders' social cognitive and communicative performance.* Unpublished doctoral dissertation, University of Illinois at Urbana-Champaign.

Scarlett, H.H., Press, A.N., & Crockett, W.H. (1971). Children's descriptions of peers: A Wernerian developmental analysis. *Child Development, 42,* 439–453.

Shepherd, G.J., & O'Keefe, B.J. (1984a, November). *Interpersonal construct differentiation and the production of messages addressing multiple aims in persuasive situations.* Paper presented at the Speech Communication Association convention, Chicago.

Shepherd, G.J., & O'Keefe, B.J. (1984b). The relationship between the developmental level of persuasive strategies and their effectiveness. *Central States Speech Journal, 35,* 137–152.

Shepherd, G.J., & O'Keefe, B.J. (1985, November). *Securing task, interactional, and relational objectives in interpersonal persuasive interactions.* Paper presented at the Speech Communication Association convention, Denver.

Snyder, M. (1974). The self-monitoring of expressive behavior. *Journal of Personality and Social Psychology, 30,* 526–537.

Streufert, S., & Streufert, S.C. (1978). *Behavior in the complex environment.* New York: Wiley.

Sypher, B.D., Sypher, H.E., & Leichty, G.B. (1983, May). *Cognitive differentiation, self-monitoring, and individual success in organizations.* Paper presented at the Fifth International Congress on Personal Construct Psychology, Boston.

Sypher, B.D., & Zorn, T.E. (1986). Communication-related abilities and upward mobility: A longitudinal investigation. *Human Communication Research, 12,* 420–431.

Sypher, H.E., & Applegate, J.L. (1982). Cognitive complexity and verbal intelligence: Clarifying relationships. *Educational and Psychological Measurement, 49,* 537–543.

Sypher, H.E., & Applegate, J.L. (1984). Organizing communication behavior: The role of schemas and constructs. In R.N. Bostram (Ed.), *Communication Yearbook* (Vol. 8, pp. 310–329). Beverly Hills, CA: Sage.

Sypher, H.E., Nightingale, J., Vielhaber, M., & Sypher, B.D. (1981). The interpersonal constructs of Machiavellians: A reconsideration. *British Journal of Social Psychology, 20,* 219–220.

Sypher, H.E., & O'Keefe, D.J. (1980, May). *The comparative validity of several cognitive complexity measures as predictors of communication-relevant abilities.* Paper presented at the International Communication Association convention, Acapulco.

Sypher, H.E., Witt, B.E., & Sypher, B.D. (1986). The comparative validity of three interpersonal cognitive differentiation measures as predictors of written communication abilities. *Communication Monographs, 53,* 376–382.

Tripodi, T., & Bieri, J. (1963). Cognitive complexity as a function of own and provided constructs. *Psychological Reports, 13,* 26.

Wegner, D.M. (1977). Attribute generality: The development and articulation of attributes in person perception. *Journal of Research in Personality, 11,* 329–339.

Werner, H. (1957). The concept of development from a comparative and organismic point of view. In D.B. Harris (Ed.), *The concept of development* (pp. 125–146). Minneapolis: University of Minnesota Press.

CHAPTER 2

Cognitive Processes: Methods for Probing the Black Box

John O. Greene

While philosophers have speculated on the nature of mind and its relation to behavior for millennia, it was not until the end of the nineteenth century that scholars undertook the systematic study of cognition (Flanagan, 1984; Mischel, 1975). It is only over the last 25 years, or since the waning of behaviorism and the return to the use of humans rather than rats as experimental subjects, that cognitive science has come into its own as an approach to the study of human behavior.

Despite the relatively recent development of cognitive science, questions concerning the nature of mental processes have emerged as essential theoretical issues throughout the social sciences. The impetus for this surge of interest stems, in part, from the growing realization that human social behavior is inextricably tied to cognitive structures and events. Consider that all social activity involves two fundamental functions, making sense of environmental inputs and the production of actions, and that scientific pursuit of these functions directly implicates the study of mind (Greene, 1984a; Greene & Cody, in press). With respect to the interpretation of the environment, it is recognized that raw stimulus inputs are detected, categorized, and evaluated in the mind of the individual social actor. Similarly, it is in the mind that intentions are formulated, potential courses of action considered, and efferent commands generated.

At the same time that social scientists have come to recognize the central role of cognitive processes in social interaction, advances in artificial intelligence and computer science have provided conceptual tools for addressing issues of meaning and action (Flanagan, 1984; Norman, 1980). Thus, the general orientation toward cognitive accounts has been given particular form and structure by technological advances in information processing. As a result, cognitive science is currently dominated by the human information processing perspective (Anderson, 1976, 1985). The aim of this approach is to explain observed behavioral regularities by describing the nature of the cognitive system which produced those regularities (Simon, 1980). Such description involves three types of components: Specification of cognitive structures, content, and processes (Anderson, 1976; Greene, 1984a). Cognitive structure refers to the form in which information is represented in the mental system, while content refers to the information itself. In contrast to conceptions of structure and content, cognitive processes involve those operations by which information is acquired, transformed, stored, and utilized.

There are a few points concerning this tripartite scheme which merit note here. It is important to keep in mind that specific conceptions of structure, process, and content are simply inferred on the basis of observed input-output regularities. As a result, they assume the status of "convenient fictions" which permit explanation, prediction, and/or control. Further, it is assumed that it is possible to articulate multiple structure-process models capable of yielding the same predictions regarding input-output relations. Thus, the task of the cognitive scientist is not to develop *the* model of the mental system responsible for some phenomenon, but rather to articulate *a* model sufficient to account for the behavior of interest.

The notion of a system defined in terms of structure, process, and content provides a potential means of addressing one of the more persistent problems of the social sciences. A fundamental goal of scientific inquiry is to discover powerful principles which apply over a number of instantiations of some particular phenomenon and also across a range of distinct phenomena. In the social sciences, this goal is manifested in attempts to ascertain explanatory principles which hold across people and situations and which make explicit points of commonality among diverse behaviors. Given this general goal of discerning more powerful, general explanatory principles we might ask what lines of theoretical inquiry are likely to yield such principles. The structure-process-content schema suggests one approach to this issue because, although cognitive content is the result of experience and thus varies across individuals, various conceptions of structure and process may well hold over individuals, situations, and diverse behavioral phenomena (Greene & Cody, in press; Fiske & Taylor, 1984).

The Nature Of Cognitive Processes

The general aim of the human information processing perspective is to articulate models of the cognitive system which serves to link inputs to outputs. In effect, then, the task is to trace the flow of information from the time it impinges on the cognitive system until some response is exhibited. One way to think about cognitive processes, then, is in terms of those general functions which occur between input and response. Such a functional orientation suggests three broad classes of processes which must transpire in the mind: (a) input, involving those processes of perception, attention allocation, and pattern recognition which allow the selection and interpretation of raw stimuli; (b) retention of information subsequent to the initial input processing—the storage and retrieval of information from some long-term repository; and utilization, whereby information made available by the operation of the input and memory functions is employed to produce responses. These three functions—input, memory, and utilization—comprise a rudimentary model of the human information processing system which, due to the fundamental and ubiquitous nature of the functions, is useful as an organizational device for structuring a complex literature.

Despite this, it should be clear that such a general scheme is of limited use as an explanatory and predictive tool. These ends require the specification of processes for executing the general functions. Such specific conceptions of cognitive processes lend themselves to test via three general types of response variables. First, an essential aspect of any process, cognitive or otherwise, is that it occurs over time (see Swinney, 1984). As a result, a variety of chronometric measures may be employed to examine the temporal characteristics of proposed cognitive processes. Second, any process is always applied over some specific content. This necessarily follows from the conception of a cognitive process as a procedure for manipulating information in some way. Thus, because processes operate on specific content, the characteristics of output information may provide a means of exploring the focal process. It is commonly observed that humans are quite limited in their ability to carry out multiple processes at any particular time (e.g., James, 1890). This fact is typically explained by recourse to the conception of finite processing resources which effectively limit the number of processes that can be executed simultaneously (see Kahneman, 1973). This notion of limited processing resources suggests that a third essential characteristic of a cognitive process is the demand that process makes upon the pool of resources. Measures of processing-capacity requirements, then, comprise the final class of response variables.

In summary, we can distinguish two general orientations toward a discussion of cognitive processes. One orientation emphasizes a sequential, functional view of the input, memory, and output systems. The other focuses upon processes in terms of their temporal characteristics, information transformations, and demands on processing capacity. These two approaches can be seen as orthogonal dimensions defining a functions-by-properties space. That is, for any given function there must exist some process (or set of processes) for executing that function which can be examined in terms of its operating characteristics.

Both of these dimensions are significant in the context of this chapter because they each suggest points critical to the study of cognitive processes. Viewing cognitive processing in terms of sequential functions serves to emphasize the systemic nature of the mind. From this perspective it should be clear that any investigation of a particular process actually involves the entire processing system. For example, an experimenter may wish to study the perceptual system by use of letter presentations via tachistoscopic display, but performing such a task will also involve the memory and output functions. One practical implication of this fact is that experimental conclusions concerning a particular process are warranted only to the extent that the operation of other processes have been controlled or assessed. A second, related, point arising from the systemic perspective concerns the familiar dictum that a particular conception of process can only be evaluated within the context of a specified structure over which that process applies (Anderson, 1976, 1978). As a result, any test of a proposed cognitive process is more accurately seen as a test of a structure-process complex.

A focus upon chronometric measures, output information, and/or processing capacity demands, as a means of assessing some process, also suggests a critical point. Rather than being independent, these variables are characterized by interrelationships such that a change in one index may result in changes in the others. It is quite common to observe speed-accuracy tradeoffs (see McClelland, 1979; Murdock, 1982; Schmidt, Zelaznik, Hawkins, Frank, & Quinn, 1979), and processing capacity-accuracy tradeoffs (see Fromkin, 1980; Kahneman, 1973; Siegman, 1979) among a variety of behavioral phenomena. One implication of this point is that, while it is useful for expository purposes to treat these measures as independent, in practice it may be necessary to examine their interrelations.

Organization and Scope of the Chapter

This chapter is intended as a general guide, to apprise the researcher of possibilities and drawbacks in the study of cognitive processes, particularly as they relate to social behavior. The tremendous breadth of this domain necessitates that in many cases the reader be referred to other treatments of issues which cannot be developed in detail here. Indeed, some of the topics discussed here are the focus of entire volumes devoted solely to a single issue. Thus, the essential orientation is more one of overview than detailed explication.

Because the emphasis of this volume is on research methods, the discussion is organized in terms of the three major classes of response variables, rather than by the functions of the information processing system. Nevertheless, where appropriate, attempts are made to alert the reader to specific applications in the study of input, memory, and utilization functions by reference to reviews, collected papers, and overview treatments which address these substantive domains.

Time as an Index of Cognitive Processing

The use of temporal measures in experimental investigations dates from the earliest systematic studies of human cognition (Brebner & Welford, 1980). This use of timed responses stems from the fact that defining the temporal characteristics of a process and the factors which impact upon its time course are crucial to understanding that process. Indeed, it can be shown that chronometric measures can be used to rule out erroneous conceptions of process which appear feasible when such measures are lacking (e.g., Swinney, 1984).

Measures of Duration, Response Latency, and Inter-Event Intervals

Because the purview of the information processing approach includes all human behavior (Greene, 1984a), virtually any response may be subjected to chronometric analysis. The simplest of these temporal measures involves the duration of some behavioral event. For example, a study by Greene and his associates (Greene, O'Hair, Cody, & Yen, 1985) revealed that individuals delivering a spontaneous (i.e., unplanned) lie exhibited shorter message durations than subjects delivering a truthful response. Such measures of response duration are thus useful as an index of cognitive processing in those situations where the conception of the process under study indicates that some independent variable will affect the duration of response.

Although some responses, such as persistence on a task or duration of a monologue, may lend themselves to a single timed observation, many social behaviors are relatively brief and recurrent, so that measures of cumulative duration may be more appropriate. This is particularly true where theory yields no strong predictions about the location or duration of individual behavioral events. As an example, such behaviors as smiling or leg and foot movements might be expected to occur sporadically as a person engages in deception (Zuckerman, DePaulo, & Rosenthal, 1981).

In contrast to measures of duration which involve the length of a behavioral event, it is possible to identify a number of measures of the time between some initiating event and the onset of a response. These response latency measures would include traditional reaction time variables (see Welford, 1980) as well as measures of speaker-turn latency, voice-onset duration, and the like (see Siegman & Feldstein, 1979; Feldstein & Welkowitz, 1978). Similar to such response latency measures are inter-event intervals which involve the duration of time elapsed between a series of similar events, such as keystrokes in typing (e.g., Long, Nimmo-Smith, & Whitefield, 1983; Ostry, 1983) or lexical items in a monologue (e.g., Grosjean, Grosjean, & Lane, 1979; Gee & Grosjean, 1984).

Issues in the Analysis of Chronometric Data as an Index of Cognitive Processing

To this point I have characterized the types of chronometric variables typically found in cognitive research in very general terms. Attendant to these various measures are a number of issues concerning the treatment of temporal data.

Where the total elapsed time of observation differs across subjects, it is typically necessary to convert cumulative measures of duration to some ratio of event duration to total elapsed time. Alternatively, a researcher can select a portion of the total observation period which is equal for all subjects (e.g., the first 15 seconds of each subject's response). Each of these techniques potentially presents a problem. The latter is limited by the fact that not all the data for each subject is employed, and further, the amount discarded for each subject is not equal. As a result, certain critical events (topic shifts, summary statements, etc.) may be included for some subjects and not others.

Procedures for controlling for differences in elapsed time by computing a ratio of event time to total elapsed time are also subject to methodological criticism. These criticisms stem from possible part-whole correlations between total elapsed time and the ratio of cumulative event duration to total elapsed time. Due to this possibility, computing such a ratio does not necessarily control for variations in total elapsed time. For this reason, it may be necessary to employ procedures other than cumulative duration/elapsed time ratios in some cases (Marsden, Kalter, & Ericson, 1974).

A second issue relevant to the analysis of temporal data concerns the fact that each of the variables outlined above might reasonably be treated in terms of mean group responses. So, a researcher might compare mean response latencies for two experimental groups. However, certain cognitive models allow predictions concerning not just group means, but also the entire distribution of reaction times (see McNicol & Stewart, 1980; Ratcliff, 1979; Smith, 1980). For this reason, in some cases it may be necessary to examine variance, skew, and kurtosis in order to determine the relative adequacy of competing models (e.g., Ratcliff, 1978; Ratcliff & Murdock, 1976).

A third methodological point concerns the desirability of cumulative statistics in examining inter-event intervals and brief, recurrent responses. When employing cumulative indices of recurrent behaviors (e.g., self-adaptors per second) or mean inter-event intervals (e.g., average duration of silent pauses), potentially valuable information concerning the location and duration of individual events is lost. For this reason, time-series techniques which preserve individual event durations and inter-event intervals may be preferred over cumulative statistics (see Davis & Lee, 1980).

An additional issue of note concerns the use of reaction time decomposition via the additive factors method. Since its introduction by Sternberg (1969a, 1969b), the additive factors method has been a cornerstone in the analysis of reaction time data. Its basic intent is to provide a means of assessing the properties of a cognitive process by determining whether some variable impacts upon that process in predicted ways. An example is useful to illustrate the logic of the additive factors method. Suppose that an investigator is concerned with the process of facial recognition and adopts a general two-stage conception of this process in which stimulus faces are held to be analyzed according to their constituent features and then compared to long-term memory representations in order to determine whether a face is familiar or not. To study these processes our investigator designs an experiment in which subjects are presented with a series of photographs of a number of different faces. At some later time subjects are shown a second series of photographs and asked to determine whether each is "new" or "old." In this basic design two factors are manipulated. We should expect that a degraded stimulus (e.g., a random pattern of dots superimposed on the photograph) will affect the feature analysis stage of processing. Further, the number of photographs in the initial session might impact upon the comparison process in that larger numbers of stimulus photographs would be associated with longer response times. For these reasons, the experimenter employs a factorial design in which the number of initial photographs and the quality of the test photographs (degraded versus normal) is varied. If the reaction times to produce correct, positive responses (for purposes of expository clarity let us ignore erroneous and negative responses) reveal independent effects of stimulus degradation and number of photographs, then we may conclude that these factors affect two distinct stages of processing. Following the logic of the additive factors method, an interaction effect between these independent variables would indicate that they are affecting at least one stage of processing in common.

Despite the apparent usefulness of the additive factors method, it is subject to several criticisms and practical limitations (McClelland, 1979; Taylor, 1976; Taylor & Fiske, 1981). Perhaps most important in this regard is the assumption of serial stages of processing. While the additive factors method is based upon the assumption that one stage of processing is completed before the second begins (e.g., feature analysis followed by memory comparison), it is equally possible that the output of one stage is continuously available to the next. In such cases the logical conclusions of the additive factors method would not hold as an accurate characterization of the focal processes (McClelland, 1979).

A final methodological point relevant to the analysis of chronometric data concerns individual differences in temporal response characteristics. Response durations and latencies are affected by a wide range of factors, such as age, sex, fatigue, familiarity with the task, and personality factors (Brebner, 1980; Newell & Rosenbloom, 1981; Sabin, Clemmer, O'Connell, & Kowal, 1979; Welford, 1980). For this reason, it is often desirable to control for individual response characteristics by employing covariates, repeated measures, or blocking designs. Alternatively, and consistent with the recommendation for use of time-series techniques given above, rather than using group means, the individual may serve as the primary unit of analysis (see Kail & Bisanz, 1982; Newell, 1973 for a related point).

Demand on Processing Capacity as an Index of Cognitive Processing

We have all experienced cases in which we were so intent upon some task that we were oblivious to other events transpiring in our immediate environment. This ubiquitous phenomenon has long been recognized as a fundamental property of attention (see James, 1890). Early attempts at explicating the nature of this limitation typically invoked a conception of some structural filter or bottleneck in the processing system which served to restrict the number of inputs that could be attended at any time (e.g., Broadbent, 1958; Treisman, 1964). Such filter models have generally given way (see Massaro, 1975; Norman, 1976) to an alternative conception of attention which involves the notion of a limited amount of processing resources that can be flexibly allocated throughout the information processing system to execute different tasks (e.g., Kahneman, 1973; Norman & Bobrow, 1975). As a result, demand on processing capacity is seen as an important property of a cognitive process.

Perhaps most common as a means of investigating resource demands is the primary task-secondary task paradigm. The rationale of such investigations is relatively straightforward. A typical experiment involves giving subjects a primary task which is assumed to make considerable demands upon processing resources, such that little capacity remains for executing additional tasks. A second task can then be introduced and the subject's performance on that task assessed. Heavy demands on processing capacity are assumed to be reflected in the speed and accuracy with which the secondary task is performed. This basic method allows the researcher to ascertain the factors that lead to greater or lesser demands on processing capacity in the performance of a particular type of task.

Among the earliest and most common of the techniques employing the primary task-secondary task rationale are shadowing experiments. In these investigations subjects are presented with an auditory message and asked to repeat, or shadow, that message as it occurs. This shadowing task generally proves quite difficult, and, for this reason, is assumed to make heavy demands on central processing capacity. Simultaneous with the message to be shadowed, the subject is given a second task on which performance is assessed. Dichotic listening situations are often used in shadowing experiments, and subjects are given the task of shadowing the message presented in one ear. Performance on the secondary task is assessed by measures of recall of information in the unshadowed ear (e.g., Cherry, 1953; Moray, 1959; Norman, 1969). Although reports of information in the unattended channel are a common means of assessing secondary task performance, practically any secondary task could be used in order to examine demand on processing capacity. Additionally, tasks other than shadowing can be used as the primary task. One alternative to shadowing that has received increasing use is that of giving subjects some memory task such as retaining a list of five lexical items while also performing the secondary task (e.g., Lansman & Hunt, 1982; Logan, 1979; Reitman, 1974). In these experiments the number of items to be retained is typically on the order of 5–7, so that the capacity of retention is approached but not exceeded.

As noted above, the dependent variables of interest in the primary task-secondary task paradigm are typically the speed and/or accuracy with which the secondary task is executed. This follows from the assumption that as one task makes increasing demands on central processing capacity there will be fewer resources leftover for performing the second task, so that it will be executed more slowly and/ or with more errors. Although examination of mean reaction times is the most common method for analyzing temporal data collected in this way, these data are subject to the same considerations developed above in the discussion of analysis of chronometric measures. Further, because of the possibility of speed-accuracy tradeoffs in such experiments, both types of data are desirable.

Other procedures for examining demand on processing capacity merit note. Among these are studies which require subjects to monitor one versus two or more inputs or sensory modalities simultaneously in order to examine potential decrements in performance that occur when monitoring multiple spatial locations or modalities. These experiments differ from the paradigm discussed above in that no input is designated as the primary stimulus. These simultaneous monitoring techniques have been used to study attentional demands of low-level perceptual processing (see Massaro, 1975, pp. 299–335).

Two other classes of methods for studying demand on processing capacity are particularly relevant for social behavior. Because heavy demands upon processing capacity are held to result in slower responses, experiments often examine the time required to produce a response in order to draw inferences about the amount or complexity of processing preceding that response. Thus, studies of acquisition of skilled behavior reveal increasing speed of performance over practice trials (e.g., Newell & Rosenbloom, 1981; Schneider & Shiffrin, 1977; Shiffrin & Schneider, 1977). This fact is commonly attributed to increasing automaticity of the skill, such that its execution demands less processing resources (Anderson, 1982; Greene, 1984c; Levin, Silverman, & Ford, 1967; Neves & Anderson, 1981).

Temporal Measures of Speech Production and Demand on Processing Capacity

Particularly relevant in the current context is the fact that the effects of repetition and practice on speed of response are revealed in speech behaviors as well as in other perceptual, motor, and cognitive tasks. Thus, temporal measures of speech production can be used to draw inferences concerning demand on processing capacity. These temporal speech variables include speech rate, speaker-turn latency, sound-silence ratio, filled pause ratio, and the like (see Siegman, 1979). Such variables are particularly appealing because, in addition to providing a means of assessing demand on processing capacity, they also have been shown to be related to social perceptions of deception (Zuckerman, DePaulo, & Rosenthal, 1981), competence (Brown, Strong, & Rencher, 1973; Lay & Burron, 1968; Street & Brady, 1982), and social attractiveness (Brown, Strong, & Rencher, 1973; Street & Brady, 1982). Thus, objective measures of speech production can be seen to have significance for both cognitive and social levels of analysis.

Although there are a number of specific temporal indices employed to investigate the cognitive processes underlying the production of speech, the various measures can be grouped into three general classes according to the type of speech behavior on which they focus: (a) silent pause variables (including response latency, and speaker-turn latency); (b) filled-pause variables; and (c) speech-disruption variables. The speech behaviors indexed in each of these classes can be used to manipulate the temporal course of speech production, and, for this reason, each provides an indication of demand on processing capacity. This line of reasoning has led Siegman (1978, 1979) to suggest that these objective measures of speech production are characterized by a "symptom equivalence." The notion that the speed of speech production can be modulated in a variety of different ways suggests three significant implications. First, we should expect that silent pausing, filled pausing, and speech disruptions will be related, such that when one means of delaying production is constrained, another will become more prominent, and, indeed, there is evidence of such a compensatory effect (e.g., Beattie & Bradbury, 1979). Second, the functional equivalence of these speech behaviors suggests the possibility that individuals will have characteristic modes of pausing, such that they rarely exhibit certain other modes (e.g., filled pauses). Finally, these two points suggest a practical recommendation for research. Due to the compensatory relationships among these variables, the investigator should examine a number of objective measures rather than focus on a single index (Siegman, 1978, 1979).

Although these various speech phenomena are characterized by a symptom equivalence, they are not strictly equivalent in the sense that in a particular situation an individual is as likely to exhibit one of these as the others. Instead, various situational and individual factors will impact upon the display of these objective measures. The nature of these limitations on functional equivalence are sketched below.

Silent pauses. In addition to response latency and speaker-turn latency, silent pausing includes those periods after the onset of speech during which there is no phonation. There is implicit in the conception of silent pausing the issue of just how long a period of silence will constitute a "pause." In practice, studies of cognitive processing in speech production (as opposed to investigation of articulatory mechanisms) will typically employ an operational definition of pauses as a period of silence on the order of 250–300 msec or greater (e.g., Beattie, 1978, 1980; Boomer, 1965; Butterworth, 1980; Cappella & Streibel, 1979; Jaffe & Feldstein, 1970; Siegman, 1979). Measures of this size are particularly appropriate in light of the social significance of silent pausing, due to the fact that people are able to detect pauses on this order of magnitude (Walker & Trimboli, 1982).

There are a number of distinct measures of silent pausing that are often employed. These include various pause ratios which attempt to adjust for monologue length by computing a ratio of silent pausing to speech duration. However, such indices are subject to the criticisms reviewed above concerning part-whole correlations in temporal ratios. Alternatively, one might employ average pause duration or measures of pause frequency (e.g., Siegman, 1979). Closely related to silent pausing are measures of speech rate. Because speech rate is primarily determined by amount of silent pausing these measures are highly correlated (Goldman-Eisler, 1956, 1958). Indeed, correlation coefficients between speech rate and the frequency and duration of silent pausing are on the order of .8–.9 in magnitude (see Sabin et al., 1979).

Filled pauses. Filled pauses refer to nonlinguistic vocalizations ("er," "uhm," "ah," etc.) which accompany speech (Maclay & Osgood, 1959; Mahl, 1956). As in the case of silent pauses, filled pauses can be used to slow speech production while cognitive operations are carried out. Filled pauses and silent pauses are not, however, strictly equivalent. Brotherton (1979) suggests that while silent pausing reflects semantic planning, filled pauses are related to lexical choice. Further, Maclay and Osgood (1959) note that filled pauses serve to prevent interruption while speech is delayed.

Speech disruptions. Speech disruptions refer to any of a number of disturbances in speech, including: repetitions, sentence incompletions or reconstructions, omissions, slips of the tongue, stuttering, and incoherent sounds (Mahl, 1956). Again, such behaviors may reflect cognitive planning, in that heavy cognitive loads will increase their frequency (Siegman, 1979). Despite this, speech disruptions are not strictly equivalent with silent pauses, because such disturbances are associated with state anxiety as well as speech preparation processes (Cook, 1969; Feldstein, Brenner, & Jaffe, 1963; Mahl, 1956; Siegman & Pope, 1965).

These preceding paragraphs suggest that the researcher needs to employ those measures most appropriate to his/her research hypotheses and design. In addition to theoretical considerations stemming from the functional role of objective speech measures, there are some practical considerations of note for the collection of such data. These objective speech variables are influenced by a number of factors which the experimenter needs to control or measure in order to reduce error variance and eliminate possible alternative interpretations of the data. Among these potential confounding factors are familiarity with the material and the opportunity to plan output in advance of speech. Because these factors will reduce pausing (e.g., Butterworth, 1980; Deese, 1978, 1980; Greene, 1984b; Lindsley, 1975), it is important to insure that they are controlled. Similarly, because pausing decreases with age over the early part of the life span (Sabin et al., 1979), it may be necessary to include age as a factor when studying the speech production of younger subjects. Finally, there is some evidence of individual stability in the tendency to employ faster speech rates, filled pauses, and the like (e.g., Goldman-Eisler, 1956) and, for this reason, covariate designs which remove individual variations in such tendencies may be especially appropriate.

Finally, a caveat is in order concerning response time as an indicant of demand on processing capacity. Such measures are probably more accurately characterized as indicants of the amount or complexity of processing preceding a response, and only indirectly as measures of cognitive load. Thus, a response may be slower because more operations were required for its execution, even though these operations made no more demands on processing capacity than another, faster response. For this reason, claims concerning demand on processing resources made on the basis of simple response time data should be scrutinized carefully, taking into account potential task differences and speed-accuracy tradeoffs.

Physiological Measures as an Index of Demand on Processing Capacity

Like the temporal characteristics of behavioral production, the final means of assessing demand on processing resources also has unique social significance. Kahneman (1973), in his landmark treatment of capacity models, shows that cognitive effort is reflected in measures of physiological arousal, particularly pupil dilation. Physiological variables, then, may be used to draw inferences about cognitive load. As an example, the fact that liars tend to show greater degrees of pupil dilation than truth-tellers (Zuckerman, et al., 1981), is to be expected, given that the process of formulating a lie is more difficult, ceteris paribus, than telling the truth. The limitations of such measures stem from the fact that factors other than mental effort can lead to heightened arousal. For this reason, the strength of claims about demand on processing capacity based on physiological indices may be weakened unless the effect on contaminating factors can be ruled out.

In concluding this discussion of processing capacity, a pair of general assumptions should be made explicit. Many of the techniques mentioned are predicated on the assumption of a single source of processing capacity that can be allocated throughout the information processing system (Logan, 1979). If, in the future, this assumption does not prove to be viable, then these techniques will need to be revised in light of conceptions of multiple processing capacities. The other key point concerns the distinction between capacity limitations and structural limitations (Kahneman, 1973). As noted above, the notion of limited processing resources is an outgrowth of observed limitations in ability to execute multiple tasks simultaneously. It should be clear, however, that in addition to finite processing capacity, people are limited in their performance by the physical structure of the body and nervous system. Such structural limitations arise when two tasks require the same perceptual or response architecture (Kahneman, 1973). Because of the possibility of structural limitations, conclusions about processing capacity requirements based on demonstrated interference effects are warranted only to the extent that structural limitations are not present.

Output Information as an Index of Cognitive Processing

At the outset of this chapter we noted that the fundamental aim of cognitive science is to explain input-output regularities by describing the structures and processes of the information processing system responsible for those regularities. In effect, the individual is seen as an information transducer, and the assumption is that by examining the relationship of input information to output information one can draw inferences concerning the nature of the system. A typical strategy for experimentation, then, is to provide the subject with a particular configuration of inputs (via instructions and controlled stimuli) and then to observe the pattern of information produced in response. Although such an orientation permits the examination of virtually any class of responses, in practice, four major types of output information represent the bulk of cognitive research. The first of these concern simple "yes/no," "stop," or stimulus identification responses given either verbally or manually, which are amenable to analysis in terms of reaction times and accuracy. Beyond such simple responses employed in studies of low-level perceptual processing (see Massaro, 1975; Vickers, 1980; Welford, 1980), output information is usually assessed by use of recognition and recall responses, self-reports, and production errors.

Memory Phenomena: Recognition and Recall

The most common procedures for examining output information involve recognition and recall techniques. In part, the widespread use of these procedures is due to the fact that they can be used to study memory for virtually any type of input information, including word lists (see Murphy & Puff, 1982; Pellegrino & Hubert, 1982), prose passages (see Voss, Tyler, & Bisanz, 1982), interpersonal interactions (e.g., Keenan, MacWhinney, & Mayhew, 1977; Stafford & Daly, 1984), and visual inputs (see Loftus, 1982).

The distinction between recognition and recall tasks is typically considered to hinge upon whether the subject is presented with a copy of the stimulus at time of test (e.g., Glass, Holyoak, & Santa, 1979; but see Murdock, 1982). Thus, a recognition task involves presenting the subject with a stimulus and asking whether that input has been encountered before. In contrast, recall tasks do not provide a copy of the information to be retrieved from memory. Recognition tests, then, simply require that the subject evaluate the stimulus in terms of its likelihood of having occurred before, while recall tasks involve both generation and evaluation of information. A practical consequence of this distinction is that performance in recognition tasks is usually, but not always, better than in recall tasks, due to the fact that recognition procedures provide more cues for searching memory (Anderson, 1985).

Recognition. Performance in recognition tasks is assessed via measures of response accuracy and latency (and, sometimes, confidence) (Murdock, 1982). Issues in the analysis of response latency data and the possibility of speed-accuracy tradeoffs in recognition tasks have both been discussed above. The analysis of accuracy of recognition responses presents several alternatives, but before reviewing these, some terminology is necessary to establish a framework for this discussion.

Any item presented in a recognition test can be considered "old" or "new" depending upon whether it has been encountered before. Further, subjects may give either affirmative or negative responses to the question of whether they recognize each item. These two factors define a 2 × 2 matrix of item type (old-new) by subject response (yes-no). There are thus two types of correct responses the subject can make: "yes" responses to old items (termed "hits") and "no" responses to new items ("correct rejections"). Similarly, two types of errors are discernable: "yes" responses to new items ("false alarms") and "no" responses to old items ("misses").

One way to proceed in reporting accuracy data is to report the hit rate. In recognition tasks which require a single, forced-choice among multiple alternatives (as in multiple-choice exams) this is probably an acceptable procedure (Murdock, 1982). However, Murdock argues that hit rate is not an appropriate measure of performance in cases where subject responses are limited to dichotomous (yes/no) responses for each item. He notes that such a procedure reflects only a portion of the data: responses to old items. A more desirable procedure would be to report both hit rate and false alarms rate. An alternative is to compute a d' statistic derived from signal detection theory (Green & Swets, 1966) which incorporates the distributions for both old and new items. Although an exposition of the underlying logic of d' goes beyond the limitations of the current forum, succinct introductions can be found in a number of sources (e.g., Lindsay & Norman, 1977; Massaro, 1975).

In addition to issues of data analysis, there are a number of practical concerns involved in collecting recognition data. The researcher needs to be cognizant of accuracy due to chance; this possibility makes it a good idea to balance the number of old and new items at time of test, so that random guessing will not produce extremely high accuracy rates. Further, the value of any recognition test is a function of the nature of the foils employed. False items which are too easily distinguished may provide little information about the process of interest. More generally, subjects' recognition of naturalistic stimuli may be phenomenally high in some cases (e.g., Haber & Standing, 1969; Shepard, 1967; Standing, 1973), so that ceiling effects become a problem. Finally, any memory study involving either recognition or recall presents the possibility of set-size effects (e.g., Hastie & Kumar, 1979), in which differential performance over stimulus conditions is due strictly to the difference in number of stimulus items of each type presented.

Recall. In contrast to recognition tasks, recall tasks require that the subject generate information without the aid of a copy of a previously presented stimulus. Recall tasks can be divided into two general classes, depending upon the eliciting conditions employed. Free-recall procedures involve nothing more in the way of instructions than asking the subject to recollect some previously input information. The second type of recall task, cued recall, involves giving the subject eliciting information which previously has been associated with the information to be remembered.

Orthogonal to the free-recall versus cued-recall distinction is that between warned- and incidental-recall techniques. Warned recall involves telling the subject, prior to exposure to the focal stimuli, that there will be a subsequent recall task. Incidental-recall experiments involve no such prior warning. The effect of warned recall is to lead the subject to employ deliberate mnemonic techniques. As a result the experimenter may wish to avoid warned-recall procedures when such methods might reduce the ecological validity of the investigation by changing the nature of the operations used to process stimulus information (Taylor & Fiske, 1981).

The most common means of assessing performance in recall tasks is the percentage of items correctly recalled. This measure lends itself well to situations in which word lists are used as stimulus materials. When prose passages (or utterances and interactions) are employed, proportion of information recalled may be more difficult to assess. This is due to the fact that people are generally poor at reproducing the surface form of such inputs (e.g., Keenan et al., 1977; Stafford & Daly, 1984). For this reason, scoring recall for prose in terms of "idea units" or "gist" may be more appropriate than examining recall of surface form (see Voss et al., 1982). Additionally, one must develop explicit coding procedures for dealing with information incorrectly recalled or added to the original material (e.g., Stafford & Daly, 1984).

In addition to measures of accuracy, performance in recall tasks can be assessed according to the sequence and organization of information recalled. These techniques are particularly significant from a conceptual standpoint. The sequence with which information is recalled should provide an index of the relative availability of that information in memory, in that items easily retrieved should be recalled sooner. The organization or clustering of information should yield insights concerning the relations among items stored in memory. The conceptual significance of clustering in free recall has given rise to a range of specific techniques for analyzing such data, and while explication of these methods is not possible here, some general reviews of issues in this domain are available (e.g., Friendly, 1979; Murphy & Puff, 1982; Pellegrino & Hubert, 1982; Puff, 1979; Voss, 1979).

The nature of recall experiments permits subjects to generate information which was not a part of the original input information; in view of this fact, a final class of approaches to the analysis of recall data involves the examination of errors, generalizations, inferences, and intrusions. Examination of such additions potentially provides a means of assessing structural properties and inferential processes in memory (e.g., Bartlett, 1932; Bower, Black, & Turner, 1979; Loftus, 1979), but, as noted above, the value of such analyses lies not with showing that recall errors occur, but with ascertaining theoretically meaningful classes of additions, such that the relative frequency of these errors can be manipulated in predictable ways.

Self-Reports on Cognitive Processes

Self-reports have been employed as a means of exploring cognitive processes since the pioneering work of Wundt and the advent of introspectionism in the late nineteenth century (Boring, 1950; Lieberman, 1979; Mischel, 1975). Problems of replicability in verbal reports of cognitive processes and arguments against theories based on unobservable constructs eventually led to the waning of introspective psychology and the rise of behaviorism. With the development of cognitive science came renewed interest in the individual's subjective experience of the world and the contents of consciousness as legitimate data for psychological theories (Miller, Polson, & Kintsch, 1984). One manifestation of this shift has been a series of articles addressing the usefulness of subject self-reports as a means of assessing cognitive processes (e.g., Ericsson & Simon, 1980; Kellogg, 1982; Nisbett & Wilson, 1977; Smith & Miller, 1978; see also Bem, 1972; Tybout & Scott, 1983; Wilson, Hill, & Johnson, 1981).

Nisbett and Wilson (1977) have attempted to show that individuals have virtually no introspective access to cognitive processes. Instead, verbal reports are made on the basis of a priori theories the person possesses concerning cause-effect relationships. As a result, introspective reports on cognitive processes are accurate only when the person's naive causal theories correspond to the process actually operating. In their treatment, Nisbett and Wilson emphasize the distinction between cognitive processes and cognitive content which results from those processes. For example, a person given the task of solving sequential puzzles such as the "Tower of Hanoi" problem (Simon, 1975) may report intermediate states leading to the eventual solution. Nisbett and Wilson argue that such intermediate results represent cognitive content, and not the process underlying solution of the problem. An alternative interpretation is offered by Smith and Miller (1978), who argue that cognitive processes can be characterized at a number of levels of abstraction, and that the sequence of intermediate results effectively describes the process at higher levels of abstraction.

To date, the most compelling and influential treatment of this issue is that of Ericsson and Simon (1980). These authors begin with the assumption that a general theory of verbal production is required in order to determine under what conditions self-reports are to be considered valid. They then propose a general human information processing model emphasizing the short-term memory (STM) long-term memory distinction as a means of meeting this requirement. On the basis of this model, Ericsson and Simon conclude that two factors are of primary importance in contributing to the validity of self-reports. First, the time of verbalization is crucial, in that retrospective reports, because they require information which no longer resides in STM, are unlikely to provide accurate accounts of cognitive processes. Second, verbal reports which require information transformations, such as inferences and generalizations from direct experience, are less likely to be valid than reports that require no such transformation. These authors add that, because low-level, automatic processes are not specified in STM, accurate verbal reports of such procedures are rarely possible. This final point is consistent with the position taken by Kellogg (1982), who invokes the controlled versus automatic processing distinction (Schneider & Shiffrin, 1977; Shiffrin & Schneider, 1977) in suggesting that introspection will be accurate only when subjects have allocated conscious attention to performance of some task.

On the basis of their model, Ericsson and Simon (1980) argue for verbal protocols produced by instructions to "think aloud" during structured tasks, as a means of assessing relevant cognitive processes (see also Genest & Turk, 1981; Newell & Simon, 1972). It is important to note, however, that protocol analysis is subject to several limitations in application. First, such techniques have traditionally been employed in highly structured task environments where initial states, end states, and legitimate transitions are well-specified (e.g., Newell & Simon, 1972). Protocol analysis may be less useful in more unstructured situations. Further, such protocols are most valuable in those cases where the processes of interest are amenable to verbal expression; automatic and sensory-motor processes are unlikely candidates for investigation in this way. Taylor and Fiske (1981) suggest that an additional limitation of protocol analysis is that such procedures are difficult to apply in studies of social interaction which necessitate that people produce other verbal outputs rather than concurrent reports of their thought processes. In light of this limitation, other researchers have opted for retrospective reports by having subjects list the thoughts which occurred to them as they processed a message (see Cacioppo & Petty, 1981).

Production Errors as an Index of Cognitive Processes

Ten years ago, Turvey noted that "while theories of perception abound, theories of action are conspicuous by their absence" (Turvey, 1977, p. 211). As if in response to this assessment, the intervening period has witnessed an explosion in cognitive approaches to issues of behavioral production (e.g., Bock, 1982; Greene, 1984c; Mackay, 1982; Newell & Rosenbloom, 1981; Norman & Shallice, 1980; Rosenbaum, 1980, 1984; Rosenbaum, Kenny, & Derr, 1983). As a result of this growing emphasis on the nature of the output system, production errors have assumed considerable conceptual significance, due to the fact that output errors provide an invaluable source of information concerning the structures and processes responsible for such errors (Fromkin, 1980; Norman, 1981; Reason, 1979). Thus, production errors are assumed to reveal much about the processes underlying normal, errorless performance.

Given the desirability of studying production errors, there are two general courses of action one might pursue. One is to accumulate a corpus of errors gleaned over time from observation of naturalistic occurrences (e.g., Motley, 1973; Norman, 1981; Zwicky, 1979). Alternatively, experimental techniques can be employed to increase the likelihood that production errors will be made. Some of these techniques are general, in that they can be used to induce a range of errors, while others are designed to produce a particular class of production failures.

Among the general techniques for inducing errors in performance are methods of manipulating demands on processing capacity. As noted above, performance on virtually any task deteriorates when the processing capacity requirements of that task exceed available resources. A second general technique involves the relation of arousal level to performance. It has long been recognized that the relation of physiological arousal and performance is given by an inverted-U function such that very low and very high levels of arousal are associated with increased errors while moderate arousal facilitates optimal performance (Yerkes & Dodson, 1908; see also Easterbrook, 1959; Hebb, 1955; Kahneman, 1973; Näätänen, 1973). This basic phenomenon makes it possible to induce errors by manipulating the arousal level of the subject. It is important to note, however, that the inflection point of the arousal-performance curve is displaced toward higher arousal for simple and automatic tasks (Kahneman,

1973). Thus, a level of arousal which disrupts performance on complex tasks may actually facilitate the execution of simpler operations.

These general techniques have the advantage of being applicable to a wide range of behaviors. However, the primary limitation of these methods lies in the fact that they provide little control over the types of errors that the subject is likely to exhibit.

In contrast to these general methods, a number of techniques have been developed for inducing a specific type of error. This second class of techniques includes a number of methods which are well-documented and need not be explicated in detail here. Among these specific methods are those for inducing the familiar Stroop (Cohen & Martin, 1975; Dyer, 1973; Logan, 1980; Stroop, 1935) and Einstellung phenomena (Luchins, 1942; Luchins & Luchins, 1959).

In addition to these techniques, a number of methods have been developed for inducing errors in speech production (see Fromkin, 1973, 1980). Particularly noteworthy in the present context are the techniques employed by Motley and his associates (see Motley, Baars, & Camden, 1983) for producing slips of the tongue. These methods have the advantage of having been employed in a number of studies so that one can be reasonably confident of their efficacy and feasibility.

In concluding this discussion on methods of eliciting production errors, we might ask what task characteristics should be incorporated in developing any such technique. Review of extant methods and current theory reveals a relatively small number of factors which seem crucial to inducing a particular class of errors (see Logan, 1980; Mackay, 1980; Motley et al. 1983; Norman, 1981). To begin, we can distinguish two general types of errors: (a) errors of selection, in which improper output constituents are employed, and (b) errors of execution, in which constituent elements are not correctly utilized or integrated. With respect to selection, the familiarity of constituents is crucial in that familiar information is more likely to be retrieved. The important notion here is that familiarity does not necessarily imply more accurate performance; as in the case of the Einstellung phenomenon, it is quite possible that more familiar constituents will be employed where they are not appropriate, precisely because they are more readily available. Also relevant to the issue of selection is the availability of other, similar constituents. Where more than one output unit might be employed, errors of transposition and inappropriate combination are more likely to occur. With errors of execution, time and demand on processing capacity are key factors. The subject should be placed under some time constraint to prevent detection and correction of mistakes. By the same token, because of time-processing capacity tradeoffs, it may be necessary to employ more demanding tasks in order to elicit frequent execution errors.

Conclusion and Some General Admonitions

Much of the work on social behavior currently being conducted under the rubric of "cognitivism" or "social cognition" does not rely on constructs suitable for examination via the variables outlined here. The reason is that many research efforts invoke cognitive terminology which is so general that no clear predictions for time or processing load are possible. Indeed, in many cases the same data could have been justified and interpreted without any reference to cognitive structures or processes. The disadvantage of such treatments is that they provide a sense of theoretical substance, while not introducing sufficient detail to allow falsification of the constructs employed. As a final comment, I want to argue for greater precision and specificity in cognitive models employed in the study of social interaction. In order to be falsified, a cognitive model must specify both structure and the process(es) which operate over that structure (Anderson, 1976, 1978; Greene, 1984a). Specification of process involves delineating those attributes discussed here: temporal characteristics, processing capacity requirements, and information transformations. Thus, when cognitive models are specified in requisite detail, they will be amenable to analysis in the ways suggested here.

The call for increased precision in conceptions of cognitive processes raises a very practical problem. Any cognitive process can always be explicated in terms of other, more fundamental, processes (Taylor & Fiske, 1981). The problem, then, is one of how far to pursue this reduction. As an answer, I suggest that one couch his/her conception of process at the most fundamental level which is still effective in yielding predictions about the social phenomena of interest. In this way, it should be possible to garner the benefits of cognitivism for the study of social behavior while relying upon theoretical constructs which permit test and falsification.

References

Anderson, J.R. (1976). *Language, memory, and thought.* Hillsdale, NJ: Erlbaum.
Anderson, J.R. (1978). Arguments concerning representations for mental imagery. *Psychological Review, 85,* 249–277.
Anderson, J.R. (1982). Acquisition of cognitive skill. *Psychological Review, 89,* 369–406.

Anderson, J.R. (1985). *Cognitive psychology and its implications* (2nd ed.). New York: Freeman.

Bartlett, F.C. (1932). *Remembering: A study in experimental and social psychology.* New York: Cambridge University Press.

Beattie, G.W. (1978). Floor-apportionment and gaze in conversational dyads. *British Journal of Social and Clinical Psychology, 17,* 7–15.

Beattie, G.W. (1980). The role of language production processes in the organization of behaviour in face-to-face interaction. In B. Butterworth (Ed.), *Language production: Vol. 1. Speech and talk* (pp. 69–107). London: Academic Press.

Beattie, G.W., & Bradbury, R.J. (1979). An experimental investigation of the modifiability of the temporal structure of spontaneous speech. *Journal of Psycholinguistic Research, 8,* 225–248.

Bem, D.J. (1972). Self-perception theory. *Advances in experimental social psychology, 6,* 1–62.

Bock, J.K. (1982). Toward a cognitive psychology of syntax: Information processing contributions to sentence formulation. *Psychological Review, 89,* 1–47.

Boomer, D.S. (1965). Hesitation and grammatical encoding. *Language and Speech, 8,* 148–158.

Boring, E.G. (1950). *A history of experimental psychology.* New York: Appleton Century.

Bower, G.H., Black, J.B., & Turner, T.J. (1979). Scripts in memory for text. *Cognitive Psychology, 11,* 177–220.

Brebner, J.M.T. (1980). Reaction time in personality theory. In A.T. Welford (Ed.), *Reaction times* (pp. 309–320). London: Academic Press.

Brebner, J.M.T., & Welford, A.T. (1980). Introduction: An historical background sketch. In A.T. Welford (Ed.), *Reaction times* (pp. 1–23). London: Academic Press.

Broadbent, D.E. (1958). *Perception and communication.* London: Pergamon.

Brotherton, P. (1979). Speaking and not speaking: Processes for translating ideas into speech. In A.W. Siegman & S. Feldstein (Eds.), *Of speech and time: Temporal speech patterns in interpersonal contexts* (pp. 179–209). Hillsdale, NJ: Erlbaum.

Brown, B.L., Strong, W.J., & Rencher, A.C. (1973). Perceptions of personality from speech: Effects of manipulations of acoustical parameters. *Journal of the Acoustical Society of America, 54,* 29–35.

Butterworth, B. (1980). Evidence from pauses in speech. In B. Butterworth (Ed.), *Language production: Vol. 1. Speech and talk* (pp. 155–176). London: Academic Press.

Cacioppo, J.T., & Petty, R.E. (1981). Social psychological procedures for cognitive response assessment: The thought-listing technique. In T.V. Merluzzi, C.R. Glass, & M. Genest (Eds.), *Cognitive assessment* (pp. 309–342). New York: Guilford Press.

Cappella, J.N., & Streibel, M.J. (1979). Computer analysis of talk-silence sequences: The FIASSCO system. *Behavior Research Methods and Instrumentation, 11,* 384–392.

Cherry, E.C. (1953). Some experiments on the recognition of speech, with one and with two ears. *Journal of the Acoustical Society of America, 25,* 975–979.

Cohen, G., & Martin, M. (1975). Hemisphere differences in an auditory stroop test. *Perception and Psychophysics, 17,* 79–83.

Cook, M. (1969). Anxiety, speech disturbances and speech rate. *British Journal of Social and Clinical Psychology, 8,* 13–21.

Davis, D.K., & Lee, J. (1980). Time-series analysis models for communication research. In P.R. Monge & J.N. Cappella (Eds.), *Multivariate techniques in human communication research* (pp. 429–454). New York: Academic Press.

Deese, J. (1978). Thought into speech. *American Scientist, 66,* 314–321.

Deese, J. (1980). Pauses, prosody, and the demands of production in language. In H.W. Dechert & M. Raupach (Eds.), *Temporal variables in speech: Studies in honour of Frieda Goldman-Eisler* (pp. 69–84). The Hague: Mouton.

Dyer, F.N. (1973). The stroop phenomenon and its use in the study of perceptual, cognitive, and response processes. *Memory and Cognition, 1,* 106–120.

Easterbrook, J.A. (1959). The effect of emotion on the utilization and the organization of behavior. *Psychological Review, 66,* 83–201.

Ericsson, K.A., & Simon, H.A. (1980). Verbal reports as data. *Psychological Review, 87,* 215–251.

Feldstein, S., Brenner, M.S., & Jaffe, J. (1963). The effect of subject sex, verbal interaction, and topical focus on speech disruption. *Language and Speech, 6,* 229–239.

Feldstein, S., & Welkowitz, J. (1978). A chronography of conversation: In defense of an objective approach. In A.W. Siegman & S. Feldstein (Eds.), *Nonverbal behavior and communication* (pp. 329–378). Hillsdale, NJ: Erlbaum.

Fiske, S.T., & Taylor, S.E. (1984). *Social cognition.* Reading, MA: Addison-Wesley.

Flanagan, O.J., Jr. (1984). *The science of the mind.* Cambridge, MA: MIT Press.

Friendly, M. (1979). Methods for finding graphic representations of associative memory structures. In C.R. Puff (Ed.), *Memory organization and structure* (pp. 85–129). New York: Academic Press.

Fromkin, V.A. (Ed.) (1973). *Speech errors as linguistic evidence.* The Hague: Mouton.

Fromkin, V.A. (Ed.) (1980). *Errors in linguistic performance: Slips of the tongue, ear, pen, and hand.* New York: Academic Press.

Gee, J.P., & Grosjean, F. (1984). Empirical evidence for narrative structure. *Cognitive Science, 8,* 59–85.

Genest, M., & Turk, D.C. (1981). Think-aloud approaches to cognitive assessment. In T.V. Merluzzi, C.R. Glass, & M. Genest (Eds.), *Cognitive assessment* (pp. 233–269). New York: Guilford Press.

Glass, A.L., Holyoak, K.J., & Santa, J.L. (1979). *Cognition.* Reading, MA: Addison-Wesley.

Goldman-Eisler, F. (1956). The determinants of the rate of speech output and their mutual relations. *Journal of Psychosomatic Research, 1,* 137–143.

Goldman-Eisler, F. (1958). Speech production and the predictability of words in context. *Quarterly Journal of Experimental Psychology, 10,* 96–106.

Green, D.M., & Swets, J.A. (1966). *Signal detection theory and psychophysics.* New York: Wiley.

Greene, J.O. (1984a). Evaluating cognitive explanations of communicative phenomena. *Quarterly Journal of Speech, 70,* 241–254.

Greene, J.O. (1984b). Speech preparation processes and verbal fluency. *Human Communication Research, 11,* 61–84.

Greene, J.O. (1984c). A cognitive approach to human communication: An action assembly theory. *Communication Monographs, 51,* 289–306.

Greene, J.O., & Cody, M.J. (in press). On thinking and doing: Cognitive science and the production of social behavior. *Journal of Language and Social Psychology.*

Greene, J.O., O'Hair, H.D., Cody, M.J., & Yen, C. (1985). Planning and control of behavior during deception. *Human Communication Research, 11,* 335–364.

Grosjean, F., Grosjean, L., & Lane, H. (1979). The patterns of silence: Performance structures in sentence production. *Cognitive Psychology, 11,* 58–81.

Haber, R.N., & Standing, L.G. (1969). Direct measures of short-term visual storage. *Quarterly Journal of Experimental Psychology, 21,* 43–54.

Hastie, R., & Kumar, P.A. (1979). Person memory: Personality traits as organizing principles in memory for behaviors. *Journal of Personality and Social Psychology, 37,* 25–38.

Hebb, D.O. (1955). Drives and the C.N.S. (Conceptual nervous system). *Psychological Review, 62,* 243–254.

Jaffe, J., & Feldstein, S. (1970). *Rhythms of dialogue.* New York: Academic Press.

James, W. (1890). *The principles of psychology,* Vol. 1. New York: Holt.

Kahneman, D. (1973). *Attention and effort.* Englewood Cliffs, NJ: Prentice Hall.

Kail, R.V., Jr., & Bisanz, J. (1982). Cognitive strategies. In C.R. Puff (Ed.), *Handbook of research methods in human memory and cognition* (pp. 229–255). New York: Academic Press.

Keenan, J.M., MacWhinney, B., & Mayhew, D. (1977). Pragmatics in memory: A study of natural conversation. *Journal of Verbal Learning and Verbal Behavior, 16,* 549–560.

Kellogg, R.T. (1982). When can we introspect accurately about mental processes? *Memory and Cognition, 10,* 141–144.

Lansman, M., & Hunt, E. (1982). Individual differences in secondary task performance. *Memory and Cognition, 10,* 10–24.

Levin, A., Silverman, I., & Ford, B. (1967). Hesitation in children's speech during explanation and description. *Journal of Verbal Learning and Verbal Behavior, 6,* 560–564.

Lieberman, D.A. (1979). Behaviorism and the mind: A (limited) call for a return to introspection. *American Psychologist, 34,* 319–333.

Lindsay, P.H., & Norman, D.A. (1977). *Human information processing* (2nd ed.). New York: Academic Press.

Lindsley, J.R. (1975). Producing simple utterances: How far ahead do we plan? *Cognitive Psychology, 7,* 1–19.

Loftus, E.F. (1979). *Eyewitness testimony.* Cambridge, MA: Harvard University Press.

Loftus, G.R. (1982). Picture memory methodology. In C.R. Puff (Ed.), *Handbook of research methods in human memory and cognition* (pp. 257–285). New York: Academic Press.

Logan, G.D. (1979). On the use of concurrent memory load to measure attention and automaticity. *Journal of Experimental Psychology: Human Perception and Performance, 5,* 189–207.

Logan, G.D. (1980). Attention and automaticity in Stroop and priming tasks: Theory and data. *Cognitive Psychology, 12,* 523–553.

Long, J., Nimmo-Smith, I., & Whitefield, A. (1983). Skilled typing: A characterization based on the distribution of times between responses. In W.E. Cooper (Ed.), *Cognitive aspects of skilled typewriting* (pp. 145–195). New York: Springer-Verlag.

Luchins, A.S. (1942). Mechanization in problem solving. *Psychological Monographs, 54,* No. 248.

Luchins, A.S., & Luchins, E.H. (1959). *Rigidity of behavior: A variational approach to the effects of Einstellung.* Eugene, OR: University of Oregon.

Mackay, D.G. (1980). Speech errors: Retrospect and prospect. In V.A. Fromkin (Ed.), *Errors in linguistic performance: Slips of the tongue, ear, pen, and hand* (pp. 319–332). New York: Academic Press.

Mackay, D.G. (1982). The problems of flexibility, fluency, and speed-accuracy trade-off in skilled behavior. *Psychological Review, 89,* 483–506.

Maclay, H.J., & Osgood, C.E. (1959). Hesitation phenomena in spontaneous English speech. *Word, 15,* 19–44.

Mahl, G.F. (1956). Disturbances and silences in the patient's speech in psychotherapy. *Journal of Abnormal and Social Psychology, 53,* 1–15.

Marsden, G., Kalter, N., & Ericson, W.A. (1974). Response productivity: A methodological problem in content analysis studies in psychotherapy. *Journal of Consulting and Clinical Psychology, 42,* 224–230.

Massaro, D.W. (1975). *Experimental psychology and information processing.* Chicago: Rand McNally.

McClelland, J.L. (1979). On the time relations of mental processes: An examination of systems of process in cascade. *Psychological Review, 86,* 287–330.

McNicol, D., & Stewart, G.W. (1980). Reaction time and the study of memory.

In A.T. Welford (Ed.), *Reaction times* (pp. 253–307). London: Academic Press.

Miller, J.R., Polson, P.G., & Kintsch, W. (1984). Problems of methodology in cognitive science. In W. Kintsch, J.R. Miller, & P.G. Polson (Eds.), *Method and tactics in cognitive science* (pp. 1–18). Hillsdale, NJ: Erlbaum.

Mischel, T. (1975). Psychological explanations and their vicissitudes. In W.J. Arnold (Ed.), *Nebraska symposium on motivation: Conceptual foundations of psychology*, Vol. 23. (pp. 133–204). Lincoln, NE: University of Nebraska Press.

Moray, N. (1959). Attention in dichotic listening: Affective cues and the influence of instructions. *Quarterly Journal of Experimental Psychology, 11,* 56–60.

Motley, M.T. (1973). An analysis of spoonerisms as psycholinguistic phenomena. *Speech Monographs, 40,* 66–71.

Motley, M.T., Baars, B.J., & Camden, C.T. (1983). Experimental verbal slip studies: A review and an editing model of language encoding. *Communication Monographs, 50,* 79–101.

Murdock, B.B., Jr. (1982). Recognition memory. In C.R. Puff (Ed.), *Handbook of research methods in human memory and cognition* (pp. 1–26). New York: Academic Press.

Murphy, M.D. & Puff, C.R. (1982). Free recall: Basic methodology and analyses. In C.R. Puff (Ed.), *Handbook of research methods in human memory and cognition* (pp. 99–128). New York: Academic Press.

Näätänen, R. (1973). The inverted-U relationship between activation and performance: A critical review. In S. Kornblum (Ed.), *Attention and performance IV* (pp. 155–174). New York: Academic Press.

Neves, D.M., & Anderson, J.R. (1981). Knowledge compilation: Mechanisms for the automatization of cognitive skills. In J.R. Anderson (Ed.), *Cognitive skills and their acquisition* (pp. 57–84). Hillsdale, NJ: Erlbaum.

Newell, A. (1973). Production systems: Models of control structures. In W.G. Chase (Ed.), *Visual information processing* (pp. 463–526). New York: Academic Press.

Newell, A., & Rosenbloom, P.S. (1981). Mechanisms of skill acquisition and the law of practice. In J.R. Anderson (Ed.), *Cognitive skills and their acquisition* (pp. 1–55). Hillsdale, NJ: Erlbaum.

Newell, A., & Simon, H. (1972). *Human problem solving.* Englewood Cliffs, NJ: Prentice-Hall.

Nisbett, R.E., & Wilson, T.D. (1977). Telling more than we can know: Verbal reports on mental processes. *Psychological Review, 84,* 231–259.

Norman, D.A. (1969). Memory while shadowing. *Quarterly Journal of Experimental Psychology, 21,* 85–89.

Norman, D.A. (1976). *Memory and attention: An introduction to human information processing* (2nd ed.). New York: Wiley.

Norman, D.A. (1980). Copycat science or does the mind really work by table look-up? In R.A. Cole (Ed.), *Perception and production of fluent speech* (pp. 381–395). Hillsdale, NJ: Erlbaum.

Norman, D.A. (1981). Categorization of action slips. *Psychological Review, 88,* 1–15.

Norman, D.A., & Bobrow, D.G. (1975). On data-limited and resource-limited processes. *Cognitive Psychology, 7,* 44–64.

Norman, D.A., & Shallice, T. (1980). *Attention to action: Willed and automatic control of behavior* (Tech. Rep. No. 99). San Diego: University of California, Center for Human Information Processing.

Ostry, D.J. (1983). Determinants of interkey times in typing. In W.E. Cooper (Ed.), *Cognitive aspects of skilled typewriting* (pp. 225–246). New York: Springer-Verlag.

Pellegrino, J.W., & Hubert, L.J. (1982). The analysis of organization and structure in free recall. In C.R. Puff (Ed.), *Handbook of research methods in human memory and cognition* (pp. 129–172). New York: Academic Press.

Puff, C.R. (1979). Memory organization research and theory: The state of the art. In C.R. Puff (Ed.), *Memory organization and structure* (pp. 3–17). New York: Academic Press.

Ratcliff, R. (1978). A theory of memory retrieval. *Psychological Review, 85,* 59–108.

Ratcliff, R. (1979). Group reaction time distributions and an analysis of distribution statistics. *Psychological Bulletin, 86,* 446–461.

Ratcliff, R., & Murdock, B.B., Jr. (1976). Retrieval processes in recognition memory. *Psychological Review, 83,* 190–214.

Reason, J. (1979). Actions not as planned: The price of automatization. In G. Underwood & R. Stevens (Eds.), *Aspects of consciousness* (vol. 1, pp. 67–89). London: Academic Press.

Reitman, J.S. (1974). Without surreptitious rehearsal, information in short-term memory decays. *Journal of Verbal Learning and Verbal Behavior, 13,* 365–377.

Rosenbaum, D.A. (1980). Human movement initiation: Specification of arm, direction, and extent. *Journal of Experimental Psychology: General, 109,* 444–474.

Rosenbaum, D.A. (1984). The planning and control of movements. In J.R. Anderson & S.M. Kosslyn (Eds.), *Tutorials in learning and memory: Essays in honor of Gordon Bower* (pp. 219–233). San Francisco: Freeman.

Rosenbaum, D.A., Kenny, S.B., & Derr, M.A. (1983). Hierarchical control of rapid movement sequences. *Journal of Experimental Psychology: Human Perception and Performance, 9,* 86–102.

Sabin, E.J., Clemmer, E.J., O'Connell, D.C., & Kowal, S. (1979). A Pausological approach to speech development. In A.W. Siegman & S. Feldstein (Eds.), *Of speech and time: Temporal speech patterns in interpersonal contexts* (pp. 35–55). Hillsdale, NJ: Erlbaum.

Schmidt, R.A., Zelaznik, H., Hawkins, B., Frank, J.S., & Quinn, J.T., Jr. (1979). Motor-output variability: A theory for the accuracy of rapid motor acts. *Psychological Review, 86,* 415–451.

Schneider, W., & Shiffrin, R.N. (1977). Controlled and automatic human information processing: I. Detection, search and attention. *Psychological Review, 84,* 1–66.

Shepard, R.N. (1967). Recognition memory for words, sentences, and pictures. *Journal of Verbal Learning and Verbal Behavior, 6,* 156–163.

Shiffrin, R.M., & Schneider, W. (1977). Controlled and automatic human information processing: II. Perceptual learning, automatic attending, and a general theory. *Psychological Review, 84,* 127–190.

Siegman, A.W. (1978). The telltale voice: Nonverbal messages of verbal communication. In A.W. Siegman & S. Feldstein (Eds.), *Nonverbal behavior and communication* (pp. 183–243). Hillsdale, NJ: Erlbaum.

Siegman, A.W. (1979). Cognition and hesitation in speech. In A.W. Siegman & S. Feldstein (Eds.), *Of speech and time: Temporal speech patterns in interpersonal contexts* (pp. 151–178). Hillsdale, NJ: Erlbaum.

Siegman, A.W., & Feldstein, S.F. (Eds.) (1979). *Of speech and time: Temporal speech patterns in interpersonal contexts.* Hillsdale, NJ: Erlbaum.

Siegman, A.W., & Pope, B. (1965). Effects of question specificity and anxiety-producing messages on verbal fluency in the initial interview. *Journal of Personality and Social Psychology, 2,* 522–530.

Simon, H.A. (1975). The functional equivalence of problem solving skills. *Cognitive Psychology, 7,* 268–288.

Simon, H.A. (1980). How to win at twenty questions with nature. In R.A. Cole (Ed.), *Perception and production of fluent speech* (pp. 535–548). Hillsdale, NJ: Erlbaum.

Smith, E.R., & Miller, R.D. (1978). Limits on perception of cognitive processes: A reply to Nisbett and Wilson. *Psychological Review, 85,* 355–362.

Smith, G.A. (1980). Models of choice reaction time. In A.T. Welford (Ed.), *Reaction times* (pp. 173–214). London: Academic Press.

Stafford, L., & Daly, J.A. (1984). Conversational memory: The effects of recall mode and memory expectations on remembrances of natural conversations. *Human Communication Research, 10,* 379–402.

Standing, L. (1973). Learning 10,000 pictures. *Quarterly Journal of Experimental Psychology, 25,* 207–222.

Sternberg, S. (1969a). Memory-scanning: Mental processes revealed by reaction-time experiments. *American Scientist, 57,* 421–457.

Sternberg, S. (1969b). The discovery of processing stages: Extensions of Donder's method. *Acta Psychologica, 30,* 276–315.

Street, R.L., Jr., & Brady, R.M. (1982). Speech rate acceptance ranges as a function of evaluative domain, listener speech rate, and communication context. *Communication Monographs, 49,* 290–308.

Stroop, J.R. (1935). Studies of interference in serial verbal reactions. *Journal of Experimental Psychology, 18,* 643–662.

Swinney, D. (1984). Theoretical and methodological issues in cognitive science: A psycholinguistic perspective. In W. Kintsch, J.R. Miller, & P.G. Polson (Eds.), *Method and tactics in cognitive science* (pp. 217–233). Hillsdale, NJ: Erlbaum.

Taylor, D.A. (1976). Stage analysis of reaction time. *Psychological Bulletin, 83,* 161–191.

Taylor, S.E., & Fiske, S.T. (1981). Getting inside the head: Methodologies for process analysis in attribution and social cognition. In J.H. Harvey, W. Ickes, & R.F. Kidd (Eds.), *New directions in attribution research,* Vol. 3 (pp. 459–524). Hillsdale, NJ: Erlbaum.

Treisman, A.M. (1964). Verbal cues, language and meaning in selective attention. *American Journal of Psychology, 77,* 206–219.

Turvey, M.T. (1977). Preliminaries to a theory of action with reference to vision. In R. Shaw & J. Bransford (Eds.), *Perceiving, acting, and knowing: Toward an ecological psychology* (pp. 211–265). Hillsdale, NJ: Erlbaum.

Tybout, A.M., & Scott, C.A. (1983). Availability of well-defined internal knowledge and the attitude formation process: Information aggregation versus self-perception. *Journal of Personality and Social Psychology, 44,* 474–491.

Vickers, D. (1980). Discrimination. In A.T. Welford (Ed.), *Reaction times* (pp. 25–72). London: Academic Press.

Voss, J.F. (1979). Organization, structure, and memory: Three perspectives. In C.R. Puff (Ed.), *Memory organization and structure* (pp. 375–400). New York: Academic Press.

Voss, J., Tyler, S.W., & Bisanz, G.L. (1982). Prose comprehension and memory. In C.R. Puff (Ed.), *Handbook of research methods in human memory and cognition* (pp. 349–393). New York: Academic Press.

Walker, M.B., & Trimboli, C. (1982). Smooth transitions in conversational interactions. *Journal of Social Psychology, 117,* 305–306.

Welford, A.T. (1980). Relationships between reaction time and fatigue, stress age and sex. In A.T. Welford (Ed.), *Reaction times* (pp. 321–354). London: Academic Press.

Wilson, T.D., Hill, J.G., & Johnson, J. (1981). Awareness and self-perception: Verbal reports on internal states. *Journal of Personality and Social Psychology, 40,* 53–71.

Yerkes, R.M., & Dodson, J.D. (1908). The relation of strength of stimulus to rapidity of habit-formation. *Journal of Comparative Neurology of Psychology, 18,* 459–482.

Zuckerman, M., DePaulo, B.M., & Rosenthal, R. (1981). Verbal and nonverbal communication of deception. *Advances in experimental social psychology, 14,* 2–59.

Zwicky, A.M. (1979). Classical malapropisms. *Language Sciences, 1,* 339–348.

CHAPTER 3

Communication Competence: Measures of Perceived Effectiveness

Brian H. Spitzberg

The "back-to-basics" competency movement of recent years has forced us to ask some difficult questions. Among the most difficult to ask—and answer—is how literate our society is. The fact that the question needs asking testifies to the potential seriousness of the problem. The headlines, and to a large extent, our political and educational institutions, still seem captured by the traditional literacies of reading, writing, and arithmetic. However, the consciousness of our day-to-day existence seems more captivated by the fourth "R" of relating.

Just how literate, or competent, are people in their ability to communicate? While the answers to this question vary considerably, taken as a whole the estimates are staggering in their social implications. In studies of applicants and patients in mental health facilities, estimates of "social inadequacy" range from 7% (Curran, Miller, Zwick, Monti, & Stout, 1980a) to 16.3% (Bryant, Trower, Yardley, Urbieta, & Letemendia, 1976) to 28% (Trower, Bryant, & Argyle, 1978). These findings alone might not seem surprising, except that estimates in normal populations range even higher. Hogarty and Katz (1971) estimate that 5% of the population is socially inadequate. Argyle (1981) estimates that 7% of the normal adult population is likely to experience serious difficulties in their social behavior. The Adult Performance Level Study (1977) estimates that approximately 20% of the normal adult population is functionally incompetent (although this estimate includes the traditional literacies as well). Dow (1985) found that 40% of subjects reported high in social anxiety were perceived as having distinct conversational deficits, while Rubin (1981a) discovered that, depending upon which of 19 specific communication competencies was being tested, between 10 and 49% of college students were incompetent.

The reason these estimates are staggering in their implications is because inadequacy in social and communicative skills has been related to loneliness (Spitzberg & Canary, 1985; Zakahi & Duran, 1982), depression (Haley, 1985; Wierzbicki, 1984), stress and anxiety (Wrubel, Benner, & Lazarus, 1981), hypertension (Morrison, Bellack, & Manuck, 1985); poor academic adjustment and outcomes (Kohn, 1977), sexual violence (Segal & Marshall, 1985), psychological well-being (Rook, 1984), and a host of mental illnesses (Curran et al., 1980b; Griffiths, 1980; Martin & Chapman, 1982; Rosen, Klein, Levenstein, & Shahinian, 1969; Zigler & Phillips, 1961). The traditional competencies may seem more tangible; they hardly seem more important. With these ideas in mind, issues of assessment in communicative competence take on considerable importance. The purpose of this chapter is to identify existing measures of communicative competence, and to review the available evidence for their research utility.

Taken very broadly, communicative competence is the ability to interact well with others. The term "well" refers to a positively valenced judgment of quality. Characteristics commonly associated with quality in communication include accuracy, clarity, comprehensibility, coherence, expertise, effectiveness, and appropriateness. Of these, appropriateness and effectiveness appear to be the most accepted criteria, partly because they subsume many of the other characteristics. However, which of these two, if either, should be accorded primary significance in defining competence is still very much in contention. It is not the purpose of this chapter to enter headlong into the theoretical debates concerning how competence in communicating should be defined and conceptualized.[1] However, a review must have boundaries, and the admittedly broad boundaries of this chapter will be to examine methods of assessing competent (i.e., appropriate and effective) communication. Competent communication is interaction that is perceived as effective in fulfilling certain rewarding objectives in a way that is also appropriate to the context in which the interaction occurs. The review of instruments assessing such constructs will be further aided by a series of critical assumptions.

First, it is not particularly productive to treat the competence research in different academic disciplines differently. Interest in communicative competence is alive and well in the literatures of social

---

[1] The interested reader is referred to several significant reviews of theoretical issues in the following sources: (Bochner & Kelly, 1974; Bradac & Wiemann, 1985; Brandt, 1979; Diez, 1984; Furnham, 1983; Hymes, 1972; McFall, 1982; Spitzberg, 1983; Spitzberg & Cupach, 1984; Wiemann & Backlund, 1980; Wiemann & Kelly, 1981).

psychology, clinical psychology, behavioral therapy, education, and business. I have drawn heavily upon reviews both within and without the communication discipline in the hope of locating the most relevant and promising assessment methods available (see, for example, Bellack, 1979, 1983; Curran, 1979a, 1979b; Curran & Mariotto, 1980; Eisler, 1976; Hersen & Bellack, 1977; Kelly, Chase, & Wiemann, 1979; Liberman, 1982; McFall, 1982; Rubin, R.B., 1981a; Schroeder & Rakos, 1983; Spitzberg, 1986a; Spitzberg & Cupach, 1984; Wiemann & Bradac, 1983). Reviews of assessment in areas peripherally related to interpersonal competence have also been examined (e.g., mental health, behavioral rigidity, and counseling; see Coulter & Morrow, 1978; Hefele & Hurst, 1972; Jackson, King, & Heller, 1981; Katz & Lyerly, 1963; Salzman, Kochansky, & Shader, 1972; Scofield & Yoxtheimer, 1983; Sundberg, Snowden, & Reynolds, 1978; Walls, Werner, Bacon, & Zane, 1977).

Second, numerous instruments have been developed for the express purpose of evaluating classroom performance. While these instruments may have potential theoretical utility, this review seeks to include them only if issues of reliability, validity, and theoretical relevance are addressed in the research literature. Most classroom performance evaluation measures have been subjected to minimal systematic investigation (Rubin, Sisco, Moore, & Quianthy, 1983). The exclusion of classroom performance measures is also justified by the existence of several extant reviews (e.g., Backlund, VanRheenan, Moore, Parks, & Booth, 1981; D. Rubin, 1981; D. Rubin, Daly, McCroskey, & Mead, 1982; R. Rubin, 1981a; D. Rubin & Mead, 1984).

Third, this review is influenced strongly by Cone's (1978) Behavioral Assessment Grid (BAG). It is necessary, therefore, to provide a brief overview of the BAG, since it will guide much of the subsequent review. According to Cone, any approach to behavioral assessment can be classified along the three dimensions of content, method, and universes of generalization. Content refers to the type of "behavior" referred to or observed. Content is commonly analyzed according to cognitive, physiological, and motor domains. This review is concerned solely with the motor domain, because it is assumed that communication behavior is the primary object of assessment when examining communication competence. While motivation and knowledge are integral to a complete understanding of communicative competence (see Spitzberg & Cupach, 1984), it is ultimately the overt behavior that is judged as competent or incompetent.

The method dimension is divided into two basic categories of "direct" and "indirect." Indirect methods include interviews, self-reports, and other reports. These are considered indirect because the actual behavior of interest usually is inferred or recalled from previous time periods and the time elapsed between the events referred to, and the recording of inferences is highly variable. Direct methods include self-observation, analog role-play, analog free behavior, naturalistic role-play, naturalistic free-behavior, and a category not envisioned by Cone (1978), objective criterion. Objective criterion refers to measures with objective "correct" responses.

The third dimension reflects the universes of generalization for the assessment method. Cone (1977) elaborates six universes of generalization: dimension, method, setting, time, item, and scorer. Dimension generality refers to the extent to which the behavioral dimension measured generalizes to other dimensions of behavior. Method generality concerns the degree of commonality among different methods of measuring the same behavior. Setting generality refers to the degree to which assessment in one context generalizes to other contexts. Time generality is the extent to which a measurement at one point in time is stable or replicated at another point in time. Scorer generality typically would be referred to as interrater reliability, and concerns the convergence of ratings of the same stimulus across raters. Finally, a subject category is added to Cone's (1978) grid to represent the degree to which a measure generalizes beyond a specific subject population.

The BAG will serve to provide a "standard usage" of terms in the remainder of this review. It also allows for specification of several decision rules in addition to the ones already developed. Those applied in this review are summarized below. These rather severe decision rules are necessary, both to provide replicability and to narrow this review to a manageable number of measurement approaches. A measure will be excluded from review if:

1. It is strictly designed for classroom assessment and has not been used in theoretical research.
2. It is concerned primarily with cognitions, feelings, demographics, or global, subjective characteristics (rather than overt, motor behaviors).
3. It is context-restricted in content or prior usage (rather than context-free), or is population-restricted in content or prior usage (rather than population-free).
4. It is primarily an outcome measure (rather than a process measure).
5. It attempts narrow or undimensional assessment (rather than a comprehensive assessment) of communicative competence.
6. It attempts to assess dimensions or constructs extraneous to

communicative competence (rather than communicative competence exclusively).
7. It attempts to describe communicative behavior (rather than evaluate its quality).
8. It is a small (i.e., less than eight items), "one-shot" operationalization (rather than a systematically developed and validated measure).
9. It is unavailable upon request, or is not replicable from published or unpublished sources.
10. It is examined in only one unpublished study.
11. It is used in a format different from its originally intended form.
12. It has yet to generate sufficient validity evidence to recommend further investigation of the measure.

The sample of potential measures was obtained from an unpublished bibliography containing 1245 entries relevant to competence in communicating (Spitzberg & Cupach, 1985a). The bibliography represents the product of several computer searches and reviews of numerous interdisciplinary articles on the subject. Each original source in the bibliography was examined to determine what operationalizations, if any, were used in assessing competence. This produced a list of 140 measures or measurement approaches that appeared a priori as potential measures of interactional or social competence. This figure does not include numerous measures of anxiety, assertiveness, children's competence, or basic social functioning.[2] Neither does it include 22 studies which used small measures (two to eight items) to operationalize competence.[3] Three initial screening passes were made of this list to exclude measures that were related only peripherally to competence. This left a list of 128 measurement approaches, comprised of measures potentially relevant to communicative competence,

---

[2] The implementation of these decision rules automatically results in the exclusion of four areas closely associated with communicative competence: (a) children's communicative competence, (b) basic social functioning, (c) social anxiety, and (d) assertiveness. Interested readers are referred to reviews of children's measures (Foster & Ritchey, 1979; Green & Forehand, 1980; Gresham, 1981; Hops, 1983; Van Hasselt, Hersen, Whitehill, & Bellack, 1979), basic social functioning measures (Doucette & Freedman, 1980; Jackson et al., 1981; Katz & Lyerly, 1963; Salzman et al., 1972; Walls et al., 1977; Weissmann, 1975), assertiveness measures (Bourque & Ladduceur, 1979; Galassi, Galassi, & Fulkerson, 1984) and social anxiety measures (Leary, 1983, ch. 15, this book; McCroskey, 1977, 1978) and the listing of measures referred to in Footnote 5.

[3] All studies located in this review process which consisted of eight items or less were either a priori constructions or single-item measures. In no case was there a systematic attempt to validate such a measure.

although clearly some are more relevant than others. The decision rules were then applied to each entry to determine the final sample for this review.[4] Application of the decision rules to the list of competence measures resulted in eight measurement approaches to be reviewed in this chapter.

Before the measures can be reviewed, a few terminological distinctions need to be clarified. Several measures originally developed for other-report have been converted to self-report measures, and vice versa. I choose to use the terms "self-reference" (SR) and "other-reference" (OR) because of the confusion that has surrounded the terms "self-report" and "other-report." Part of the problem is that "report," as both a noun and a verb, is ambiguous with regard to who reports and who is reported about. While "self-reference" and "other-reference" are targeted, they do not designate the "reportee." In this review an effort is made to identify three experimental "persons" of interest consistently: subject, partner, and observer. The "subject" of the investigation is generally the primary focus of most assessment efforts. Most subjects interact with partners, although in the case of recalled conversation and trait measures, the partners are more or less implicit. In practice the partners may be subjects as well, but for the purpose of discussion, in studies of dyadic interaction one member of a dyad arbitrarily is referred to as the "subject" and the other as the subject's "partner" (frequently a confederate). In many instances, the interaction between subject and partner(s) is coded, rated, or otherwise evaluated by third-parties not directly involved in the interaction itself. These are the observers, often referred to as "judges" in the literature.

Second, measures may be viewed on a continuum from molar to molecular. Molar items are general evaluations, such as "cooperative," "open," "trustworthy," and so on. They are subjective and global. Molecular items are specific, relatively discrete, behaviors, such as "gestured frequently," "maintained eye contact," and "asked questions." Most measures represent a mixture of these types of items. The more molar the item composition of a measure, the more generally applicable it tends to be to a variety of communicative encounters. However, the more molar the items, the less diagnostically useful the measure tends to be. That is, molecular items provide specific information regarding the precise nature of an interactant's skill proficiencies and deficiencies, whereas a molar measure does not.

One final distinction needs to be made. Some measures refer to a

---

[4] The table listing all measures and the decision rules applied is available upon request from the author.

particular time, place, and encounter. Other measures seek to generalize over entended periods of time, across many situations, and over many episodes of interaction. The former are usually called state measures, and the latter are usually called trait measures. While other terms may be more accurate (e.g., episodic/dispositional, event-focused/tendency-focused), the terms "state" and "trait" are used in this review.

Measurement Approaches to Communicative Competence: Self-Reference Measures

Communicative Adaptability Scale (CAS-SR)

Development. Duran and Wheeless (1980) originally generated 67 items, 31 of which were drawn from existing measures and the remaining written to tap the dimensions of social experience, adaptability, empathy, and rewarding impression. The items were set in a five-point Likert-type response format, and administered along with McCroskey's (1978) Personal Report of Communication Apprehension (PRCA) and a measure of social self-esteem. The measures were given to 831 college students. Factor analysis with oblique rotation produced three factors explaining 33% of the variance. *Social adaptability* (e.g., "I am sensitive to others' needs of the moment") was correlated .40 with *rewarding impression* (e.g., "I find it easy to get along with new people") and .39 with *meaning-centered empathy* (e.g., "I am a good listener"). Factors II and III correlated .34. Factors I and III correlated significantly with the PRCA, and factors I, II and III correlated positively with social self-esteem. In a subsequent report on these 67 items in a sample of 830 students a similar two-factor solution accounted for 48% of the variance. The apparent reason for the discrepancy is a stricter requirement for factor definition in the latter report.

This measure, referred to as the Social Management Scale and as the initial Communicative Adaptability Scale, played a significant role in a subsequent elaboration of the CAS-SR. Duran (1983) added items to represent dimensions of *social composure, wit, appropriate disclosure,* and *articulation* (see Appendix 1). The scale was administered to two samples: 162 primary and secondary teachers and 697 college students. The CAS-SR produced a five factor oblique solution in the first sample (social confirmation, articulation, social experience/composure, wit, appropriate disclosure) explaining 55% of the variance. In the second sample, a six-factor oblique solution emerged explaining 40% of the variance (social composure and experience loaded as separate factors).

Validity. In the development and validation study Duran (1983) found the six CAS-SR factors were strongly related to the PRCA and social self-esteem in both the first and second sample. Duran, Zakahi and Mumper (1982) had 214 college student dyads interact over five 30-minute sessions, after which the CAS-SR, CAS-OR (other-reference), Norton's (1983) Communicator Style Measure (CSM), and Hecht's (1978) Communication Satisfaction (COMSAT) scale were administered. The factor structure of the CAS-SR replicated previous studies. Self-rated social confirmation, social experience, and appropriate disclosure were significantly related to COMSAT. However, using communicator style as a covariate and partialling out its variance, the CAS-SR factors explained only 2% of COMSAT variance, and only 8% without controlling for communicator style. Very similar results are reported by Ballard-Reisch (1984). Duran et al. (1982) concluded that given the level of empirical interrelationships observed, "no conclusive statements can be made as to the superiority of the CAS vs the CSM" (p. 22). Indeed, in a different data set (n=426, see Duran & Zakahi, 1984), a canonical correlation of the CAS-SR factors and the CSM scales revealed considerable overlap of the constructs.

In Cupach and Spitzberg's (1983) sample of 49 college student dyads, CAS-SR correlated significantly with trait versions of Wiemann's (1977) Communicative Competence Scale-SR, Cupach and Spitzberg's (1981) Self-Rated Competence scale, and a measure of social self-esteem. The CAS also correlated with the state measures of Prisbell's (1979) Feeling Good scale, and Cupach and Spitzberg's (1981) Self-Rated Competence and Rating of Alter-Competence scales.

Finally, Kelly and Duran (1984) found that 94 college students self-reported as shy or not shy significantly varied in the expected direction on three of six factors of the CAS-SR, and Zakahi and Duran (1982) found in a sample of 287 college students that the two-factor CAS (Wheeless & Duran, 1982) predicted 25% of the variance of self-reported loneliness. In a later report, Zakahi and Duran (1985) observed similar results in 398 college students. The factors of the CAS-SR combined to explain about 20% of the variance in self-referenced loneliness, almost all of which was accounted for by the social experience factor.

Reliability. Coefficient *alpha* reliability for the CAS-SR factors have ranged from .70 to .89 (Duran, 1983). Coefficient *alpha* for the entire measure was reported as .81 by Cupach and Spitzberg (1983).

Evaluation. The research background of the CAS is not entirely clear. The factor-structure of the CAS has been generally supportive of the predicted structure, but the precise item content of the subscales has varied considerably across studies. Despite these reservations, the

CAS has generally revealed supportive relationships with other trait measures of competence and related constructs. It offers the advantage of a subscale structure which permits the examination of several distinct interpersonal skill constructs commonly associated with competent interaction. However, its item content is not very molecular, and therefore cannot provide diagnostically specific information.

Self-Rated Competence (SRC) Scale

Development. Cupach and Spitzberg (1981) developed the SRC partly out of a desire to validate an event-focused measure of communicative competence. The SRC items were drawn from 18 existing instruments conceptually related to competence (including Wiemann's 1977 and Lowe and Cautela's 1978 measures reviewed in this chapter), representing such constructs as empathy, listening, self-disclosure, interaction management, behavioral flexibility, and communication anxiety. An original pool of over 300 items was reduced to 66 by eliminating redundant, ambiguous, irrelevant, and trivial items. In addition, only items that could be written in both self-reference and other-reference format were retained. This pool was set in both SR and OR formats, and administered to 109 college students in a five-point Likert-type response scale. Reliability and exploratory factor analysis allowed the SRC to be reduced to 28 items (see Appendix 2). Phase two then involved 289 college students asked to recall a recent extended face-to-face conversation. Respondents completed the SRC, the Rating of Alter-Competence (RAC) developed with the SRC, and Hecht's (1978) Communication Satisfaction scale (COMSAT). SRC revealed a three-factor oblique solution. The factors were labeled *other-orientation, conversation skills,* and *self-centered behavior.* These three factors explained over 16% of COMSAT variance.

Validity. Since the validation study, the SRC has been investigated in over 11 studies involving almost 3000 college subjects. Situations have ranged from conflict and problem-solving to get-acquainted conversations. The SRC consistently correlates in the expected direction and generally demonstrates moderate to strong relationships with state or event-focused constructs. For example, SRC correlates significantly with reported use of constructive and destructive conflict tactics, interaction involvement, attentiveness, knowledge, motivation, interpersonal communication apprehension, reported behavioral anxiety, self-monitoring, social self-esteem, loneliness, and a number of measures of communication quality, including communication satisfaction, perceived confirmation, and perceived appropriateness and effectiveness. In addition, in one of the few studies examining the role of response bias, SRC was found to be unrelated to social desirability (Spitzberg & Cupach, 1983). Its relationships to trait constructs is less dramatic than with state constructs, but this would be expected from the state-trait literature (Spitzberg, 1986a). Related to this point, when the SRC was adapted into a trait format, it revealed substantial relationships with other trait competence scales, including the CAS-SR, CCS-SR, and a measure of social self-esteem. For a review of much of the research associated with the SRC, see Spitzberg and Cupach (1983).

Reliability. Coefficient *alpha* reliability for SRC has ranged from .87 to .92, with a mean of .90 across nine studies in which it was reported for the entire scale.

Evaluation. The SRC appears to have excellent construct validity. It is highly reliable and strongly related to episode-based perceptions of satisfaction, confirmation, appropriateness, and effectiveness. However, despite an apparent factor structure, the utility of the factors has not been investigated. In addition, the SRC only seems useful in generating a molar-level impression of competence, rather than providing diagnostically specific information.

Social Performance Survey Schedule (SPSS-SR)

Development. Lowe and Cautela (1978) asked three classes of college students to list all of the social traits they could use to describe their behavior or the behavior of another. The authors added traits not listed by the students. The authors then generated behavioral items reflecting the trait terms. For example, a "warm" person descriptor trait was behaviorally translated into "has eye contact when speaking," "talks readily to people (s)he hasn't met before," and "shows interest in what another is saying (e.g., with appropriate facial movements, comments, and questions)." This process resulted in 100 items written in a format allowing both self-reference and other-reference. The rating scale is a five-point (0-4) Likert-type usage scale (indicating the degree to which the target person engages in each behavior from "not at all" to "very much"). The SPSS-SR was designed with 50 positive items (Part A) and 50 negative items (Part B).

Validity. In the development study, 303 college students referenced themselves on the SPSS-SR and a measure of social anxiety. SPSS scores correlated in the predicted direction with social anxiety. Lowe (1985) administered the measure to 326 college students, and collected a number of other measures to assess the validity of the SPSS. First, students were selected who could be designated as either high skill (HS>80th percentile) or low skill (LS<20th percentile) on Part A of the SPSS-SR. There were 10 HS males, 12 HS females, 10 LS males, and 11 LS females. These subjects were given a social contact monitoring form (SCM) to keep records of their social contacts for the next five days. They also completed a measure of social anxiety and the Hopkins Symptom Check List (SCL), a measure of disturbance symptoms. Two subject-nominated peers were sent peer rating forms (PRF) assessing social skill, anxiety, likability, conversational initiation, and items such as "fun to be with," "easy to talk to," and interest in the peer. Finally, subjects were videotaped in a five-minute get-acquainted interaction with confederates trained to interact in a standardized manner. After the interaction, subjects rated their own skill and anxiety on two seven-point scales. Observers rated the videotapes on seven categories of behavior (frequency of self-disclosures, questions about the confederate, smiles, minimal encourages, gestures, duration of talk-time, and eye contact). In all, the validity support was fairly consistent and convincing. Relative to the low skill subjects, high skill subjects had more interactions, more peer initiated activities, more total time spent in interaction, more friends, higher peer SPSS Part A other-reference ratings, higher peer likability ratings, and lower anxiety scores. High skilled subjects smiled more, talked more, had more eye contact, rated their own performance higher in skill, and were rated by observers as higher in skill and lower in anxiety. All effects were significant at the .05 level.

In a sample of 65 psychiatric patients, Lowe (1978) found the SPSS-SR to be positively related to measures of depression, staff ratings of patient social skills, self-referenced social introversion, social desirability, and the number of psychiatric hospitalizations.

Miller and Funabiki (1983) administerd the SPSS-SR to 282 college students. From this sample, 30 HS and 30 LS subjects were defined. The subjects were videotaped responding to 30 analog role-play situations. Subjects were then videotaped in a free behavior situation with a confederate. Subjects completed self-reference measures of anxiety and depression. For the entire pre-experiment sample, the low competent subjects rated themselves significantly higher in depression and anxiety. Ratings of the videotaped interactions revealed that HS subjects displayed significantly more smiles, open-ended questions, specific questions, self-disclosing statements, positive statements, neutral statements, and were rated by experimentally blind observers as more competent and likable than the LS subjects.

Wessberg, Curran, Monti, Corriveau, Coyne, and Dziadosz (1981) conducted a contrasted group study in which a sample of 60 National Guardsmen and a sample of 81 psychiatric patients were compared on the SPSS-SR. The Guardsmen were significantly higher in their

SPSS-SR scores than the patient group. In the second study reported, 38 psychiatric patients rated themselves on the SPSS-SR, and were rated by judges evaluating patient performance on the Simulated Social Interaction Test (SSIT; Curran, 1982). SPSS-SR scores correlated significantly to judges' ratings of patient performance on the SSIT. This is in contrast to results in a sample of 63 psychiatric inpatients, in which Fingeret, Monti and Paxson (1983) found no significant relationships between Forms A and B of the SPSS-SR and SSIT scores. Similarly, in a study of 43 psychiatric patients, Monti, Corriveau and Curran (1982) found no significant relationships between patient self-reports on an abbreviated SPSS-SR, and either judges' or interviewers' ratings of patients' SSIT performance of SPSS-OR ratings.

Fingeret, Monti and Paxson (1985) found that in a sample of 27 male psychiatric inpatients and 18 nonpsychiatric males, that patients rated themselves lower on SPSS-SR Part A and Part B. In addition, ratings of the subjects' performance on the SSIT correlated significantly with SPSS-SR Part A. This is in contrast to Monti's (1983) study in which 87 male psychiatric patients were involved in a structured social skills interview (SSIT performance). Monti obtained staff other-reference and patient self-reference ratings on the SPSS. Self-referenced SPSS scores did not correlate significantly to interviewer ratings.

Reliability. Lowe and Cautela (1978) report a four-week test-retest correlation of .87 for 177 college students. Coefficient *alpha* was .94 for the entire sample of 303. Lowe (1985) reports a one-month test-retest correlation of .81 for a sample of 43 college students. Coefficient *alpha* was .93. Monti (1983) calculated both mean interrater correlations on the SPSS-OR and coefficient alpha. For the day hospital staff, mean $r=.31$ $(p<.05)$ and $alpha=.70$. For the inpatient staff mean $r=.47$ $(p<.01)$ and $alpha=.86$.

Evaluation. Of the self-reference measures reviewed, the SPSS-SR has been the most systematically and comprehensively investigated. The measure is flexible (having both positive and negative subscales, and having been used both as a self-reference and other-reference measure) and diagnostically useful (comprised as it is of relatively molecular level items). Despite its predictive and discriminant validity evidence, the SPSS-SR has limited convergent and discriminant validity evidence. Nevertheless, the SPSS-SR should find much more usage in the area of communicative competence research.

Measurement Approaches to Communicative Competence: Other-Reference Measures

Communicative Competence Scale (CCS-OR)

Development. Wiemann (1975, 1977) generated 57 Likert-type items from a thorough review of the literature and extant measures. The items were written to reflect five components of competence in interpersonal interaction: general competence, empathy, affiliation/support, behavioral flexibility, and social relaxation. After a review by three experts, four items were dropped. A total of 239 college students used the instrument to rate a videotaped confederate enact any one of four role-played interaction management conditions (high, medium, low, rude) in a conversational episode. Factor analysis revealed a strong first factor (e.g., "S is easy to talk to,"). A second factor loaded three relaxation items (e.g., "S enjoys social gatherings where s/he can meet new people"). The items that discriminated most successfully among interaction management conditions were used in formulating the CCS-OR dependent variable. That is, the items from each dimension with the largest t-values differentiating the four experimental conditions, along with two additional items retained for variety, were retained to comprise the final form of the dependent competence measure. The competence measure was shown to be significantly different among the four conditions of interaction management. The better the management of interaction was, the higher the rating of competence.

Validity. In addition to Wiemann's (1977) results, the entire CCS-OR has been investigated in at least three other studies. McLaughlin and Cody (1982) audiotaped get-acquainted conversations among 90 college student dyads. After the conversations subjects completed a 30-item version of the CAS-OR and Hecht's (1978) Communication Satisfaction scale (for acquaintances). In addition, the conversations were coded for conversational lapses and pre- and post-lapse utterances. A total of 40 dyads were classified as multiple lapse dyads (three or more lapses) and 41 dyads had two or fewer lapses. Total scores on the CAS-OR and COMSAT for each dyad were averaged to produce a dyadic score. Multiple lapse dyads mutually rated their conversations lower in competence than fewer lapse dyads, and lower in satisfaction, although this difference failed to reach statistical significance.

Backlund (1977) had 82 college students engage in a 10-minute conversation. Students were rated by their partners on the CCS-OR, and also completed measures of dogmatism, affective sensitivity, social insight, willingness to communicate, and semantic habits. In addition, students were rated by trained observers on the Purdue Basic Oral Communication Evaluation Form, a measure of communicative competence based on a 10-minute interview. The resulting correlation between CCS-OR and the Purdue measure was nonsignificant, and when the CCS-OR was treated as a dependent variable, only two variables achieved statistical significance (dogmatism and social insight), resulting in a small overall effect size.

Kelly and Duran (1984) had 47 dyads interact for 10-minute videotaped get-acquainted conversations. The subjects completed Duran's (1983) CAS-SR, a measure of shyness, and two 30-item forms of Wiemann's (1977) CCS. One form was the original CCS-OR, whereas the other form had the subjects rate the impression they believed their partners had of the subject doing the rating (CCS-META). Accuracy scores were then computed by subtracting each subject's CCS-META score from the CCS-OR score given them by their partners. A median split was performed to create shy and nonshy groups. Finally, two observers rated each videotape interactant on Wiemann's (1977) CCS-OR scale. Shy and nonshy groups did not differ on the observers' CCS-OR ratings. In all-female dyads, self's CCS-META explained 24% of the variance in partner's CCS-OR. That is, person A's perception of partner B's impression of A predicted 24% of B's actual impression of A. However, this effect was not replicated in the predominately male group of dyads. Shy and nonshy female dyads did not differ in their accuracy scores, while the predominantly male dyad groups did.

Reliability. Wiemann (1975) reports a coefficient *alpha* of .96 for the CCS-OR. McLaughlin and Cody (1982) report a coefficient *alpha* of .91. Kelly and Duran (1984) found a coefficient *alpha* of .92, and an interrater reliability of .81 for the observer measure.

Evaluation. The CCS-OR items emerged from a well-conceived rationale. The empirical validation efforts have thus far been largely supportive. The item content of the CCS-OR contains primarily molar evaluations, some of which are trait-like in their levels of inference. This produces a mixed-inference measure in which an interactant is judged both within a particular episode and across episodes, and both in terms of molecular behaviors and molar evaluations. Thus, while the CCS-OR was designed as a state or episode-specific measure, it appears to provide an inferred evaluation of an interactant's typical competence. Given its generally molar item content, the CCS-OR does not provide diagnostically specific data. Despite these qualifications, the CCS-OR is highly reliable and reveals fairly consistent experimental validity as a measure of another person's competence in interacting.

Communicative Competency Assessment Instrument (CCAI)

Development. The CCAI represents a mixed mode assessment package developed (and reviewed extensively) by Rubin (1981a, 1981b, 1982, 1985). It provides five-point ratings scales on 19 communication competencies: pronunciation, facial expression/tone of voice, articulation, persuasiveness, clarity of ideas, ability to express and defend viewpoint, recognize misunderstanding, distinguish fact from opinion, understand suggestions for improvement, identify instructions, summarize, introduce self to others, obtain information, answer questions, express feelings, organize messages, give accurate directions, describe another person's viewpoint, describe differences of opinion. The behavior assessed is generated by a variety of techniques. A subject presents a three-minute extemporaneous persuasive speech, listens to a brief videotape-based lecture representing a first-day class lecture, provides directions to a location known to the subject and interviewer, and responds to several natural and hypothetical prompts. As this suggests, the CCAI was developed to assess "the appropriateness of communication behaviors within a particular setting (the college environment)" (Rubin, 1985, p. 174). While the stimulus materials are clearly college-based, the competencies appear to be general. In addition, while it was primarily motivated by needs for pedagogical assessment (e.g., competency requirements in education), it subsequently has been investigated in a theoretical framework.

Initially, 57 "items" were generated. These items were "sorted" by five experts into the 19 competency areas identified by the Speech Communication Association's 1978 Task Force on Minimal Speaking/Listening Competencies (Bassett, Whittington & Staton-Spicer, 1978). Pilot testing allowed the selection of the 19 most reliable and face-valid items (see Rubin, 1981a, 1981b, 1982).

Validity. The validity of the CCAI is reviewed elsewhere (Rubin, 1982, 1985). A few highlights are acknowledged here for their relevance to general communicative competence. The CCAI has been found to correlate significantly with a self-reference version of the CCAI, communication apprehension, and instructor molar ratings of student communicative skills. As would be expected, the CCAI was uncorrelated to argumentativeness (Rubin, 1985). Rubin and Feezel (1984) found less supportive results with a similar set of variables. Two studies have examined the relationship between the CCAI and cognitive complexity (Henzl, Mabry, & Powell, 1983; Rubin & Henzl,

1984). Contrary to expectations, neither study found a strong effect of complexity on CCAI scores, although differences were found on various individual competencies. Finally, there is some suggestion that the CCAI is culturally biased (Powell & Avila, 1985), although the effect of culture was not great, and Rubin (1982) indicates that experts can find no such bias.

Reliability. Rubin (1981a) reports coefficient *alphas* in the pretesting phase of the CCAI from .78 to .83. Interrater reliabilities range from .92 for relatively untrained raters to .97 for trained raters (Rubin & Henzl, 1984, p. 266).

Evaluation. Despite a substantial amount of work done on the CCAI, there are still questions that need to be addressed. The competencies were drawn from the recommendations of an academic task force examining the question of what competencies are critical for students. While this provided a good conceptual grounding for the development of the CCAI, it still remains to be seen whether or not these competencies make a "real difference" outside the academic setting. Since the measure was designed to assess communicative competence in the classroom context, its relevance to interpersonal settings is not known. In addition, several of the stimulus prompts may not be assessing *ability to perform* so much as the subject's comprehension of the prompts. Differentiating fact from opinion, introducing self, expression of feelings, and ability to express and defend point of view may be highly dependent on the phrasing of the stimulus prompts. If asked to perform in reference to the scaling criteria, subjects might be more competent in responding. While there is no direct evidence that the CCAI is contaminated by demand effects, other measures using less complex situational prompts have been shown to suffer from such effects (see Mahaney & Kern, 1983; Martinez-Diaz & Edelstein, 1979; Nietzel & Bernstein, 1976; Steinberg, Curran, Bell, Paxson & Munroe, 1982).

Conversational Skills Rating Scale (CSRS-OR)

Development. The objective in developing the CSRS was to provide an instrument that diagnosed molecular behaviors, that could be used by self or other, expert or layperson, and could be adapted to state-trait uses and virtually any face-to-face interpersonal context (Spitzberg, 1985; Spitzberg & Hurt, 1987). The items for the CSRS were initially refined in four stages. Stage one involved a qualitative pilot study of open-ended responses of college students regarding competent and incompetent behaviors. Stage two involved a literature search of studies examining molecular behaviors and competence (e.g., Conger,

Wallander, Mariotto, & Ward, 1980; Dillard & Spitzberg, 1984, Romano & Bellack, 1980; Royce, 1982; Spitzberg & Cupach, 1985b). Stage three consisted of item reduction on the basis of redundancy, observability, clarity and relevance across interpersonal contexts. Stage four provided an empirical test of the resulting 40-item instrument. The items were classified a priori into four skill clusters (interaction management, expressiveness, composure, altercentrism). In the study (Spitzberg, 1985), 372 college students were engaged in 7-minute get-acquainted conversations. These conversations were rated by an instructor observer, by student observers (different observers for each interactant and for each dyad), and by a subsample of the interactants themselves (subsample n=107). In addition, the students obtained ratings on the measure by an acquaintance involved in an out-of-class natural conversation. The composite instructor skills ratings correlated significantly with the in-class student ratings, interactant communication apprehension, interactants' self-referenced expressiveness, but, interestingly, were negatively related to out-of-class acquaintance ratings and several measures of listening ability.

Based on this extensive pilot study, the CSRS was further refined into a 30-item measure consisting of 25 molecular behavioral items and 5 molar evaluation items. The molecular items reflect altercentrism (e.g., "asking of questions"), composure (e.g., "shaking or nervous twitches"), expressiveness (e.g., "use of humor and/or stories"), and interaction management (e.g., "maintenance of topics and follow-up comments"). The rating scale is a 5-point Likert-type dimension anchored by "INADEQUATE (use was awkward, disruptive, or resulted in a negative impression of communicative skills)," "ADEQUATE (use was sufficient but neither very noticeable nor outstanding—Produced neither strong positive impression nor strong negative impression)," and "EXCELLENT (use was smooth, controlled, and resulted in positive impression of communicative skills)."

Validity. The CSRS-OR subsequently has been used in four studies. In study one (Spitzberg & Hurt, 1987), 623 students were engaged in seven-minute get-acquainted conversations which were rated by instructors on the 30-item CSRS-OR. An analysis of variance compared the mean scores of the total 30-item measure by instructor (i.e., rater). Results indicated significant differences, suggesting rater idiosyncracies. In addition, female instructors provided significantly higher ratings than male raters. Regressing the 25 molecular items onto the summed molar items produced a regression model explaining 64% of the variance. Controlling for rater sex and rater differences, the 25 behavioral items still explained 31% unique variance in the molar impression of student competence.

Study two (Spitzberg, 1986b) replicated study one with 258 college students involved in get-acquainted conversations. In addition, students rated their own conversational performance in terms of their motivation, knowledge, CSRS-SR, and rated their partner on the CSRS-OR. Finally, the students also reported on their current loneliness, and number of friends. Rater effects (differences and gender) were again significant (combining to explain 23% of the variance in rater molar evaluation of the students' competence). However, the CSRS-OR molecular items explained 42% unique variance. In all, observer ratings of skills were correlated .79 with observer molar ratings of student performances. Student self-reference CSRS ratings on the 25 molecular skills explained 34% unique variance in student self-reference molar evaluation of performance, controlling for motivation, loneliness, number of friends, and knowledge. The zero-order correlation between student CSRS-SR skills to molar self-reference rating of competence was .72. These variables combined to explain 68% of student self-reference molar impressions of competence. In addition, student other-reference CSRS ratings of partners' molecular behaviors explained between 67% and 77% of other-reference molar evaluations of partners' competence.

In a study of the role of contexts in competence inferences, Brunner and Spitzberg (1986) gave 287 college students one of two instructions. Subjects were asked to recall either the most satisfying or most dissatisfying conversation of the past two weeks. They rated themselves on the CSRS-SR, motivation, knowledge, and a single-item (1-100) satisfaction scale. They also rated their recalled conversation partner on the CSRS-OR. Finally, subjects rated the conversational context along primary dimensions of interpersonal communication (e.g., formal-informal, cooperative-competitive, etc.) both in terms of expectancies and expectancy fulfillment. It was predicted that degree of expectancy violation would be negatively correlated to CSRS-OR. Contextual expectancy discrepancy was correlated negatively to CSRS-OR. CSRS-OR was also correlated to satisfaction, CSRS-SR, and positively-valenced ratings of the context.

In a small-scale study, Powers and Spitzberg (1987) videotaped 10 dyads interacting in get-acquainted conversations. The interactants rated self and partner on the CSRS, rated their self-motivation and knowledge in the conversation, rated the degree to which they thought they had put forward a positive impression in the conversation, and were subsequently rated on the CSRS by four observers each. Observer CSRS ratings of the subjects were significantly related to an average of their scores, but were related only to the observers' molar positive impressions of competence and the accuracy of interactants at assessing their own impression relative to that of the observers. Self's rating of partner correlated significantly with post-conversation positive impressions of partner, self-referenced competence, and was negatively related to a deviation score representing the discrepancy between self's initial *desired* impression and post-conversation perceptions of *accomplished* impression management. Thus, the less able self was in accomplishing the impression she or he desired, the less competent her or his conversational partner was perceived to be.

Reliability. The molecular items produced a coefficient *alpha* of .94 and .91 in studies one and two, respectively.

Evaluation. The CSRS fills a gap in the assessment of communicative competence by providing diagnostically specific information that can be obtained in virtually any interpersonal context. It can be used for self-reference or other-reference, and it can be used by trained or untrained raters. However, despite its relatively objective item content, the research thus far suggests that raters apply their own idiosyncratic subjective standards to the items. This is less a limitation of the measure, and more a limitation of the procedures for using it. Its utility will depend largely upon the intentions of the researcher using it. If "objective" information is desired, rater training and further scaling refinement is likely to be necessary for the raters to provide consistent information. On the other hand, if interest is in the role of behavior in producing layperson inferences of competence, then rater training may be counterproductive (see Bernadin & Pence, 1980).

Rating of Alter-Competence (RAC)

Development. Development of the RAC scale paralleled that of the Self-Rated Competence (SRC) scale (Cupach & Spitzberg, 1981) reviewed earlier. The objectives were basically twofold. First, it was determined that an alternative to trait measures was needed to tap perceptions of the process of interaction within an actual episode of communication. The solution was to develop a measure that references a specific conversation (see Appendix 3). In this way, even though a particular context is not specified, the measure is imbued with the respondent's own sense of context. Second, it was deemed important to attempt to reference both interactants involved in an interpersonal encounter. Since it is assumed that interpersonal communication is an interdependent process, it is important that both self and alter (i.e., other or conversational partner) be assessed. Thus, 66 items were generated to reference self, and 66 items referenced alter, in a particular communicative situation. The initial pilot study suggested that the RAC could be reduced to 27 items without impairing its reliability or dimensionality.

The 27-item RAC was administered along with the SRC and Hecht's (1978) Communication Satisfaction (COMSAT) scale to 289 college students asked to rate a recent, extended, face-to-face conversation. Like the results with the CCS-OR (Wiemann, 1977) and CAS-OR (Ballard-Reisch, 1984), the RAC displayed a very strong general evaluation factor accounting for 85% of the explained variance. Oblique rotation produced a second factor that at first appeared similar to the first factor. In a later analysis (Cupach & Spitzberg, 1982) confirmatory factor analysis supported the existence of the second factor, and the two factors were labeled *other-orientation* (e.g., "S/he was respectful"), and *expressiveness* (e.g., "Her/his voice was monotone and boring"). The two factors were correlated and the scale has generally been treated as a summed score variable. The RAC shares 15 items with the SRC, meaning therefore, that 12 of its items loaded differently when the locus of reference was alter rather than self.

Validity. The RAC has now been used in 14 studies. Subjects typically are college students, although one study sampled adults. Situations studied range from conflict and problem solving to get-acquainted and interrupted natural conversations. It is significantly related to self-referenced use of constructive and destructive conflict tactics, interaction involvement, attentiveness, interpersonal communication apprehension, reported anxiety behaviors, communicative adaptability scale, social self-esteem, knowledge, motivation, and its companion, SRC. RAC is also related to a number of measures of communication quality, including communication satisfaction, conversational appropriateness and effectiveness, perceived confirmation, feeling good, immediacy, and ratings of conversational partner's skills on the Social Interaction Test developed by Trower et al. (1978). Like the SRC, the RAC is unrelated to social desirability response set. A review of its development and validity evidence is available in Spitzberg and Cupach (1983).

Reliability. Coefficient *alpha* reliability for the RAC has ranged from .90 to .94, and averages .93 across 11 studies in which it has been reported.

Evaluation. The RAC, as a relatively general, molar evaluation of competence in a specific episode, is strongly supported by the research literature. It is highly reliable, suitable for virtually any context, and substantially related to criteria of competent interaction, as well as other measures of competence. The RAC does not provide diagnostically specific information, and is therefore most useful when interest is in exploring the process of inferring others' overall competence in a given episode of interaction.

Simulated Social Interaction Test (SSIT)

Development. The developmental history, research, and training procedures for the SSIT up to 1982 are summarized by Curran (1982). The SSIT consists of eight problematic interpersonal situations which are introduced by a narrator and then prompted by a confederate. The situation descriptions and prompts typically are presented on videotape, but they could be performed live or on audiotape. While the scenes are designed for male respondents, the situations are general enough that simple pronoun changes could be made without seriously affecting the validity of the test. Ratings are made (sometimes by the respondent, always by observers) on two 11-point Likert-type items; one anxiety item and one social skill item.

Validity. Research indicates that the situations are generalizable (*G* coefficients range from .76 to .87) as are ratings across observers (*G* coefficients range from .94 to .98), but do not generalize well from self-reference ratings to observer other-reference ratings (*G* coefficients range from .46 to .61; see Curran, 1982 et al., 1980b). Monti et al., (1982) assessed the correspondence of SSIT ratings by observers to clinic staff naturalistic free-behavior ratings and 43 psychiatric patients' self-reference ratings on the SSIT. The SSIT observer ratings correlated significantly to clinic staff ratings, but not to patient self-reference ratings.

Wallander, Curran, and Myers (1983) also attempted to assess the social validity of the SSIT. Videotapes of 20 research assistants acting as bogus patients, and 52 actual psychiatric patients served as stimulus materials. Three groups of judges were used to compare ratings (50 "community representatives," 17 untrained assistants, and three extensively trained research assistants). Briefly put, the three judge groups rated the bogus patients similarly, and generally rated the psychiatric patients similarly on skill ratings.

Monti, Wallander, Ahern, Abrams, and Munroe (1983) assessed SSIT generalizability across samples of male college students, non-college adults, and psychiatric patients. The subjects made self-reference SSIT ratings and were rated by two trained judges. The authors concluded: "In summary, the findings of this investigation suggest that the SSIT is a highly reliable procedure for obtaining measures of anxiety and social skills for non-clinic male college student population as well as with adult male psychiatric patients and non-college normal adult males" (p. 23).

Another generalizability study was conducted by Monti (1983). In this study, 77 male psychiatric patients (inpatients, day hospital patients) were interviewed on a structured social skills interview and assessed on the SSIT by observer ratings. Interviewer skill ratings correlated significantly with SSIT observer ratings.

In an ambitious attempt to address issues of replicability and generalizability, Curran, Wessberg, Farrell, Monti, Corriveau and Coyne (1982) sent stimulus tapes of National Guardsmen responding to the SSIT to six different social skills training laboratories around the nation. Despite differences in orientation and training, the ratings were moderately generalizable across different labs.

Studies more relevant to discriminant validity have also been performed on the SSIT. For example, the SSIT significantly discriminated a group of National Guardsmen from a group of psychiatric patients (Curran, 1982). Convergent validity was addressed by Wessberg et al. (1981). In this study, observer SSIT ratings correlated significantly to subjects' self-reference ratings, nurses' global ratings of patients, interviewer global ratings of patients, and a research assistant's global ratings of the patients.

Studies bearing on the construct validity of the SSIT include two by Fingeret et al. (1983, 1985) and one by Monti et al. (1984). Fingeret et al. (1983) assessed 63 psychiatric patients on the SSIT, had patients rate themselves on the SPSS-SR Forms A and B (Lowe & Cautela, 1978), and had subjects respond to a videotape-based measure of social knoweldge. SSIT observer-ratings of patient skills correlated significantly with the measure of social knowledge. SSIT observer-ratings of patient skills correlated significantly with the measure of social knowledge, but did not correlate significantly with either SPSS rating form. Fingeret et al. (1985) tested 27 male psychiatric patients and 18 "normal" males on a measure of nonverbal sensitivity, SSIT, and a skill-rating task in which subjects rated previously determined skilled and unskilled interactants responding to the SSIT. SSIT scores correlated significantly with ratings of unskilled SSIT interactants for patient sample, and the measure of nonverbal sensitivity for the entire sample. Monti et al. (1984) developed molecular rating scales consisting of 11-point Likert-type ratings of nine nonverbal behaviors (extremity movements, voice, gestures, facial expressions, self-manipulations, orienting, posture, sense of timing, and speech rate pressure). Seven of these molecular behavior ratings correlated significantly ($p < .01$) with SSIT ratings for the patient sample (n=37). However, only the "voice" ratings correlated significantly to SSIT ratings in the college student sample (n=27).

Finally, in one of the few studies of demand characteristics associated with a competence assessment approach, Steinberg et al. (1982) found that different confederate prompt styles (unreceptive, neutral, or receptive) produced differences in performance competence of 30 male college students, with the unreceptive style resulting in generally lower rated social skills of students.

Reliability. In the seven studies and 14 samples in which reliability coefficients were reported, interrater reliability ranged from .47 to .94 with a mean of .71. When raters received training, reliabilities were consistently around .90 or better. In the 10 samples in which internal consistency estimates were reported, coefficient *alpha* ranged from .76 to .98, with a mean of .85. Both the interrater and the internal consistency estimates represent an extremely diverse population of raters across these studies.

Evaluation. The SSIT is clearly the most comprehensively validated assessment procedure examined in this review. It has revealed respectable content, construct, discriminant, and predictive validity. Its generalizability across rater and situation types is generally good, and its interrater reliabilities, especially for trained raters, has been high. The major weakness of the SSIT is that the information it provides is not diagnostically specific. Ratings on 11-point "socially-skilled" to "socially-unskilled" items only indicates a subject's overall skill in responding to the situations. Such a rating procedure does not indicate particular skill deficiencies or competencies. Thus, the SSIT would appear especially useful as either a screening device or in the validation of other measures.

Conclusion

Limitations

Like any other study, this review is limited by its sample. Despite all efforts to locate the entire domain of communicative competence measures relevant to theoretical research, it is almost inevitable that this goal cannot be accomplished. Just as importantly, in an effort to focus this review, some worthy measures were left to the reader to explore. Several measurement approaches are clearly noticeable by virtue of their exclusion from this review. Argyris' (1965) Interpersonal Competence Scoring System is an elaborate and theoretically grounded system for coding communication. However, it is strictly designed for group interaction. Mead's (1980a, 1980b) elaboration of the Massachusetts Basic Skills Assessment of Listening and Speaking was another measurement system excluded. While there is clearly evidence of the validity of the system, it is focused on the educational and public contexts and has yet to be taken into theoretical areas of research.

Assessments of "organizational" communication competence unfortunately also were excluded because of their context restrictions. Monge, Bachman, Dillard, and Eisenberg (1982) and Stricker (1980, 1982, 1983) have developed what appear to be outstanding assessment approaches for studying competence in the organizational context. Similarly, assertiveness measures (e.g., Goldsmith & McFall, 1973, Levenson & Gottman, 1978, McFall & Lillesand, 1971), heterosocial competence measures (Barlow, Able, Blanchard, Bristow, & Young, 1977; Kolko, & Milan, 1985; Perri, Richards, & Goodrich, 1978), and behavior-analytic measures (e.g., Fisher-Beckfield & McFall, 1982; Gaffney & McFall, 1981; Gaffney, 1984) were excluded either due to context restriction or population restriction, despite the promise their respective research has shown.

Finally, there is a class of assessment techniques excluded because they represent outcome measures or narrow dimensions of competence. Specifically, many measures use a criterion of interpersonal perception, accuracy, or understanding as an indicator of competence (e.g., Block & Bennett, 1955; Brilhart, 1965; Cahn & Shulman, 1984; Gottman & Porterfield, 1981; Kahn, 1970; Martin & Chapman, 1982; Powers & Lowry, 1984; Rosenberg & Cohen, 1966; Ruesch, Block, & Bennett, 1953). These assessment approaches were not reviewed for two reasons. First, strictly speaking, they are outcome measures rather than process measures. Second, understanding or accuracy is an overly narrow dimension of communicative competence given that a person can get an idea across in a very precise, yet inappropriate, way.

Taking Stock

Taking stock of such a diverse and multifaceted topic is not an easy task. The literature on communicative and interpersonal competence is spread out in a wide array of disciplines. It would be nice to be able to say that the measures located for this review are merely slightly different maps of the same behavioral terrain. Unfortunately, such a conclusion is not warranted by the available evidence, partly because little of such evidence exists, and partly because what evidence there is often suggests otherwise. So what can be said of the state of measurement in the area of interpersonal communicative competence? The following conclusions can be drawn from this review.

First, while we have a fairly precise understanding of what behaviors and characteristics people *believe* are competent, we know relatively little about how people form such inferences and what actual behaviors influence these inference processes. Much of the reason for this state of affairs is that our measurement approaches tend not to be behaviorally focused.

Second, trait measures of competence are generally only trivially, or at best moderately, related to episode-specific (i.e., state) measures of communicative competence. In other words, measures of interactants' typical competence in interacting do not appear to be strong predictors of their actual communicative competence in a specific encounter. In Cone's (1978) terms, the evidence of generality across setting, time, dimension, and method is insufficient.

Third, the inferences derived about a person's competence depend greatly upon the person making the judgment. When directly compared, A's rating of A share only a small amount of variance with B's rating of A. This appears to hold true if the ratings are of A's state or trait competence, or if B is an observer or a conversational partner of A. The disturbing implication is that each of us walks around with our own idiosyncratic standards for judging our own competence and the competence of others. While some studies have found high interrater reliability, this still leaves the self-other discrepancy unaccounted for. Progress in the science of communicative competence is likely to hinge significantly on the question of disparities between perceptions of self and other. Until this question is addressed, and fruitful inroads made, the credibility of any single measurement approach will be limited. Until that time, if a researcher's interest is in how laypersons form inferences of competence, then both self-reference and other-reference measures appear to be needed. On the other hand, if diagnostic information is desired, other-reference measures used by raters trained to an acceptable degree of interrater reliability are needed. In other words, the best chance of obtaining an "objective" assessment of a person's competence is a "consensus" approach in which two or more persons using the same assessment device in a similar fashion make similar inferences. This unfortunately suggests a very cumbersome and labor-intensive form of assessment, but as the need for accuracy in diagnosis increases, so too does the demand for this kind of rigor.

Fourth, related to this issue, it appears that who is referenced in a measure makes an important difference in what construct is being assessed. Self-reference measures that have been subsequently transformed into other-reference measures frequently reveal distinct factor structures, higher reliabilities, and higher correlations to such criteria as communication satisfaction, perceived confirmation, and perceived appropriateness. This should suggest caution when considering such conversions of existing measures.

Fifth, with a few notable exceptions, research has been strong on construct self-report validity, and weak in experimental, predictive, and discriminant validity. Much remains to be done in these areas before confidence in our measures is assured.

Finally, I would be remiss if I did not make note of a disturbing tendency that was revealed in this review. There is a strong narcissism in the area of communicative competence research. Most studies conducted in the area use the measures developed by the investigator performing the study. Such a tendency is easily understood, but it makes comparison of measures very difficult. Results cannot be compared in an effort to develop theoretic statements if the constructs being measured have never been compared empirically. Until more research is done to compare the measures available in direct empirical investigations, there will continue to be considerable uncertainty in the area of competence research.

APPENDIX 1.

Communicative Adaptability Scale

The following are statements about communication behaviors. Answer each item as it relates to your general style of communication (the type of communicator you are most often) in social situations.

Please indicate the degree to which each statement applies to you by placing the appropriate number (according to the scale below) in the space provided.

5 = Always true of me.
4 = Often true of me.
3 = Sometimes true of me.
2 = Rarely true of me.
1 = Never true of me.

Social Composure

_____ 1. I feel nervous in social situations. (R)
_____ 2. In most social situations I feel tense and constrained. (R)
_____ 3. When talking, my posture seems awkward and tense. (R)
_____ 4. My voice sounds nervous when I talk with others. (R)
_____ 5. I am relaxed when talking with others.

---

[5] Duran, R.L. & Zakahi, W.R. (1984). Competence or style: What's in a name? *Communication Research Reports, 1,* 42–47.

Social Confirmation

_____ 6. I try to make the other person feel good.

_____ 7. I try to make the other person feel important.

_____ 8. I try to be warm when communicating with another.

_____ 9. While I'm talking I think about how the other person feels.

_____ 10. I am verbally and nonverbally supportive of other people.

Social Experience

_____ 11. I like to be active in different social groups.

_____ 12. I enjoy socializing with various groups of people.

_____ 13. I enjoy meeting new people.

_____ 14. I find it easy to get along with new people.

_____ 15. I do not "mix" well at social functions. (R)

Appropriate Disclosure

_____ 16. I am aware of how intimate my disclosures are.

_____ 17. I am aware of how intimate the disclosures of others are.

_____ 18. I disclose at the same level that others disclose to me.

_____ 19. I know how appropriate my self-disclosures are.

_____ 20. When I self-disclose I know what I am revealing.

Articulation

_____ 21. When speaking I have problems with grammar. (R)

_____ 22. At times I don't use appropriate verb tense. (R)

_____ 23. I sometimes use one word when I mean to use another. (R)

_____ 24. I sometimes use words incorrectly. (R)

_____ 25. I have difficulty pronouncing some words. (R)

Wit

_____ 26. When I am anxious, I often make jokes.

_____ 27. I often make jokes when in tense situations.

_____ 28. When I embarrass myself I often make a joke about it.

_____ 29. When someone makes a negative comment about me I respond with a witty comeback.

_____ 30. People think I am witty.

_____ R = Before summing the items to create dimensions, reverse the score where indicated by (R). If the person indicated 5 for that item, give it a score of 1. If the person indicated a 4, give it a 2. If a person indicated a 2, give it a 4. If a person indicated a 1 for that item, give it a 5.

APPENDIX 2.

Self-rated Competence

1 = STRONGLY DISAGREE   *Regarding*
2 = MILDLY DISAGREE   *YOURSELF*
3 = UNDECIDED   *in the Conversation.*
4 = MILDLY AGREE
5 = STRONGLY AGREE

_____ 1. I was relaxed and comfortable when speaking.
_____ 2. I was a likable person.
_____ 3. I expressed myself clearly.
_____ 4. I gave positive feedback.
_____ 5. I was trustworthy.
_____ 6. I was assertive.
_____ 7. I was a good listener.
_____ 8. I was supportive.
_____ 9. I showed an interest in the conversation.
_____ 10. I was sarcastic.
_____ 11. I was awkward in the conversation.
_____ 12. I was socially skilled.
_____ 13. I was confident.
_____ 14. I found it difficult to express my true feelings.
_____ 15. I ignored the other person's feelings.
_____ 16. I lacked self-confidence.
_____ 17. I was an effective conversationalist.
_____ 18. I talked too much about myself.
_____ 19. I pretended to listen when I actually didn't.
_____ 20. I was shy.
_____ 21. I was nervous during the conversation.
_____ 22. My facial expressions were abnormally blank and restrained.
_____ 23. I was a competent communicator.
_____ 24. I was respectful.
_____ 25. I interrupted too much.
_____ 26. I understood the other person.
_____ 27. I was sensitive to the needs and feelings of the other person.

---

[6] Cupach, W.R., & Spitzberg, B.H. (1981). *Relational competence: Measurement and validation.* W.S.C.A., San Jose, CA.

——— 28. I was cooperative.

APPENDIX 3.

Rating of Alter Competence

1 = STRONGLY DISAGREE   *Regarding the*
2 = MILDLY DISAGREE   *OTHER PERSON*
3 = UNDECIDED   *in the Conversation.*
4 = MILDLY AGREE
5 = STRONGLY AGREE

——— 1. S/he was versatile.
——— 2. S/he was sympathetic.
——— 3. S/he was likable.
——— 4. S/he gave positive feedback.
——— 5. S/he was trustworthy.
——— 6. S/he was assertive.
——— 7. S/he was a good listener.
——— 8. S/he was supportive.
——— 9. S/he appeared tired and sleepy.
——— 10. S/he was awkward in the conversation.
——— 11. S/he spoke too rapidly.
——— 12. S/he was confident.
——— 13. S/he ignored my feelings.
——— 14. S/he lacked self-confidence.
——— 15. S/he spoke too slowly.
——— 16. S/he could easily put her/himself in another person's shoes.
——— 17. Her/his voice was monotone and boring.
——— 18. Her/his facial expressions were abnormally blank and restrained.
——— 19. S/he was adaptable.
——— 20. S/he had an accurate self-perception.
——— 21. S/he was easy to confide in.
——— 22. S/he was respectful.
——— 23. S/he understood me.
——— 24. S/he paid attention to the conversation.
——— 25. S/he was sensitive to my needs and feelings in the conversation.

[7] Cupach, W.R., & Spitzberg, B.H. (1981). *Relational competence: Measurement and validation.* W.S.C.A., San Jose, CA.

_____ 26. S/he was polite.
_____ 27. S/he was cooperative.

References

Adult Performance Level Study. (1977). *Final report: The adult performance level study.* U.S. Office of Education, Department of Health, Education, and Welfare.

Argyle, M. (1981). The contribution of social interaction research to social skills training. In J.D. Wine and M.D. Smye (Eds.), *Social Competence* (pp. 261–286). New York: Guilford Press.

Argyris, C. (1965). Explorations in interpersonal competence—I. *Journal of Applied Behavioral Science, 1,* 58–83.

Backlund, P.M. (1977). *Speech communication correlates of perceived communication competence.* Unpublished doctoral dissertation, University of Denver, Denver, CO.

Backlund, P.M., Brown, K.L., Gurry, J., & Jandt, F. (1982). Recommendations for assessing speaking and listening skills. *Communication Education, 31,* 10–17.

Backlund, P.M., VanRheenen, D., Moore, M., Parks, A.M. & Booth, J. (1981). *Perspectives on the assessment of speaking and listening skills for the 1980s.* Proceedings of a symposium presented by the Clearinghouse for Applied Performance Testing, Portland, OR.

Ballard-Reisch, D. (1984). *Communication competence and satisfaction: Knowledge, skill and feelings in acquaintanceship dyads: An exploratory analysis.* Paper presented at the Speech Communication Association Conference, Chicago, IL.

Barlow, D.H., Able, G.G., Blanchard, B.B., Bristow, A.R., & Young, L.D. (1977). A heterosocial skills behavior checklist for males. *Behavior Therapy, 8,* 229–239.

Bassett, R.E., Whittington, N., & Staton-Spicer, A. (1978). The basics in speaking and listening for high school graduates: What should be assessed? *Communication Education, 27,* 293–303.

Bellack, A.S. (1979). A critical appraisal of strategies for assessing social skill. *Behavioral Assessment, 1,* 157–176.

Bellack, A.S. (1983). Recurrent problems in the behavioral assessment of social skill. *Behavior Research and Therapy, 21,* 29–41.

Bernadin, H.J., & Pence, E.C. (1980). Effects of rater training: Creating new response sets and decreasing accuracy. *Journal of Applied Psychology, 65,* 60–66.

Block, J., & Bennett, L. (1955). The assessment of communication: Perception and transmission as a function of the social situation. *Human Relations, 8,* 317–325.

Bochner, A.P., & Kelly, C.W. (1974). Interpersonal competence: Rationale, philosophy, and implementation of a conceptual framework. *Speech Teacher, 23,* 270–301.

Bourque, P., & Ladduceur, R. (1979). Self-report and behavioral measures in the assessment of assertive behavior. *Journal of Behavioral Therapy and Experimental Psychiatry, 10,* 287–292.

Bradac, J.J., & Wiemann, J.M. (1985). *Communicative competence: A behavioral perspective.* Paper presented at the International Communication Association Conference, Honolulu, HI.

Brandt, D.R. (1979). On linking social performance with social competence: Some relations between communicative style and attributions of interpersonal effectiveness. *Human Communication Research, 5,* 223–237.

Brilhart, B.L. (1965). The relationship between some aspects of communicative speaking and communicative listening. *Journal of Communication, 15,* 35–46.

Brunner, C.C. & Spitzberg, B.H. (1986). *Measuring interpersonal communication competence across situations: Toward a theoretical integration of context and competence inference research.* Paper presented at the Central States Speech Communication Association Conference, Cincinnati, OH.

Bryant, B., Trower, P., Yardley, K., Urbieta, H., & Letemendia, F.J. (1976). A survey of social inadequacy among psychiatric outpatients. *Psychological Medicine, 6,* 101–112.

Cahn, D.D., & Shulman, G.M. (1984). The perceived understanding instrument. *Communication Research Reports, 1,* 122–125.

Cone, J.D. (1977). The relevance of reliability and validity for behavioral assessment. *Behavior Therapy, 8,* 411–426.

Cone, J.D. (1978). The Behavioral Assessment Grid (BAG): A conceptual framework and a taxonomy. *Behavior Therapy, 9,* 882–888.

Conger, A.J., Wallander, J.L., Mariotto, M.J., & Ward, D. (1980). Peer judgments of heterosexual-social anxiety and skills: What do they pay attention to anyhow? *Behavioral Assessment, 2,* 243–295.

Coulter, W.A., & Morrow, H.W. (1978). A collection of adaptive behavior measures. In W.A. Coulter and H.W. Morrow (Eds.), *Adaptive behavior: Concepts and measurements* (pp. 141–152). New York: Grune and Stratton.

Cupach, W.R., & Spitzberg, B.H. (1981). *Relational competence: Measurement and validation.* Paper presented at the Western Speech Communication Association Conference, San Jose, CA.

Cupach, W.R., & Spitzberg, B.H. (1982). *A reanalysis of the measure of relational competence.* Unpublished manuscript, Illinois State University, Normal, IL.

Cupach, W.R., & Spitzberg, B.H. (1983). Trait versus state: A comparison of dispositional and situational measures of interpersonal communication competence. *Western Journal of Speech Communication, 47,* 364–379.

Curran, J.P. (1979a). Pandora's box reopened? The assessment of social skills. *Journal of Behavioral Assessment, 1,* 55–71.

Curran, J.P. (1979b). Social skills: Methodological issues and future directions. In A.S. Bellack and M. Hersen (Eds.), *Research and practice in social skills training* (pp. 348–398). New York: Plenum.

Curran, J.P., (1982). A procedure for the assessment of social skills: The

Simulated Social Interaction Test. In J.P. Curran and P.M. Monti (Eds.), *Social skills training* (pp. 348–398). New York: Guilford.

Curran, J.P., & Mariotto, M.J. (1980). A conceptual structure for the assessment of social skills. *Progress in Behavioral Modification, 10,* 1–37.

Curran, J.P., Miller, I.W., III, Zwick, W.R., Monti, P.M., & Stout, R.L. (1980a). The socially inadequate patient: Incidence rate, demographic and clinical features, and hospital and posthospital functioning. *Journal of Consulting and Clinical Psychology, 48,* 375–382.

Curran, J.P., Monti, P.M., Corriveau, D.P., Hay, L.R., Hagerman, S., Zwick, W.R., & Farrell, A.D. (1980b). The generalizability of a procedure for assessing social skills and social anxiety in a psychiatric population. *Behavioral Assessment, 2,* 389–401.

Curran, J.P., Wessberg, H.W., Farrell, A.D., Monti, P.M., Corriveau, D.P., & Coyne, N.A. (1982). Social skills and social anxiety: Are different laboratories measuring the same constructs? *Journal of Consulting and Clinical Psychology, 50,* 396–406.

Diez, M.E. (1984). Communicative competence: An interactive approach. *Communication Yearbook, 8,* 56–79.

Dillard, J. &, Spitzberg, B.H. (1984). Global impressions of social skills: Behavioral predictors. *Communication Yearbook, 8,* 446–463.

Doucette, J., & Freedman, R. (1980). *Progress tests for the developmentally disabled: An evaluation.* Cambridge, MA: Abt Books.

Dow, M.G. (1985). Peer validation and idiographic analysis of social skill deficits. *Behavior Therapy, 16,* 76–86.

Duran, R.L. (1983). Communicative adaptability: A measure of social communicative competence. *Communication Quarterly, 31,* 320–326.

Duran, R.L., & Wheeless, V.E. (1980). *Social management: Toward a theory based operationalization of communication competence.* Paper presented at the Speech Communication Association Conference, New York.

Duran, R.L., & Zakahi, W.R. (1984). Competence or style: What's in a name? *Communication Research Reports, 1,* 42–46.

Duran, R.L., Zakahi, W.R. & Mumper, M.A. (1982). *Competence vs style: A dyadic assessment of the relationship among communication performance variables and communication satisfaction.* Paper presented at the International Communication Association Conference, Boston, MA.

Eisler, R.M. (1976). Behavioral assessment of social skills. In M. Hersen and A.S. Bellack (Eds.), *Behavioral assessment: A practical handbook* (pp. 369–395). Oxford, England: Pergamon.

Fingeret, A.L., Monti, P.M., & Paxson, M. (1983). Relationships among social perception, social skill, and social anxiety of psychiatric patients. *Psychological Reports, 53,* 1175–1178.

Fingeret, A.L., Monti, P.M., & Paxson, M.A. (1985). Social perception, social performance, and self-perception. *Behavior Modification, 9,* 345–356.

Fisher-Beckfield, D., & McFall, R.M. (1982). Development of a competence inventory for college men and evaluation of relationships between competence and depression. *Journal of Consulting and Clinical Psychology, 50,* 699–705.

Foster, S.L., & Ritchey, W.L. (1979). Issues in the assessment of social competence in children. *Journal of Applied Behavior Analysis, 12,* 625–638.

Furnham, A. (1983). Research in social skills training: A critique. In R. Ellis and D. Whittington (Eds.), *New directions in social skill training* (pp. 267–298). London: Croom Helm.

Gaffney, L.R. (1984). A multiple-choice test to measure social skills in delinquent and nondelinquent adolescent girls. *Journal of Consulting and Clinical Psychology, 52,* 911–912.

Gaffney, L.R., & McFall, R.M. (1981). A comparison of social skills in delinquent and nondelinquent adolescent girls using a behavioral role-playing inventory. *Journal of Consulting and Clinical Psychology, 49,* 959–967.

Galassi, J.P., Galassi, M.D., & Fulkerson, K. (1984). Assertion training in theory and practice: An update. In C.M. Franks (Ed.), *New developments in behavior therapy: From research to clinical application* (pp. 319–376). New York: Haworth.

Goldsmith, J.B., & McFall, R.M. (1975). Development and evaluation of an interpersonal skill-training program for psychiatric inpatients. *Journal of Abnormal Psychology, 84,* 51–58.

Gottman, J.M., & Porterfield, A.L. (1981). Communicative competence in the nonverbal behavior of married couples. *Journal of Marriage and the Family, 43,* 817–824.

Green, K.D., & Forehand, R. (1980). Assessment of children's social skills: A review of methods. *Journal of Behavioral Assessment, 2,* 143–159.

Gresham, F.M. (1981). Assessment of children's social skills. *Journal of School Psychology, 19,* 120–129.

Griffiths, R.D.P. (1980). Social skills and psychological disorder. In W.T. Singleton, P. Spurgeon, and R.B. Stammers (Eds.), *The analysis of social skill* (pp. 39–78). New York: Plenum.

Haley, W.E. (1985). Social skills deficits and self-evaluation among depressed and nondepressed psychiatric inpatients. *Journal of Clinical Psychology, 41,* 162–168.

Hecht, M.L. (1978). The conceptualization and measurement of interpersonal communication satisfaction. *Human Communication Research, 4,* 253–264.

Hefele, T.J., & Hurst, M.W. (1972). Interpersonal skill measurement: Precision, validity, and utility. *Consulting Psychologist, 3,* 62–70.

Henzl, S., Mabry, E.A., & Powell, R.G. (1983). *The effects of cognitive complexity and gender on assessments of communication competence.* Paper presented at the International Communication Association Conference, Dallas, TX.

Hersen, M., & Bellack, A.S. (1977). Assessment of social skills. In A.R. Ciminero, K.S. Calhoun, & H.S. Adams (Eds.), *Handbook of behavioral assessment* (pp. 509–544). New York: John Wiley and Sons.

Hogarty, G.E., & Katz, M.M. (1971). Norms of adjustment and social behavior. *Archives of General Psychiatry, 25,* 470–480.

Hops, H. (1983). Children's social competence and skill: Current research practices and future directions. *Behavior Therapy, 14,* 3–18.

Hymes, D.H. (1972). On communicative competence. In J.B. Pride and J. Holmes (Eds.), *Sociolinguistics* (pp. 269–293). Middlesex, England: Penguin.

Jackson, H.J., King, N.J., & Heller, V.R. (1981). Social skills assessment and training for mentally retarded persons: A review of research. *Australian Journal of Developmental Disabilities, 7,* 113–123.

Kahn, M. (1970). Non-verbal communication and marital satisfaction. *Family Process, 9,* 449–456.

Katz, M.M., & Lyerly, S.B. (1963). Methods for measuring adjustment and social behavior in the community: I. Rationale, description, discriminative validity and scale development. *Psychological Reports, 13,* 503–535.

Kelly, C.W., Chase, L.J., & Wiemann, J.M. (1979). *Interpersonal competence: Conceptualization, measurement, and future considerations.* Paper presented at the Speech Communication Association Conference, San Antonio, TX.

Kelly, L., & Duran, R.L. (1984). *An investigation of the relationship of shyness to self-, partner-, observer-, and meta-perceptions of communication competence.* Paper presented at the Speech Communication Association Conference, Chicago, IL.

Kohn, M. (1977). *Social competence, symptoms and underachievement in childhood: A longitudinal perspective.* Washington, DC: V.H. Winston & Sons.

Kolko, D.J., & Milan, M.A. (1985). A woman's heterosocial skill observational rating system: Behavior-analytic development and validation. *Behavior Modification, 9,* 165–192.

Leary, M.R. (1983). Social anxiousness: The construct and its measurement. *Journal of Personality Assessment, 47,* 66–75.

Levenson, R.W., & Gottman, J.M. (1978). Toward the assessment of social competence. *Journal of Consulting and Clinical Psychology, 46,* 453–462.

Liberman, R.P. (1982). Assessment of social skills. *Schizophrenia Bulletin, 8,* 62–83.

Lowe, M.R. (1978). *The validity of a measure of social performance in an inpatient population.* Unpublished manuscript, Washington University, St. Louis, MO.

Lowe, M.R. (1985). Psychometric evaluation of the Social Performance Survey Schedule: Reliability and validity of the positive behavior subscale. *Behavior Modification, 9,* 193–210.

Lowe, M.R., & Cautela, J.R. (1978). A self-report measure of social skill. *Behavior Therapy, 9,* 535–544.

Mahaney, M.M. & Kern, J.M. (1983). Variations in role-play tests of heterosocial performance. *Journal of Consulting and Clinical Psychology, 51,* 151–152.

Martin, E.M., & Chapman, L.J. (1982). Communication effectiveness in psychosis-prone college students. *Journal of Abnormal Psychology, 91,* 420–425.

Martinez-Diaz, J.A., & Edelstein, B.A. (1979). Multivariate effects of demand characteristics on the analogue assessment of heterosocial competence. *Journal of Applied Behavior Analysis, 12,* 679–689.

McCroskey, J.C. (1977). Oral communication apprehension: A summary of recent theory and research. *Human Communication Research, 4,* 78–96.

McCroskey, J.C. (1978). Validity of the PRCA as an index of oral communication apprehension. *Communication Monographs, 45,* 192–203.

McFall, R.M. (1982). A review and reformulation of the concept of social skills. *Behavioral Assessment, 4,* 1–33.

McFall, R.M. & Lillesand, D.B. (1971). Behavioral rehearsal with modeling and coaching in assertion training. *Journal of Abnormal Psychology, 77,* 313–323.

McLaughlin, M.L., & Cody, M.J. (1982). Awkward silences: Behavioral antecedents and consequences of the conversational lapse. *Human Communication Research, 8,* 299–316.

Mead, N.A. (1980a). *Assessing speaking skills: Issues of feasibility, reliability, validity and bias.* Paper presented at the Speech Communication Association Conference, New York.

Mead, N.A. (1980b). *The Massachusetts basic skills assessment of listening and speaking.* Paper presented at the Speech Communication Association Conference, New York.

Miller, L.S., & Funabiki, D. (1983). Predictive validity of the Social Performance Survey Schedule for component interpersonal behaviors. *Behavioral Assessment, 6,* 33–44.

Monge, P.R., Bachman, S.G., Dillard, J.P., & Eisenberg, E.M. (1982). Communicator competence in the workplace: Model testing and scale development. *Communication Yearbook, 5,* 505–528.

Monti, P.M. (1983). The Social Skills Intake Interview: Reliability and convergent validity assessment. *Journal of Behavior Therapy and Experimental Psychiatry, 14,* 305–310.

Monti, P.M., Boice, R., Fingeret, A.L., Zwick, W.R., Kolko, D., Munroe, S., & Grunberger, A. (1984). Midi-level measurement of social anxiety in psychiatric and non-psychiatric samples. *Behavior Research and Therapy, 22,* 651–660.

Monti, P.M., Corriveau, D.P., & Curran, J.P. (1982). Assessment of social skills in the day hospital: Does the clinician see something other than the researcher sees? *International Journal of Partial Hospitalization, 1,* 245–250.

Monti, P.M., Wallander, J.L., Ahern, D.K., Abrams, D.B., & Munroe, S.M. (1983). Multi-modal measurement of anxiety and social skills in a behavioral role-play test: Generalizability and discriminant validity. *Behavioral Assessment, 6,* 15–25.

Morrison, R.L., Bellack, A.S., & Manuck, S.B. (1985). Role of social competence in borderline essential hypertension. *Journal of Consulting and Clinical Psychology, 53,* 248–255.

Nietzel, M.T., & Bernstein, D.A. (1976). Effects of instructionally mediated demand on the behavioral assessment of assertiveness. *Journal of Consulting and Clinical Psychology, 44,* 500.

Norton, R.W. (1983). *Communicator style.* Beverly Hills, CA: Sage.

Perri, M.G., Richards, C.S., & Goodrich, J.D. (1978). Heterosocial Adequacy Test (HAT): A behavioral role-playing test for the assessment of heterosocial skills in male college students. *JSAS Catalog of Selected Documents in Psychology, 8,* (Ms. 1650).

Powell, R.G., & Avila, D.R. (1985). *Ethnicity, communication competency and classroom success.* Paper presented at the International Communication Association Conference, Honolulu, HI.

Powers, W.G., & Lowry, D.N. (1984). Basic communication fidelity: A fundamental approach. In R.M. Bostrom (Ed.), *Competence in communication: A multidisciplinary approach* (pp. 57–71). Beverly Hills, CA: Sage.

Powers, W.G., & Spitzberg, B.H. (1986). Basic communication fidelity and image management *Communication Research Reports, 3,* 60–63.

Prisbell, M. (1979). *Feeling good: Conceptualization and measurement.* Paper presented at the Western Speech Communication Association Conference, Los Angeles, CA.

Romano, J.M., & Bellack, A.S. (1980). Social validation of a component model of assertive behavior. *Journal of Consulting and Clinical Psychology, 48,* 478–490.

Rook, K.S. (1984). The negative side of social interaction: Impact on psychological well-being. *Journal of Personality and Social Psychology, 46, 1097–1108.*

Rosen, B., Klein, D.F., Levenstein, S., & Shahinian, S.P. (1969). Social competence and posthospital outcome among schizophrenic and nonschizophrenic psychiatric patients. *Journal of Abnormal Psychology, 74,* 401–404.

Rosenberg, S., & Cohen, B.D. (1966). Referential processes of speakers and listeners. *Psychological Review, 73,* 208–231.

Royce, W.S. (1982). Behavioral referents for molar ratings of heterosocial skill. *Psychological Reports, 59,* 139–146.

Rubin, D.L. (1981). Using performance rating scales in large-scale assessments of oral communication proficiency. *Perspectives on the assessment of speaking and listening skills for the 1980's* (pp. 51–67). Proceedings of a symposium presented by Clearing House for Applied Performance Testing, Northwest Regional Educational Laboratory, Portland, OR.

Rubin, D.L., Daly, J., McCroskey, J.C., & Mead, N.A. (1982). A review and critique of procedures for assessing speaking and listening skills among preschool through grade twelve students. *Communication Education, 31,* 285–304.

Rubin, D.L., & Mead, N.A. (1984). *Large scale assessment of oral communication skills: Kindergarten through grade 12.* Annandale, VA: Speech Communication Association/ERIC.

Rubin, R.B. (1981a). Assessment of college-level speaking and listening assessment. *Perspectives on the assessment of speaking and listening skills for the 1980's* (pp. 25–42). Proceedings of a symposium presented by Clearing

House for Applied Performance Testing, Northwest Regional Educational Laboratory, Portland, OR.

Rubin, R.B. (1981b). *The development and refinement of a Communication Competency Assessment Instrument.* Paper presented at the Speech Communication Association Conference, Anaheim, CA.

Rubin, R.B. (1982). Assessing speaking and listening competence at the college level: The Communication Competency Assessment Instrument. *Communication Education, 31,* 19–32.

Rubin, R.B. (1985). The validity of the Communication Competency Assessment Instrument. *Communication Monographs, 52,* 173–185.

Rubin, R.B., & Feezel, J.D. (1984). *Elements of teacher communication competence: An examination of skills, knowledge, and motivation to communicate.* Paper presented at the Speech Communication Association Conference, Chicago, IL.

Rubin, R.B., & Henzl, S.A. (1984). Cognitive complexity, communication competence, and verbal ability. *Communication Quarterly, 32,* 263–270.

Rubin, R.B., Sisco, J., Moore, M.R. & Quianthy, R. (1983). *Oral communication assessment procedures and instrument development in higher education.* Annandale, VA: Speech Communication Association.

Ruesch, J., Block, J., & Bennett, L. (1953). The assessment of communication: I. A method for the analysis of social interaction. *Journal of Psychology, 35,* 59–80.

Salzman, C., Kochansky, G.E., & Shader, R.I. (1972). Rating scales for geriatric psychopharmacology—A review. *Psychopharmacology Bulletin, 8,* 3–50.

Schroeder, H.E., & Rakos, R.F. (1983). The identification and assessment of social skills. In R. Ellis and D. Whittington (Eds.), *New directions in social skill training* (pp. 117–188). London: Croom Helm.

Scofield, M.E., & Yoxtheimer, L.L. (1983). Psychometric issues in the assessment of clinical competencies. *Journal of Counseling Psychology, 30,* 413–420.

Segal, Z.V., & Marshall, W.L. (1985). Heterosexual social skills in a population of rapists and child molesters. *Journal of Consulting and Clinical Psychology, 53,* 55–63.

Spitzberg, B.H. (1983). Communication competence as knowledge, skill, and impression. *Communication Education, 32,* 323–328.

Spitzberg, B.H. (1985). *Loci of perception in the domain of interpersonal skills.* Paper presented at the International Communication Association Conference, Honolulu, HI.

Spitzberg, B.H. (1986b). *Validating of a measure of perceived conversational skills.* Paper presented at the Speech Communication Association Conference, Chicago, IL.

Spitzberg, B.H. (1986a). Issues in the study of communicative competence. *Progress in Communication Sciences, 8,* 1–46.

Spitzberg, B.H., & Canary, D.J. (1985). Loneliness and relationally competent communication. *Journal of Social and Personal Relationships, 2,* 387–402.

Spitzberg, B.H., & Cupach, W.R. (1983). *The relational competence construct:*

Development and research. Paper presented at the Speech Communication Association Conference, Washington, D.C. (ERIC #ED 246–490).

Spitzberg, B.H., & Cupach, W.R. (1984). *Interpersonal communication competence.* Beverly Hills, CA: Sage.

Spitzberg, B.H., & Cupach, W.R. (1985a). *A bibliography on competence in communicating.* Unpublished manuscript, North Texas State University, Denton, TX.

Spitzberg, B.H., & Cupach, W.R. (1985b). Conversational skill and locus of perception. *Journal of Psychopathology and Behavioral Assessment, 7,* 207–220.

Spitzberg, B.H., & Hurt, H.T. (1985). The measurement of interpersonal skills in instructional contexts. *Communication Education, 36,* 28–45.

Steinberg, S.L., Curran, J.P., Bell, S., Paxson, M.A., & Munroe, S.M. (1982). The effects of confederate prompt delivery style in a standardized social simulation test. *Journal of Behavioral Assessment, 4,* 268–273.

Stricker, L.J. (1980). *Interpersonal competence instrument: Development and preliminary findings.* Princeton, NJ: Educational Testing Service (Research Report 80–24).

Stricker, L.J. (1982). Interpersonal competence instrument: Development and preliminary findings. *Applied Psychological Measurement, 6,* 69–81.

Stricker, L.J. (1983). *Interpersonal competence, social intelligence, and general ability.* Research Report, Education Testing Service, Princeton, NJ.

Sundberg, N.D., Snowden, L.R., & Reynolds, W.M. (1978). Toward assessment of personal competence and incompetence in life situations. *Annual Review of Psychology, 29,* 179–221.

Trower, P., Bryant, B., & Argyle, M. (1978). *Social skills and mental health.* Philadelphia, PA: University of Pennsylvania Press.

Van Hasselt, V.B., Hersen, M., Whitehill, M.B., & Bellack, A.S. (1979). Social skill assessment and training for children: An evaluative review. *Behavior Research and Therapy, 17,* 413–437.

Wallander, J.L., Curran, J.P., & Myers, P.E. (1983). Social calibration of the SSIT: Evaluating social validity. *Behavior Modification, 7,* 423–445.

Walls, R.T., Werner, T.J., Bacon, A., & Zane, T. (1977). Behavior checklists. In J.D. Cone and R.P. Hawkins (Eds.), *Behavioral assessment: New directions in clinical psychology* (pp. 77–146). New York: Brunner/Mazel.

Weissman, M.M. (1975). The assessment of social adjustment: A review of techniques. *Archives of General Psychiatry, 32,* 357–365.

Wessberg, H.W., Curran, J.P., Monti, P.M., Corriveau, D.P., Coyne, N.A., & Dziadosz, T.H. (1981). Evidence for the external validity of a social simulation measure of social skills. *Journal of Behavioral Assessment, 3,* 209–220.

Wheeless, V.E., & Duran, R.L. (1982). Gender orientation as a correlate of communicative competence. *Southern Speech Communication Journal, 48,* 51–64.

Wiemann, J.M. (1975). *An explication of communicative competence in initial interaction: An experimental study.* Unpublished doctoral dissertation, Purdue University.

Wiemann, J. (1977). Explication and test of a model of communicative competence. *Human Communication Research, 3,* 195–213.

Wiemann, J.M., & Backlund, P.M. (1980). Current theory and research in communicative competence. *Review of Educational Research, 50,* 185–199.

Wiemann, J.M., & Bradac, J.J. (1983). *Some issues in the study of communicative competence.* Paper presented at the Speech Communication Association Conference, Washington, D.C.

Wiemann, J.M., & Kelly, C.W. (1981). Pragmatics of interpersonal competence. In C. Wilder-Mott and J.H. Weakland (Eds.), *Rigor and imagination: Essays from the legacy of Gregory Bateson* (pp. 283–297). New York: Praeger.

Wierzbicki, M. (1984). Social skills deficits and subsequent depressed mood in students. *Personality and Social Psychology Bulletin, 10,* 605–610.

Wrubel, J., Benner, P., & Lazarus, R.S. (1981). Social competence from the perspective of stress and coping. In J.D. Wine and M.D. Smye (Eds.), *Social competence* (pp. 61–99). New York: Guilford Press.

Zakahi, W.R., & Duran, R.L. (1982). All the lonely people: The relationship among loneliness, communicative competence, and communication anxiety. *Communication Quarterly, 30,* 203–209.

Zakahi, W.R., & Duran, R.L. (1985). Loneliness, communicative competence, and communication apprehension: Extension and replication. *Communication Quarterly, 33,* 50–60.

Zigler, E., & Phillips, L. (1961). Social competence and outcome in psychiatric disorder. *Journal of Abnormal and Social Psychology, 63,* 264–271.

CHAPTER 4

Communication Networks: Measurement Techniques*

*Peter R. Monge and
Noshir S. Contractor*

The idea of structure is one of the fundamental issues that any science must address. In its broadest sense, structure refers to the arrangement of the parts of the system that the science studies. Structure is fundamental because it significantly determines the processes of the system, that is, the ways in which the system can function or behave.

The science of human communication studies the communication systems that people use as they live their daily lives. Like every other scientific object, structure is a fundamental part of every communication system. Identification of this structure requires that we identify the people that comprise the various elements of the system and determine the arrangement of information exchange among these parts. In the science of human communication, the study of structure is usually undertaken under the rubric of network analysis.

The general idea of a network is one that is familiar to most people since we have all had frequent contact with concrete networks such as telephones, highways, and electrical power lines. But networks of social structure, of which communication is one type, are harder to identify. The difficulty stems from the fact that communication networks are comprised of abstract human behavior over time, rather than concrete physical material such as wires, pipes, and macadam.

Communication networks, then, are the regular patterns of person-to-person contacts that we discern as people exchange information in a human social system. By observing the communication behavior of people we can infer who is informationally connected to whom, and

* The authors wish to express their appreciation to Ron Rice for his helpful comments on an earlier draft of this manuscript.

thus, we can infer the communication network. Once we know the people who comprise the elements of the communication system and discern how they are arranged (i.e., the structure or network), we can describe how the overall communication system will operate and how it is related to other important variables.

Observing and inferring these regular patterns of human communication is not easy, but it is interesting and challenging. Because the task requires that we observe human communication and often assign numbers to what we observe, it falls within the proper domain of measurement. In this chapter we describe the measurement alternatives that are currently available and provide a summary of the current wisdom about their advantages and limitations. The selection of the appropriate network analysis method and computer program is also important. This chapter, however, concentrates primarily on the measurement process. (For a detailed review of network methods and programs, see Rice & Richards, 1985.)

The chapter is divided into three parts. The first section discusses properties of linkage data that have been used in network studies in general, and communication network studies in particular. The next section deals with two boundary specification problems: space and time. The third section focuses on various ways that network data are collected.

Properties of Network Linkages

The fundamental difference between network analysis and most other social science research is the emphasis placed on the relationship between two or more objects rather than the attributes of the objects. The objects, often called nodes in network analysis, may be individuals, roles, categories of individuals, groups, organizations, or even entire societies. Researchers in different disciplines have used network analysis to study such diverse phenomena as the transaction or flow of goods, money, information, power, influence, acquaintance, affection, and kinship patterns (Knoke & Kuklinski, 1982). While communication research may find one or more of these networks useful, the flow of information through communication networks is of primary concern.

Properties of Communication Linkages

The *strength* of a communication link is an important property of communication linkages. The strength of a link is a numerical description of the amount of the relationship between two nodes. There are three typical measures of strength. First, in some cases simply the presence or absence of a communication link is of interest. Such a measure is referred to as *binary*. This approach would suffice, for instance, if the aim of the network analysis is only to identify the isolates (Reitz, 1983). To obtain information on a binary link between A and B, respondent A may be asked to respond to a question such as, "Do you talk with B?." Second, the research question may require information about the *frequency* of communication over a fixed period of time. To obtain information on the frequency, the question may read, "How often do you talk with B?" Response options could include monthly, weekly, daily, or several times per day. The third measure of strength is the *duration* of each interaction. For example, a network measure of duration might be, "The last time you talked with this person, how long did your conversation last? less than 5 minutes, 5 to 15 minutes, 15 to 30 minutes, 30 minutes to an hour, more than an hour." Alternatively, if information is sought on the average duration of the interactions, the question, "How long, on the average, are your interactions with B?" must be asked. Sometimes, a researcher is interested in a combined measure of both frequency and duration. Typically, interactions of short durations will be assigned lower strengths as compared to equally frequent interactions of longer durations.

In some cases, the strength may be weighted by perceptual variables, such as satisfaction with, or importance of, the communication linkage. In such instances, it may be more appropriate to use an ordinal scaling scheme rather than an interval or ratio level measure (Killworth & Bernard, 1974). Finally, a strength can be assigned based on the level of distortion that occurs during a communication between the two nodes, or the amount of time required for a message to be sent from one node to another (Edwards & Monge, 1975).

The second property of network relations is the *symmetry* of the link. A link is defined as symmetric if the two nodes share information, both giving and taking equally. In contrast, an asymmetric link is defined as one in which information is primarily given by one node to the other, such as when one person instructs another or one person reprimands another. Thus, it may be of interest to know if a communication link between two nodes, say, A and B, implies that, A sends a message *to* B (an asymmetric link), or if A talks *with* B (a symmetric link).

Closely related to the concept of symmetry of a link is a property of network relations known as *directionality*. Directionality pertains to the flow of the substance of the relation from one person to another. Typically, there are two values to directionality. First a directional link refers to a link in which information or communication flows from person A to person B. A directional link can only be defined for an asymmetric relation. Second, an undirected link refers to one in which the direction of the flow of information or communication between two is unspecified. Undirected links occur only for symmetrical relations. For example, if A discusses politics with B, the link is undirected and they engage in a symmetric relationship. To obtain information on a symmetric link, an individual must be asked specifically to report undirected linkages. For example, "How often do you discuss politics with B?" If on the other hand, A informs B about politics, the link is directed and they engage in an asymmetric relationship. In such cases, individual A must be asked "How often do you talk to B about politics?"

A third property of network relations that may be of interest is *reciprocation*. Reciprocation is defined as the degree to which two individuals agree on the strength of the communication linkage between them. For instance, if A reports a high level of interaction with B, while B disagrees and reports a low volume of interaction with A, the link is said to have a low degree of reciprocation. As can be seen from this example, reciprocation is a property that is only defined for symmetric links. If information is required on the degree of reciprocation for links, it is imperative that the network question be posed to all members of the network.

Finally, a fourth property of network relations, proposed by Rice and Richards (1985) is *confirmation*. Confirmation is defined as the degree of agreement between two individuals involved in an asymmetric link. For instance, if A reports that he/she instructs B on how to conduct a network analysis and B indicates that he/she was taught how to conduct a network analysis by A, the link is said to have a high degree of confirmation. Clearly, confirmation is a property defined only for asymmetric links. To obtain information on the degree of confirmation, it is necessary for the researcher to ask an additional question. For example, the question, "How often do you initiate communication with B?" must be accompanied with the question, "How often does B initiate communication with you?"

Content of Communication Linkage

The properties of network linkages described above provide a framework for studying a generic communication network. However, in practice, most researchers restrict their attention to specific forms of communication. In this section we examine ways in which network researchers have isolated or categorized the forms of communication which are relevant to the research question. First, a communication network instrument may need to identify the *content* or *function* of the communication, based on the research questions being posed. For instance, one functional classification applied to messages in organizations distinguishes between production (getting the job done), innovation (exploring new alternatives), and maintenance (keeping the system and its components operating) (Farace, Monge, & Russell, 1977). In a social setting, studies on content-specific communication networks have been wide-ranging. For instance, research has examined communication networks pertaining to the diffusion of a specific innovation, to a particular hobby, and to taboo issues such as abortion or contraception (Rogers & Kincaid, 1981).

Second, network analysis has also been used to answer research questions dealing with the differential effects of the communication *media* being used. One approach would be to study a network of verbal communication and compare it with one based on written communication. With the growing interest in effects of various communication technologies, a communication network instrument might distinguish between mass communication technologies (such as radio, television, and computer bulletin boards), various point-to-point communication technologies (such as telephone and electronic mail), and face-to-face communication (e.g., Rice, 1982).

While most studies focus on a single communication network, some studies attempted to study networks where individuals are connected by more than one form of linkage. Such relationships are referred to as multiplex linkages. It must be pointed out that, even though a network instrument may be able to collect data on multiplex relationships, their subsequent analysis may be limited by the analytic algorithms currently available. To date, almost none of the network programs using graph-theoretic algorithms can analyze multiplex networks. However Burt (1980) argues that algorithms using the positional approach allow the analysis of multiplex networks.

Boundary Specification

In this section, we address two issues. For what membership and over what duration of time are these relationships being studied? The first question would imply specifying a boundary in space, while the latter would require the specification of a boundary in the time domain. The boundary of a system, therefore, is defined by a set of criteria that result in the specification of membership over a particular period of time.

Space Boundary

The selection of a spatial boundary for the network is accompanied by very specific assumptions about the object of explanation. Consider for a moment, a biologist who observes an exotic collection of acquatic organisms in a petri dish through a microscope. After some focusing the biologist will zero in on a clear picture. However, this view of the acquatic world is largely determined by the order of magnification to which the microscope has been adjusted. The biologist could switch to a higher or lower power of magnification. By doing so, new levels of the acquatic community come into focus. Switching to a higher order of magnification would allow the study of cells within a single organism. A lower order of resolution might be appropriate to study colonies of organisms. Just as in this example the object of explanation (e.g., a cell or a colony) determined the order of magnification chosen, so also in network research the object of explanation (e.g., a department, an organization, or an industry) will determine the specification of a boundary.

Historically, network studies have often provided little or no theoretical rationale for their choice of system boundaries. Laumann, Marsden, & Prensky (1983) have argued that an error in the specification of the boundary can result in fundamental misrepresentations of the structure abstracted from an analysis of an ill-defined network. They propose that membership in a network could be based on any of three broad criteria. The first focuses on the people, the second on the relationship, and the third on a common activity.

In the first approach, all people having a common attribute, such as membership in an organization, club, or village, could be considered members. A variation is to include people recommended by knowledgeable informants. A large proportion of network studies in organizations fall into this first category. Laumann et al. (1983) have pointed out that in this approach the nodal characteristics have been fixed and cannot be studied. However, the patterns of participation and the levels of interconnectedness can be empirically analyzed.

The second alternative specifies people participating in a particular type of relationship. A variation restricts membership to those who have a minimum frequency of interaction in this type of a relationship. In this approach, the form of the network is fixed, but the nodal attributes and patterns of participation are free to vary.

Finally, some researchers (such as Pfeffer & Salancik, 1978) define the boundary of the system as a set of events or activities. For instance, Dahl (1961) chose to study only those members of the New Haven community elite who were involved in a controversy. In this case, the level of interconnectedness and the nodal attributes are both allowed to vary, while the participation in the event is empirically fixed.

Time Boundary

Let us return for a moment to the example of the biologist. After having chosen the appropriate level of magnification required the biologist would still need to decide on the duration of the observation. For some research questions, the biologist may need to make an observation at one point in time. In other cases, the observation may need to be made continuously for a long period of time. In still other cases, the observations may need to be made intermittently. The time intervals may vary from seconds to months, even years! Like the biologist, the communication scientist must also decide on the temporal boundary of the study based on the research question being posed.

As in other social science research, network analysis has traditionally been cross-sectional in design. However, since the objective of network analysis is to describe the structure based on patterns of interaction over time, all network analysis has a built-in time component. Cross-sectional network research has been classified into concrete-time network analysis and abstract-time network analysis (Edwards & Monge, 1975). Concrete-time network analysis is based on aggregating and reporting actual interactions over a specified period of time (say, a week). For instance, the researcher may ask the question, "How often did you talk to A in the past week?" Abstract-time network analysis, on the other hand, requires the respondent to extrapolate from reality to provide estimates of interactions for a hypothetical or an average time period. For instance, the researcher may ask the question, "How often do you talk to A in a typical week?"

The choice of the duration of the time period in cross-sectional network analysis may affect the data collected significantly. Choosing too short a time duration may leave the researcher with data too sparse to ascertain patterns of communication. For instance, asking individuals to report the frequency of interactions in the past day may exclude all those linkages that occur less frequently than daily. On the other hand, choosing too large a time duration might mask any recent changes in the communication patterns. Further, the choice of the words "short" and "large" to describe the time durations is relative and varies with the context. This dilemma can be resolved individually for each study, based on the theoretical rationale of the process being examined, and by pretesting the instrument.

As with other cross-sectional research, cross-sectional network analysis is often not appropriate to capture change. Ironically, despite the fact that theorists of social structure have often described the unfolding of structure as a processual phenomenon, most network researchers have used cross-sectional instruments to measure network structure. Consequently, they have had considerable difficulty describing the process of network change. Fortunately, researchers have recently begun to correct this problem by conducting longitudinal communication network studies (Rice & Barnett, 1986).

There are two principal approaches to designing a longitudinal network instrument. The feature that distinguishes them is the timing of their administration. The first approach would be to aggregate the number of interactions (just as in the concrete-time network analysis) periodically. The time period would need to coincide with the duration for which the interactions were aggregated. The second approach would not collect data at equal intervals of time. Instead, the instrument would be used at specific stages. These stages, for example, the life cycle of an organization, or stages of the diffusion of innovations, may be theoretically determined (Monge & Miller, in press).

The time span of longitudinal studies would be governed by the nature of the phenomena being studied. Researchers interested in microphenomena, such as interactions during a group discussion, would conduct their study over a relatively short time span. On the other hand, those interested in macrophenomena, such as formation of alliances, or maintenance of stratification, conduct their studies over fairly large time spans (Barnes, 1979).

Data Collection

Methodologies for the collection of communication data were developed more than half a century ago. Different techniques were utilized in laboratory and field settings. Further, they either relied on self-reports or on external observers to provide the data. The external observer could range from a participant observer to a mechanized monitor keeping logs. In the next few pages, these techniques are briefly described, with special emphasis on the assumptions and limitations accompanying each technique. (For more detailed descriptions of these techniques, see Farace et al., 1977, Rogers & Kincaid, 1981).

Laboratory Studies

Laboratory data collection techniques were developed by Bavelas (1948, 1950) and Leavitt (1951). Working in a small-group laboratory, they imposed a variety of communication network configurations on their subjects. The configurations allowed some of the subjects to communicate directly, while preventing direct communication between others. The subjects (rarely more than five) were then given a task, while the experimenter measured the number of interactions between the members in the group before a certain decision or outcome was achieved. These interactions were often in the form of written messages exchanged by members connected in the specified network. These researchers, therefore, primarily used data collected by external observers.

There are several fairly stringent limitations to this technique. First, laboratory groups are typically small, and extrapolating findings to larger groups may not be valid (Farace et al., 1977). Second, the laboratory group is a closed group in a closed system, and findings in such a setting may not be applicable to groups which are embedded in larger systems (e.g., Cohen, Robinson, & Edwards, 1969; Bernard & Killworth, 1979). Finally, most laboratory groups do not have a history of working together, and hence may not reflect communication patterns that are associated with groups which have been in existence for some time (Fortes, 1957).

Traditionally, experimental techniques have been used to study outcomes of imposed networks. This approach, however, does not permit researchers to study easily the processes whereby networks emerge (Monge and Eisenberg, in press). This shortcoming reflects a deficiency in the way the technique has been used and does not represent an inherent limitation of the experimental approach.

Field Studies

Techniques to collect network data from the field itself have existed since the first half of this century. Two traditions have developed within field studies. The first relies on self-report of communication activities through sociometric surveys or diary studies. The second relies on data collected either by an observer in the field or by unobtrusive methods.

Self-report using sociometric techniques. Moreno (1934) was among the first to develop a self-report technique for the study of communication networks. He proposed a sociometric-based survey questionnaire to collect network data. Barnes (1954) and Bott (1955, 1957) used sociometric network data for the first time to explain individual behavior. The technique was also used by anthropologists from "the Manchester School" (Rogers & Kincaid, 1981, p. 95) in their study of small networks (e.g., Mitchell, 1969; Boissevain & Mitchell, 1973; Boissevain, 1974).

The self-report technique is most closely related to conventional social science survey techniques. The members of a system are asked to report on their interaction with each of the other members of the system. In some cases, they are provided with a roster, listing all the members, while in other cases they are asked to recall the names of all the people with whom they have interacted. The former technique is referred to as "recognition" or "aided-recall," while the latter is referred to simply as the "recall" technique.

Following the lead of Barnes (1954) and Mitchell (1969), researchers have proposed the use of network instruments in conjunction with instruments that describe social attributes of the individual. The incorporation of network items in traditional social science surveys is described by Burt (1984). These items provide information on the demographics of the respondent's significant contacts and the level of communication between the respondent's significant links.

The use of network items in conjunction with the standard social science survey enables the use of social variables to predict network attributes of the individual. For instance, respondent background variables such as socioeconomic status, have been used to determine network range—the degree to which an individual's contacts are socially diverse (e.g., Laumann, 1973; Fischer, 1982). It is also possible to study the extent to which network variables, such as range, can be used to predict sociometric variables such as stress, leadership skills, reliance on stereotyping (Burt, 1984). Finally, it is possible to include network variables as an interaction term. For instance, in a study conducted by Ruan, and reported by Burt (1984), "interpersonal environments of especially close sexually homogeneous people created significant sex bias in the respondent's opinion" (Burt, 1984, p. 309). The General Social Survey, one of the nation's largest sociological data bases, included network items in its questionnaires for the first time in 1985.

Self-report using the diary technique. A second form of self-report technique is referred to as the diary (or duty) study. Among the early researchers who used this technique were Burns (1954), Hinrichs (1964) and Farace and Morris (1969). In this technique each individual is requested to keep a diary for a specified period of time. During this period of time they are expected to report their interactions with each other person immediately. Variations of this technique allow for the diary entry to be made at specified time intervals, which may be fixed or random.

The two approaches described above have one feature in common.

They both rely on the individual to provide the information. Hence, they are likely to be influenced by the individuals' perceptions of their interactions. Before deciding whether this is an asset or a liability, it is important to identify specific ways in which this influence can occur.

First, the nature of data obtained may be determined by the *salience* of the communication being studied. Salience is the degree to which the topic of communication is central or relevant to the individual. For instance, asking people to report their conversations on sporting issues may not elicit perfect recall if sports is not a salient issue for those people (Richards, 1985).

Sudman and Bradburn (1974) proposed two outcomes related to the salience of the communication. The first, telescoping, refers to misremembering the date on which an event occurred and including it in the time period being discussed. Sudman (1985) points out that this problem is especially germane to events of low salience in short time periods. The problem of telescoping can be significantly reduced by the use of abstract-time network analysis rather than concrete-time network analysis. By doing so, the exact date on which a communication occurred is less pertinent than the "typical" frequency of that communication. If the respondents were questioned about acquaintance patterns over a long period of time, telescopinig is not likely to result in a severe problem. However, in such cases, the second outcome, namely omission, is likely to be an issue. Omission occurs, in such cases, because "the less recent the last meeting, the more likely respondents are to forget" (Sudman, 1985, p. 131).

Second, the *sensitivity* of the content may also be a determining factor. Sensitivity of the content is reflected in the degree of reticence expressed by an individual in disclosing information about that issue. This problem is especially serious when the study is related to taboo issues, such as abortion or contraception. Even in an organizational setting, people tend to underreport communication on personnel issues as compared to production issues (Burns, 1954). Bradburn, Sudman, and Associates (1979) showed that larger errors were associated with responses to questions that were considered threatening. Higgins, McClean, & Conrath (1985) also found that personal phone calls, even when not prohibited, were often not reported. The problem was further accentuated when the personal call was to someone outside the organization. The collection of data on sensitive issues is greatly facilitated by assurances of confidentiality or anonymity. For data collected by interview, a good rapport between the interviewer and the respondent is crucial (Rogers & Kincaid, 1981).

Third, the *specificity* of the communication also influences the data that respondents provide. Asking about too specific a content topic might yield a network that has too few links to be of any use. Rogers and Kincaid (1981) cite a study by Braun (1975) in which most of those sampled in the five Colombian villages in his study simply did not discuss the two specific issues dealt with in the network instrument. On the other hand, too large or ambiguous a topic might yield a network that could be saturated and inaccurate (McCallister & Fischer, 1978).

Fourth, the *directionality* of communication may also affect what is reported. As mentioned earlier, a directional communication link refers only to communication initiated by the respondent. Since a higher status is often associated with the receiver than with the initiator of a communication (Blau & Scott, 1962), initiated communication may be under reported. Higgins et al. (1985) provide empirical evidence supporting this hypothesis.

Fifth, the *total volume* of communication is also likely to influence the respondents' perceptions of their communication patterns. Webber (1970) showed that individuals who received a large volume of communication often underestimated their communication with specific individuals. On the contrary, those with a small net volume of communication overestimated their communication activity.

Sixth, *individual characteristics* of respondents also affect their perceptions of their communication interaction. Individual characteristics were first suggested as a mediating variable by Webber (1970). More recently, Sudman (1985) found evidence that respondent characteristics affected recall of network size. In particular, errors were greater among older respondents, among those with higher education, and among those who had been with the organization for a longer period of time. No evidence was found for differences based on gender, marital status, or supervisory status, though Webber's (1970) study contradicted the latter findings.

Finally, the respondents' perceptions are mediated by the *size and structure* of the instrument itself. Interviewee fatigue, a concern of most social science research, may become a very serious problem in network instruments. In a typical sociometric-type survey, respondents are confronted with the task of naming and/or providing information on their relationships with each other. Therefore, their task is directly related to the size of the network. The task is enlarged if information is requested on the mode of communication used, the initiation pattern, and the volume of communication in each of many content categories. Conrath, Higgins, & McClean (1983) suggest that a self-recording diary should require no more than five to 10 minutes per day to complete. In their study each subject logged their communication for a period of one week. The diary was open-ended and "the data gathered included: the identification of the other party to the communication, who initiated it, the estimated elapsed time in minutes and the mode used" (Conrath et al., 1983, p. 178). Erickson, Nosanchuk, & Lee (1981) recommend that a survey listing could be as high as 150, but not higher than 200. Knoke and Kuklinski (1982) note that a list of 130 names should take about 15 minutes to complete.

There have been many attempts at simplifying the task of the respondent. The appropriate simplification depends on the nature of the questions being posed. One solution, suggested by Laumann (1973), was that each individual be asked only about their three most important contacts. Such an approach was criticized for not being able to identify "the strength of weak ties" (Liu & Duff, 1972; Granovetter, 1973; Rogers, 1973). The "strength of weak ties" refers to the informational strength associated with weak sociometric ties. A weak tie between two individuals, A and B, signifies that with the exception of their link, there exists little overlap between members of their respective personal networks (Rogers & Kincaid, 1981). Collecting data on only three important contacts would ignore sociometrically weak ties, that are informationally rich. Exclusion of these ties would significantly hinder efforts at describing the true communication structure of the network. Empirical evidence of this problem was provided by Killworth and Bernard (1974). They recommended that individuals should be asked to report on at least seven, rather than three contacts. Further refinements described by McCallister and Fischer (1978) and Fischer (1982) allow collection of detailed information on up to 30 individuals within 20 minutes.

A second solution does not place any limit, such as three or seven, on the number of contacts to be reported by an individual. Instead it facilitates the gathering of information on a large number of an individual's contacts. Generally it does so by providing closed coding schemes. A self-recording diary used by Conrath et al. (1983), for instance, required no more than four to eight check marks, besides identifying the communication contact. They collected information on the initiator, the mode used, the elapsed time, and the process involved. Erickson et al. (1981) make several recommendations on improving the response to a sociometric network instrument. These include the making of a brief statement of purpose, including the respondent's name on the list, and pretesting the questionnaire to detect any ambiguities.

Participant observation; full time/intermittent. The field studies discussed so far have all relied on individuals to report their own communication. However, there are a number of techniques that rely on external observers to provide the data. Observational techniques were first used in the famous Hawthorne studies of the 1920s and 1930s (Roethlisberger & Dickson, 1946; Davis, 1953). In these studies, trained participant observers recorded the communication behavior of the subjects.

Participant observation is a technique that grew from the anthropological tradition and often uses ethnographic techniques. One study using this technique in communication network analysis is Marshall's (1971) observation of the communication in the diffusion of two innovations in an Indian village. Bernard and Killworth (1973, 1977, 1978), Killworth and Bernard (1974) and Bernard, Killworth, and Sailer (1980) have also reported the use of participant observation in describing the communication that occurred on two ships, two offices, a women's prison, students in a fraternity, and faculty, graduate students and secretaries in a graduate program. In all these cases, a "trained" person observed verbal interactions for a specified period of time.

There are several potential problems with research that uses a participant observer. First, it is physically impossible for a single observer to be everywhere all the time. As a result, a single participant observer cannot comprehensively document all interactions in the system. Two solutions have been suggested to overcome this problem. In some studies the system is observed intermittently. For instance, in one of the studies by Bernard et al. (1980), the observer walked through the office at 15-minute intervals. However, this interval may be too large and could therefore provide an inadequate description of communication activities within the time period (Rogers & Kincaid, 1981). A second solution would be to use more than one observer, so as to observe communication at two or more places at the same time, at more frequent time intervals, or both. However, in these cases, the different observers must be trained to encode communication in a standardized way (Richards, 1985).

Second, observational studies may require the collection of data over a large period of time. This may present some very exacting demands on the researcher. For instance, Marshall's (1971) study of communication patterns in an Indian village, required the observer to stay in the village for a year.

Third, Richards (1985) argues that an observer is not likely to record all that is observed. This is because "only a small subset of the total range of behavior is significant" (Richards, 1985, p. 116). As a result, the recorded behavior may not mirror the actual behavior with sufficient accuracy. This criticism is closely related to the larger argument presented by Richards that observers will, as a rule, not be cued in to the context surrounding the interactions they observe. Richards argues:

> What is of interest with the outside observer approach to measurement is the actual behavioral sequences in which the participants engage. It is not necessary for there to be anything behind that behavior. Because internal events such as feelings, perceptions and the like are not considered in the processes of collecting and analyzing, or interpreting the data, this might be called the "external event" view. (p. 116)

One way of minimizing this problem would require the observer to gather information on the content being discussed, the duration of the interactions and possibly the directionality and symmetry of the communication. However, any attempts at gleaning information of this nature may result in the observer being perceived as overly obtrusive.

Fourth, these studies require the presence of an outsider, the observer. Two strategies have been used to minimize this problem. In one strategy, the observers are included in the network and are therefore participant observers. For instance, Bernard and Killworth (1978) included themselves in the communication network on board the ship they were studying. The second strategy is to keep the observer as unobtrusive as possible. One way of accomplishing this goal is to allow the observer to make only infrequent "walks" through the system being studied. This would certainly help to keep the observer less obtrusive, but, as mentioned earlier, there are problems associated with observations that are too infrequent. Further, neither of these strategies is particularly effective in preventing the differential effects of an obtrusive observer on different forms of communication. For instance, it is less likely for two or more individuals to discuss a sensitive organizational rumor in the presence of an observer than it is to discuss routine task-related issues.

Observational data using unobtrusive methods. There are a growing number of studies that collect observational data with strategies that resolve some of the problems described above. Typcially, this is achieved by studying some "trace" left by communication interactions. In the case of computer-mediated communication (Rice, 1982), it is possible for researchers to monitor a large amount of information about the communication. The information could include complete transcripts, the dates and times of the communication, the duration, as well as information about who initiated the communication. Killworth and Bernard (1976) monitored the communication of a group of deaf persons via teletype. Bernard et al. (1980) unobtrusively monitored communication of 44 HAM radio operators over a 27-day time period by recording the conversations they held over the public air waves. Higgins et al. (1985) monitored telephonic communication in an organization using a Traffic Data Analyzer (TDA) attached to the office's local PBX (private branch exchange). Other studies have relied on appointment calendars and inter- and intra-organizational mail envelopes.

Burt (1983) has proposed an unobtrusive technique for gathering network data from archived documents such as court records and newspapers. In an example of the technique, Burt used information in newspaper reports of events. The actors were categorized based on specified typologies. Therefore, Burt studied types rather than individuals. The prominence of the association between categories of actors (a linkage strength) was determined by the proportion of the news reports that discussed a relationship between actors in different categories. It is important to note that the network data derived from these records were based on the assumption that "actors embroiled in the same events are more likely to have relations with one another than actors involved in different events" (Burt, 1983, p. 163).

There are three main advantages associated with these techniques. First, they are not likely to influence the communication patterns being observed. Second, they often provide detailed descriptions of the interactions, and these could be used to provide context to the communication. Third, unobtrusive monitors can often be used to obtain data from very large systems and over long periods of time at a minimal cost. As a result, it is possible to study archival records about communication among individuals who may be inaccessible, even dead. Further, there is a great deal of flexibility on the time periods and time intervals used in archival studies (Burt, 1983).

However, the unobtrusive techniques discussed above are not without shortcomings. In addition to Richard's (1985) criticism described above, there are four further problems that must be considered. The first shortcoming stems from the fact that unobtrusive techniques lend themselves only to certain types of communication network studies. The examples provided above illustrate this selection bias. Most of these examples relied on technology to provide information on technologically mediated communication such as electronic mail. Clearly, these techniques are of great use in understanding the communication structure associated with various technologies. However, there remains the difficulty involved in teasing out those findings that are common to all forms of communication from findings that are unique to the use of specific communication technologies.

Second, unobtrusive studies of technologically-mediated communication would be greatly enhanced if they were combined with data on other forms of nonmediated communication such as face-to-face dicussion. Obviously, many communication network studies may need to incorporate communication via the various existing media. Unfortunately at present, disparity in the quality of data received from the different sources hinders its utility.

Third, even research that is confined to a single communication technology often discovers that the technology is not as "cooperative" as desired. Rice and Borgman (1983) describe three problems associated with collection of computer-monitored data. Monitoring a large system and converting the raw data into an analyzable form often involves high cost and time investments; further, they often require a high level of computer expertise on the part of the researcher.

Fourth, there remain a large number of unresolved ethical issues related to the use of technologically monitored data. Researchers so far have studied communication that occurs in the public domain. Monitoring HAM radio operators was one such example. However, data from public domain communication may have limited generalizability. This problem has diminished as organizations seeking to improve the effectiveness of their communication-technology systems allow researchers access to data within their offices (Rice & Borgman, 1983). One of the compromises struck by many of these researchers is to restrict information monitored to exclude the content of the communication. However, this strategy is at best only a compromise. There remains a modest but significant invasion of privacy, coupled with data that is now even more bereft of context.

Sampling Procedures Used in Field Studies

In our discussion of experimental techniques for data collection it was pointed out that generalizing the findings of an experiment to a large social system was a serious problem. In this section we examine ways to generalize the findings of a field study. Ideally, a researcher would like to collect data from all members within the boundaries specified. Studies which collect data from all members of the system utilize what is referred to as saturated sampling or a census. For example, many organizational studies define a single organization as the population and collect information from all members in the organization as the sample. (A more valid interpretation of this procedure is that the population of interest is the network in all organizations and that the particular organization being studied is a sample of one. Obviously, it is not easy to generalize to such a large population on the basis of a single sample.) However, in large social systems, such as a village, collecting information from all members may become extremely unwieldy. In such cases, sampling techniques are often used to collect information from a few of its members and then extrapolate to all members in the system.

Sampling techniques have been routinely used in survey-based social science research. The notion of sampling in network research was first proposed by Moreno and Jennings (1938). However, the development of procedures remained primitive. The development of sampling techniques can be traced to two different analytical approaches used to study network models. The first analytical approach, referred to as the "relational" approach, describes the intensity of relationship between pairs of actors. The second analytical approach, referred to as the "positional" approach, focuses on the pattern of relationships between positions or role-sets. These positions may be occupied by one or more individuals who share a set of social attributes (Burt, 1980).

Sampling techniques in network research based on the relational approach have been used to estimate the density of a large system from a sample. The density of a system is defined as the ratio between the *actual* number of links that people report using to the total number of *possible* links that can exist between all members in the system. They have also been used to identify and study the flow of messages in a system. Network research based on the positional approach, on the other hand, has developed techniques to estimate the relationship between different social positions based on network items and general sociometric variables.

Sampling Techniques Based on the Relational Approach

Estimation of system characteristics. It is often unwieldy to collect network information from all members in the network. In many of these cases, the aim of the research is to obtain an estimate of the level of connectedness of the entire network, that is the density of the network. An appropriate sampling procedure to provide density estimates was developed by Proctor (1967) and Frank (1971). They described "the sample selection scheme, giving an estimator, finding its bias and variance, and finally giving an estimator of variance" (Proctor, 1979, p. 313). Granovetter (1976) also provided a formula for the confidence interval of density estimates. However, the formula assumes the presence of multiple equivalent random samples. Erickson and Nosanchuk (1983) support the use of multiple network samples for two reasons. First, multiple samples (six, in their study) allow researchers to assess the amount of bias introduced by pragmatic problems associated with the administration of a network instrument, such as missing names. Second, multiple samples provide some description of the sampling distribution.

This procedure is appropriate only if the objects of explanation are characteristics of the system as a whole. The procedure fails to provide estimates at the individual level, such as individual network involvement (Morgan & Rytina, 1977).

"Snowball Sampling". Another frequently used network sampling technique is called "snowball sampling" (Goodman, 1961). This technique requires the initial identification of a random sample of members in the system. The researcher then asks these respondents to report their communication contacts. Those individuals named as communication contacts in this phase are now included in the sample. They are referred to as first-stage respondents. The researcher next obtains information about the communication contacts of these first-stage respondents, generating in the process a group of second-stage respondents. The researcher might then repeat the process several times until only some small number of new respondents is added to the sample. The typical exponential increase in the sample as the process continues resulted in the technique being named "snowball sampling."

The snowball sampling technique has been used to study the process whereby communication of specific issues occurs within a social system. Snowball sampling can also be used to provide information about the way in which individuals influence and are influenced by others.

Like other sampling techniques, snowball sampling cannot capture the complete network structure. However, its success can be judged by its ability to adequately, and parsimoniously, provide a description of the entire network structure. In survey-based sampling procedures this judgment is often made on the basis of specific criteria such as the standard error of the estimates. In the case of snowball sampling, Frank (1979) has discussed the merits of alternative variance estimators, for example, the Horvitz-Thompson variance estimator and the Sen-Yates-Grundy variance estimator using a constant-probability Bernoulli sampling design. (A constant-probability Bernoulli sampling design is normally a good approximation of simple random sampling.) Despite considerable research (e.g., Holland & Leinhardt, 1975; Wasserman, 1977; and Capobianco, 1972, 1974) estimation problems continue to remain formidable. For instance, in the absence of rigorous algorithms, there is little certainty about the number of stages that must be conducted in a snowball sampling procedure in order to obtain an adequate description of the population. The distortion that may result from insufficient sampling continues to remain a serious concern. A hypothetical example of how insufficient snowball sampling could incorrectly identify opinion leaders is provided by Knoke and Kuklinski (1982).

Sampling Procedures Based on the Positional Approach

As was mentioned earlier, the aim of sampling in this approach is to help understand the relationship between positions or role-sets in the system. This procedure was first proposed by Beniger (1976) and further developed by Burt (1981). In this procedure the researcher collects data from a random sample. Each respondent is required to furnish information on the attributes of the people they contact for specific issues. The respondents also provide information on their own attributes. It is clearly not the aim of this sampling procedure to provide estimates of individual linkages among people. In fact, the actual names of the individuals need not be collected. Instead, this sampling procedure helps provide infromation about the likelihood of there being a relationship between two "positions." The "positions" may be defined by the presence of one or more attributes. For instance, Laumann (1979) discusses the likelihood of a marital relationship between members of the Protestant working class (PWC) and the Protestant middle class (PMC) and compares it to the likelihood of a marital liaison between a PWC and a Catholic working class (CWC). In communication research, this procedure could be used, for instance, to describe the likelihood of communication between doctors in surgery and pediatrics, and compare it with the likelihood of communication between doctors and nurses in surgery.

Clearly, the efficacy of this sampling procedure is determined largely by the selection of the attributes that are used to define the positions. The inclusion of irrelevant attributes might result in unwanted differentiation, while the exclusion of a crucial attribute might cause undesired aggregation of people in the same position.

Reliability and Validity of the Data Collected

In the past decade there has been a great deal of debate surrounding the reliability and validity of data obtained from different techniques. The debate was triggered to a large degree by a series of studies by Bernard, Killworth, and their colleagues in the late 1970s (Bernard & Killworth, 1977, 1978; Bernard, Killworth, & Sailer, 1980, 1981, 1982, 1984). They pointed out significant differences between the communication reported by the individuals (perceived communication) and the communication reported by other recording techniques. Based on these findings, they questioned the validity of self-reporting techniques for describing network characteristics and communication behavior. There have been two lines of criticism of the Bernard, Killworth, and Sailer (hereafter designated BKS) studies.

The first group of critics accept the fact that there may be significant differences between actual communication and reported communication. However, they argue that this difference should be expected and does not undermine the utility of perceived data. They attribute the differences to the fact that perceived communication, unlike actual communication, is mediated by the individuals' beliefs, perceptions, and interpretations. They suggest that collection of data on perceived communication permits the inclusion of context, which they argue, is of paramount importance (Richards, 1985).

Second, there are those who argue that the differences proposed by BKS were in fact not as significant as suggested. They point to differences as being artifacts of the methodology used. For instance, Romney and Faust (1982) report a significant structural similarity between the communication patterns that were reported and those recorded by observers in one of the BKS studies. Romney and Faust defend their findings by suggesting that BKS "were looking for error" while they were "looking for regularities" (Romney & Faust, 1982 p. 300). As a result, the null model for Romney and Faust was one of "pure chance association" between the two forms of data, while the null model used by BKS was one of "perfect association." Burt (1983) has shown that the "evidence presented by Bernard and his colleagues does not warrant their conclusion . . . Of course, rejecting their methodology is not the same as accepting the hypothesis that cognitive and behavioral relations are one and the same," (pp. 299–301).

A partial resolution of this debate may be obtained by a closer examination of the metatheoretical orientations of network scholars. Richards (1985) has proposed that the controversy stems from two opposing epistemological paradigms. The dichotomy follows from "the time-honored controversy in the social sciences between nominalist and realist views of the ontological status of social phenomena" (Laumann et al., 1983, p. 20). The realist view has alternatively been referred to as "objectivist," "positivist," or "functionalist," while the nominalist view is sometimes labeled "subjectivist," "interpretivist," or "cognitive constructivist" (Richards, 1985; Putnam, 1983).

Notwithstanding the plausibility of this dichotomy, most theories in social science draw upon assumptions that are not unequivocally nominalist or realist. A theory may, for instance, propose that a phenomena is best explained in terms of a set of antecedent variables, some of which may be considered "subjective" while others would be regarded as "objective." Further, there is often considerable debate as to the degree of "objectivity" or "subjectivity" of the variables considered.

Therefore the two approaches described above represent two "ideal" and opposing viewpoints that are rarely obtained in network research. They are useful insofar as they represent the logical extremities of a continuum. Most theories and research, we argue, lie not at one or the other end of these extremities, but somewhere on the continuum between them. It seems logical, then, to propose that any evaluation of the quality of data would depend jointly on the technique used and the metatheoretical position of the researcher on the objective-subjective continuum.

The arguments presented above apply broadly to the study of human communication networks. Within the domain of measurement in particular, the above debate can be couched in somewhat different terms. In the next few paragraphs we introduce and define a few concepts used in measurement theory. These concepts will then be applied to examples from network research.

As was mentioned earlier, measurement of human communication networks entails the assigning of numbers to observed phenomena, based on certain rules. The numbers assigned to these phenomena are referred to as observed responses. All of the data collection techniques described in the previous section, therefore, provide the researcher with observed responses.

According to measurement theory observed responses are generated by an underlying theoretical variable. The observed responses represent an attempt at measuring the "true score" on a theoretical variable, X. The difference between the true score and the observed response is defined as measurement error. Hence,

Measurement error = True Score on X − Observed Score on X

or,

Observed score on X = True Score on X + Measurement error.

Let us examine for a moment the nature of the "true score." In the social sciences there are a large number of behavioral responses for which there exist, at least in theory, a verifiable true score. For instance, the amount of time an individual spends communicating on the telephone is a behavioral response which is verifiable. Sutcliffe (1965) calls a verifiable true score a Platonic score.

However, there are a large number of variables for which it would be meaningless to conceive of a real "true score" that is verifiable.

Most cognitive or affective responses fall in this category. Sudman and Bradburn (1974) refer to these as psychological states. Bohrnstedt (1983) points out that, in these cases, a Platonic true score makes little sense because "true psychological states can only be inferred indirectly" (p. 71). True scores belonging to this category are often referred to as non-Platonic scores or classical true scores.

We now see how these concepts are used in an example from communication network research. Suppose two studies, A and B, asked each individual in a group to report the number of times they initiated a telephonic communication with each of the other members in the group. Clearly, the observed responses in the two studies would be identical. To estimate the measurement error associated with the studies, the nature of the true score must be sought. The first study conceived the true score to be a Platonic. true score, that is, actual behavioral data on the number of times the individual initiated communication. These obtained values can be verified, at least in principle, by the use of a system like the traffic data analyzer which records all calls at the PBX (Private Branch exchange, see, e.g., Higgins et al., 1985). The second study, however, may estimate the true score to be somewhat different. Despite the fact that the question elicited information on discrete behavioral acts, this study assumes that the information provided by the respondents would actually be based on their perception of the ongoing relationship with each other individual. This perception is no longer a Platonic true score since it cannot be verified, at least in theory. It is important to recognize, therefore, that the two studies using the same observed responses may be attempting to measure two different true scores based on the study's theoretical assumptions. Therefore, the measurement errors incurred by the two studies will not be identical.

From a measurement perspective, therefore, any debate on the accuracy of data using different techniques must begin by identifying the true scores being sought by the researcher. Having identified the nature of the true score, measurement theory provides two ways, reliability and validity, in which one can assess the quality of the data.

Reliability

Reliability, in general terms, refers to the degree to which an instrument consistently measures the same variable in the same way at one or more points in time. Operationally, it is defined as the ratio of the variance in the true score to the variance in the observed response (Bohrnstedt, 1983).

Reliability measures can be of two types. The first, a measure of stability, requires the administration of the instrument at more than two points in time. First, we examine a measure of stability, under the assumption that the true score remains constant over time. Under this assumption, the correlation of the items at two (or more) points in time provide a measure of stability. However, in many cases, the assumption that the true score remains constant over time may not be true. In these cases, there have been many attempts to isolate real change from the lack of reliability. All these approaches require the collection of data at a minimum of three points in time. (For a detailed description of these methods and their assumptions, see Bohrnstedt, 1983.)

There have been very few instances in communication network research where the stability of an instrument has been assessed. However, the growing interest in longitudinal network studies would provide an opportunity to measure the stability of an instrument while simultaneously hypothesizing change in the true score components of the scores.

The second approach used to assess reliability is with a measure of equivalence. This method requires the administration of two or more items (or scales) at one point in time that are assumed to be measuring the same true score. An estimate of reliability, in such cases, is computed in terms of the number of items used and the covariance between the items. (For a detailed description of specific algorithms and the accompanying assumptions, see Cronbach et al., 1972).

Traditionally, in network research all variables are single-item scales. However, based upon arguments provided by Weinshall (1966) and Hesseling (1970), Conrath et al. (1983) present a measure of reliability of the linkage between pairs of individuals. The estimate is computed from reports of communication provided by both members of the pair. However, based on our earlier discussion, we suggest that this measure of reliability will only hold for those cases where the values reported by the two individuals are assumed to measure the same underlying score. Conceivably there could be a research question that examines the differences in perceptions by two individuals of the same communication and therefore cannot make the above mentioned assumption. In such cases, the technique proposed by Conrath et al. (1983) should not be used.

In addition to Conrath et al's estimate of reliability there are four other alternative strategies that can be used. First, if two or more data collection techniques are used to yield measures of the same underlying score, a measure of equivalence can be obtained. For instance, combining a sociometric-based survey with an unobtrusive traffic data analyzer can provide two measures of a single underlying variable, say, telephonic communication. Clearly, in this study the sociometric surveys would elicit information specifically on telephonic communication. Further, the study would assume that the survey responses would provide a measure of actual (rather than perceived) telephonic communication. Second, if the respondent is asked to report on a series of sociometric questions measuring the same underlying communication variable, a measure of equivalence can be computed. This second approach may run into respondent resistance if people are required to fill in responses to many items for each of a large number of contacts. Third, in the case of data gathered by observation, measures of equivalence can be estimated by comparing the data obtained by two or more different observers or coders of the same event (Burt, 1983). Finally, for studies using archival data, the reliability of the linkages can be estimated by using data collected from two separate archival sources that describe the same variable, for example, two newspapers.

In the past, most network researchers have not attempted to assess the reliability of their measures. More recently, network analysts have raised several concerns about the reliability of these measures and have called for a "systematic research attempt to determine the quality of network measurement" (Rogers & Kincaid, 1981, p. 120). Computing a measure of reliability is one way of determining the quality of network measurement.

Validity

Validity is conceptually defined as the degree to which an instrument measures the theoretical construct it has been designed to measure. Operationally, the correlation between the observed response and the true score is defined as the theoretical validity. Empirical validity, on the other hand, is defined as the degree to which an instrument measures an underlying theoretical variable as well as another instrument measuring the same underlying variable. Therefore, operationally, empirical validity is the correlation between two observed responses measuring the same true score (Bohrnstedt, 1983).

The relationship between the validity and reliability of a measure is an important one. For a measure to be theoretically valid, it must also be reliable. In fact, as Bohrnstedt (1983) has shown, the theoretical validity of a measure is exactly equal to the square root of its reliability. On the other hand, a measure that is reliable is not necessarily empirically valid.

We began this section with a brief discussion of the debate, triggered by the BKS studies on the reliability and validity of data obtained by different techniques. We also said that the criticism that has been made against the BKS studies falls into two categories. First, there were those who felt that there was no reason why they should have expected similar results because the different techniques were measuring different underlying variables. Second, there were those who agreed that the reason they did not obtain similar results was because of methodological problems. For instance, their tests of similarity for the data obtained from different techniques were considered too conservative (Romney & Faust, 1982).

The first criticism has already been discussed extensively in this section. To summarize, therefore, the validity of data comparing two or more different techniques can only be conducted if one assumes that the same underlying theoretical variable is being measured by the different techniques.

The second criticism, however, makes the assumption that a single underlying theoretical variable can in fact be measured by different techniques. The use of multiple measures to study a system of variables is referred to as triangulation. Only a handful of network studies have adopted triangulation procedures (e.g., Lievrouw, Rogers, Lowe, & Nadel, 1986). Campbell and Fiske (1959) proposed the use of a multitrait—multimethod matrix to study the degree to which different data collection techniques yield similar results for the same theoretical variable, that is, convergent validity (Campbell, 1954), and the degree to which the same data collection techniques yield different results for different theoretical variables, that is, discriminant validity. Confirmatory factor analytic methods (Fink & Monge, 1985; Jöreskog, 1971; Werts, Jöreskog, & Linn, 1972) provide statistical criteria for establishing convergent and discrimant validity (Alwin, 1974; Bohrnstedt, 1983; Schmitt, Coyle, & Saari, 1977). Using this method, it is possible to simultaneously study the difference between the variables being measured and the effect of the measurement techniques being used. In the short term this approach would help resolve the debate generated by the work of BKS. In the long term, its continued use would contribute to the development of network measurement.

Conclusion

The measurement process, as presented in this chapter, necessitates that the researcher make a large number of informed decisions. Each of these decisions, it was shown, is directly related to the nature of the research question being posed and the assumptions of the researcher. The consequences and limitations accompanying each of these decisions are, as yet, only partially understood, and it continues to remain the focus of a great deal of research and debate. In this chapter we have attempted to capture the essence of the findings as well as the spirit of the debate, in order to provide a basis for future progress in the measurement of communication networks.

References

Alwin, D.F. (1974). Approaches to the interpretation of relationships in the multitrait-multimethod matrix. In H.L. Costner (Ed.), *Sociological methodology: 1973–74*. San Francisco, CA: Jossey Bass.

Barnes, J.A. (1954). Class and committees in the Norwegian island parish. *Human Relations, 7,* 39–58.

Barnes, J.A. (1979). Network analysis: Orienting notion, rigorous technique or substantive field of study? In P. Holland and S. Leinhardt (Eds.), *Perspectives on Social Network Research.* New York: Academic Press.

Bavelas, A. (1948). A mathematical model for group structures. *Applied Anthropology, 7,* 16–30.

Bavelas, A. (1950). Communication patterns in task oriented groups. *Journal of the Acoustical Society of America, 22,* 271–282.

Beniger, J.R. (1976). Sampling social networks: The subgroup approach. *Proceedings of the Business and Economics Statistics Section, American Statistical Association,* 226–231.

Bernard, H.R., & Killworth, P.D. (1973). On the social structure of an ocean-going research vessel and other important things. *Social Science Research, 2,* 145–184.

Bernard, H.R., & Killworth, P.D. (1977). Informant accuracy in social network data, II. *Human Communication Research, 4,* 3–18.

Bernard, H.R., & Killworth, P.D. (1978). On the structure and effective sociometric relations in a closed group over time. *Connections,* 1–44.

Bernard, H.R., & Killworth, P.D. (1979). Deterministic models of social networks. In P. Holland and S. Leinhardt (Eds.), *Perspectives on social network research.* New York: Academic Press.

Bernard, H.R., Killworth, P.D., & Sailer, L. (1980). Informant accuracy in social network data, IV. A comparison of clique-level structure in behavioral and cognitive data. *Social Networks, 2,* 191–219.

Bernard, H.R., Killworth, P.D., & Sailer, L. (1981). A note on inferences regarding network subgroups: Response to Burt and Bittner. *Social Networks, 2,* 191–218.

Bernard, H.R., Killworth, P.D., & Sailer, L. (1982). Informant accuracy in social network data, V. An experimental attempt to predict actual communication from recall data. *Social Science Research, 11,* 30–66.

Bernard, H.R., Killworth, P.D., & Sailer, L. (1984). The problem of informant accuracy: The validity of retrospective data. *Annual Review of Anthropology, 13,* 495–517.

Blau, P.M., & Scott, W.R. (1962). *Formal organizations.* San Francisco, CA: Chandler.

Bohrnstedt, G.W. (1983). Measurement. In P.H. Rossi, J.D. Wright, and A.B. Anderson (Eds.), *Handbook of survey research.* New York: Academic Press.

Boissevain, J. (1974). *Friends of friends: Networks, manipulators and coalitions.* Oxford, England: Basil Blackwell.

Boissevain, J., & Mitchell, J.C. (1973). *Network analysis: Studies in human interaction.* The Hague, Amsterdam: Mouton.

Bott, E. (1955). Urban families: Conjugal roles and social networks. *Human Relations, 8,* 345–384.

Bott, E. (1957). Family and social networks: Roles, norms and external relationships in ordinary urban families. London: Tavistock (first ed.) and New York: Free Press (second ed., 1971).

Bradburn, N.M., Sudman, S., & Associates (1979). *Improving interview method and questionnaire design: Response effects to threatening questions in survey research.* San Francisco, CA: Jossey-Bass.

Braun, J.R. (1975). *Communication, non-formal education, and national development: The Colombia Radio Schools.* Unpublished doctoral dissertation, Michigan State University.

Burns, T. (1954). The directions of activity and communication in a departmental executive group. *Human Relations, 7,* 73–97.

Burt, R. (1980). Models of network structure. *Annual Review of Sociology, 6,* 79–141.

Burt, R. (1981). Studying status/role-sets as ersatz network positions in mass surveys. *Sociological Methods & Research, 9,* 313–337.

Burt, R. (1983). Network data from archival records. In R. Burt and M.J. Minor (Eds.), *Applied network analysis.* Beverly Hills, CA: Sage.

Burt, R. (1984). Network items and the general social survey. *Social Networks, 6,* 293–339.

Burt, R., & Bittner, W.M. (1981). A note on inferences regarding network subgroups. *Social Networks, 3,* 71–83.

Campbell, D.T. (1954). Operational delineation of "what is learned" via the transposition experiment. *Psychological Review, 61,* 167–174.

Campbell, D.T., & Fiske, D.W. (1959). Convergent and discriminant validity by the multitrait-multimethod matrix. *British Journal of Statistical Psychology, 15,* 113–128.

Capobianco, M.F. (1972). Estimating the connectivity of a graph. In Y. Alavi, D.R. Lick, and A.T. White (Eds.), *Graph theory and applications.* Berlin: Springer.

Capobianco, M.F. (1974). Recent progress in stagraphics. *Annals of the New York Academy of Sciences, 231,* 139–141.

Cohen, A.M., Robinson, E.L., & Edwards, J.L. (1969). Experiments in organizational embeddedness. *Administrative Science Quarterly, 14,* 208–221.

Conrath, D.W., Higgins, C.A., & McClean, R.J. (1983). A comparison of the reliability of questionnaire versus diary data. *Social Networks, 5,* 315–322.

Cronbach, L.J., Gleser, C.C., Nanda, H., & Rajaratnam, N. (1972). *The dependability of behavioral measurements.* New York: Wiley.

Dahl, R. (1961). *Who governs?* New Haven, CT: Yale University Press.

Davis, K. (1953). A method of studying communication patterns in organizations. *Personnel Psychology, 6,* 301–312.

Edwards, J.A., & Monge, P.R. (1975). *A comparison of data collection procedures for the study of communication networks and structure.* (Technical Report #6.) Arlington, VA: Office of Naval Research.

Erickson, B.H., & Nosanchuk, T.A. (1983). Applied network sampling. *Social Networks, 5,* 367–382.

Erickson, B.H., Nosanchuk, T.A., & Lee, E. (1981). Network sampling in practice: Some second steps. *Social Networks, 3,* 127–136.

Farace, R.V., & Morris, C. (1969). *The communication system of Justin Morrill College.* Unpublished paper, Department of Communication, Michigan State University.

Farace, R.V., Monge, P.R., & Russell, H.M. (1977). *Communicating and organizing.* Reading, MA: Addison Wesley.

Fink, E.L., & Monge, P.R. (1985). An exploration of confirmatory factor analysis. *Progress in Communication Sciences, 6,* 167–197.

Fischer, C.S. (1982). *To dwell among friends.* Chicago, IL: University of Chicago Press.

Fortes, M. (1957). Malinowski and the study of kinship. In R.W. Firth (Ed.), *Man and culture: An evaluation of the work of Bronislaw Malinowski.* London: Routledge and Kegan Paul.

Frank, O. (1971). *Statistical inference in graphs.* Stockholm: FOA Repro.

Frank, O. (1979). Population estimation by use of snowball samples. In P. Holland and S. Leinhardt (Eds.), *Perspectives on Social Network Research.* New York: Academic Press.

Goodman, L.A. (1961). Snowball sampling. *Annals of Mathematical Statistics, 32,* 148–170.

Granovetter, M.S. (1973). The strength of weak ties. *American Journal of Sociology, 73,* 1361–1380.

Granovetter, M.S. (1976). Network sampling: Some first steps. *American Journal of Sociology, 81,* 1287–1303.

Hesseling, P. (1970). Communication and organization structure in a large multi-national company. In Heald, (Ed.), *Approaches to the study of organizational behavior.* London: Tavistock.

Higgins, C.A., McClean, R.J., & Conrath, D.W. (1985). The accuracy and biases of diary communication data. *Social Networks, 7,* 173–187.

Hinrichs, J.R. (1964). Communication activity of industrial research personnel. *Personnel Psychology, 17,* 193–204.

Holland, P., & Leinhardt, S. (1975). Local structure in social networks. In D. Heise (Ed.), *Sociological methodology.* San Francisco, CA: Jossey Bass.

Jöreskog, K.G. (1971). Statistical analysis of sets of congeneric tests. *Psychometrika, 36,* 109–134.

Killworth, P.D., & Bernard, H.R. (1974). CATIJ: A new sociometric and its application to a prison living unit. *Human Organization, 33,* 335–350.

Killworth, P.D., & Bernard, H.R. (1976). Informant accuracy in social network data. *Human Organization, 35,* 269–86.

Knoke, D., & Kuklinski, J.H. (1982). *Network analysis.* Beverly Hills, CA: Sage.

Laumann, E.O. (1973). *Bonds of pluralism.* New York: John Wiley.

Laumann, E.O. (1979). Network analysis in large social systems: Some theoretical and methodological problems. In P.W. Holland and S. Leinhardt (Eds.), *Perspectives on social network research.* New York: Academic Press.

Laumann, E.O., Marsden, P., & Prensky, D. (1983). The boundary specification problem in network analysis. In R. Burt and M.J. Minor (Eds.), *Applied network analysis.* Beverly Hills, CA: Sage.

Leavitt, H.J. (1951). Some effects of certain communication patterns on group performance. *Journal of Abnormal and Social Psychology, 46,* 38–50.

Lievrouw, L.A., Rogers, E.M., Lowe, C.U., & Nadel, E. (1986, February). *Triangulation as a research strategy for identifying invisible colleges among biomedical scientists.* Paper presented at Sunbelt Social Networks Conference, Santa Barbara, CA.

Liu, W.T., & Duff, R.W. (1972). The strength of weak ties. *Public Opinion Quarterly, 36,* 361–366.

Marshall, J.F. (1971). Topics and networks in intra-village communication. In S. Polgar (Ed.), *Culture and population: A collection of current studies.* (Carolina Population Center, Monograph 9.) Chapel Hill, NC: University of Northern Carolina.

McCallister, L., & Fischer, C.S. (1978). A procedure for surveying personal networks. *Sociological Methods & Research, 9,* 267–285.

Mitchell, J.C. (1969). *Social networks in urban situations.* Manchester, England: University Press.

Monge, P.R., & Eisenberg, E.M. (in press). Emergent communication networks. In L. Porter, L. Putnam, K. Roberts, and F. Jablin (Eds.), *Handbook of organizational communication.* Beverly Hills, CA: Sage.

Monge, P.R., & Miller, K.I. (in press). Alternative conceptualizations and analytic techniques for the study of communication processes. In G. Goldhaber (Ed.), *Handbook of organizational communication.* Norwood, NJ: Ablex.

Moreno, J.L. (1934). *Who shall survive?* Washington, DC: Nervous and Mental Disease Monograph.

Moreno, J.L., & Jennings, H. (1938). Statistics of social configurations. *Sociometry, 11,* 262–286.

Morgan, D.L., & Rytina, S. (1977). Comment on "Network sampling: Some first steps," by Mark Granovetter. *American Journal of Sociology, 83,* 722–727.

Pfeffer, J., & Salancik, G. (1978). *The external control of organizations: A resource dependence perspective.* New York: Harper & Row.

Proctor, C.H. (1967). The variance of an estimate of linkage density from a simple random sample of graph nodes. *Proceedings of the Social Statistics Section. American Statistical Association,* 457–465.

Proctor, C.H. (1979). Graph sampling compared to conventional sampling. In P.W. Holland and S. Leinhardt (Eds.), *Perspectives on social network research.* New York: Academic Press.

Putnam, L. (1983). The interpretive perspective: An alternative to functionalism. In L. Putnam and M. Pacanowsky (Eds.), *Communication and organizations: An interpretive approach.* Beverly Hills, CA: Sage.

Reitz, K.P. (1983). *Social groups, a network approach.* Unpublished dissertation, University of California, Irvine.

Rice, R.E. (1982). Communication networking in computer-conferencing systems: A longitudinal study of group roles and system structure. *Communication Yearbook, 6,* 925–944.

Rice, R.E., & Barnett, G. (1986). Group communication networking in an information environment: Applying metric multidimensional scaling. *Communication Yearbook, 9,* 319–338.

Rice, R.E., & Borgman, C.L. (1983). The use of computer-monitored data in information science and communication research. *Journal of the American Society for Information Science, 34,* 247–256.

Rice, R.E., & Richards, W.D. (1985). An overview of network analysis methods and programs. *Progress in Communication Sciences, 5,* 105–165.

Richards, W.D. (1985). Data, models and assumptions in network analysis. In R.D. McPhee and P.K. Tomkins (Eds.), *Organizational communication: Traditional themes and new directions.* Beverly Hills, CA: Sage.

Roethlisberger, F.J., & Dickson, W.J. (1946). *Management and the worker.* Cambridge, MA: Harvard University Press.

Rogers, E.M. (1973). Communication strategies for family planning. New York: Free Press.

Rogers, E.M., & Kincaid, D.L. (1981). *Communication networks: Toward a new paradigm for research.* New York: Free Press.

Romney, A.K., & Faust, K. (1982). Predicting the structure of a communications network from recalled data. *Social Networks, 4,* 285–304.

Schmitt, N., Coyle, B.W., & Saari, B.B. (1977). A review and critique of analysis of multitrait-multimethod matrices. *Multivariate Behavioral Research, 12,* 447–478.

Sudman, S. (1985). Experiments in the measurement of the size of social networks. *Social Networks, 7,* 127–151.

Sudman, S., & Bradburn, N.M. (1974). *Response effects in surveys: A review and synthesis.* Chicago: Aldine.

Sutcliffe, J.P. (1965). A probability model for errors of classification 1. General considerations. *Psychometrika, 30,* 73–96.

Wasserman, S. (1977). Random directed graph distributions and the triad census in social networks. *Journal of Mathematical Sociology, 5,* 61–86.

Webber, R.A. (1970). Perceptions of interactions between superiors and subordinates. *Human Relations, 23,* 235–248.

Weinshall, T.D. (1966). The communicogram. In J.R. Lawrence (Ed.), *Operational research and the social sciences.* London: Tavistock.

Werts, C.E., Jöreskog, K.G., & Linn, R.L. (1972). A multitrait-multimethod model for studying growth. *Educational and Psychological Measurement, 32,* 655–678.

CHAPTER 5

Communication Style: Considerations for Measuring Consistency, Reciprocity, and Compensation

Richard L. Street, Jr.

Communication style refers to a characteristic way of communicating. A "style of communicating" consists of an identifiable pattern of linguistic, vocal, and nonverbal behaviors which are distinguishable from the behavioral patterns of other communication styles. Communication style also refers primarily to "how" one communicates rather than "what" is said (Giles & Powesland, 1975) and to those behaviors which give "form" to literal meaning (Norton, 1983).

Approaches to the study of communication style have varied greatly depending on the researcher's theoretical context or research question. For example, Joos (1962) examined *linguistic* variations as a function of the perceived formality of a setting. Giles and Powesland (1975) focused on *speech* characteristics which were contingent upon context (e.g., setting, partner's speech style) and class (e.g., upper, middle, and lower). Norton (1983) identified distinctive *communicator* styles which are reflected in presumed behavioral, affective, and cognitive differences. Researchers of *self-presentation* styles have focused on cross-situationally consistent verbal and nonverbal behaviors which are related to psychological, cultural, and motivational factors (Arkin, 1981; Giles & Street, 1985). Linguists have sought to describe various *dialects*, patterns of phonological and linguistic usages, characteristic of particular cultures (see, e.g., Labov, 1966) or regions (see, e.g., Wells, 1970).

This chapter has two broad objectives: a discussion of behavioral approaches for studying communication style and an examination of statistical methods for assessing the stability (i.e., consistency vs. adaptability) of a communicator's style during social interaction. The remainder of this discussion unfolds as follows: (a) justification for a behavioral approach to communication style, (b) behavioral indices of communication style, (c) a comparison of statistical procedures for assessing interactants' communication behavior consistency and adaptations, (d) the effect of the size of the analysis unit on measuring communicators' style consistency and adaptations, and (e) concluding comments.

Why a Behavioral Approach for Studying Communication Style?

There are several self-report measures of communication style which assess respondents' perceptual judgments of their own or other's communication behaviors (Cegala, 1981; Deethardt & McLaughlin, 1976; Norton, 1983). The primary advantage of gathering respondents' perceptions of communication style is the ease with which a large amount of data can be collected in a variety of contexts. Relative to laborious behavioral coding methods, judgments of communicators' styles can be quickly gathered and subsequently analyzed in relation to personal characteristics (e.g., personality, sex, education level), situational features, or interaction outcomes (e.g., persuasiveness, likeability). Also, with self-report measures the researcher usually does not encounter the limitations plaguing behaviorists such as transporting and setting up recording equipment and subject anxiety-reluctance about being recorded. Norton's (1983), Cegala's (1981), and Deethardt and McLaughlin's (1976) measures have demonstrated sufficient reliability, and their predictive and construct validity have been shown in numerous empirical tests. Additionally, the wording of the measures can be easily adapted to various targets (i.e., self, partner, or observed other) and situations (e.g., classrooms, physician-patient interaction, managerial communication).

Nevertheless, there are also several disadvantages of using perceptual measures of communication style. The most significant is that the measures are grounded in an insufficient behavioral foundation. The self-report measures usually employ items addressing behavioral *inferences* rather than *actual behaviors* (e.g., "I am a precise communicator," Norton, 1983, p. 280; "I listen very carefully to others during conversation," Cegala, Savage, Brunner, & Conrad, 1982, pp. 232–233; "nervous-relaxed," Deethardt & McLaughlin, 1976). This problem is compounded by the fact that the same interaction style may behaviorally manifest itself differently for different individuals. For example, Cegala et al. (1982) reported that nonverbal behavior indicators of involvement differed for men and women. Street and Murphy (1987) observed that conversants' responsiveness toward others, as measured by their interpersonal orientations (Swap & Rubin, 1983), was related to different speech styles but only for males. There were few differences in the females' speech behavior regardless of interpersonal orientation. In short, while interactants may differ regarding *judgments* of their communication styles, we know little about the actual *behaviors* constituting these style perceptions. Also, differences in receivers' expectations (Cappella & Greene, 1982) and preferences (Street & Giles, 1982) for interlocutors' communicative behaviors may produce discrepant perceptions of the same behavior (see, e.g., Thakerar & Giles, 1981). Second, responses to self-report measures often reflect perceptual distortions or discrepancies. For example, Daly and Street (1980) reported that respondents tended to produce socially desirable responses when completing various social-communicative anxiety measures. Self-report instruments usually produce greater consistency if they are completed at one sitting as opposed to over several sittings (Campbell & Stanley, 1963). Subjects often wish to appear self-consistent (Bem & Allen, 1974; Hewes & Haight, 1980). Finally, some self-report questionnaires require participants to report on cognitive states or behaviors which are typically produced subconsciously (Cappella, 1985a; Jaccard & Daly, 1980). Third, the correlations between self-reports of behaviors and actual behaviors are often low (Hewes & Haight, 1980) or, when high, only at extreme behavioral levels (e.g., very fast speech or very slow speech, Street, 1982).

In sum, researchers should not totally rely on self-report measures of communicative behavior when developing models of social interaction or communication behavior evaluation. This is not to say that self-report instruments are without merit. To the contrary, when used in conjunction with behavioral measures, self-report instruments can provide information on perceptual correlates of certain behaviors. Also, certain cognitive, relational, and motivational states can create differing judgments of the same behavior (Larsen, Martin, & Giles, 1977; Street & Hopper, 1982). The joint use of behavioral and self-report measures can produce data on the nature of these discrepancies. Fortunately, the labor-intensive methods for coding actual communication behavior have been simplified with the advent of microcomputer technologies and programs.

Behavioral Measures of Communication Style

Interactants' communicative predispositions manifest themselves in at least two forms. First, and most commonly investigated, individuals may differ in their characteristic communication behavior *levels* (for reviews, see Giles & Street, 1985; Patterson, 1983). There is substantial empirical evidence that interactants are rather consistent across situations in their self-presentations and communication behavior styles (Arkin, 1981; Cappella, 1983; Patterson, 1982; Street, 1986). Second, communicators also may differ in their proclivities to *modify* communication behavior given partner and task contingencies (for reviews, see Cappella & Greene, 1982, 1984; Street & Giles, 1982). Relative to methods for measuring communication behavior levels, assessments of communication behavior adaptations have received less critical attention. Thus, though discussing methodological approaches to both, I will provide a more detailed account of considerations when measuring communication behavior modifications.

Measuring Communication Behaviors

Communication behaviors are generally operationalized as verbal, vocal, and nonverbal behaviors coded for particular analyses units such as speaking turns, 250 milliseconds, one minute intervals, interactions, or across several interactions. Typically, two variables are of interest, rate and duration. Rate refers to the frequency of a particular behavior. Historically, researchers have been interested in rates of gestural movements, interruptions, vocal back channels, posture shifts, word repetitions, powerless speech acts, modifiers, glances, vocalizations, to name a few. Duration represents how long a behavior was enacted and has been used to measure gaze, floortime, response latency, body orientation, vocalization, and so on. Obviously, some behaviors may be measured by some combination of the two such as speech rate (e.g., word frequency divided by speech duration) or relative to other rate and frequency scores such as percentage of talk time (e.g., person A's talk time divided by the duration of the interaction).

Thus, an interactant's communication style can be reflected in his or her verbal, vocal, and nonverbal behavior scores for a particular unit of analysis. Two limitations to this approach to communication style are immediately apparent. First, the potentially large number of style variables is too cumbersome to be of theoretical or empirical utility. In other words, given that communication style manifests itself in various nonverbal, vocal, and verbal behaviors, the number of variables potentially warranting attention are endless. There are at least three solutions to this problem. First, some researchers have limited their behavioral domain to a particular channel, such as gaze (Rutter, Pennington, Dewey, & Swain, 1984), language (Bradac, Konsky, & Davies, 1976), or vocalics (Street, 1982, 1983, 1984). While arguing that these behaviors are significant factors influencing a particular feature of communication process, these authors usually acknowledge the limited scope of their investigations. Second, researchers have measured numerous behaviors and then employed factor analytic techniques to inductively reduce the number of behavioral dimensions. For example, Cappella and Greene (1984) employed factor analytic methods to categorize 10 behaviors into four behavioral groups: affiliative response (eye gaze, posture, and orientation), gesture (body-focused gestures minus object-focused gestures), speech (vocalization duration minus pause duration minus latency duration), and smiles/laughter (see also, Cappella, 1985a). Finally, researchers have isolated a single interaction function (e.g., control, coherence, intimacy) and investigated only those behaviors contributing to that function (see, for example, Hale & Burgoon, 1984; Tracy, 1985).

A second limitation of the behavioral approach to studying communication style is the labor-intensive, time-consuming coding procedures. Traditionally, behaviorists have relied on stopwatches, transcripts, videotapes, pencils, and coding sheets to quantify their data. However, recent software technologies have made this process more facile and efficient. SLCA III (Cummings & Renshaw, 1979) and DICTION (Hart, 1985) compute numerous verbal measures from a text sample. FIASSCO (Cappella & Streibel, 1979) and SPECO (Anderson & Street, 1984) are software programs for coding vocal behaviors on mini- and microcomputers. Though not all are designed for computer technologies, there are numerous techniques for coding nonverbal behavior. Event recorders (e.g., the DATAMYTE 900) or event recording programs such as PLEXYN (Stephenson, 1979) and WRATS (White, 1971) are useful for measuring duration and rate data for various behaviors. FACS (Ekman & Friesen, 1978) and MAX (Izard, 1979) are noncomputerized methods for coding facial expressiveness. Exline and Fehr (1982), Rosenfeld (1982), and Jones and Yarbrough (1985) discuss strategies for measuring gaze behavior, body movement, and touching behavior, respectively.

Researchers of communication behavior must also choose between exhaustive sampling (i.e., coding the behaviors of the entire message sample or interaction) or selective sampling (i.e., systematically coding select periods—such as every fifth minute—of the message or interaction). Considerations when sampling have been addressed in detail by Scherer and Ekman (1982), Fagen and Young (1978), Sackett (1978), and Rosenthal (1982). Also, Cappella (1985b) has been developing microcomputer software which performs various sampling operations and subsequently codes behaviors for the particular time period being sampled.

The previous discussion on behavioral coding procedures, sampling, and deriving behavioral dimensions of communication style admittedly has been sketchy. This was justified given space limitations and that other chapters in this volume (see, e.g., Bradac, Chapter 12), as well as other readily available sources (Bowers & Courtright, 1984; Cairns, 1979; Lamb, Suomi, & Stephenson, 1979; Scherer & Ekman, 1982) present these issues coherently and in sufficient detail. The methodological area that has received much less attention concerns procedures for assessing the stability of an interactant's communication style; that is, the extent to which one maintains or adapts communication behavior levels during social interaction.

Measuring Communication Behavior Adaptations

Communication researchers are increasingly turning away from the study of self-reported or single-event behaviors and are becoming more interested in verbal, vocal, and kinesic *patterns* evolving during the course of social interaction and in the functional impact of these behavioral arrays. This latter orientation is principally concerned with mutual influence among communicative behavior; that is, the extent to which a participant's behavior relates to a partner's behavior for a given time period (e.g., turn, minute, dyad). Researchers examining interaction *processes* and using *time* as a variable are faced with at least two significant methodological decisions: size of the analysis unit and statistical procedures to test hypotheses and research questions. These choices must be made carefully, guided by statistical and conceptual considerations. As I will demonstrate, different statistical procedures and various analysis units often generate different, even contradictory, statistical findings.

Substantive Findings as a Function of Statistical Method and Analysis Unit

Overview

Reciprocity (or convergence, congruence, response matching, pattern matching) and *compensation* (or divergence, response mismatching) are two response patterns frequently characterizing an array of social interaction contexts including conversation (Cappella & Planalp, 1981; Feldstein & Welkowitz, 1978), interviews (Matarazzo & Wiens, 1972; Street, 1984), adult-child interactions (Street, 1983; Welkowitz, Cariffe, & Feldstein, 1976), and family interactions (Fitzpatrick, 1985; Watzlawick, Beavin, & Jackson, 1967). Discussions of theoretical positions explicating reciprocal and compensatory behavioral patterns are available elsewhere (Argyle & Dean, 1965; Cappella, 1983; Cappella & Greene, 1982; Feldstein & Welkowitz, 1978; Hale & Burgoon, 1984; Hewes, 1979; Patterson, 1983; Street & Giles, 1982) and are beyond the scope of this paper.

Reciprocity refers to A and B performing similar behaviors within a given time period or in some temporal contingency to one another. For example, if A self-discloses and B follows with self-disclosures, then self-disclosure reciprocity has occurred (Dindia, 1982). Likewise, reciprocity occurs when A and B adapt a particular behavior in corresponding directions as when B increases rate subsequent to an increase in A's rate (Street, 1983; Webb, 1972). For reciprocity to occur, the behaviors of A and B need not be identical but may be functionally equivalent. For example, A's expression of increased intimacy (e.g., increased gaze, increased proximity) may be reciprocated by B via different but functionally similar behaviors (e.g., forward lean, touch) (see, e.g., Patterson, 1983).

Compensation refers to A and B performing dissimilar behaviors, functionally dissimilar behaviors, or adapting behavior in opposite directions. For example, A's use of a particular dialect may be followed by B's use of a different dialect (i.e., language divergence, Giles & Powesland, 1975). Likewise, an increase in A's turn duration may be followed by B's decrease in turn duration (Matarazzo, Wiens, Matarazzo, & Saslow, 1968; Street, Street, & Van Kleeck, 1983). Finally, A's effort to increase intimacy by touching B may produce compensatory responses from B such as gaze aversion and increasing distance (Patterson, 1983).

Communication behaviors may also vary little during the course of interaction. These circumstances characterize behavioral *consistency* or *maintenance*. Consistency and adaptation are not necessarily contradictory trends. For example, a communicator's behavior may remain relatively stable, not varying greatly from previous levels. Yet these variations may constitute moves toward or away from partner behavior levels. While findings of communication behavior consistency are quite robust (Cappella, 1984; Patterson, 1982; Street, 1984), the relatively smaller trends of reciprocity and compensation are often statistically significant (Cappella & Planalp, 1981; Dindia, 1982; Jaffe & Feldstein, 1970; Street, 1983, 1984).

Substantive conclusions of behavioral consistency, reciprocity, and compensation during social interaction can be contingent upon the statistical procedure employed. The following comparison is limited to the analysis of *continuous* data which are coded for particular time units. Because Hayes, Meltzer, and Wolf (1970) and Van Lear (1983) have addressed similar issues regarding Markov models testing reciprocity and consistency among *discrete* behaviors, this topic will not be addressed in this chapter. Also, this comparison is initially limited to examining reciprocity and compensation. The issue of consistency is addressed later.

Differing Results as a Function of Statistical Method

Differing statistical procedures are often grounded on varying assumptions and logics (Cappella, 1980; Van Lear, 1983). The use of assorted statistical techniques poses two potential problems. First, researchers' efforts to reach substantive conclusions about reciprocity and compensation are constrained by the statistical analysis of the data. Second, generalizing across studies may be impeded, if not impossible, due to conclusions based on different statistical methods. Similarly concerned, Van Lear (1983) recently compared the results of Markov analysis and of multiple-regression procedures with repeated measures on relational control move data coded from dyadic interaction. Van Lear found that for one comparison, the Markov and regression analyses yielded similar conclusions that the data were best characterized by a multiphasic model.[1] However, in a second data set, there were differences as the Markov analysis suggested a uniphasic model, and the regression procedures implicated a multiphasic model.

A similar observation can be raised regarding correlational analysis of reciprocity and compensation among continuous variables, particularly communication style. Three common statistical procedures are the Pearson product-moment correlation (r), intraclass correlation (r'), and time-series regression procedures. Depending on which technique is employed, researchers are imposing differing assumptions regarding what counts as evidence of reciprocity and compensation.

Pearson-product moment correlation. The Pearson correlation (r) has

---

[1] Van Lear (1983) cogently discusses the different assumptions underlying Markov and regression statistics: (a) Markov is a stochastic statistic, and regression is a correlational statistic. (b) Markov analyses apply to distributions within a transition matrix, whereas regression procedures are appropriate for continuous and proportional data.

been used by Matarazzo and Wiens (1972) and Street et al. (1983) to measure speech convergence and divergence. The r statistic is bivariate in nature; that is, r measures the association between pairs of measures which do not share the same unit of measurement (e.g., height and weight). In the case of speech patterns, person A's behavior represents one variate and B's another. As Haggard (1958) points out, r measures degree of covariation between the two variates but is not sensitive to differences in means within the pairs of scores. In sum, r reflects the degree to which A and B adapted behavior in a *similar or dissimilar direction* for a particular time period, but nothing about their degree of similarity.

Intraclass correlation. The intraclass correlation (r') has been used by Feldstein, Welkowitz, and their associates (see Feldstein & Welkowitz, 1978, for review) to measure speech matching ("congruence" in their terminology) and presumably speech compensation. These researchers usually determine speech behavior means for each participant in each interaction and then compute r' across interactions. However, it is also possible to score speech behaviors for particular time units (e.g., for each minute of interaction) and correlate these within and across dyads.

Each unit of analysis—dyad number, occasion 1, minute 1—represents the "classes" or levels of the independent variable—dyads, occasions, time. The number of observations within a class typically corresponds to the number of participants in the interaction. For example, there would be two observations in a study of dyadic interaction, three for triads, four or more for groups. Since the computation of r' is computed with the F-test, the degrees of freedom for the r' statistic are the same as that of the appropriate F-test. For example, if a researcher is using dyads for analysis units and there are 10 dyads, then the degrees of freedom for r' would be 9/10. In other words, there are ten levels (i.e., dyads) for the variable "dyad" with two observations within each level.

According to Haggard (1958), r' is maximally positive when intraunit scores are the same and the scores differ from level to level (i.e., dyad to dyad, minute to minute, etc.). The r' statistic is maximally negative when heterogeneity of intraunit scores is maximal and the means are similar across units (i.e., different dyads, time periods, etc.). Thus, r' assesses both similarity of means and shapes of distributions (Feldstein & Welkowitz, 1978) but ignores individual differences between partners (Warner, Kenny, & Stoto, 1979). The significance of r' is determined by the F ratio of between-class-mean-square (BCMS)/ within-class-mean-square (WCMS). When BCMS < WMS, a negative

r' results and the significance of r' corresponds to the reciprocal of F and the degrees of freedom interchanged (Haggard, 1958).

In sum, when employing r' to assess reciprocity and compensation, the researcher is measuring not only variations among A's and B's behaviors across time intervals, but also the degree of difference between A's and B's behavior levels within each interval.

Time-series regression. Cappella (1980) has argued that time series regression methods are appropriate for the examination of reciprocal and compensatory interaction patterns. A typical regression model would be the following:

$$Y_{(t)} = Y_{(t-1)} + X_{(t-1)} + Y_{(t-2)} + X_{(t-2)} + E$$

where Y_t represents person A's (or B's) behavior at t, $Y_{(t-1)}$ is A's (or B's) behavior for the previous time period, $X_{(t-1)}$ is B's (or A's) behavior at the previous time period, $Y_{(t-2)}$ consists of A's (or B's) behavior for the second previous time period, $X_{(t-2)}$ is B's (or A's) behavior for the second previous time period, and E is the error term.

Conceptually, time-series regression differs from r and r' in three respects. First, rather than a *dyadic* measure of reciprocity or compensation, time-series regression computes the direction and degree to which an *individual* participant adapted behavior relative to the partner's behavior.

Second, autoregressive order is accounted for prior to assessing the influence of predictor variables on the criterion variables. When regressing a participant's current speech behavior level on the participant's own preceding performance of that behavior (that is, the self influence) and on the partner's current or preceding level of that behavior (that is, the partner influence), several assumptions of ordinary least squares regression procedures are violated. These assumptions are that (a) the error terms are uncorrelated over time, (b) the error term has constant variance over all observations, and (c) predictor variables are independent of error terms. When the third assumption is violated, the error process is autoregressive (Cappella, 1980; Ostrom, 1978). The consequences of using OLS procedures when these assumptions are violated (inflated significance tests, biased effects, etc.) are considered in depth by Hibbs (1974) and Kmenta 1971). As a result, the researcher must determine which order of autoregressive processes characterizes the data. Time series data for turn, vocalization, and pause durations are generally first-order autoregressive (Jaffe & Feldstein, 1970; Hayes et al., 1970), though second-order autoregression has been observed for speech coded for one-minute intervals (Street, 1983, 1984; Street & Murphy, 1987). Cappella (1980) recommended that the autoregressive order of each analysis first be ascertained and, given these results, appropriate data transformations made as suggested by Kmenta (1971) and Hibbs (1974).

Third, time-series regression allows the researcher to take into account participants' baseline behavior levels by including self-influences (e.g., Y_{t-1}) in the model (i.e., using previous levels of the participant's behavior to predict current levels of the participant's behavior). According to Cappella (1980), this is an important inclusion because participants may mutually but independently change behavior in similar or dissimilar directions (e.g., changes in task involvement; incremental arousal changes). Without first controlling for previous or baseline behavioral levels and then ascertaining the independent influence of B's behavior on A's behavior (or vice-versa), statistical evidence of reciprocity or matching may only be an artifact. Self-influences are also representative of consistency effects (see, e.g., Cappella, 1980; Street, 1983, 1984). Thus, time series regression allows the researcher to examine *both* behavioral consistency and adaptation in the same statistical model.

A Comparison of Statistical Analyses

Overview of the data sets. Three different data sets were individually analyzed using r, r', and time series regression. These data sets represent a diverse set of interaction contexts including adult-child interaction (Street, 1983), fact-finding interviews (Street, 1984), and adult conversation (Street & Murphy, 1987). Detailed descriptions of the subjects and procedures were provided in the original sources and are not repeated here. The initial comparison only includes the adult-child and the interview interaction data. The conversation data are presented later when comparing the influence of size of the analysis unit on substantive findings.

Overview of speech behavior coding system. While the methodological details of these three studies will not be mentioned here, information about the speech behavior coding procedures should be discussed briefly. For this comparison, three behaviors were chosen: turn duration, response latency, and speech rate. *Turn duration* was defined as the amount of time an interactant held the floor during a speaking turn. *Response latency* refers to the period of time following one interactant's vocalization to assume the floor. The response latency is credited to the person about to take the floor (Matarazzo and Wiens, 1972). *Speech rate* was measured two ways. In the adult-child interaction study, speech rate was measured in syllables per second by dividing the number of syllables uttered by the time in seconds needed to produce the utterance. In the fact-finding interview and conversation studies, speech rate was measured by dividing the speaker's vocalization time within a speaking turn by the turn duration itself (which includes both vocalization time and internal pause time). This measure of speech rate was reported to be highly correlated with rate measured as words per minute (Crown, 1982; Feldstein, 1976) and syllables per second (Street, 1984).

Each behavior was coded for each participant for each minute of interaction. Thus, each participant had an average turn duration, response latency, and speech rate for each minute of the interaction.

The comparison. For each type of interaction, the within-dyad speech scores were pooled across dyads. Thus, the total number of data points for each analysis represents the number of minute intervals coded for each dyad multiplied times the number of dyads. Pooling data in this fashion is advantageous in that it enahnces statistical power and takes into account both intra- and inter-dyad variance (Cappella, 1980).

Table 1 presents the results of the three statistical procedures. While some similarity is evident, there are also instances of findings implicating contradictory conclusions.

Regarding similarities, the response latency results are comparable across statistical procedures. All indicate a significant matching effect. Second, the Pearson correlations and the time-series regression pro-

Table 1. Comparison of Statistical Analyses for Speech Behavior and Type of Interaction

Interaction/Speech Behavior				Statistic					
	Pearson			Intraclass		Time-series regression			
Adult-Child	r	df prob.	r'	df	prob.	B	df	t	prob.
Response Latency	.34	149 .0001	.33	150,149	.0001	A(+)C .38	1,144	3.98	.0001
						C(+)A .26	1,144	4.01	.0001
Speech Rate	.33	149 .0001	−.23	150,149	.0001	A(+)C .27	1,143	2.23	.027
						C(+)A .11	1,143	2.08	.039
Turn Duration	−.11	149 n.s.	−.09	150,149	n.s.	A(0)C−.04	1,144	−.87	n.s.
						C(0)A−.14	1,144	−.82	n.s.
Interview									
Response Latency	.40	679 .0001	.49	455,456	.0001	ER(+)EE .32	1,671	9.42	.0001
						EE(+)ER .35	1,671	9.36	.0001
Speech Rate	.37	679 .0001	.09	455,456	.027	ER(+)EE .23	1,671	5.50	.0001
						EE(+)ER .16	1,671	4.88	.0001
Turn Duration	.04	679 n.s.	−.35	456,455	.0001	ER(0)EE .00	1,671	.27	n.s.
						EE(0)ER .02	1,671	.21	n.s.

cedures produced comparable results in terms of the degree and direction of participants' speech adaptations. The only noticeable difference between the two, concerned speech rate among the adult-child interactions. Using the Pearson correlation, the matching effect for the dyad itself appears larger than the adults' and children's individual rate adaptations toward partners, as measured by time-series regression.

Regarding differences, computation of the intraclass correlation implicated speech adjustments contradictory to those of the other statistical procedures. These include significant *negative* relationships between adult-child speech rate adjustments and between interview participants' turn duration levels. Also, for the interviews, the highly significant speech rate matching effect, as indexed by the Pearson correlation and time series regression, appears attenuated when the intraclass correlation was employed.

Why does r' differ so dramatically from the results of the other statistical procedures? Quite simply, the intraclass correlation is grounded in assumptions quite different from the other two. The use of r' assumes data are univariate; that is, both scores in the pair (in this case both participants' speech levels for a particular time interval) are derived from the same unit of measurement. This, of course, appears to be true for the calculations of speech levels in these data. Yet, there are substantive implications, given these assumptions. Recall that r' is generated by dividing BCMS (variance among scores across analysis units) by WMS (variance between scores within analysis units). Thus, scores different across and similar within classes create a positive r'. This indeed indexes speech similarity as well as concordant speech moves across time intervals.

On the other hand, while speech differences between participants within a time unit *may* indicate moves opposite one another, some speech differences may reflect individual differences between participants due to age, role, or personality, even though the same unit of measurement was used for both participants' speech. These individual speech differences contribute to intraclass variance and influence r' toward greater negativity. In short, r' may be negative when two interactants adapt speech opposite one another *or* when the interactants produce speech at different levels.

If our reasoning is accurate, the results presented in Table 1 may reflect differences among speech rates between adults and children and between interview participants, and among floorholdings between interview participants. This was indeed the case as adults and interviewers spoke significantly faster than children ($F(1,298) = 239.28$, $p < .0001$) and interviewees ($F(1,1349) = 52.27$), $p < .0001$. Interviewers also held the floor for significantly shorter periods than did interviewees ($F(1,1249) = 787.04$, $p < .0001$). Likewise, one would expect minimal differences between participants for those analyses in which r' was consistent with the Pearson and time-series statistics. Interview participants, and adults and children indeed did not significantly differ in their response latencies ($F(1,1349) = 2.55$, n.s.) and turn durations ($F(1,298) = .39$, n.s.), respectively. However, adults did produce latencies significantly shorter than the children's ($F(1,298) = 6.61$, $p < .02$).

Thus, it would appear that small differences between interactants' speech levels do not greatly affect consistency among conclusions yielded by these three statistical procedures. However, individual differences can become large enough to influence r' toward greater negativity even though the Pearson correlation and time series regression methods indicate that participants may be adapting speech in similar directions. In short, r' is a function of behavioral similarity and of direction of behavioral adjustments. Pearson correlation and time-series regression are dependent only upon the direction of behavioral adaptations by participants. Therefore, the intraclass correlation can be appropriate when investigators assume that reciprocal and compensatory interaction patterns are contingent upon similarities and differences among behavioral *levels* or assume (and verify) that participants' behavioral levels do not significantly differ. The Pearson correlation and time-series regression are suitable if reciprocity and compensation are defined in terms of direction of behavior *adaptations.*

Measuring consistency among communication behaviors. To this point, I have limited discussion to the assessment of reciprocity and compensation among communication behaviors during dyadic interaction. As previously explicated, time series regression can be designed to take into account the influence of an interactant's previous behavior levels (i.e., Y_{t-1}, the consistency effect) and subsequently the influence of partner behavior (i.e., X_t) within the same statistical model. If the researcher chooses to use r or r' to examine both consistency and reciprocity/compensation, two *separate* statistical analyses must be conducted. One correlation would assess the relationship between participant behavior scores at t with participant behavior scores at t-1. Another correlation would then test the relationship between a participant's behavior at t and a partner's behavior at t or t-1.

I recommend time-series regression because one model is used to examine self-influences initially and subsequently the *independent* partner effect (that is, after self-influences are accounted for, systematic variance in a participant's behavioral levels can be attributed solely to the partner's behavioral levels). The use of r and r' to measure consistency and reciprocity/compensation requires two separate statistical computations, and, also, the researcher is unable to conveniently separate how much influence can be attributed to behavioral consistency and how much is due to behavioral adaptation.

Differing Results as a Function of Size of the Analysis Unit

Researchers of social interaction processes must also choose a particular unit of analysis. For continuous behavior, this often entails a decision regarding time or unit intervals for which the behavior is coded. Among studies of vocal behavior patterns, the unit size has varied greatly, including 300 milliseconds (Cappella & Planalp, 1981; Jaffee & Feldstein, 1970), speaking turn (Cappella & Planalp, 1981; Street, 1983), averages per five speaking turns (Street et al., 1983), one-minute intervals (Street, 1983, 1984), five-minute intervals (Matarazzo & Wiens, 1972) and dyads (Dabbs, Evans, Hopper, & Purvis, 1980; Feldstein & Welkowitz, 1978). Results of speech matching and compensation appear to differ systematically depending on the unit size for which the behavior was coded. It appears that the larger the unit, the more likely that evidence of speech matching and compensation emerges. For example, convergence and divergence effects have been regularly observed for response latency, switching pauses, vocalization duration, turn duration, internal pauses, and interruptive speech when units of one-minute or larger have been employed (see, e.g., Feldstein & Welkowitz, 1978; Matarazzo & Wiens, 1972; Street, 1983, 1984). However, for units the size of individual speaking turns and less (e.g., 300 milliseconds), speech matching and compensation has occurred less regularly (Cappella & Planalp, 1981; Street, 1983, 1984).

These studies do not allow for direct comparisons because of their methodological and statistical differences. For example, Cappella and Planalp (1981) and Street (1983, 1984) used speaking turns as analysis units and examined speech convergence in *individual* dyads. Feldstein, Welkowitz, and their associates (see Feldstein & Welkowitz, 1978) usually compute behavior scores per interactant per dyad and assess congruence across dyads or across groups of dyads (e.g., younger vs. older children; perceived similar vs. perceived dissimilar conversants). Street (1983, 1984) and Cappella (1980) have computed scores per time unit within a dyad, then pooled these scores across dyads.

To assess differences more directly as a function of the analysis unit, a subset of conversational speech data from Street and Murphy, (1987) was coded using three different analysis units: intervals of 30, 60, and 120 seconds. Interval scores for the 19 conversations were pooled. The Pearson correlation was employed to make the comparison. Time-series regression (as described above) was not used because previous levels of an interactant's behavior may differentially influence current behavior levels as a function of the analysis unit which in turn will not provide a comparable test of partner behavior influence for each comparison. Thus, for the sake of illustrating the sole impact of analysis unit size, correlations were computed assessing consistency and matching effects separately. Speech consistency was assessed by correlating a conversant's behavior at t with the conversant's behavior at t-1. Speech matching was measured by correlating the conversant's behavior at t with partner's behavior at t.

For these data, there are three consequences of the use of the different analysis units. First, as the coding interval increases in size, so does statistical evidence of speech consistency. Evidence of speech rate matching also appears to increase with the size of the analysis unit. Third, evidence of response latency matching decreases as the coding interval increases. The first two differences are likely due to the instability of continuously coded behaviors constituting speech structure and tempo. Behaviors coded within brief intervals may reflect significant perturbations or variation due to momentary hesitations, arousal or other physiological changes, topic transition periods, etc. Increasing the coding interval appears to stabilize this error variance and thus may provide clearer evidence of speech consistency and reciprocity/compensation.

Why is the response latency matching comparison contrary to the

Table 2. Analysis Unit Comparisons Among Correlations of Conversants' Speech Behaviors

Effect/Speech Behavior	30 seconds (N=890)	60 seconds (N=445)	120 seconds (N=222)
Consistency			
Turn Duration	.16***	.24***	.28***
Speech Rate	.02	.24***	.15*
Response Latency	.18***	.17***	.36***
Adaptation			
Turn Duration	−.02	−.08	−.04
Speech Rate	.11**	.14**	.26***
Response Latency	.08*	.06	.02

*p<.05
**p<.01
***p<.001

others?[2] First, the correlations are quite small and the difference could be due to chance. Second, relative to the other coding intervals, the 30-second interval has much greater power given the increase in number of observations. However, it does not seem reasonable to think that increasing the size of the analysis unit diminishes evidence of response latency matching since such matching has been observed among studies using speaker turns (Cappella & Planalp, 1981; Street, 1984), one-minute intervals (Street, 1983, 1984), five-minute intervals (Matarazzo & Wiens, 1972), and entire interactions (Feldstein & Welkowitz, 1978) as analysis units.

Conclusions

The researcher should recognize the substantive implications of various statistical indices of communication style consistency and adaptation and of the size of the analysis unit. The Pearson correlation assesses only the extent to which two variables covary. The intraclass correlation assumes data are univariate and is an index of the similarity of means and the shapes of their distributions. Time series regression initially takes into account the autoregressive order of the data, then places various predictors in the model such as previous levels of a partner's behavior (reciprocity or compensation effect). Also, whereas the Pearson and intraclass correlations measure degree of dyadic reciprocity or compensation, time series regression allows the researcher to assess these moves by individual interactants. As revealed in Table 2, differences in the size of the coding interval may create statistical results implicating inconsistent substantive conclusions. Researchers should carefully choose analysis units given empirical and theoretical concerns. In short, I offer the following guidelines for choosing statistical procedures and analysis units to measure consistency, reciprocity, and compensation of communication behaviors which are coded as continuous variables.

1. The researcher should use time-series regression if interested in the extent to which adaptations in an interactant's behavior level and direction are due to the interactant's previous behavior level and

---

[2] The absence of response latency convergence in these data is likely due to the manipulation of the partner's (i.e., confederate's) behavior. During the middle of the interaction, the confederate would change from low (or high) activity (i.e., long pauses, slow rates, little expressiveness) to high (or low) activity (i.e., fast speech, few pauses, high expressiveness). This manipulation may have inhibited the subjects' proclivities to achieve greater convergence.

to the partner's behavior level for a given time period. Time-series regression is not appropriate if the researcher is interested in similarity among behavioral means or is only interested in a participant's average behavior score for an entire interaction.

2. The researcher should use the intraclass correlation if interested in behavioral similarity or differences across time periods, occasions, or dyads. If behaviors are coded in time units (i.e., not, for example, as means for an entire interaction), then a positive r' will reflect similarity of interactants' behavioral levels *and* adaptations. However, a negative r' only reflects behavioral dissimilarity and not whether participants compensated or diverged behaviors. As indicated in Table 2, participants who characteristically produce behaviors at significantly different levels, generated negative r' values, though they actually adapted behavior in similar directions.

3. The researcher should use an analysis unit that sufficiently enables garnering representative samples of the data. While this statement may seem common-sensical, I do not forward it lightly. Some communication behaviors, such as self-disclosures and conversational topic shifts, often require a larger coding unit interval than others such as gaze direction and disfluency rate. In my own research on speech behavior, I have found that intervals smaller than 60 seconds (e.g., speaking turns, 30-second intervals) are often insufficient for measuring the relatively subtle patterns of reciprocity and compensation. As depicted in Table 2, there was also greater speech consistency among these continuous behavior variables when analysis units larger than 30 seconds were used. However, with Markov models, interactants usually demonstrate greater behavioral consistency and less partner influence the faster the sampling rate (e.g., taking a sample every 200–300 milliseconds; see Cappella & Planalp, 1981; Hayes et al., 1970). Thus, researchers must carefully consider the theoretical and empirical context when selecting the size of the analysis unit and not take it for granted.

References

Anderson, D., & Street, R.L., Jr. (1984). SPECO: A microcomputer program for coding speech behavior. Unpublished manuscript. Texas Tech University.

Argyle, M., & Dean, J. (1965). Eye contact, distance, and affiliation. *Sociometry, 38,* 289–304.

Arkin, R.M. (1981). Self-presentation styles. In J.T. Tedeschi (Ed.), *Impression management theory and social psychological research.* New York: Academic Press.

Bem, D., & Allen, A. (1974). On predicting some of the people some of the time: The search for cross-situational consistencies in behavior. *Psychological Review, 31*, 506–520.

Bowers, J.W., & Courtright, J. (1984). *Communication research methods.* Glenview, IL: Scott, Foresman, and Company.

Bradac, J., Konsky, C., & Davies, R. (1976). Two studies of the effects of linguistic diversity upon judgments of communicator attributes and message effectiveness. *Communication Monographs, 43*, 70–79.

Cairns, R.B. (1979). *The analysis of social interactions: Methods, issues, and illustrations.* Hillsdale, NJ: Erlbaum.

Campbell, D.T., & Stanley, J.C. (1963). *Experimental and quasi-experimental designs for research.* Chicago: Rand McNally.

Cappella, J.N. (1980). Structural equation modeling: An introduction. In P.R. Monge and J.N. Cappella (Eds.), *Multivariate techniques in human communication research,* (pp. 57–109). New York: Academic Press.

Cappella, J.N. (1983). Conversational involvement: Approaching and avoiding others. In J.M. Wiemann and R.P. Harrison (Eds.). *Nonverbal interaction,* (pp. 113–148). Beverly Hills, CA: Sage.

Cappella, J.N. (1984). The relevance of microstructure of interaction to relationship change. *Journal of Social and Personal Relationships, 1*, 239–264.

Cappella, J.N. (1985a). The management of conversations. In M.L. Knapp and R. Miller (Eds.), *The handbook of interpersonal communication.* Beverly Hills, CA: Sage.

Cappella, J.N. (1985b). Reciprocal and compensatory reactions to violations of distance norms for high and low self-monitors. In M.L. McLaughlin (Ed.), *Communication Yearbook 9.* Beverly Hills, CA: Sage.

Cappella, J.N., & Greene, J.O. (1982). A discrepancy-arousal explanation of mutual influence in expressive behavior for adult-adult and infant-adult interaction. *Communication Monographs, 49*, 80–114.

Cappella, J.N., & Greene, J.O. (1984). The effects of distance and individual differences in arousability of nonverbal involvement. A test of discrepancy-arousal theory. *Journal of Nonverbal Behavior, 8*, 259–286.

Cappella, J.N., & Planalp, S. (1981). Talk and silence sequences in informal conversations III: Interspeaker influence. Human Communication Research, 7, 117–132.

Cappella, J.N., & Streibel, M. (1979). Computer analysis of talk-silence sequences: The FIASSCO system. *Behavior Research Methods and Instrumentation, 11*, 384–392.

Cegala, D.J. (1981). Interaction involvement: A cognitive dimension of communicative competence. *Communication Education, 30*, 109–121.

Cegala, D.J., Savage, G.T., Brunner, C.C., & Conrad, A.B. (1982). An elaboration of the meaning of interaction involvement: Toward the development of a theoretical concept. *Communication Monographs, 49*, 229–248.

Crown, C.L. (1982). Impression formation and the chronography of dyadic interactions. In M. Davis (Ed.), *Interaction rhythms: Periodicity in communication behavior* (pp. 225–248). New York: Human Sciences Press.

Cummings, H.W., & Renshaw, S.L. (1979). SLCA III: A metatheoretic approach to the study of language. *Human Communication Research, 5,* 291–300.

Dabbs, J.M., Jr., Evans, M.S., Hopper, C.H., & Purvis, J.A. (1980). Self-monitors in conversation: What do they monitor? *Journal of Personality and Social Psychology, 39,* 278–284.

Daly, J.A., & Street, R.L., Jr. (1980). Measuring social-communicative anxiety: Social desirability and the fakability of scale responses. *Human Communication Research, 8,* 79–90.

Deethardt, J.F., & McLaughlin, M.L. (1976). A study of communicator types and styles. Presented at the meeting of International Communication Association, Berlin.

Dindia, K. (1982). Reciprocity in self-disclosure: A sequential analysis. In M. Burgoon (Ed.), *Communication Yearbook 6* (pp. 506–528). Beverly Hills, CA: Sage.

Ekman, P., & Friesen, W.V. (1978). *The facial action coding system: A technique for the measurement of facial movement.* Palo Alto, CA: Consulting Psychologists Press.

Exline, R.V., & Fehr, B.J. (1982). The assessment of gaze and mutual gaze. In K.R. Scherer & P. Ekman (Eds.), *Handbook of methods in nonverbal behavior research* (pp. 91–135). Cambridge: Cambridge University Press.

Fagen, R.M., & Young, D.Y. (1978). Temporal patterns of behavior: Durations, intervals, latencies, and sequences. In P.W. Colgan (Ed.), *Quantitative etiology.* New York: Wiley.

Feldstein, S. (1976). Rate estimates of sound-silence sequences in speech. *Journal of the Acoustical Society of America, 60* (Supplement No. 1), 546 (Abstract).

Feldstein, S., & Welkowitz, J. (1978). A chronography of conversation: In defense of an objective approach. In A.W. Siegman & S. Feldstein (Eds.), *Nonverbal behavior and communication* (pp. 329–378). Hillsdale, NJ: Erlbaum.

Fitzpatrick, M.A. (1985). A typological approach to marital interaction: Recent theory and research. In L. Berkowitz (Ed.), *Advances in experimental social psychology.* New York: Academic Press.

Giles, H., & Powesland, P.F. (1975). *Speech style and social evaluation.* London: Academic Press.

Giles, H., & Street, R.L., Jr. (1985). Communicator characteristics and behavior: A review, generalizations, and model. In M.L. Knapp & G.R. Miller (Eds.), *Handbook of interpersonal communication.* Beverly Hills, CA: Sage.

Haggard, E.A. (1958). *Intraclass correlation and the analysis of variance.* New York: Dryden.

Hale, J.L., & Burgoon, J.K. (1984). Models of reactions to changes in nonverbal immediacy. *Journal of Nonverbal Behavior, 8,* 287–314.

Hart, R. (1985). Systematic analysis of political discourse: The development of DICTION. In K. Sanders et al. (Eds.), *Political Communication Yearbook 1984* (pp. 97–134). Carbondale, IL: Southern Illinois University Press.

Hayes, D., Meltzer, L., & Wolf, G. (1970). Substantive conclusions are dependent upon techniques of measurement. *Behavioral Science, 15,* 265–269.

Hewes, D.E. (1979). The sequential analysis of social interaction. *Quarterly Journal of Speech, 65,* 56–73.

Hewes, D.W., & Haight, L. (1980). Multiple act criteria in the validation of communication traits: What do we gain and what do we lose? *Human Communication Research, 6,* 352–366.

Hibbs, D.A. (1974). Problems of statistical estimation and causal inference in time-genes regression models. In H.L. Costner (Ed.), *Sociological methodology 1973–1974.* San Francisco: Jossey-Bass.

Izard, C. (1979). *The maximally discriminative facial movement coding system (MAX).* Unpublished manuscript. Instructional Resources Center. University of Delaware.

Jaccard, J., & Daly, J. (1980). Personality traits and multiple act criteria. *Human Communication Research, 6,* 367–377.

Jaffe, J., & Feldstein, S. (1970). *Rhythms of dialogue.* New York: Academic Press.

Jones, S.E., & Yarbrough, E.A. (1985). A naturalistic study of the meanings of touch. *Communication Monographs, 52,* 19–58.

Joos, M. (1962). The five clocks. *International Journal of American Linguistics, 28,* part 5.

Kmenta, J. (1971). *Elements of econometrics.* New York: MacMillan.

Labov, W. (1966). *The social stratification of English in New York City.* Washington, D.C. Center for Applied Linguistics.

Lamb, M.E., Suomi, S.J., & Stephenson, G.R. (Eds.) (1979). *Social interaction analysis: Methodological issues.* Madison, WI: University of Wisconsin Press.

Larsen, K.S., Martin, H.J., and Giles, H. (1977). Anticipated social cost and interpersonal accommodation. *Human Communication Research, 3,* 303–308.

Matarazzo, J.D., & Wiens, A.N. (1972). *The interview: Research on its anatomy and structure.* Chicago: Aldine-Atherton.

Matarazzo, J.D., Wiens, A.N., Matarazzo, R.G., & Saslow, G. (1968). Speech and silence behavior and its laboratory correlates. In J. Schlien, H. Hunt, J.D. Matarazzo, & C. Savage (Eds.), *Research in psychotherapy* (Vol. 3) (pp. 347–394). Washington: American Psychological Association.

Norton, R. (1983). *Communicator style.* Beverly Hills, CA: Sage.

Ostrom, C.W., Jr. (1978). *Time series analysis: Regression techniques.* Beverly Hills, CA: Sage.

Patterson, M.L. (1982). Personality and nonverbal involvement: A functional analysis. In W.J. Ickes & E.S. Knowles (Eds.), *Nonverbal behavior: A functional perspective* (pp. 141–164). New York: Springer-Verlag.

Patterson, M.L. (1983). *Nonverbal behavior: A functional perspective.* New York: Springer-Verlag.

Rosenfeld, H.M. (1982). Measurement of body motion and orientation. In

K.R. Scherer & P. Ekman (Eds.), *Handbook of methods in nonverbal behavior research* (pp. 199–286). Cambridge: Cambridge University Press.

Rosenthal, R. (1982). Conducting judgment studies. In K.R. Scherer & P. Ekman (Eds.), *Handbook of methods in nonverbal behavior research* (pp. 287–361). Cambridge: Cambridge University Press.

Rutter, D.R., Pennington, D.C., Dewey, M.E., & Swain, J. (1984). Eye contact as a chance product of individual looking: Implications for the intimacy model of Argyle and Dean. *Journal of Nonverbal Behavior, 8,* 250–258.

Sackett, G.P. (Ed.) (1978). *Observing behavior* (Vols. 1–2). Baltimore, MD: University Park Press.

Scherer, K.R., & Ekman, P. (Eds.) (1982). *Handbook of methods in nonverbal behavior research.* Cambridge: Cambridge University Press.

Stephenson, G.R. (1979). PLEXYN: A computer compatible grammar for coding complex social interactions. In M.E. Lamb, S.J. Suomi, & G.R. Stephenson (Eds.), *Social interaction analysis: Methodological issues* (pp. 157–184). Madison, WI: University of Wisconsin Press.

Street, R.L., Jr. (1982). Evaluation of noncontent speech accommodation. *Language and Communication, 2,* 13–31.

Street, R.L., Jr. (1983). Noncontent speech convergence in adult-child interactions. In R.N. Bostrom (Ed.), *Communication Yearbook 7* (pp. 369–395). Beverly Hills, CA: Sage.

Street, R.L., Jr. (1984). Speech convergence and speech evaluation in fact-finding interviews. *Human Communication Research, 11,* 139–169.

Street, R.L., Jr. (1986). Interaction processes and outcomes in interviews. *Communication Yearbook, 9,* 215–250.

Street, R.L., Jr. & Giles, H. (1982). Speech accommodation theory: A social-cognitive approach to language and speech behavior. In M.E. Roloff & C.R. Berger (Eds.), *Social cognition and communication* (pp. 193–226). Beverly Hills, CA: Sage.

Street, R.L., Jr. & Hopper, R. (1982). A model of speech style evaluation. In E.B. Ryan & H. Giles (Eds.), *Attitudes toward language variation: Social and applied contexts* (pp. 175–188). London: Edward Arnold.

Street, R.L., Jr. & Murphy, T. (1987). Interpersonal orientation and speech behavior. *Communication Monographs, 54,* 42–62.

Street, R.L., Jr., Street, N.J., & Van Kleeck, A. (1983). Speech convergence among talkative and reticent three year-olds. *Language Sciences, 5,* 79–96.

Swap, W.C., & Rubin, J.Z. (1983). Measurement of interpersonal orientation. *Journal of Personality and Social Psychology, 44,* 208–219.

Thakerar, J.N., & Giles, H. (1981). They are-so they speak: Noncontent speech stereotypes. *Language and Communication, 1,* 251–256.

Tracy, K. (1985). Conversational coherence: A cognitively grounded rules approach. In R.L. Street, Jr. & J.N. Cappella (Eds.), *Sequence and pattern in communicative behavior* (pp. 30–49). London: Edward Arnold.

Van Lear, C.A., Jr. (1983). Analysis of interaction data. In R.N. Bostrom (Ed.), *Communication Yearbook 7* (pp. 282–303). Beverly Hills, CA: Sage.

Warner, R.M., Kenny, D.A., & Stoto, M. (1979). A new round robin analysis of variance for social interaction data. *Journal of Personality and Social Psychology, 37,* 1742–1757.

Watzlawick, P., Beavin, J.H., & Jackson, D.D. (1967). *Pragmatics of human communication.* New York: W.W. Norton.

Webb, J.T. (1972). Interview sychrony: An investigation of two speech rate measures. In A.W. Siegman and B. Pope (Eds.), *Studies in dyadic communication* (pp. 115–133). New York: Pergamon.

Welkowitz, J., Cariffe, G., & Feldstein, S. (1976). Conversational congruence as a criterion for socialization in children. *Child Development, 47,* 269–272.

Wells, J.C. (1970). Local accents in England and Wales. *Journal of Linguistics, 6,* 231–252.

White, R.E.C. (1971). WRATS: Computer compatible system for automatically recording and transcribing behavioral data. *Behavior, 40,* 135–161.

CHAPTER 6

Conversation: Data Acquisition and Analysis

Stuart J. Sigman,
Sheila J. Sullivan,
and Marcley Wendell[1]

Unlike the topics discussed in most of the other chapters, conversation analysis does not evidence a single recognizable or uniform method. Further, the systematic study of conversation is not securely rooted in the communication discipline as an integral research enterprise. The debate regarding the value of conversation scholarship has, with few exceptions (e.g., Hopper, Koch, & Mandelbaum, 1986), avoided detailed methodological pronouncements. In addition, an implicit claim for the validity of individual research reports, which also lack descriptions of procedure, rests on the background or taken-for-granted cultural knowledge presumably shared by analysts, participants, and readers (see Sacks, 1984). Conversation analysis is said to be best learned in the doing of analysis—in the actual confrontation by a researcher of his/her background understandings with various conversational materials.

Granting some validity to these observations on the state of conversation research, the resulting situation represents a problem for any serious review of contemporary methods. In the absence of univocal methodological statements in the literature, we have reviewed a sample of existing empirical research papers to determine the implicit perspectives, investigative procedures, and research vocabularies likely to have produced these studies. We recognize the potential danger of reading the literature from our own vantage point (in this regard,

[1] A grant to the senior author from the New York State/United University Professions Professional Development and Quality of Working Life Committee for preparation of this chapter is gratefully acknowledged. We also appreciate the critical readings provided by Anne Donnellon, Robert Hopper, Charles Petrie, and Robert Sanders.

see Sigman, 1985), yet we hope that this stab at elucidating and articulating method will also bring some initial order to the nascent field. To delimit our task, we are concerned here only with research aimed at uncovering the guiding behavioral "rules," "patterns," "programs," "structures," and/or "organization" of everyday conversation and conversational events. This chapter does not consider examinations of verbal data in the service of cognitive (see Daly, 1985; Delia, 1985) or social systems analysis (Millar & Bavelas, 1985), but concentrates instead on scholarship treating conversation as "a phenomenon in its own right" (Litton-Hawes, 1977, p. 2), "an activity in its own right" (Schegloff & Sacks, 1973, pp. 289–290), and "worth studying in itself rather than as an indicator of [i.e., independent or dependent variable for] something else" (Nofsinger, 1977, p. 12).

Analytic Perspective

The list of topics which form part of conversation scholarship is long, representing interest in a diverse array of conversational units, relationships between units, functions, and practices (for excellent anthologies, reviews, and recent texts, see Craig & Tracy, 1983; McLaughlin, 1984; Psathas, 1979; Schenkein, 1978; Stubbs, 1983; Tannen & Saville-Troike, 1985; West & Zimmerman, 1982). Despite the diversity in the literature, we have been able to read several themes extending across individual studies and investigators. Taken as a whole, the following five themes serve as an "ideal type" description of the goals and analytic perspective associated with conversation analysis.[2]

Theme (1). Conversation as Structured Social Activity

As noted above, students of conversation consider talk to be an organized or rule-governed activity whose patterns can be discerned. Stubbs (1983) writes in this regard:

Connected discourse is clearly not random. People are quite able to

---

[2] The conflict over "conversation(al) analysis" and "discourse analysis" as appropriate labels for the enterprise is further evidence of the infancy of the field (cf., Litton-Hawes, 1977; Nofsinger, 1977; Stubbs, 1983; Levinson, 1983). This chapter does not enter the debate, and makes the somewhat arbitrary decision to gloss over the differences between the two terms and refers only to "conversation analysis." We recognize the danger of thus lumping together scholars who disagree on fundamental methodological and theoretical issues, and hope that future reviews will be devoted to these substantive differences.

distinguish between a random list of sentences and a coherent text, and it is the principles which underlie this recognition of coherence which are the topic of study for discourse analysts (p. 15).

Instead of correlating features of talk with participant demographics, or considering the affective and information-processing states producing talk, conversation analysts examine the *behavioral building blocks* of talk. The structure of a given stretch of conversation is said to rest on speaker/hearers' abilities to manipulate—that is, produce and interpret—sequences of behavioral units. However, conversation analysts do not concentrate on the "abilities" (in this regard, see Chapter 3), but rather on the nature of the units and the sequences of units themselves, for example, on "turns" (Sacks, Schegloff, & Jefferson, 1974), "adjacency pairs" (Schegloff, 1968), states of "fission" (Sigman, 1981) and "fragmentation" (Parker, 1984), "insertions" (Jefferson, 1972), "compliment responses" (Pomerantz, 1978), "overlaps" and "interruptions" (Jefferson, 1973), "pre-invitations" (Schegloff, 1980), and "stories" (Sacks, 1972). There is a "preoccupation with units that exceed the limits of a single sentence" (Thompson, 1984, p. 99), and/ or that function to connect speakers' discrete utterance contributions.

At the same time that this microstructural perspective on conversation is stressed, we must also note that the early ethnomethodologists responsible for developing conversation analysis as an enterprise within sociology declare that the object of focus is ultimately not talk. Cicourel (1980b) observes:

> Language structure and use are not peripheral to the study of social life but instead provide a central concept for understanding notions such as social organization and social structure (p. 2).

According to Schegloff (1980), conversation analysis makes possible an action theory of social structure and social organization which does not require abstractions from behavior such as "group" and "role": "[The analysis of social structure] can be undertaken on action in the primordial scene of sociality—interaction" (p. 151). Thus, it is important to keep in mind that *talk as an aspect of social activity* is the concern of the ethnomethodological approach to conversation.

There is a particularly important implication of this perspective. While talk is seen by ethnomethodologists to serve as an exemplary instantiation of social organizing processes, neither language nor the coherent conversations with which language is associated are held to have a "theoretical primacy" of study over other communication modalities (Schegloff & Sacks, 1973, pp. 289–290). Thus, the scarcity of research concerned with nonlexical features of interaction and multichannel interdependencies (cf., Goodwin, 1981; Kendon, 1985; Schegloff, 1984b) is accidental and theoretically unmotivated. As West and Zimmerman (1982) write: "Existing [conversation] analyses yield several particular parameters of conversational organization that might profitably be examined in the situated context of nonverbal exchanges" (p. 528). The assumption here is that the mode of analysis for verbal behavior can be applied to gestural components of communication.

Theme (2). Interactional Vocabulary

Despite the close affinity between talk and social organization, a guiding principle of conversation analysis seems to be that investigators must rely on a descriptive vocabulary which is interactionally based, rather than social structurally-based. Instead of explaining conversational regularities in terms of the social identities or personalities of the individuals producing talk, analysts legitimately make appeals only to the readers' willingness to see the behavior as organized in its own terms, and apart from the social-psychological features of particular speaker/hearers. In his article on pre-sequences, for example, Schegloff (1980) writes: "There may be differential allocation of turn types in interviews or differential status in doctor-patient clinical interactions. . . . Caution is in order in too readily taking such materials as evidence of differential allocation or differential status, when an alternative, empirically well-grounded analysis is available" (p. 146)[3] Coulthard and Montgomery (1981) comment on their research: "While initially it was essential to use concepts like 'status,' . . . the hope was that eventually it would be possible to come full circle and define roles like 'chairman' as a set of linguistic options" (cited in Thompson, 1984, p. 104). This principle is reminiscent of earlier descriptive

---

[3] It is our position that conversation analysis is no more or less empirical than other forms of social science scholarship. There is a "face valid" sense in which the data and interpretations of conversation analysis are "closer" to, and less an abstraction from, behavior as actually performed and lived by social actors; for example, one can "see" a greeting in talk, whereas differential status can only be abstracted (inferred) from observable behavior. Nevertheless, the empiricist claim fails to recognize: (a) the interpretive work actually engaged in by the analyst in the process of rendering a transcript meaningful; (b) the investigator's language structure which frames his/her reading of the data; and (c) the selective presentation of transcription segments in published research reports which serves to lead readers toward certain interpretations and away from others. In this respect, compare the different treatments of conversation by Sacks (1972), Sinclair and Coulthard (1974), Labov and Fanshel (1977), and Gumperz (1982).

linguistic (Pike, 1967) and context analytic (Birdwhistell, 1970; Scheflen, 1973) procedures which suggest that behavioral data must be thoroughly exhausted in terms of structural explanations before appeals are made to "randomness," "free-variation," "individuality," or "idiosyncracy."

Thus, the literature draws upon a distinction between what can be considered participants' "interaction role(s)" and their "social role(s)" (cf., Goffman, 1983). Within the conversation analysis framework, one goal of research is to consider the interaction role(s) constructed by participants when producing and/or eliciting particular behavioral units, rather than the predictive value of previously abstracted social role(s) for produced behavior.[4] (See Harré, Clarke, & DeCarlo, 1985, for a further discussion of the implications of talking about actors versus behavior.)

Theme (3). Non-Deterministic Understanding

Conversation scholarship is compatible with, and is further evidence for, the general social science departure from deterministic, covering-laws explanations for human behavior, and the movement toward rules and interpretive understanding (cf., Cushman and Whiting, 1972; Geertz, 1983; Gergen, 1982; Harré & Secord, 1972; Shimanoff, 1980). Harré et al. (1985) suggest: "There is a very great difference between the workings of simple causal mechanisms and the way human beings act. . . . Human beings' actions are typically performed *in accordance with* rules, rather than *determined by* causes" (pp. 9–10, emphasis in original). With specific reference to conversation analysis, Nofsinger (1979) writes: "Remember that at first, the researcher should not study episodes with the expectation of immediately [sic] formulating laws of nature, but with the hope of identifying the details of non-random patterns in everyday life" (p. 15). Levinson (1983) suggests that the goal is not to study norms which constrain participants' behavior, but rather the options available to speaker/hearers when constructing talk sequences and the entailments or co-occurrences associated with particular option selections.

The researcher's aim is to study those options for behaving that are available to social actors, given the delimitations imposed by the larger behavioral sequence unfolding at a given moment. Conversation

---

[4] This chapter does not assess the success of the ethnomethodological program with regard to the relationship between interactional and social structural data. Thompson (1984) critiques this research for its failure "to explore the ways in which the analysis of language can be integrated with the study of the institutional and structural dimensions of the social world" (p. 100).

analysts are concerned with the abstract set of procedures available to interactants and stress that speakers' choices are made on a moment-by-moment basis and do not automatically lead to a single interpretation and response. Thus, conversation analysts consider that numerous functions can be served by interactants' behavior and multiple interpretations by participants of the same behavior are possible. In Gergen's (1982) terminology, conversation analysts eschew studying a bit of talk as an exogenic stimulus causing a particular reaction, and encourage considering the potential information value(s) of behavior and the endogenic processing practices of individuals.

This third feature of the conversation analysis perspective is evidenced in the following discussion of a sequence comprised of units labeled by Jefferson (1972) "A" and "B":

> The possibility for a B-to-some-prior-A, A-for-the-next-B object provides that an A-speaker cannot necessarily control what will be done with some utterance he makes. He can—merely or however—project a possible sequence (p. 307).

For example, research by Keenan and Schieffelin (1976) and Litton-Hawes (1977) on topic construction suggests that, given a speaker's production of a topic-related utterance, a next speaker's turn-at-talk will make use of one or more devices from a limited set for developing a relevant and coherent follow-up utterance. However, there is no basis within the conversational system itself for judging which interpretation or topical focus of the previous utterance will be selected (but cf. Sigman, 1983a). Thus, rather than account for the probabalistic features of each talk device, conversation researchers consider the following: (a) the range of permissible (and nonpermissible) alternative behaviors; (b) limitations placed on participants' selections from these alternatives given the structure and content of the earlier turn(s); and (c) the consequences of the "responding" speaker's selection for (his/hers and others') subsequent turns a talk.

Theme (4). Local Orientation

The behavioral forms that are used to construct conversation are considered by many analysts to be both "context-free" and "context-sensitive" (see Sacks et al., 1974; cf. Hymes, 1974; Parker, 1984; Sigman, 1981 for alternative views). From this viewpoint, the conversational model is said to be, respectively, applicable across interaction situations, yet adaptable to the real-time exigencies and contingencies of actual interaction events. "By virtue of its context-free property, the turn-taking mechanism is a general and abstract resource usable by *any* conversationalist in *any* conversation" (West & Zimmerman, 1982, p. 527, emphasis added).

The context-sensitive position is supported by an additional claim, namely that conversation is a locally-oriented, locally-managed, and locally-produced phenomenon (Sacks et al., 1974). This is to suggest that the structure of conversation at any one time is dependent on, and is emergent from, speaker/hearers' moment-by-moment behavioral selections. Levinson (1983) notes that many of the variations observable across conversations—e.g., lapses between interactants' turns may or may not occur, turns may consist of verbal units as small as "y'know" or "yeah," or as large as a multi-sentential story— "are allowed for basically because the system is locally managed, i.e., it operates on a turn-by-turn basis, organizing just the transition from current speaker" (p. 300).

This conception of conversation as a locally-managed activity has largely precluded coordination with an earlier research tradition studying the hierarchical, contextualized, and preprogrammed features of face-to-face interaction (Scheflen, 1968). That is, current conversation scholarship seems not to have integrated research on interaction from a structural linguistic perspective (e.g., Birdwhistell, 1970; McQuown, 1971; Scheflen, 1973). This earlier research emphasized the a priori contextual constraints on interaction and the multilevel organization of behavior.

We do not intend these remarks to serve as criticism of contemporary conversation scholarship; rather, we use this opportunity to acknowledge the existence of alternative approaches to interaction analysis, and to suggest methodological consequences of the various approaches. What are some of the methodological implications of a local management view of conversation? First, several research topics are more conducive to a contextual and hierarchical view of communication; these topics are not prominently displayed by contemporary scholarship. We can briefly note three such lacunae in the literature: (a) the creation, invocation, and reinvocation of interaction agendas or programs across multiple episodes; (b) procedures for establishing the social acceptability, as opposed to interaction relevance or situatedness, of conversational topics; and (c) processes by which locally-managed behavior serves to segment and organize the multiple phases and levels of communication events (cf. Scheflen, 1968; Sigman, 1983a; Sinclair & Coulthard, 1975; see also Gallant & Kleinman, 1983, for a discussion of the differences between ethnomethodological and symbolic interactionist approaches to talk).

A second methodological concomitant of conversation analysts' local orientation concerns data generation. Currently, little conversation scholarship is carried out within a fieldwork tradition emphasizing long-term contact and familiarity with one interacting group or community. The empiricist and localist notions that behavioral organization can be developed, respectively (a) from the talk itself, (b) as it unfolds, leads to an emphasis on texts—i.e., iconic traces of conversation, see below—as a basis for analysis. Although there are exceptions, most conversation analysts do not engage in prolonged observation sessions prior to taping (or filming), or conduct interviews prior or subsequent to making the audio-visual records. Our discussion will sketch work by those researchers (Corsaro, 1982; Grimshaw, 1982; Gumperz, 1979, 1982; Mathiot, 1982; Stubbs, 1983) who differ from the Sacks-Schegloff-Jefferson tradition in the use of, and rationale for, conducting ethnographic fieldwork and informant questioning.

On average, conversation researchers tend to draw upon various transcripts of naturally occurring conversation for analyses of features of whole conversations (cf. the papers in Craig & Tracy, 1983; also Labov and Fanshel, 1977), or select out instances of particular units of behavior—conduct "data runs"—across conversations (e.g., Jefferson, 1972; Schegloff, 1980). Noteworthy, in this regard, the University of Texas at Austin has recently established a library of conversational tapes and transcripts (Koch, Glenn, & Hopper, 1985), and the Speech Communication Association has assembled a comparable directory of materials available to interested research groups (Shimanoff, 1983). One assumption of such practices is that "secondary research" on materials not originally observed and/or recorded by the analyst is acceptable. Indeed, a further assumption is that research on talk without benefit of direct observational knowledge of the community and its communication events is feasible. (See Corsaro, 1982, and Sigman, 1985, for discussions on integrating ethnographic data with conversational data.)

Theme (5). Continuous and Emergent Categorization

Finally, conversation analysis must be conceptually distinguished from other investigations exploring verbal data, especially from one technique with which it shares superficial resemblance—content analysis. Speier (1973) contrasts the two enterprises with the case of topic analysis in this manner: *"For us, topic is but another element of conversational structure around which participants organize their concerted interactions.* Accordingly we are led to ask: *What does a topic do in a conversation,* rather than what are the topics?" (p. 19, emphasis in original). The former question is addressed by conversation analysis, the latter by content analysis.

Content analysis (see Bowers, 1970) typically begins with a set of categories for listing what the conversation (or other text) under study is about; it tabulates the frequency of the various topic categories discussed, and, perhaps also, the transitional probabilities between and among topics. In contrast, conversation analysis makes problematic the notion of "topic," asking how speakers construct utterances about a given topic, how they signal topic shifts and terminations, and how they mark the relevance (or nonrelevance) of their turns for the topic. Such questions lead to the kind of "nonintuitive descriptions" which Schenkein (1978, p. 7) characterizes as the commitment of conversation analysis. Generally, this goal is held to be attainable only when close scrutiny is laid on the details of talk, which requires that the analyst bring a probing and continuous openness to the transcripts, rather than an arbitrary and predetermined set of categories (see the discussion below on conversation analysis as an iterative procedure).

There are several additional problems left unexplored by content analysis which are keystones of conversation analysis. First, the emergent nature of conversation analysis permits the discovery of novel features of talk by having the investigator constantly make the comprehensibility of language problematic (see Atkinson & Drew, 1979). Second, it recognizes that talk is composed of a variety of units, for example, single turns, adjacency pairs, insertion sequences, moves, and so on and that consideration of each type may be appropriate at different stages of analysis and for different research topics. Third, conversation analysts contend that there are no a priori formal criteria for establishing analytic units; in most cases, the "meaning" and "function" of utterances can not be judged on the basis of previously defined syntactic and/or semantic features of the utterances (see below). Rather, establishing the unit identity(ies) of utterances may require reference to subsequent turns at talk, including not immediately adjacent ones, as part of a determination of what they "accomplished," that is, how the various potential meanings were selected upon by subsequent participants' talk. As Schegloff (1984a) notes: "The use of the sheer occurrence of the lexical items, without regard to the placement of the utterances in which they occur in the sequential organization of conversation, can be badly misleading, though not implausible" (p. 30). An invitation, for example, can be accomplished by a question ("Why don't you come and visit me?"), an imperative ("Come and visit me"), and even a declarative statement ("You haven't visited me in months")—yet each one of these syntactic forms can be placed (and can be seen to be systematically placed by speakers) in the service of other conversational functions. Units for conversation analysis can not be specified, therefore, via a priori formal operationalizations, but rather only by the examination of the sequential placement and consequences of each utterance in its turn and across turns.

An additional consideration here is that most content analysis coding schemes are unable to recognize the multifunctionality of utterances, and the multiple rule systems generating utterances (Cicourel, 1980a,b). Conversation analysis, in contrast, aims to take behavioral multifunctionality into account (see *Theme 1* above): "The philosopher of language and the linguist must face the problem that the classification of an utterance is based on several sources of information, and . . . an utterance can be construed as indicating more than one message" (Cicourel, 1980b, p. 15). We will see how such recognition is accomplished.

Finally, a related criticism of coding schemes is that they represent an imposition on the verbal data of categories operating within the researcher's sphere. As such, they do not model the interpretive procedures likely to have been employed by speaker/hearers in the production and reception of talk. Although it is certainly the case that conversation analysts place interpretive overlays of their own on conversation, there is a nontrivial sense in which *these explanations are assumed to represent actions engaged in by the participants and grounded in a life-world shared by analysts and participants.* More specifically, the orderliness analyzed by conversation investigators is said to be oriented to, and sustained by, the participants themselves; and the problems regarded by researchers as worthy of study are considered practical (interactional) problems that the participants must resolve. This places clear methodological constraints and obligations on researchers. Jefferson (1972) points to these methodological issues in discussing the analysis of a conversational sequence:

> Ordered letters will be used to mark a possible "sequence" where, then, it will remain to be shown that something more than arbitrary notation is involved; that these "sequences" are mechanisms in which orientation to parts and to the relationship of these parts is involved (p. 316).

In keeping with the empiricist notions warranting an interactional vocabulary as described above, West and Zimmerman (1982) note: "Getting close to an empirical social world and understanding it from the point of view of the member does not require empathetic understanding or access to the subjectivity of actors" (p. 527). Rather, the transcripts represent "public materials" (p. 524) which can be seen "to *display* speakers' understanding . . ., [and which] thereby make available to the *analyst* a basis in the data for claiming what the coparticipants' understanding is of prior utterances, for as they display it to one another, we can see it too" (Schegloff, 1984a, p. 38, emphasis in original).

In summary, the above five themes abstracted from the conversation analysis literature emphasize the goals of a nondeterministic description of conversational structure developing out of a non-a piori inquiry into the locally-managed character of conversation. It was further suggested that such analysis needs to be grounded in how participants themselves orient to conversational phenomena. This emphasis on participant orientation leads to a consideration of conversations as containing public materials for inquiry. In the following section we present some of the critical issues concerning the acquisition of such data.

Data Sources and Transcription

Ochs (1979) suggests that the transcription process, inasmuch as it provides the analyst with his/her primary manipulable data, must be handled with "care." The following is a brief discussion of key considerations in this area: source selection; recording techniques; notation; and formatting.

McLaughlin (1984) indentifies five sources of data which are commonly used in conversation research: (a) "naturalistic" conversation in everyday, ordinary settings; (b) "natural" speech obtained in laboratory or other controlled environments; (c) specific speech samples that are elicited by direct request of the researcher; (d) samples of "spoken" discourse taken from literary and/or historical sources; and (e) apocryphal examples of interactional behavior constructed by the researcher him/herself. Conversation analysts tend to rely on spontaneously generated talk. For instance, some of the early studies relied on telephone calls, one of the easiest social contexts for such data collection (see Schegloff, 1968).

Once a source for data acquisition has been decided upon, a recording technique must be chosen. Conversation analysis has traditionally involved audio-channel recordings. McLaughlin (1984) assesses this tendency thus: "There is evidence that nonverbal behaviors may play a critical role in (certain) features of conversational interaction. . . . For this reason, videotaping is recommended, even though for most conversation researchers it has not been the technique of choice" (p. 247). No matter what event and recording focus is finally chosen by the researcher, emphasis should be placed on one key methodological point: "Adhere to the criterion of *naturalness*. . . . Minimize the intrusiveness of [the] recording equipment" (Hopper et al., 1986, p. 174, emphasis in original).

Having collected some audio/video traces of interaction, the analyst begins the transcription process proper. West and Zimmerman (1982) note that the process of "transcribing conversational data for analytical purposes entails strictest attention to what is heard as it is heard, in fine detail. The job is time-consuming and painstaking, to be sure (it may very well require 8 to 10 hours of time to transcribe each hour of audiotape; the ratio increases with video)" (p. 518). Transcription is not easily turned over to research assistants for often in this phase of the contact with data many of the hunches regarding how the talk "works" and "is held together" first emerge. Indeed, researchers generally listen to tapes accompanied by transcripts as part of the analysis phase of their projects.

As regards the actual details of transcription notation, researchers are urged to familiarize themselves with the work of Gail Jefferson (summarized in Schenkein, 1978, pp. xi-xvi), whose conventions are now widely used by contributors to the research literature. Although her system can in no way be considered "complete," Jefferson's conventions are useful in that they allow for the use of standard typewriter symbols. As the researcher develops some experience, he/she can modify the transcription system to focus on conversational objects of concern. For example, Labov and Fanshel (1977) graph intonation patterns alongside a transcript of the conversation. Goodwin's study (1981) on the negotiated construction of turns by speakers and hearers required distinguishing shifts in eye gaze directed to different conversational participants and coordinating these shifts with the utterance output.

A key question regarding notation and the process of transcription concerns the degree of naturalistic detail to be included. There are no simple answers. For example, Ochs (1979) points out: "One of the important features of a transcript is that it should not have too much information. . . . Selectivity, then, is to be encouraged. . . . The transcript should reflect the particular interests—the hypothesis to be examined—of the researcher" (p.44). In contrast, Jefferson (1971) argues that the transcription process is never complete, but should be performed as minutely as possible so that the transcripts can be used repeatedly: "A task we have undertaken is to provide transcripts that not only serve for current research interests, but are 'research generative' " (cited in West & Zimmerman, 1982, p. 515). This second orientation is especially recommended for researchers intending to create permanent files of conversations for future data runs (see above).

A related issue concerns the different amounts of detail generated by transcriptions which attempt some approximation of phonetic production using standard orthography, versus those which engage in "normalization," the practice of rendering what was said into "proper" language. With regard to the former methodological choice, Treichler (1984) points out that too detailed a phonetic transcript can do violence to readers' ability to understand the text; she criticizes stereotyped attempts to capture the sounds of the talk as being superfluous. Stubbs (1983) also questions the value of micro-detailed transcriptions; "There is a danger that such conventions are a kind of folk phonetics, marking, for example, stress and intonation in an *ad hoc* way, without reference to any theory of phonology" (p. 229).

From another perspective, however, the failure to indicate particular pronunciations, to provide phoneticized transcripts, can result in "lost data" and "lost research problems" (West & Zimmerman, 1982, p. 517). In addition, Ochs (1979) points out that there is an underlying assumption regarding communication in the application of normalization procedures. "Utterances are pieces of information, and this, in turn, assumes that language is used to express ideas [through words]" (p. 45).

Finally, a brief note regarding transcription format or page layout. Ochs (1979) argues: "The format of a transcript influences the interpretation process carried out by the reader [researcher]" (p. 47). For example, "the standard 'script' format . . . tends to impose a contingent relation between immediately adjacent utterances of different speakers" (p. 47). Such a contingency may not be appropriate to the theoretical concerns being addressed by the research. This format contrasts with the one developed by Scheflen (1973), which plots out the verbal contributions by all participants simultaneously through time; the latter method emphasizes the collaborative and coordinating efforts of each participant in the total event. Similarly, Koch's use of musical notation in the study of video arcades blurs the distinction between turn alternations in order to focus on the embeddedness of talk in the total noise environment (Hopper et al., 1986).

Stubbs' (1983) conclusion is that there is "no method of transcription which is appropriate for all studies of discourse" (p. 229). Therefore, it seems reasonable that individual research reports specify the type of transcription conventions employed and the rationale for the particular choice. The following works are recommended as representative of the variety of transcription systems and formats available:

McQuown (1971); Kendon (1977); Ochs (1979); Pittenger, Hockett, and Danehy (1960); Scheflen (1973); and Zivin (1978).

Units and Relations

As noted above, there is no published set of uniform procedures for analyzing and interpreting conversational data. Reading across the diverse contributions to the literature, several methodological "styles" seem evident to us. For example, Speier (1972) recognizes two strategies for the analysis of a particular transcript (from mealtime conversation) available to him:

> One strategy of analyzing our data, then, could consist of examining the natural progression of the meal through its stages to see how that temporal organization also organizes the ongoing speech of participants. The other strategy would be to concentrate entirely upon the utterance-by-utterance exchanges that sequentially occur and treat each participant's turn at talking for the general properties that exist in the exchanges, whether or not they are relevant for the particular type of practical activity at hand (p. 417).

The latter approach is the one more commonly taken by conversation analysts. It reflects the previously discussed concern for isolating local organizing features of interaction which are not context-specific.

The distinctions made by Speier are similar to the "from below" and "from above" perspectives articulated by Sigman (1983b), and the "bottom up" and "top down" views of Cicourel (1980b). The from-below and bottom-up approaches are ones "in which the dialogue is parsed and speech act units are identified according to criteria developed by philosophers and linguists" (Cicourel, 1980b, p. 20), and sequential organization is assessed on a turn-by-turn basis. There is little regard for the social context in which the conversation(s) occur, for as Handel (1982) observes: "So long as the appropriate [conversational] practices are employed in the conversations studied, there is no need for the conversations to have occurred in a single setting or among a single group of individuals" (p. 131). In contrast, from-above and top-down approaches, having been strongly influenced by ethnographic theory and method, represent attempts to examine how particular conversational units are tied to organizing principles or features of the larger context, i.e., the event. These approaches are concerned with the structure of interaction episodes, and how this structure serves to frame or constrain the moment-by-moment utterance contributions of speaker/hearers (cf., Kendon, 1982; Scheflen, 1974).

Despite the different foci of bottom-up and top-down approaches to conversation analysis, the two must address a common set of procedural questions: From where do the initial insights, interpretations, and explanations concerning the data emerge? What are the "recognition" or "intelligibility rules" (Gergen, 1982) for establishing units for conversation analysis?

It is convenient to think of conversation research as being initially constituted by three analysis activities: (a) the generation or abstraction of units of talk from the transcripts; (b) the establishment of the various relationships between and among the units under consideration; and (c) the development of a warrant for claiming "that such sequential expectations actually are oriented to by participants" (Levinson, 1983, p. 326). These three activities are interrelated.

Our reading of the ever emerging research literature indicates at least three sources for explanations of the data: (a) some analysts approach the transcripts with a hunch as to the phenomenon to be studied, perhaps as a result of naturalistic observation—either formal or informal—or personal interaction experience; (b) some analysts set out to extend previous lines of research, either disagreeing with prevailing sentiments expressed in the literature (e.g., Parker, 1984; Sigman, 1981) or hoping to refine previous formulations; and (c) multiple replayings of taped conversations and multiple readings of accompanying transcripts may lead to the questioning of *what* is taking place in the interaction and *how* this is being accomplished. The latter strategy is especially recommended by Sacks (1984), who writes: "Treating some actual conversation in an unmotivated way, that is, giving some consideration to whatever can be found in any particular conversation we happen to have our hands on, subjecting it to investigation in any direction that can be produced from it, can have strong payoffs" (p. 27).

One initial unitization consideration is "the size of the units to be studied: basically smaller or larger than sentences" (Stubbs, 1983, p. 10). The units typically studied by conversation analysts include single lexical items ("mm-hmm"), multiple lexical strings constituting a speaker's single turn at talk ("John, it's your turn to speak"), and utterances across two or more speakers' turns ("What are you doing tonight?"/"Nothing much"/"Want to catch a movie?").

Although there is no single rule for generating units of analysis, several conversation analysts argue that it is functional categories of discourse which ultimately must be elucidated, not syntactic or semantic features of sentences. It is the analyst's ability to "read" functions into the various units isolated in a transcript that is the hallmark of conversation analysis.

The analyst uses the aforementioned means of parsing a transcript only as a preliminary step in sorting out what the dialogue "consists of" and what "is happening" therein. As noted, the linguistic units must at some point be transformed into conversationally-relevant ones. The analyst must be alert to the functional slots being filled by the particular behavioral units initially isolated. Once a given conversational function (or functional position) has been developed, the analyst must then search for other examples of the function in the original as well as other transcripts, and for additional behavioral units which appear to serve it.[5]

How does an investigator specifically establish the interactional function of an utterance apart from its intrasentential syntactic or semantic form? First, Sinclair and Coulthard (1975) use their knowledge of the social situation, the participants' history of shared experiences, and manifest goals of the interaction in order to arrive at the conversational uses of particular linguistic forms. Related to this, the analyst may interpret the consequences of an utterance, that is, what follows from its production, in order to establish function(s). In some cases, the existence of "repair work" (Goffman, 1971) makes transparent a disjunction between the consequential structure typically found for an utterance and that of the recipient's actual response in a particular moment (see below).[6] Finally, Thompson (1984, p. 105) notes that consistent intonational patterns can be used to disambiguate utterances.

The study of utterance functioning implies consideration of the placement of the utterance of concern in relation to "surrounding" utterances in the overall talk. Function emerges as part of an analysis of the behavior's location in a structure. In asking what a given utterance "does," it is necessary to consider the interpretations seemingly made public by responses to it. In this manner, the research activities establishing conversational units, unit functions, and relationships between units are separated in the present discussion for heuristic purposes only; in practice, they are closely related—perhaps even simultaneous—procedures. The sequence described up to this

---

[5] In addition, conversation analysts must be attentive to the possibility of unit multifunctionality (see Stubbs, 1983). Conversational functions may be hierarchically arranged, and utterances may exhibit both "primary" and "subsidiary" functions.

[6] It is easy when referring to conversation analysis to lapse into a "sender" (or "speaker") and "receiver" ("listener") vocabulary. This is unfortunate. Ultimately, conversation analysis will need to be integrated into a more contextual and transactional view of communication.

point, involving a movement from linguistic units to conversational functions, is not absolute. For example, it is also possible for the analyst, upon hearing a bit of dialogue and/or perusing a transcript, to discern an initial set of functions or actions being accomplished and then ask how these functions are carried out.

The most basic unit relationship of interest to conversation analysts, especially to those working within the Sacks-Schegloff-Jefferson tradition, is *sequentiality* (Zimmerman, 1985).[7] Jefferson (1972, 1973) notes that the term "sequential relations" is not meant to refer to all temporally or spatially adjacent utterances, but to those utterances which can be seen to have some structural and functional ties to each other, ties that are generalizable across multiple examples of the unit type. Two (or more) utterances are said to be sequentially located to the extent that the analyst is able to say, not only that the utterances "go" (i.e., appear) together, but also "belong" together. At the most rudimentary level, sequentiality involves immediately adjacent utterances produced by different speakers, in which the "first pair part" implicates a limited range of appropriate "second pair parts," as in the case of a Question/Answer Sequence (Schegloff & Sacks, 1973). (For a discussion of the sequentiality of units that are not adjacent but separated spatially and temporally, see Birdwhistell, 1970; Scheflen, 1973; and Sigman, 1983a.)

An important methodological issue concerning units found to have sequential relations with each other must be acknowledged here. The existence of standard (repetitive) sequential relationships usually gives rise in linguistics to the notion that the two (or more) sequential units actually represent constituents or subunits of some "larger" behavioral unit. To the extent that the units fully constrain or condition each other's appearance(s), so that the appearance of utterance A without the follow-up utterance B, or the appearance of B without the prior A, is "heard" or "seen" as unusual, then the more likely is the analyst to describe the two utterances as constituting a *single* conversational unit, that is, one with a complex "internal" structure. In other words, the repeated existence of certain unit relationships produces a higher order unitization of the transcript.

Conversation analysts do not necessarily proceed in quite as linear a manner as the discussion implies, that is, moving from the isolation of separate linguistic units (e.g., a question and an answer) to statements about unit sequentiality, to the emergence and establishment

---

[7] Sequentiality is not the only relationship between units. Others include: (a) embeddedness (cf., Goffman, 1971); (b) co-occurrences (cf., Schegloff, 1972); and (c) extensions and completions (cf., Speier, 1972). The analysis procedure is much the same as for sequentiality.

of the more complex unit (e.g., Question/Answer Sequence). The methodological sequence could be reversed for some researchers who begin the analysis with a sense of the larger unit and then decompose it into constituent functional units.

On this last point, a cautionary note is warranted. We recognize here the potential error of reading sequential presentations of data in final reports as indicators of the actual steps followed by conversation analysts. This danger is especially heightened by the absence of explicit methodological descriptions in most conversation analysis publications. Nevertheless, our own experiences in studying conversation bear out this characterization of the enterprise as being non-linear in direction, and as involving multiple starting points for understanding the data. The following sequential idealization of conversation analysis procedures should be understood from this perspective:

1. the researcher uncovers a unit/phenomenon of interest to be studied
2. the researcher develops an initial definition (operationalization) for recognizing this unit
3. he/she searches for additional examples
4. some sort of "structural" analysis is performed, relating how the unit functions or relates to preceding and proceeding units
5. given the analysis in (4), the researcher is likely to revise his/her definition of the unit
6. as a result of the revisions in (5), the researcher can—and should— go back over the transcript files for additional examples.

As can be seen, the process is iterative and recursive; there are likely to be a number of recyclings of steps (5) and (6). Each step repeated should serve to refine the understanding of the functional unit and of the diverse linguistic units commonly associated with this function. At each stage of this expanding recursive process researchers must ground their knowledge claims, that is, generate warrants, regarding the analytic units, unit functions, and unit relations (cf. Glaser, 1965). The procedures for warranting interpretations of the data are discussed in the following section.

Nature of Knowledge Claims

Perhaps the most frequently asked question regarding conversation analysis concerns how the researcher can substantiate the interpretive claims concerning functional relationships of units. Once again, there are no established formulae to accomplish this. However, one requirement placed on the conversation analyst's treatment of the data can be noted here: "For each substantive claim, the methodology employed in CA [conversation analysis] requires evidence not only that some aspect of conversation *can* be viewed in the way suggested, but that it actually is so conceived by the participants producing it" (Levinson, 1983, pp. 318–319, emphasis in original). Traditionally, conversation analysts have taken a text-based approach in substantiating such claims. That is, researchers have turned primarily to the transcripts (in conjunction with recordings) to inform their interpretations. This requires that the analyst find evidence *in the transcripts* that speaker/hearers orient and attend to the particular conversational device(s) in a way suggested by the analyst's interpretation. As Schegloff (1984a) writes: "Utterances are built to display speakers' understanding. . . . They also thereby make available to the *analyst* a basis in the data for claiming what the coparticipants' understanding is of prior utterances" (p. 38, emphasis in original).

Levinson (1983) suggest that the establishment of a requirement that researchers document participants' orientation in the interaction to the talk phenomenon under review, and the availability of such information in the transcripts of participants' talk, "offer us a way of avoiding the indefinitely extendable and unverifiable categorization and speculation of actors' intents" (p. 319), typical of other approaches to verbal data. However, one must be careful of a potential problem with tautological analysis: the existence of particular conversational units in the transcripts, as isolated by the researcher, are used to generate particular items that need interpretation and then to substantiate the interpretation. To our knowledge there has been no published discussion or resolution of this issue (see below).

A brief example is used here as a demonstration of the *empiricist language requirement* of conversation analysis. This excerpt is taken from Jefferson's (1972) discussion of "side sequences":

> That participants orient to such things as (O)-(S)-(R) [ongoing activity/ side activity/resumption of original activity] as "parts," and parts in relation to one another, might be initially suggested by pointing out the use of items like "Oh, Okay" (II); items that can signal "satisfactory termination" of the action they follow. That the satisfactory termination of *an* action provides for the initiating of another action, and that participants produce actions according to that fact, might be seen via the "By the way" fragment . . ., where "Okay" is something like a "pre-final" object—that is, it at least *occurs* immediately prior to "Buh bye." That it is *placed* immediately prior to "Buh bye," i.e., provides

for the initiating of "goodbyes," can be observed in that both parties use it that way (p. 317, emphasis in original).

As this example demonstrates, the researcher working within the Sacks-Schegloff-Jefferson tradition is limited to a text-based analysis, and must use the transcripts and recordings as both objects to be interpreted and as sources for indicating speaker/hearers' similar interpretations (and employment) of conversational resources. The general paradigm is to see how conversational utterances are responded to. This procedure is followed because it is assumed that participants display their own interpretations of prior utterances in subsequent ones. However, "not all problems of hearing [and interpretation] require resolution by looking at actions that are exclusively conversational, i.e., as next utterances" (Speier, 1972, p. 410). The analyst may also refer to "nonspoken action" performed by recipients of the talk, for example, smiling, passing salt, opening a window.

However, we suggest that none of the above examples of text-based analysis represents a "pure" case of a conversational understanding being portrayed empirically by speaker/hearers to their coparticipants—and so being made available to the analyst. How does Jefferson (1972) warrant, for example, the interpretation of "Oh, okay" as a witness of "satisfactory termination"? How does she know which features of the dialogue are oriented to with "Okay," "By the way," and "Buh bye?" Similarly, is it not the analyst himself who is using such terms as "Well he says" and "By what standard" to bolster an understanding of ambiguity in the Schegloff (1984) case? It is certainly conceivable for alternative understandings regarding the objects of speaker/hearers' orientation to be brought to these extracts (see Atkinson & Drew, 1979). This is not intended as criticism of the Sacks-Schegloff-Jefferson position that analysis and analytic claims be rooted in the transcripts/recordings. Rather, we wish to emphasize the preeminent role of interpretation and labeling assumed for participants by the conversation analyst, as well as for those bits of "data" subsequently used as evidence of speaker/hearer orientation.

To elaborate, it can be seen that, as a competent interactional participant, the researcher brings to the transcripts and/or recordings an ability to identify conversational devices and activities. Prior to the initial inspection of a transcript, the researcher may not have established specific search procedures, levels of investigation, or analytic categories. However, inspection of a specific utterance of talk may provide the analyst with recognition of some common or noteworthy conversational phenomenon. This sense of "ah-ha," of discovery and excavation of some already known item, emerges from the analyst's prior cultural experience and familiarity with the phenomenon as these interact with the text, albeit not in any formal way. On the existence of such prior understanding, Nofsinger (1977) correctly observes: "Some students of talk would argue that . . . a categorization must have been possible at the very beginning of the analysis phase in order for . . . an extensive set of interpretations to have been made" (p. 19).

For those following within the ethomethodological tradition, the researcher's background knowledge regarding talk cannot be eliminated; it constitutes an indispensible methodological tool. Wittgenstein (1953), much earlier, pointed out that there is no way to discuss a phenomenon without our already understanding it in some way (see Apel, 1980; Winch, 1958). However, it is advisable for there to be explicit recognition and statement of the analyst's knowledge grounding. *Conversation researchers should be asked to defend the applicability of their cultural understandings to the particular transcripts and recorded events under study.* If the analyst advances a member-of-the-culture warrant for his/her ability to do conversation analysis—i.e., to provide meaningful organization for the verbal data—then he/she should also demonstrate that the talk being investigated was in fact produced by members of the same culture for which the analyst claims membership and cultural awareness (see Nofsinger, 1977). This does not contradict the requirement that the analysis be tied to transcribed data; it only prescribes that the interpretive work on the "empirical" data be more firmly explicated by the analyst.

The alternative approach is to permit non-text-based sources to be included in conversation research. This procedure is followed by a number of conversation analysts not working within the Sacks-Schegloff-Jefferson tradition. Cicourel (1980a, p. 112) notes that Labov and Fanshel's (1977) "utterance expansions" utilize several of these data sources. (For a general discussion of ethnographic methodology, which is beyond the scope of this chapter, see Agar, 1980, Spradley, 1980; see below for a discussion regarding interview data.)

Briefly, there are a variety of non-text-based sources for the "verification"—perhaps, more accurately, "inspiration" and "adjudication"—of the researcher's interpretations, including:

1. Background knowledge of the event by the analyst based on his/her prior observation of events similar to the one currently under analysis.
2. Informant interviews, for example, eliciting their taken-for-granted knowledge regarding the goals, typical organization, and so on of particular conversational events.

3. Subjects' reactions to, and interpretations upon, viewing (or hearing) tapes and seeing the transcripts.

These data sources are not mutually exclusive, but rather are interrelated. Moreover, to varying degrees, they place the researcher in the position of weighing alternative sources in building a "case" for the interpretation. Data from textual and non-text-based sources do not serve as confirmation of one's interpretations, but they provide weight in favor or against particular interpretations. In this respect, it may be best to see conversation analysis as a rhetorical enterprise which operates to get the researcher to find some way to organize diverse verbal data. The organizational insights provided by the conversation analyst should not be thought of as "valid" or "invalid," but rather as "consistent" or "inconsistent" with the overall data, and as "plausible" or "implausible."[8]

Informant Data

As noted, conversation analysis practiced within the Sacks-Schegloff-Jefferson ethnomethodological tradition argues against the generation of, and reliance on, informant data. This practice is not accepted by all—or even most—other researchers concerned with the organization of conversation. It is to these dissenting methodologists that we turn our attention in the remainder of the chapter. Informant data emphasizing the verbalizable perspectives and meanings of members-of-the-culture have been used in a variety of ways by conversation researchers. This section concerns some of the ways informant data have been employed in recent research, and, secondly, attempts to make explicit some of the problems often overlooked by researchers relying on informant data.

Mathiot (1982) provides a framework for the analysis of face-to-face interaction which relies almost entirely on the use of "respondents" to segment the behavioral stream into culturally meaningful units. Mathiot argues: "If the analyst is a member-of-the-culture, at best he will not be 'wrong' in his meaning attribution, but he will account only for his own views. As a consequence his analytic generalizations will not be valid" (p. 3).

Mathiot's (1982) method proceeds as follows: The event being

---

[8] Stubbs (1983) argues: "Different kinds of evidence may be combined, but the account will always depend on the reader filling in knowledge, and will never be finally validated" (p. 234).

investigated is first observed via ethnographic methods, and a video-
or audio-tape is made as a representative specimen. In conjunction
with choosing the interaction event for study, the researcher also
chooses a respondent, that is, someone who is familiar with the type
of event being studied, having participated in this or similar episodes
as a cultural member. After collecting the specimen and enlisting a
respondent (or respondents), the analyst asks this individual to name
or label the event, as well as to describe it in terms of a general
mental image. This interview, which is nondirective, is recorded and
transcribed; it provides data which Mathiot labels the "recollection."
Subsequent to the initial phase of fieldwork, the specimen is transcribed and presented to the respondent in order to elicit "blow-by-
blow" descriptions. The latter data are obtained from the respondent
as he/she views or listens to the specimen tape, and consist of com-
mentary (also recorded and transcribed) about what goes on in the
specimen. Finally, the respondent is given a transcript of the blow-
by-blow account, and is asked to segment it into categories of "information" and/or "activity," that is, to outline the separate activities
and phases accomplished in the specimen episode. (Frankel and Beckman [1982] report on a method similar to that used by Mathiot [1982]
which they describe as being based on the principles of ethnography.)

Gumperz's (1978, 1979) use of informants differs somewhat from
the approach by Mathiot. Instead of using informants as the primary
means of producing or segmenting data, Gumperz employs cultural
members in an effort to corroborate or "flesh out" his own analyses
of the data. For example, he describes the methods used to discover
contextualization cues by writing:

> They rely partly on comparative analysis of a wide variety of ethnically
> homogenous in-group and ethnically mixed encounters, and partly on
> indirect elicitation procedures and role play experiments in which par-
> ticipants in a conversation, or others of similar background, listen to
> tape-recorded passages and are questioned to discover the perceptual
> cues they use in arriving at their interpretation (1979, pp. 276–277).

It must be remarked, however, that Gumperz is not always explicit
about how the use of informant data fits into, or informs, his sociolinguistic analyses. For instance, in his discussion of an interview
between a British government worker and an Indian teacher, he
comments on one segment of the transcript by noting: "Listeners of
English background who notice this shift in prosodic cues tend to
dismiss it as rather minor. Many Indian speakers, on the other hand,
readily identify it as a sign of strong affect" (1979, p. 279). Although

this reference to British and Indian speakers of English suggests that informant data are being used, the precise sample of conversationalists and the specific context of data elicitation are not made clear.

From a general ethnography of communication stance, the various uses of informants can be summarized thus:

> The subjects can be asked: (1) to assist in the segmentation of discourse behavior into appropriate units of analysis . . .; (2) to provide explanations and interpretations of their behavior; (3) to augment the number and type of cases recorded by the investigator; and (4) to validate (e.g., qualify or refute) the researcher's own interpretations. (Sigman, 1985, p. 120)

The following outlines some of the problems associated with informant questioning which serve to lessen—but not eliminate—the value of such data. First, the informant perspective elicited by interviews may not be trustworthy. Mathiot's (1978, 1982) method seems to assume, for example, that the information provided by the informants during the interview session is isomorphic with the taken-for-granted information actually employed by them while participating in conversation. The reader is urged to review the ever mounting literature for and against using informants in this way (see Harré and Secord, 1972; Zimmerman, 1976).

Second, we assume that the interview situation itself structures—in ways not as yet fully researched or understood—the information informants are able to provide. That there are demand characteristics associated with researchers' questioning seems likely (cf. Adair, 1973; Rosenthal & Rosnow, 1969). Beyond this, the nature of the question/answer session as an organized interactional event may shape what the informant tells the researcher and the manner in which it is told. (A discussion of these problems and other interview-related problems can be found in Briggs', 1983, critique of the ethnographic interview.) Just as there have been conversation analyses of teacher-student (Sinclair & Coulthard, 1975) and psychologist-client (Labov & Fanshel, 1977) interaction, the present discussion leads us to suggest a need for conversation scholarship to turn some attention to the Question-Answer formats commonly employed in ethnographic interviews (cf. Agar, 1980).

Summary

Conversation researchers have yet to grapple successfully with the issue of generalizability or universality of the conversational structures which they develop from verbal data bases. Although some cross-cultural studies have been pursued (e.g., Godard, 1977; Keenan, 1976; Moerman, 1977), the findings are at best suggestive. For example, Keenan's examination of the applicability of Grice's (1978) conversational maxims leads her to suggest: "The value of Grice's proposal is that it provides a point of departure for ethnographers who wish to integrate their observations, and to propose stronger hypotheses related to general principles of conversation" (Keenan, 1976, p. 79).

One of the problems with extending conversation analysis across cultures and across communities within the same culture may reside in the methodological gaps in the literature. It is hoped that this chapter can provide an initial crystallization of prevailing methods and that it can serve as a basis for conducting research and as a point of departure for much needed debate concerning methodology.

References

Adair, J.G. (1973). *The human subject: The social psychology of the psychological experiment.* Boston: Little Brown.

Agar, M.A. (1980). *The professional stranger: An informal introduction to ethnography.* New York: Academic Press.

Apel, K.O. (1980). *Towards a transformation of philosophy.* London: Routledge and Kegan Paul.

Atkinson, J.M., & Drew, P. (1979). *Order in court.* Atlantic Highlands, NJ: Humanities Press.

Birdwhistell, R.L. (1970). *Kinesics and context.* Philadelphia, PA: University of Pennsylvania Press.

Bowers, J.W. (1970). Content analysis. In P. Emmert and W.D. Brooks (Eds.), *Methods of research in communication* (pp. 291–314). New York: Houghton Mifflin.

Briggs, C.L. (1983). Questions for the ethnographer: A critical examination of the role of the interview in fieldwork. *Semiotica, 46,* 233–261.

Cicourel, A.V. (1980a). Three models of discourse analysis: The role of social structure. *Discourse Processes, 3,* (2), 101–132.

Cicourel, A.V. (1980b). Language and social interaction: Philosophical and empirical issues. *Sociological Inquiry, 50,* (3/4), 1–30.

Corsaro, W.A. (1982). Something old and something new: The importance of prior ethnography in the collection and analysis of audiovisual data. *Sociological Methods and Research, 11,* 145–166.

Coulthard, R.M., & Montgomery, M. (Eds.). (1981). *Studies in discourse analysis.* London: Routledge and Kegan Paul.

Craig, R.T., & Tracy, K. (1983). *Conversational coherence: Form, structure and strategy.* Beverly Hills, CA: Sage.

Cushman, D.P., & Whiting, G.C. (1972). An approach to communication theory: Toward consensus on rules. *Journal of Communication, 22*, 217–238.

Daly, J.A. (1985). *The social cognition perspective on conversation.* Paper presented to the International Communication Association, Honolulu, Hawaii.

Delia, J. (1985). *The constructivist perspective on conversation.* Paper presented to the International Communication Association, Honolulu, Hawaii.

Frankel, R.M., & Beckman, H.B. (1982). Impact: An interaction-based method for preserving and analyzing clinical transactions. In L.S. Pettegrew, with P. Arnston, D. Bush, and K. Zoppi (Eds.), *Straight talk: Explorations in provider and patient interaction* (pp. 71–85). Louisville, KY: Humana.

Gallant, M.J., & Kleinman, S. (1983). Symbolic interactionism vs. ethnomethodology. *Symbolic Interaction, 6*, 1–18.

Geertz, C. (1983). *Local knowledge: Further essays in interpretive anthropology.* New York: Basic Books.

Gergen, K.J. (1982). *Toward transformation in social knowledge.* New York: Springer-Verlag.

Glaser, B.G. (1965). The constant comparative method of qualitative analysis. *Social Problems, 12*, 436–445.

Godard, D. (1977). Same setting, different norms: Phone call beginnings in France and the United States. *Language in Society, 6*, 209–219.

Goffman, E. (1971). *Relations in public.* New York: Harper & Row.

Goffman, E. (1983). The interaction order. *American Sociological Review, 48*, 1–17.

Goodwin, C. (1981). *Conversational organization: Interaction between speakers and hearers.* New York: Academic Press.

Grice, H.P. (1978). Further notes on logic and conversation. In P. Cole (Ed.), *Syntax and semantics, Vol. 9: Pragmatics.* New York: Academic Press.

Grimshaw, A.D. (1982). Sound-image data records for research on social interaction: Some questions and answers. *Sociological Methods and Research, 11*, 121–144.

Gumperz, J.J. (1978). Dialect and conversational inference in urban communication. *Language in Society, 7*, 393–409.

Gumperz, J.J. (1979). The retrieval of sociocultural knowledge in conversation. *Poetics Today, 1*, 273–286.

Gumperz, J.J. (1982). Fact and inference in courtroom testimony. In J.J. Gumperz (Ed.), *Language and social identity* (pp. 163–195). Cambridge: Cambridge University Press.

Handel, W. (1982). *Ethnomethodology: How people make sense.* Englewood Cliffs, NJ: Prentice-Hall.

Harré, R., & Secord, P.R. (1972). *The explanation of social behavior.* Oxford, England: Blackwell.

Harré, R., Clarke, D., & DeCarlo, N. (1985). *Motives and mechanisms: An introduction to the psychology of action.* London: Methuen.

Hopper, R., Koch, S., & Mandelbaum, J. (1986). Conversation analysis methods. In D. Ellis and W. Donahue (Eds.), *Contemporary issues in discourse processes* (pp. 169–186). Hillsdale, NJ: Erlbaum.

Hymes, D. (1974). *Foundations in sociolinguistics: An ethnographic approach.* Philadelphia, PA: University of Pennsylvania Press.

Jefferson, G.A. (1971). *A report on some difficulties encountered when using pseudonyms in research generative transcripts.* Unpublished manuscript, University of California at Irvine.

Jefferson, G.A. (1972). Side sequences. In D. Sudnow (Ed.), *Studies in social interaction* (pp. 294–338). New York: Free Press.

Jefferson, G.A. (1973). A case of precision timing in ordinary conversation. *Semiotica, 9,* 47–96.

Keenan, E.O. (1976). The universality of conversational postulates. *Language in Society, 5,* 67–80.

Keenan, E.O., & Schieffelin, B.B. (1976). Topic as a discourse notion: A study of topic in the conversations of children and adults. In C.N. Li (Ed.), *Subject and topic.* New York: Academic Press.

Kendon, A. (1977). *Studies in the behavior of social interaction.* Bloomington, IN: Indiana University Research Center for Language and Semiotic Studies.

Kendon, A. (1982). The organization of behavior in face-to-face interaction: Observations on the development of a methodology. In K.S. Scherer and P. Ekman (Eds.), *Handbook of methods in nonverbal behavior research* (pp. 440–505). Cambridge: Cambridge University Press.

Kendon, A. (1985). Some uses of gesture. In D. Tannen and M. Saville-Troike (Eds.), *Perspectives on silence.* Norwood, NJ: Ablex.

Koch, S., Glenn, P., & Hopper, R. (1985). *The conversation library users' handbook.* Unpublished manuscript, Department of Speech Communication, University of Texas at Austin.

Labov, W., & Fanshel, D. (1977). *Therapeutic discourse: Psychotherapy as conversation.* New York: Academic Press.

Levinson, S.C. (1983). *Pragmatics.* Cambridge, England: Cambridge University Press.

Litton-Hawes, E.M. (1977). A foundation for the study of everyday talk. *Communication Quarterly, 25,* (3), 2–11.

Mathiot, M. (1978). Toward a frame of reference for the analysis of face-to-face interaction. *Semiotica, 24,* 199–220.

Mathiot, M. (1982). The self-disclosure technique for ethnographic elicitation. In M. Herzfeld and M. Lenhart (Eds.), *Proceedings of the 5th Annual Meeting of the Semiotic Society of America.* Lubbock, Texas (pp. 339–346). New York: Plenum Press.

McLaughlin, M.L. (1984). *Conversation: How talk is organized.* Beverly Hills, CA: Sage.

McQuown, N.A. (Ed.). (1971). *The natural history of an interview.* Chicago, IL: University of Chicago Library, Microfilm Collection of Manuscripts on Cultural Anthropology.

Millar, F., & Bavelas, J.B. (1985). *The pragmatic/interactional perspective on conversation.* Paper presented to the International Communication Association, Honolulu, Hawaii.

Moerman, M. (1977). The preference for self-correction in a Tai conversational corpus. *Language, 53,* 872–882.

Nofsinger, R.E. (1977). A peek at conversational analysis. *Communication Quarterly, 25,* (3), 12–20.

Ochs, E. (1979). Transcription as theory. In E. Ochs & B.B. Schieffelin (Eds.), *Developmental pragmatics* (pp. 251–268). New York: Academic Press.

Parker, R. (1984). Conversational grouping and fragmentation: A preliminary investigation. *Semiotica, 50,* 43–68.

Pike, K. (1967). *Language in relation to a unified theory of the structure of human behavior.* The Hague: Mouton.

Pittenger, R.E., Hockett, C.F., & Danehy, J.J. (1960). *The first five minutes: A sample of microscopic interview analysis.* Ithaca, NY: Paul Martineau.

Pomerantz, A. (1978). Compliment responses: Notes on the co-operation of multiple constraints. In J. Schenkein (Ed.), *Studies in the organization of conversational interaction.* New York: Academic Press.

Psathas, G. (Ed.). (1979). *Everyday language: Studies in ethnomethodology.* New York: Irvington.

Rosenthal, R., & Rosnow, R.L. (Eds.). (1969). *Artifact in behavioral research.* New York: Academic Press.

Sacks, H. (1972). An initial investigation of the usability of conversational data for doing sociology. In D. Sudnow (Ed.), *Studies in social interaction* (pp. 31–74). New York: Free Press.

Sacks, H. (1984). Notes on methodology. In J.M. Atkinson and J. Heritage (Eds.), *Structures of social action* (pp. 21–27). Cambridge: Cambridge University Press.

Sacks, H., Schegloff, E. A., & Jefferson, G. (1974). A simplest systematics for the organization of turn-taking for conversation. *Language, 50,* 696–735.

Scheflen, A.E. (1968). Human communication: Behavioral programs and their integration in interaction. *Behavioral Science, 13,* 44–55.

Scheflen, A.E. (1973). *Communicational structure: Analysis of a psychotherapy transaction.* Bloomington, IN: Indiana University Press.

Scheflen, A.E. (1974). *How behavior means.* Garden City, NY: Doubleday.

Schegloff, E.A. (1968). Sequencing in conversational openings. *American Anthropologist, 70,* 1075–1095.

Schegloff, E.A. (1972). Notes on a conversational practice: Formulating place. In David Sudnow (Ed.), *Studies in social interaction* (pp. 75–119). New York: Free Press.

Schegloff, E.A. (1980). Preliminaries to preliminaries: "Can I ask you a question?" *Sociological Inquiry, 50,* 104–152.

Schegloff, E.A. (1984a). On some questions and ambiguities in conversation. In J.M. Atkinson and J. Heritage (Eds.), *Structures of social action: Studies in conversation analysis* (pp. 28–52). Cambridge, England: Cambridge University Press.

Schegloff, E.A. (1984b). On some gestures' relation to talk. In J.M. Atkinson and J. Heritage (Eds.), *Structures of social action: Studies in conversation analysis* (pp. 266–296). Cambridge, England: Cambridge University Press.

Schegloff, E.A., & Sacks, H. (1973). Opening up closings. *Semiotica, 8,* 289–327.

Schenkein, J. (Ed.). (1978). *Studies in the organization of conversational interaction.* New York: Academic Press.

Shimanoff, S.B. (1980). *Communication rules: Theory and research.* Beverly Hills, CA: Sage.

Shimanoff, S.B. (1983). *Directory of conversational researchers.* Department of Rhetoric, University of California at Davis.

Sigman, S.J. (1981). Some notes on conversational fission. *Working Papers in Sociolinguistics.* No. 91. Austin, TX: Southwest Educational Development Laboratory.

Sigman, S.J. (1983a). Some multiple constraints placed on conversational topics. In R.T. Craig and K. Tracy (Eds.), *Conversational coherence: Form, structure and strategy.* Beverly Hills, CA: Sage.

Sigman, S.J. (1983b). *Conversational coherence: Views from above and below.* Paper presented to the Speech Communication Association, Washington, D.C.

Sigman, S.J. (1985). Some common mistakes students make when learning discourse analysis. *Communication Education, 34,* 119–127.

Sinclair, J.M., & Coulthard, R.M. (1975). *Towards an analysis of discourse: The English used by teachers and pupils.* Oxford, England: Oxford University Press.

Speier, M. (1972). Some conversational problems for interactional analysis. In D. Sudnow (Ed.), *Studies in Social Interaction* (pp. 397–427). New York: Free Press.

Speier, M. (1973). *How to observe face-to-face interaction: A sociological introduction.* Pacific Palisades, CA: Goodyear.

Spradley, J.P. (1980). *Participant observation.* New York: Holt, Rinehart and Winston.

Stubbs, M. (1983). *Discourse analysis: The sociolinguistic analysis of natural language.* Chicago, IL: University of Chicago Press.

Tannen, D., & Saville-Troike, M. (Eds.). (1985). *Perspectives on silence.* Norwood, NJ: Ablex.

Thompson, J.B. (1984). *Studies in the theory of ideology.* Berkeley, CA: University of California Press.

Treichler, P.A. (1984). Review of *The social organization of doctor-patient communication* edited by S. Fisher and A.D. Todd. *Journal of Communication, 34,* (3), 214–219.

West, C., & Zimmerman, D.H. (1982). Conversation analysis. In K.R. Scherer and P. Ekman (Eds.), *Handbook of methods in nonverbal behavior research* (pp. 506–541). Cambridge, England: Cambridge University Press.

Winch, P. (1958). *The idea of a social science.* London: Routledge & Kegan Paul.

Wittgenstein, L. (1953). *Philosophical investigations.* London: Blackwell.

Zimmerman, D.H. (1976). A reply to Professor Coser. *American Sociologist, 11,* 4–13.

Zimmerman, D.H. (1985). *The conversation analysis perspective on conversation.*

Paper presented to the International Communication Association. Honolulu, Hawaii.

Zivin, G. (1978). Layers of description for studying contextual relations of facial gestures. *Sociolinguistics Newsletter, 9,* (2), 44–45.

CHAPTER 7

Dyadic Personal Relationships: Measurement Options

Leslie A. Baxter

The last decade has witnessed a burgeoning interest in the study of dyadic personal relationships. Complementing the longstanding study of marriage and the family is a growing body of work in acquaintanceship, friendship, and premarital romantic relationships (for reviews see Duck, 1982, 1984; Duck & Gilmour, 1981a, 1981b, 1981c; Duck & Perlman, 1985; Kelley et al., 1983). Among other indicators of the rapid growth of this area are the formation of an interdisciplinary Society for the Study of Social and Personal Relationships in 1984 and the initiation of the *Journal of Social and Personal Relationships* in the same year. Another indicator of growth in the study of personal relationships is the expanding domain of measurement and assessment techniques available to the researcher. A computerized search of *Psychological Abstracts, Sociological Abstracts,* and *ERIC* from 1975–1985 revealed well over 100 published studies whose primary focus was the development and psychometric adequacy of measures in the area of personal relationships.

The purpose of this chapter is to provide a selective review of personal relationships measures. In particular, the focus is on the most frequently employed type of measurement technique brought to bear in the study of personal relationships—insider reports on the relationship by one or both of the relationship partners (McCarthy, 1981). Further, because much of the psychometric work prior to 1978 in this domain has been reviewed elsewhere (Straus, 1969; Straus & Brown, 1978), this chapter concentrates the bulk of its attention on measurement developments since 1978. Space does not allow an exhaustive review of all measurement work since 1978, so this chapter concentrates on the three most frequent types of relationship measures: (a) multi-attribute measures in which relationships are conceptualized as a complex system of properties; (b) unitary measures of relationship development or intimacy; and (c) evaluative unitary measures of relationship quality.

Overview of Measurement Issues

Despite the expanded repertoire of measures available to the personal relationships researcher, extant relationships research is not free of measurement concerns. A brief overview of those concerns is instructive in framing the decisions made by the author on which measures to include and relevant features by which to differentiate among measures.

From a measurement perspective, three observations can be made about the growing body of personal relationships research. First, this work is excessively reliant on operationalization through ordinary language labels alone. That is, relationships are differentiated from one another exclusively through their common usage labels such as "close friends" and "acquaintances." As Bochner (1984) has observed, ordinary language labels are problematic in the study of relationships because different terms can refer to the same relational phenomenon (e.g., a "husband" can also be a "best friend") and because the same term can be used to refer to different relational phenomena (e.g., the "husband" who is simultaneously a "best friend" differs qualitatively from the "husband" who is not a "best friend," yet both are referred to by their respective spouses as their "husband"). The result of relying on ordinary language operationalization is ambiguity concerning exactly what relational phenomena are being referenced.

The second observation about extant relationships research is that much of it ignores the complex, multi-attribute nature of relationships in favor of single-item scales which assess but a single relational property, typically intimacy or relational quality. As becomes evident below, both intimacy and relational quality are complex, multidimensional properties in and of themselves and merit more sophisticated assessment than single-item indicators. Moreover, several measures exist which provide multiple-attribute profiles of relationships, affording a more complex approach to relationships when that is appropriate to the researcher's needs.

The final observation, and by far the most problematic, is the ecological fallacy problem which plagues much research in personal relationships. Insider measurement typically involves the individual, yet the data are often generalized to the relationship level. The ecological fallacy potentially involves two issues which merit discussion:

the *target object of measurement* and the *source of the data.* The *target object* to which the individual responds can be either at the individual level (perceptions of some state, attribute, or predisposition of Self or Other) or at the relationship level (perceptions of relationship events or properties). For example, assessment of a respondent's trust in or love for the Other illustrates an individual-level target object. In contrast, assessment of a respondent's perceptions of mutual support in the relationship illustrates a relationship-level target object. Although some researchers accept measurement of such individual subjective states as trust in and love for the Other as relational phenomena (e.g., Huston & Robins, 1982), others argue that the ecological fallacy is at play in such individual-level target objects (Thompson & Walker, 1982). The author's position is that such individual subjective states as love and trust are embedded in relationships but, nonetheless, assess the individual rather than the relationship as the target object of measurement. For the purposes of this chapter, a target is the relationship if the measure asks a respondent to report on events or episodes which occur between the two parties or properties of the relationship between the parties, rather than individual states of one or the other of the relationship parties.

As we shall see below, measures are rarely pure in their target objects, often mixing individual-level attributes or states with relationship-level targets. This review includes measures which involve relationship-level target objects at least to some extent and excludes measures which contain only individual-level target objects such as attraction, trust, love, liking, and jealousy, among others (several measures with individual-level target objects are discussed elsewhere in the chapter on "Interpersonal Evaluation").

Despite the fact that many of the measures reviewed below mix individual-level target objects with relationship-level target objects, important distinctions within each of these two types of target objects can usefully be recognized. For individual-level target objects, a distinction can be made between what Davis and Todd (1985) call the *being* vs. *having* focus. Measures whose focus is the respondent *having* a relationship partner typically include items in which the partner is assessed by the respondent, for example, "I have a partner who can be depended upon." In contrast, measures whose focus is the respondent *being* a relationship partner consist of items in which the respondent assesses his or her attributes or predispositions as a relationship partner to the other, e.g., "I am a partner who can be depended upon." Obviously, a relationship consists of both *having* and *being*, but measures often favor one focus over the other.

For relationship-level target objects, a distinction can be made between measures in their level of abstraction, with relationship properties representing the more general category which in turn is comprised of a set of specific episodes or events enacted by the relationship parties. For example, a measure which asks the respondent to monitor or record instances of joint decision-making illustrates an event or episode focus. In contrast, a measure which asks the respondent to generalize about who typically makes decisions illustrates a focus on relationship properties.

The second issue related to the ecological fallacy is the *source of the data*. Some scholars (e.g., Montgomery, 1984) reject totally the validity of collecting data from the individual respondent, arguing that true dyadic-level information is obtained only in observing the joint interaction of the relationship parties. The primary concern in drawing inferences about the relationship when data are gathered from the individual respondent, even with a relationship-level target object, is one of subjective bias. Partner discrepancy in accounts of their relationship is a pervasive phenomenon (Jacobson & Moore, 1981). However, as Thompson and Walker (1982) argue, validity may not be an issue if the researcher is theoretically predisposed to focus on personal constructions of experience, for example, the uncertainty reduction theorist, the attribution theorist, the symbolic interactionist. For such theoretical orientations, it is legitimate to gather data about an individual's relationships from his or her perspective alone. Validity becomes problematic only if the individually-generated data are regarded as objective information about the relationship unit. Thus, because data collected from one of the relationship parties are not inherently lacking in validity, single-perspective measures are included in this chapter.

If the researcher seeks to infer objective information about the relationship while collecting data from the individual relationship partner, combining both partners' data into a single relationship observation or score is necessary. Such derived relationship-level data can be referred to as second-order to indicate that they are one step removed from the level at which measurement occurs, that is, first-order data (Thompson & Walker, 1982). Regardless of the target object involved in first-order data, relationship-level second-order data are possible. Although not included in this chapter, measures which consist solely of individual-level target objects can be transformed into relationship-level data at the second order. For example, if the individual-level subjective state of trust in Other is measured as first-order data, a relationship-level datum of the second order can be derived in a discrepancy score between the two parties' respective trust scores. Relationship target objects at the first order of data also can be used as the basis of relationship-level second-order data. Each partner's perceptions of the relationship property of consensus, for example, could be measured as first-order relationship-level data, with a comparison between these two perceptions constituting relationship-level data of the second-order.

Most insider report measures are intended for use as first-order data only, an observation which may or may not constitute a validity indictment, depending on the researcher's theoretical assumptions and interests. However, for those measures which are used at the second order, the combination rule must be appropriate to the variable under study. The combination rule applied to the two parties' first-order data should vary according to the researcher's theoretical orientation and the particular variables under study. The reader is referred to Baucom (1983) for a useful summary of various combination rules available to the researcher and the assumptions which accompany each type of combination principle.

Measurement Devices

Multi-Attribute Assessment Techniques

Table 1 lists five multi-attribute measures of dyadic personal relationships and summarizes relevant information concerning their use. In addition to a summary of each measure's organizing features, the table also indicates the "scope conditions" (i.e., the measure's targeted relationship(s) and population(s), the content focus of the measure, a summary of the measure's reliability and the method(s) by which validity was demonstrated, and last, the key references where the reader can find more detailed information about the measure. Because of their multi-attribute nature, these measures afford the researcher a complex and sophisticated differentiation of relationships. However, a researcher could opt to use only a certain subscale of a multi-attribute measure, as appropriate. Space limitations preclude an in-depth discussion of each of the measures listed in Table 1, but some selective observations are in order.

The two measures which can be used with the widest range of relationship types are the revised Acquaintance Description Form (ADF-F; Wright, 1969, 1974, 1985) and the Relationship Rating Form (RRF; Davis & Todd, 1982, 1985). These two measures share many features in common, but differences are apparent, as well. Both can be used to study friendship as well as romantic relationships, including marriage. The two instruments also measure some of the same re-

Table 1. Summary of Multi-Attribute Measures of Personal Relationships

Measure	Organizing Features	Scope Conditions	Content	Reliability	Validity	Key Citations
Acquaintance Description Form—Revised (ADF-F)	largely individual-level (*having* a partner) target object items with some relationship-level (properties) items; used as first-order data	applicable to any dyadic relationship, including friendships & romantic relationships; used with college & adult populations	13 dimensions, each assessed in 5 Likert-type items: person-qua-person; voluntary interdependence; maintenance difficulty; utility value; ego support value; stimulation value; self-affirmation value; security value; general favorability; exclusiveness; salience of emotional expressiveness; social regulation; permanence	internal coeff. exceeds .75 for all subscales; test-retest coeff. range from .72 to .96 for the subscales	concurrent & discriminant	Wright (1969); Wright (1974); Wright (1985)

Instrument	Description	Items	Reliability	Validity	References
Friendship Inventory Scales (FI, Friendship Inventory; CFEI, Children's Friendship Expectations Inventory)	largely individual-level (*having* a partner) target objects with some relationship-level (properties) target object items; used as first-order data applicable to same sex friendships; FI used with adolescent & college populations; CFEI used with pre-adolescents	FI assesses 7 dimensions, each through 4 Likert-type items: positive regard; authenticity; helping/support; intimacy potential; similarity; empathic understanding; strength of character CFEI includes 4 dimensions: conventional morality; mutual activities; empathic understanding; loyalty	internal coefficients for FI range from .61–.86 and from .63 to .74 for CFEI; test-retest coeff. for FI range from .65–.83	concurrent & predictive	La Gaipa (1977); La Gaipa (1979); La Gaipa (1981); La Gaipa & Wood (in press)
Network of Relationships Inventory (NRI; formerly the Social Network Questionnaire)	mix of relationship-level (properties) & individual-level (*having* a partner) target object items; used as first-order data compares a network of relationships for pre-adolescent age group; same-sex & opposite-sex friends; parents & step-parents; extended kin; sibling; teacher	30 Likert-type items which assess 10 qualities: reliable alliance; enhancement of worth; instrumental help; companionship; affection; intimacy; relative power; conflict; satisfaction; importance	mean internal consistency of .80	concurrent	Furman (1984); Furman & Buhrmester (1985)

(continued)

Table 1. Summary of Multi-Attribute Measures of Personal Relationships (Continued)

Measure	Organizing Features	Scope Conditions	Content	Reliability	Validity	Key Citations
Relationship Dimensions Instrument (RDI)	largely relationship-level (properties) with some individual-level target object items equally distributed between *having* and *being* a partner; first-order data used as basis of 3 types of relationship definitions, with second-order data providing the basis for a couple typology of relationship definitions	to date, the RDI has been used exclusively with married couples	the 77 Likert-type items assess 8 dimensions: sharing; autonomy; undifferentiated space; temporal regularity; ideology of traditionalism; ideology of uncertainty & change; conflict avoidance; assertiveness	internal consistency coefficients range from .46–.88, with 5 of the dimensions below .70	predictive & construct	Fitzpatrick (1976); Fitzpatrick (1977); Fitzpatrick (1984); Fitzpatrick & Indvik (1982)
Relationship Rating Form (RRF)	mix of individual-level (*having* and *being*) target object items and relationship level (properties) items; used as first-order data	applicable to any dyadic relationship, both friendship and romantic relationships; used with college & adult populations	the 68 Likert-type items in version 3 of the RRF assess 21 qualities, clustered into these groupings: support; intimacy; viability; passion; understanding; stability; success; equality; conflict; ambivalence; maintenance;	internal coefficients of consistency range from .51 to .98, with most greater than .70; test-retest coefficients range from .42 to .82	concurrent	Davis & Todd (1982); Davis & Todd (1985)

lationship dimensions or qualities, despite differences in the labels attached to those dimensions. Of the thirteen dimensions which comprise the ADF-F, eight appear redundant with the RRF; of the 21 qualities which comprise the RRF (version 3), eight appear in some form on the ADF-F measure. In several instances, the qualities measured in the RRF reflect finer-grained distinctions of ADF-F dimensions. For example, the RRF measure has five utilitarian qualities of relationships in contrast to the single dimension of "Utility Value" on the ADF-F. Similarly, whereas the ADF-F measure has a single dimension of "Maintenance Difficulty," the RRF has at least three qualities which relate to difficulty in maintaining the relationship. Although both of the measures mix individual-level with relationship-level target objects, the RRF probably relies more on relationship-level items than does the ADF-F; further, the RRF appears to contain a more equal balance between individual-level items which emphasize *being* a partner and *having* a partner than does the ADF-F measure. The two measures are similar in length, with 65 items (ADF-F) and 68 items (RRF). Both of the measures have been analyzed for internal consistency and test-retest reliability, with results suggesting that the ADF-F measure has slightly higher item consistency within sub-scales and somewhat higher stability than the RRF scales.

The ADF-F and RRF measures are also alike in that each is the product of an extensive program of research which has resulted in several measurement revisions over time. Wright (1969) developed the original ADF measure as a way to assess variations in friendship. Subsequently, the measure underwent two major revisions and in 1984 took its current form as the ADF-F(inal) measure applicable to friendship as well as romantic relationships (Wright, 1985). Davis and Todd (1982, 1985) have produced three versions of the RRF. With both the ADF-F and RRF measures, the researcher should work with the latest revision.

Both the ADF-F and the RRF measures have amassed substantial validation evidence. Both measures have demonstrated concurrent validity in distinguishing among various levels of friendship and among various relationship types (Davis & Todd, 1982, 1985; Davis, Todd, & Denneny, 1985; Wright, 1974, 1985). In addition, the ADF-F measure has displayed discriminant validity for several of its sub-scales (Wright, 1985; Wright & Keple, 1981; Wright & Bergloff, 1984).

Would the researcher be better served by using the ADF-F or the RRF? The answer depends on several factors. In general, the ADF-F measure appears to have a slight edge in reliability, but for many of the RRF sub-scales the two measures perform at comparable levels. The higher proportion of relationship-level items and the better balance between having-being a partner in the RRF puts the ADF-F measure at a slight disadvantage in terms of content validity. In addition, the RRF appears to offer a finer-grained measurement of relationship qualities than that afforded by the ADF-F. However, both measures have demonstrated their ability to differentiate among known groups of relationship types. Neither measure has been used as second-order data, but nothing inherent in the measures prevents their use in this manner.

Although the Relationship Dimensions Instrument (RDI) is of relevance to a narrower band of relationship types, the measure surpasses both the ADF-F and RRF measures in the quantity of validation evidence which Fitzpatrick has amassed on its behalf (for a detailed review of this research program, see Fitzpatrick, 1984). To date, the RDI has been used exclusively in the study of marital couples, although Fitzpatrick (1984) posits the potential utility of the measure for pre-marital romantic couples. Fitzpatrick's Relationship Dimensions Instrument was initially developed with a sample of more than 1000 married people (Fitzpatrick, 1976, 1977) and was subsequently re-validated with 224 married couples drawn from a standard metropolitan statistical area using stratified random sampling in order to solicit a range of demographic features (Fitzpatrick & Indvik, 1982). It has been subject to several additional validation studies, as well. Theoretically grounded in Kantor and Lehr's (1975) work, the RDI is an eight-dimensional Likert-type measure given to relationship partners from which a second-order typology of couple types has been derived. The RDI dimensions of Autonomy, Undifferentiated Space, Temporal Regularity, and Ideology of Traditionalism do not appear redundant with the ADF-F and RRF measures. In short, the RDI appears to be tapping some unique features of the marital relationship which other measures used with adult marital relationships do not gauge.

Linear typal analysis applied to individuals' scores on the eight dimensions produced three basic relational definitions which, across the various samples, accounted for all but 8% of the respondents (Fitzpatrick, 1984). The relational definitions are: (a) *Traditional*, characterized by a conventional ideology, limited autonomy, a high degree of companionship, and low assertiveness despite a tendency to engage conflict; (b) *Independent*, characterized by a nonconventional ideology, a high degree of companionship while simultaneously maintaining some privacy and autonomy, and some assertiveness coupled with a tendency to engage conflict; and (c) *Separate*, characterized by conventional ideology, autonomy over interdependence, some assertiveness but a tendency to avoid conflict.

The third measurement step employed with the RDI is the derivation of second-order data, comparing partner definitions to produce a typology of couple types. Partners can be matched or mismatched on the three relational definitions, producing a matrix of nine possible couple types. "Pure" types are those in which the couple partners agree in perceiving their relationship as Traditional, Independent, or Separate. "Mixed" types are those in which "his" classified definition does not match "hers." Approximately 60% of sampled couples to date are pure types, more or less equally distributed across the three definitional types (Fitzpatrick, 1984).

Validation of the RDI is based on the association of the RDI-derived couple types with various variables of theoretical interest. These variables have involved both self-report measures and behavioral observation of interaction. As one would expect, Separates have the least open marital communication style and Traditionals have the most open style of the pure couple types (Fitzpatrick, 1977). The couple types are also clearly discriminated by the parties' sex role orientations, with Independents displaying the least endorsement of conventionalized sex roles (Fitzpatrick & Indvik, 1982). Couple type also predicts partner accuracy in estimating how the other responded to a personal sex role orientation inventory, with Separates displaying least accuracy, as one might expect (Fitzpatrick & Indvik, 1982). Dyadic adjustment is also significantly related to couple type in a manner largely consistent with the conceptualization of the couple typology (Fitzpatrick & Best, 1979). Couple types have also been differentiated in largely expected ways in their actual communicative behaviors (Fitzpatrick, 1984; Fitzpatrick, Best, Mabry, & Indvik, 1984; Fitzpatrick, Fallis, & Vance, 1982; Fitzpatrick, Tenney, & Witteman, 1983; Fitzpatrick, Vance, & Witteman, in press; Sillars, Pike, Redman, & Jones, 1983).

The RDI reflects a decade of work by Fitzpatrick and her colleagues. The measure has many strengths and some limitations for researchers interested in studying premarital and marital relationships. Despite Fitzpatrick's (1984) claim that the RDI could appropriately be used with premarital romantic couples, many of the items would necessitate alteration because of their bias toward marital couples. Although half of the RDI dimensions have quite acceptable internal reliability, half of the dimensions have low reliability coefficients. Additional work is needed on the reliability of the Autonomy, Undifferentiated space, Ideology of Uncertainty and Change, and Conflict Avoidance dimensions. Evidence of the RDI's stability through test-retest reliability would also be welcome information. The final limitation which should be noted about the RDI is that approximately 40% of the couples studied to date are mixed types in which the partners disagree on their perceptions of the relationship's definition. This percentage is substantial, yet the conceptual work which surrounds the RDI appears to concentrate on the three pure couple types. Thus, the conceptual implications of partner disagreement are unclear. As a result, it is difficult to know what to make of the couples who are typed as "Mixed" in the second-order data from the RDI.

Despite these limitations, the RDI has several strengths. Of all of the multidimensional measures reviewed in this chapter, the RDI comes closest to a fully relationship-level measure, both with regard to the relationship as a target object and the derivation of second-order relationship data from individual respondent data. The theoretical grounding of the dimensions of the measure and the subsequent verification of those theoretical underpinnings supports the construct validity of the measure. In addition, the RDI-derived pure couple types correlate in largely expected ways with several self-report and behavioral measures. In short, the validity evidence for the RDI is very encouraging.

For the researcher interested in relationships among adolescent and pre-adolescent populations, three measures from Table 1 offer the potential of greater measurement sophistication than the simplicity afforded by the commonly used method of sociometric choice. These three measures are: La Gaipa's Friendship Inventory and Children's Friendship Expectation Inventory (FI and CFEI; La Gaipa, 1977, 1979, 1981; La Gaipa & Wood, in press) and Furman's Network of Relationships Inventory (Furman, 1984; Furman & Buhrmester, 1985). La Gaipa's FI and CFEI measures differ in the targeted age group, with the CFEI appropriate to pre-adolescents and the FI appropriate to adolescent and college populations. The dimensions assessed in the two measures are largely comparable, although a finer-grained distinction is made among friendship qualities in the FI than in the CFEI. The Network of Relationships Inventory dimensions of relative power, conflict, satisfaction, and importance are not tapped in either the FI or the CFEI measures; reciprocally, the latter two measures contain a unique dimension which assesses the character of the partner (strength of character (FI) and conventional morality (CFEI)). The FI and CFEI measures are narrowly focused in terms of same-sex friendship, whereas Furman's measure assesses same-sex friendship as well as all other important relationships held by pre-adolescents. Furman's measure contains a higher proportion of relationship-level target object items than the FI and CFEI measures. All of the measures are used as first-order data only. The validation efforts on behalf of both measures have been successful, but the work with the Network of Relationships Inventory is in its relative infancy compared to the decade-long validation work by La Gaipa with over one thousand respondents. In terms of reliability, the three measures are comparable with regard to internal consistency, and no test-retest information is yet available for either the Network of Relationships Inventory or the CFEI to allow comparison with the adequate stability of the FI measure.

Unitary Measures: Relationship Progress/Development/Intimacy

Of the relationship measures which seek to operationalize a single relational property or phenomenon, those which assess the progress of development from a state of individual independence to a state of pair interdependence among friendships and romantic relationships are among the most frequent. Because intimacy or closeness is the single property most frequently used to gauge relational development, measures of relational intimacy are included in this section, as well. It would be misleading, however, to suggest that the eight measures summarized in Table 2 exhaust the domain of instruments by which relationship development can be discerned. All of the multi-attribute measures discussed above, for example, could be used to gauge relationship development. Unlike the multi-attribute measures, however, those discussed in this section are more likely to view relationship development as a process rooted in a single property or phenomenon rather than a system of properties.

Five of the eight measures in Table 2 assess relationship intimacy. However, a comparison of these measures reveals that conceptualizations of the intimacy construct vary substantially. One of the measures conceptualizes intimacy as the occurrence of behavioral events or episodes in the relationship, whereas the other four focus on a respondent's perceptions of relationship properties and feelings about the relationship partner. To some, the intimacy construct is a unidimensional concept, whereas to others intimacy is multifaceted.

The Friendship Observation Checklist (FOC) is a 190-item inventory which refers to specific relational events or episodes which might occur in the same-sex friendship relationship (Hays, 1984, 1985). The FOC is modeled after the Spouse Observation Checklist (Patterson, 1976) with one important difference: the items of the FOC form a Guttman scalogram with three levels of friendship intimacy depth in four behavioral domains. A sample item of high intimacy value from the Affection domain is "O(ther) and I performed a ceremony of our friendship." In addition, Hays employs a simple count of the total

Table 2. Summary of Selected Unitary Measures of Relationship Progress/Intimacy

Measure	Organizing Features	Scope Conditions	Content	Reliability	Validity	Key Citations
Dyadic Formation Inventory (DFI)	largely relationship-level (properties) with some individual-level (*having* a partner) target objects; used as second-order data	applicable to heterosexual, romantic couples, both marital & non-marital; used with college & adult populations	5 dimensions assessed in 25-item measure: dyadic interaction; boundary maintenance; dyadic stability/commitment; identification as a pair; and a globalized index of dyadic crystallization	internal coefficient varies by subscale, with dyadic crystallization and identification as a pair displaying greatest reliability	predictive	Lewis (1973); Filsinger, Mc-Avoy, & Lewis (1982); also see Straus & Brown (1978) for a review of the DFI
Friendship Observation Checklist (FOC)	relationship-level events or episodes; used as first-order data	to date, has been used exclusively to monitor the development of same-sex friendships among college population	190 listed events/episodes which allow a derived index of intimacy breadth and depth in 4 content domains: companionship; consideration/utility; communication; affection	Guttman coefficients of reproducibility exceed .90 for all 4 domains and coefficients of scalability exceed .80 for all 4 domains	concurrent, predictive, & construct	Hays (1984); Hays (1985)

Scale	Data level	Applicability	Items	Reliability	Validity	Reference
Miller Social Intimacy Scale (MSIS)	largely individual-level (*having a partner* target object items; used as first-order data)	applicable to both friendship and marital/nonmarital romantic relationships; used in college and adult populations	17 items which assess frequency & intensity of intimacy behaviors or feelings	internal consistency coefficients of .86–.91 across different samples & test-retest coefficients of .84–.96 for different samples	concurrent & discriminant	Miller & Lefcourt (1982)
Personal Assessment of Intimacy in Relationships Inventory (PAIR Inventory)	a mix of relationship-level (properties) and individual-level (*having a partner* target objects; used as second-order data)	applicable to heterosexual romantic & non-romantic relationships; used in college and adult populations	36 items which measure actual & desired intimacy in 5 areas, plus a subscale for social desirability bias: emotional intimacy; social intimacy; sexual intimacy; intellectual intimacy; recreational intimacy; plus conventionality sub-scale;	internal consistency coefficients exceed .70 for all intimacy subscales	concurrent	Schaefer & Olson (1981)
Relationship Events Scale (RES)	relationship-level (events); used as first-order data	applicable to heterosexual romantic relationships; used in college & adult populations	19 event items which comprise a Guttman progression of 6 levels of relationship development	coefficient of reproducibility of .94 and coefficient of scalability of .76	concurrent & predictive	King & Christensen (1983)
Relationship World Index—2 (RWI-2)	items consist of statements about romantic relationships in general; used as second-order data	applicable to marital & nonmarital romantic relationships; used with college & adult populations	60 statements about romantic relationships in general which comprise a Q-sort	test-retest coefficient of .73	concurrent & predictive	Stephen-Markman (1983); Stephen (1984a) Stephen (1984b) Stephen (in press)

(continued)

Table 2. Summary of Selected Unitary Measures of Relationship Progress/Intimacy (Continued)

Measure	Organizing Features	Scope Conditions	Content	Reliability	Validity	Key Citations
Solidarity Scale	largely individual-level (*having* a partner) target object items with some relationship-level (properties) target object items; used as first-order data	applicable to any dyadic interpersonal relationship, romantic or non-romantic; used with college & adult populations	revised version consists of 20 Likert-type statement which address closeness or intimacy	internal consistency coefficient of .96	predictive	Wheeless (1976); Wheeless (1978)
Waring Intimacy Questionnaire (WIQ)	mix of relationship-level (properties) and individual-level (*having* a partner) target object items; can be used as first-order data or as second-order data	applicable to marital couples; used with adult population	90 items, 10 for each of 8 intimacy domains, plus a social desirability sub-scale: conflict resolution; affection; cohesion; sexuality; identity; compatibility; expressiveness; autonomy; plus desirability	internal consistency coefficients range from .52 to .87 for subscales; test-retest coefficients range from .73 to .90	concurrent & discriminant	Waring (1984); Waring & Reddon (1983); Reddon, Patton, & Waring (1985)

number of checked items as an index of intimacy breadth. Social penetration theory (Altman & Taylor, 1973) provides the framework for the measure. Whereas intimacy breadth is indexed by the total number of checked events or episodes in a given domain, intimacy depth for a given domain is determined by the highest level (super-ficial-casual-close) for which the respondent checks at least one event or episode. Although intimacy scores in the four domains are mod-erately correlated, it is possible for intimacy to develop in different ways depending on the specific domain and the specific stage of relationship development. Hays employs the FOC as first-order data.

In the initial validation work (Hays, 1984) and again in a replication study (Hays, 1985), coefficients of reproducibility for the four domains have exceeded .94, and coefficients of scalability have exceeded .80. Given the guidelines of .90 for an acceptable coefficient of repro-ducibility and .60 for an acceptable coefficient of scalability (Edwards, 1957), the FOC clearly meets the standards for an adequate Guttman scalogram.

Validation of the FOC rests to date with two longitudinal studies of friendship conducted by Hays (1984, 1985). The findings are quite consistent across the two studies and are fully compatible with social penetration theory. Relationships which were affectively rated as closer at a given point in time featured greater breadth and depth of behavioral intimacy across content domains. The FOC scores ac-counted for an impressive proportion of the variance in affective ratings of the friendship's closeness depending on the stage of rela-tionship development. Further, the developmental progression of re-lationships across the period of assessment was from less to more intimacy breadth and depth. Last, the FOC scores at the end of the academic term significantly predicted the affective rating of the friend-ship three months later. In short, the validation work on behalf of the FOC provides preliminary support for the measure's construct, concurrent, and predictive validity.

Although work with the FOC is still in its infancy, results suggest that the measure affords a useful tool by which to gauge the pro-gression of friendship intimacy. To date, the measure has been em-ployed exclusively with close, same-sex friendships, and subsequent work is needed to determine the usefulness of the FOC with cross-sex relationships. A potential difficulty with the FOC for communi-cation researchers interested in the communication correlates of friendship intimacy is that two of the four content domains deal exclusively with communication events and episodes: the communi-cation domain taps self-disclosure and the affection domain taps ex-plicit metacommunication. If communication is used to operationalize intimacy, then it would be circular to consider these two communication variables as correlates of intimacy. With these caveats, the FOC holds promise as an alternative to other measures of intimacy which have a cognitive or affective focus.

The other four intimacy measures from Table 2 focus on relationship properties and individual perceptions of and feelings for the relationship partner rather than relationship events and episodes. Two of these measures, the Miller Social Intimacy Scale (MSIS; Miller & Lefcourt, 1982) and the Solidarity Scale (Wheeless, 1976, 1978), are the broadest in scope of any of the intimacy measures, applicable to any dyadic personal relationship. These two measures are alike in other respects, as well. Both are short, unidimensional scales of globalized intimacy with a heavy proportion of individual-level target object items. Both measures are used as first-order data. The MSIS and Solidarity Scale have demonstrated more than adequate internal consistency, and the MSIS additionally has evidence on behalf of its stability. Finally, both measures have evidence on behalf of their validity, although both have generally been underutilized by researchers. The length of these two measures makes them easy to use yet with no apparent loss of psychometric adequacy.

The last two intimacy measures from Table 2 also share many features in common. In fact, the two have correlated .77 in a sample of marital couples (Waring, 1984). Both the Personal Assessment of Intimacy in Relationships Inventory (PAIR; Schaefer & Olson, 1981) and the Waring Intimacy Questionnaire (WIQ; Waring, 1984; Waring & Reddon, 1983; Reddon, Patton, & Waring, 1985) display a multifaceted operationalization of intimacy. Both measures display a mix of relationship-level items which focus on perceived relational properties and individual-level items which focus on the respondent's perceptions of and feelings about the relational partner. The WIQ is used as first-order or second-order data, whereas the PAIR is used exclusively as second-order data. Although the PAIR taps five intimacy domains compared to the eight intimacy domains of the WIQ, the content overlap is substantial between the two measures. To their credit, both measures contain a subscale designed to gauge social desirability responses from the respondent. Although both measures emerged from an applied clinical setting, they have demonstrated psychometric adequacy for research purposes. Internal consistency is adequate for both measures, and the WIQ has additionally demonstrated adequate stability, as well. Both measures correlate in expected ways with other measures of relational phenomena, and the WIQ has also demonstrated its discriminant validity. The PAIR is broader in scope than the WIQ, the former applicable to any heterosexual relationship, romantic or nonromantic, in contrast to the exclusive use of the WIQ with marital couples.

The final three measures from Table 2 provide an index of development as a dyadic unit. The Dyadic Formation Inventory (DFI; Filsinger, McAvoy, & Lewis, 1982; Lewis, 1973) assesses dyadic crystallization and its four constituent qualities. Because it is reviewed elsewhere (see Straus & Brown, 1978), the DFI will not be discussed in detail here.

On the assumption that developmental progress is indicated by the occurrence of certain objective events which take place in a predictable order between the couple partners, the Relationship Events Scale (RES; King & Christensen, 1983) consists of 19 events organized in a Guttman scalogram. These 19 events are organized into six levels of relational progress based on similar frequencies of occurrence in a pre-test sample and based on their logical cohesiveness. The RES has a coefficient of reproducibility of .94 and a coefficient of scalability of .76, both sufficient to meet the requirements for Guttman progression (King & Christensen, 1983). King and Christensen (1983) use the measure as first-order data.

Evidence of both concurrent and predictive validity for the RES is reported in King and Christensen (1983). A strong association exists between a respondent's RES score and his or her ordinal classification of the relationship into such stages as "serious dating," or "going steady." Further, the RES score correlates with the respondent's expectation that the relationship will be permanent, the respondent's love for the Other, respondent satisfaction, and the reported length of the relationship, across two different college samples. Finally, the RES score significantly predicted which relationships would still be intact at a six-month follow-up, affording better prediction than the respondent's own classification of the relationship using the folk labels described above.

The evidence on behalf of the psychometric adequacy of the RES, while preliminary, is nonetheless encouraging. Whether the events which comprise the scale generalize to other respondent groups is an empirical question for subsequent researchers.

The Relationship World Index (RWI-2) was created by Stephen and Markman (1983) to determine agreement in partners' construction of relational reality, that is, symbolic interdependence, as an index of relationship development in romantic couples. The measure is a Q-sort in which respondents sort 60 statements about relationships in general into fifteen columns in an order which would "represent [their] ideas about the important aspects of an intimate or potentially committed love relationship" (Stephen & Markman, 1983). A second-order relationship-level datum is derived for each couple in the form of the correlation of the partner sorts, and it is this which operationalizes symbolic interdependence. The measure is grounded in social exchange and symbolic interaction theories in the assumption that symbolic interdependence increases as relationships develop. However, only 16 of the 60 items about relationships are taken from extant theoretical work in social exchange and symbolic interaction, with the remainder of the items taken from other miscellaneous writings on relationships (Stephen, 1984a).

Reliability for the RWI-2 measure is evidenced by a test-retest correlation of .73 between partner sorts with a ten-day interval between test occasions (Stephen & Markman, 1983). As the measure's originators readily admit, however, determination of what constitutes an acceptable test-retest coefficient value is problematic given the fact that the RWI-2 measure was designed for assessing a dynamic change in agreement through time.

Validity evidence for the RWI-2 is largely encouraging, although the magnitudes of expected findings are generally quite modest. Symbolic interdependence increases monotonically with relationship closeness (Stephen, 1984a, in press; Stephen & Markman, 1983). Further, partner consensus correlates positively with commitment (Stephen, 1984a) and with relationship satisfaction (Stephen, 1984a; Stephen & Markman, 1983). These latter correlations appear stable across a six-month interval of time (Stephen, in press). Finally, in a study of premarital break-up, Stephen (1984b) found that symbolic interdependence was significantly, albeit modestly, correlated with whether or not a couple broke up across a six-month period of time. As predicted, symbolic interdependence was also related to the partners' post-break-up distress.

III. Unitary Measures: Evaluation of Relationship Quality

Probably the most frequently measured feature of relationships is their quality. "Quality" is an exceedingly vague construct, and captures a range of evaluative features of relationships—relationship adjustment, relationship satisfaction, relationship happiness, relationship stability, to name but a few. Although some (e.g., Lively, 1969) have recommended the abandonment of research with such obscure constructs as "quality," researchers and theorists are still very interested in distinguishing "good quality" from "poor quality" relationships. This chapter does not engage the conceptual debate which surrounds the quality construct, but instead reviews the primary ways in which quality can be measured. Table 3 presents a selective summary of the primary self-report measures of relationship quality which have gained attention during the past decade. Interestingly, none of these measures addresses relationship quality in the friendship relationship. Researchers and theorists have unfortunately displayed their bias toward the ideology of intimacy (Parks, 1982) in assuming that intimacy is the equivalent of quality in close relationships. Further, the vast majority of the measures of relationship quality address only the marital relationship, ignoring nonmarital romantic pairs. Due to space limitations, this chapter concentrates on measures designed to assess quality in both marital and nonmarital romantic couples and measures designed for marital couples which could easily be adapted to nonmarital romantic pairs with slight modification of item content. As a consequence of this selectivity, several measures of relationship quality which can be used only with the marital relationship are not discussed (e.g., the Areas of Change Questionnaire (Weiss, Hops, & Patterson, 1973; Margolin, Talovic, & Weinstein, 1983), the Spousal Inventory of Desired Changes and Relationship Barriers (SIDCARB; Bagrozzi & Atilano, 1982; Bagarozzi & Pollane, 1983), the Marital Status Inventory (Weiss & Cerreto, 1980), and the Marital Instability Index (Booth, Johnson, & Edwards, 1983)).

Since its publication in 1976, the Dyadic Adjustment Scale (DAS; Spanier, 1976) has emerged as probably the single most frequently employed evaluative measure of personal relationships, comparable to the domination of the Locke-Wallace Marital Adjustment Scale (Locke & Wallace, 1959) during the 1960s and 1970s (see Straus [1969] and Straus & Brown [1978] for reviews of the Locke-Wallace). The DAS was constructed from all items ever used in any scale of marital quality plus a pool of new items (Spanier, 1976). As a consequence, the DAS displays substantial redundancy with prior measures of quality. For example, 12 of the 15 items which comprise the Locke-Wallace measure are contained among the 32 items of the DAS. It is thus not surprising that the DAS correlates .93 with the Locke-Wallace Marital Adjustment Scale (Spanier, 1976). Unlike the unidimensional score derived from the Locke-Wallace measure, however, the DAS provides a total score of dyadic adjustment in addition to constituent scores on each of four sub-scales; consensus, cohesion, satisfaction, and affectional expression. In further contrast to the Locke-Wallace measure, the DAS is applicable to married and non-married heterosexual romantic pairs whereas the Locke-Wallace is applicable only to marital pairs. The DAS is comprised of mostly relationship-level target object items which address the four constituent subscale properties. The measure has been used as first-order data.

Table 3. Summary of Evaluative Measures of Relationship Quality

Measure	Organizing Features	Scope Conditions	Content	Reliability	Validity	Key Citations
Dyadic Adjustment Scale (DAS)	largely relationship-level (properties) target object items with some individual-level (*having a partner*) target object items; used as first-order data	applicable to marital couples as well as non-marital romantic pairs	32 items, largely 6-point Likert-type, which measure 4 components of adjustment in addition to composite score: consensus (13 items) satisfaction (10 items) cohesion (5 items) affectional expression (4 items)	internal consistency coefficient for total scale is .96 with subscale reliabilities from .73 to .94	construct, concurrent, & predictive	Spanier (1976); Spanier & Thompson (1982); Antill & Cotton (1982)
Dyadic Adjustment Scale—Abbreviated (ADAS)	relationship-level (properties) target object items from the original DAS	same as for DAS	7 items from the original DAS which form a unidimensional scale: 3 consensus items 3 cohesion items 1 satisfaction item	internal consistency coefficient of .76	concurrent	Sharpley & Cross (1982); Sharpley & Rogers (1984)
Index of Marital Satisfaction (IMS)	mix of relationship-level (properties) and individual-level (*having a partner*) target object items; used as first-order data	married couples and non-marital romantic couples	25 Likert-type items which comprise a unidimensional global measure of satisfaction with the relationship and with one's partner.	internal consistency coefficient of .95 across 3 samples	construct & concurrent	Hudson & Glisson (1976); Cheung & Hudson (1982)

son Level Index (MCLI)	(having a partner) and relationship-level (properties) target object items; used as first-order data	items could be used as well with non-marital pairs with slight modification	which form a unidimensional scale of perceived outcomes compared to expected outcomes in several relational domains	ency coefficient of .93		
Marital Satisfaction Inventory (MSI)	mix of relationship-level (properties) and individual-level (*having a partner*) target object items; used as first-order data	married couples, but only slight modification of items from the super-factors of Disaffection & Disharmony would make those two factors applicable to non-marital romantic pairs	complete MSI consists of 280 true-false items which comprise 11 subscales: conventionalization disagreement about finances sexual dissatisfaction role orientation traditionalism family history of distress dissatisfaction with children conflict over child rearing global distress affective communication problem-solving communication time together (items from the last 4 sub-scales form the super-factors of Disaffection & Disharmony)	mean internal consistency across sub-scales is .88; test-retest reliability averages .89 across sub-scales; Disaffection & Disharmony super-factors have internal consistency coefficients of .95 and .87 and test-retest coefficients of .89 and .83	concurrent	Snyder (1979); Snyder & Regts (1982); Snyder, Wills, & Keiser (1981); Scheer & Snyder (1984)

(continued)

Table 3. Summary of Evaluative Measures of Relationship Quality (Continued)

Measure	Organizing Features	Scope Conditions	Content	Reliability	Validity	Key Citations
Marital Satisfaction Scale (MSS)	mix of individual-level (*having* a partner) and relationship-level (properties) target object items; used as first-order data	married pairs, but items could be used as well with non-marital couples with slight modification	original scale has 70 items, and the revision has 48 items, which comprise a unidimensional scale of attitude favorability toward the relationship	internal consistency coefficient of .97 for both long and short versions; test-retest coefficient of .76 for 3-week interval	concurrent & discriminant	Roach, Frazier, & Bowden (1981)
Quality Marital Index (QMI)	largely relationship-level (properties) target object items with some individual-level (*having* a partner) items; used as first-order data	applicable to married couples but with slight modification can be used with nonmarital romantic pairs as well	6 Likert-type items which address the "goodness of the relationship gestalt"	internal consistency coefficient of .95	predictive	Norton (1983); Norton (1985)

| Spouse Observation Checklist (SOC) | relationship-level (episodes & events) target object items; used as either first-order or second-order data | married couples | a checklist of 406 pleasing and displeasing behavioral episodes and events in 12 content domains: companionship; affection; consideration; communication; sex; coupling activities; parenting; household responsibilities; financial decision-making; employment & education; personal habits & appearance; self/spouse independence | mean observation agreement between spouses of 48%; odd-even day stability of observation for a given spouse of .94 for pleasing and .74 for displeasing | concurrent | Weiss, Hops, & Patterson (1973); Barnett & Nietzel (1979); Christensen & Nies (1980); Jacobson & Moore (1981); Margolin (1978); Robinson & Price (1980); see also Straus & Brown (1978) |

Although the evidence on behalf of the psychometric adequacy of the DAS has been supportive, the measure is not without its critics. Certainly, no critic takes issue with the reliability of the measure; the DAS has an overall internal consistency reliability of .96, with subscale reliability coefficients which range from .73 to .94, lowest for the affectional expression subscale (Spanier, 1976). The critical debate surrounds the validity of the DAS. On the positive side of the debate, a case can be made for both construct and concurrent validity. In his initial validation study, Spanier (1976) found that the factor analysis of emergent subscales supported in large measure his a priori theoretical expectations surrounding the underlying dimensions of dyadic adjustment (Spanier & Cole, 1976). However, the affectional expression dimension was not theoretically predicted, and in fact subsequent confirmatory factor analytic work (Antill & Cotton, 1982; Spanier & Thompson, 1982) has found this to be an unstable factor. In addition to the argument for construct validity, concurrent validity has been demonstrated in the ability of the DAS to distinguish between currently married and divorced relational partners (Spanier, 1976). In addition, the DAS has usefully predicted differences in a variety of relational phenomena, including most recently conflict management (Ting-Toomey, 1983; Yelsma, 1984), interpersonal coorientational perceptions (Bochner, Krueger, & Chmielewski, 1982), and marital type (Fitzpatrick, 1984).

Criticisms of the DAS have led to the construction of several alternative measures of dyadic adjustment. The Abbreviated Dyadic Adjustment Scale (ADAS) emerged from the failure of Sharpley & Cross (1982) to replicate the factor structure of the DAS, finding instead a single globalized adjustment factor. They found that seven items from the original DAS could distinguish high vs. low adjustment groups as well as the complete DAS measure (Sharpley & Cross, 1982; Sharpley & Rogers, 1984). Although the internal reliability of the ADAS is understandably lower than for the complete 32-item DAS, its reliability coefficient of .76 suggests that it is sufficiently consistent internally.

Perhaps the most thorough critique of the DAS is provided by Norton (1983), although his critical insights are equally applicable to the Locke-Wallace Dyadic Adjustment Scale among others. Most importantly, Norton argues that relationship quality should be assessed as a "goodness of the relationship gestalt" (Norton, 1983, p. 143) rather than evaluation on several relational properties which reflect the researcher's preconceived biases of relationship "goodness." The latter measurement approach has two unfortunate outcomes: either those constituent properties are not systematically researched in their own right in conjunction with relationship quality, because they are part of the measure, or they are examined, which results in circular reasoning. In addition, the unequal number of items devoted to each of the four properties assessed in the DAS leads to the disproportionate weighting of the larger subscales over the smaller subscales with no theoretical justification for such weights. In order to free the quality concept from the implicit biases evidenced in measures such as the DAS, Norton (1983) produced a 6-item unidimensional Quality Marital Index (QMI) whose items solicit a respondent's gestalt perceptions of how "good" the relationship is (e.g., "We have a good marriage"). Because Norton (1983) was also critical of the fact that measures such as the DAS employ mixed response formats whose scaling differences are ignored in deriving score sums, the QMI involves standardization of items. The QMI has an internal reliability of .95 (Norton, 1983, 1985) and is correlated in theoretically expected ways with such relational properties as similarity in partner attitudes, estimate of relationship future, consideration of breaking up, partner coorientation in perceptions of a variety of interaction behaviors in their relationship, and partner perceptions of equitability in several interaction domains (Norton, 1983, 1985). Although the name of the QMI suggests its restriction to the marital couple, the measure has been employed in slightly modified form with premarital romantic couples, as well (Baxter & Bullis, 1985).

Sabatelli (1984) was critical of the atheoretical derivation of extant quality measures, including the DAS, and he has constructed the Marital Comparison Level Index (MCLI) as an alternative. The MCLI is derived from social exchange theory (Kelley & Thibaut, 1978) in its focus on expected relational outcomes compared to realized outcomes. The 32 items of the MCLI display a mix of individual-level and relationship-level target objects, and the measure is used as first-order data. Although the measure is designed for use with marital couples, it could be employed with nonmarital romantic couples with very little modification. The MCLI has an internal consistency coefficient of .93, supporting its reliability. Scores on the MCLI measure significantly predict perceived equitability in the relationship and reported commitment (Sabatelli, 1984). Although the psychometric evidence for the MCLI is preliminary, it is encouraging. The greatest advantage afforded by the MCLI is the fact that it is theoretically-based.

The Marital Satisfaction Scale (MSS) is also a by-product of criticism of the DAS (Roach, Frazier, & Bowden, 1981). Roach and his colleagues were critical of the multiple response formats in the DAS and its heavy reliance on respondent estimates of frequencies with which things occurred in the relationship (Roach et al., 1981). They argued that asking respondents to provide recollected frequency estimates is overly reliant on cognitive and memory processes; instead, relationship quality should be assessed more directly with affective attitudinal responses. The 70 items of the original MSS and the 48-item revision consist of a mix of relationship-level and individual-level target object items which are used as first-order data. In contrast to the heavy cognitive focus of the DAS, the MSS solicits the respondent's affective attitude toward the target object phenomena. The MSS is designed for use with marital couples, but it could be used as well with nonmarried romantic pairs with slight rewording of items. The measure has demonstrated both adequate internal consistency and adequate stability. In a series of studies summarized in Roach et al. (1981), the MSS has amassed evidence on behalf of both concurrent and discriminant validity. The MSS is significantly correlated with the Locke-Wallace, successfully distinguishes satisfied from dissatisfied criterion groups, and significantly correlates with an index of marital problems. The measure is not correlated with social desirability measures. In short, the psychometric evidence for the MSS is encouraging. For the researcher in need of a measure which will detect subtle change in relationship quality, the MSS is a promising option because of its exclusively affective orientation.

Two of the measures from Table 3 were developed at about the same time as the DAS, rather than emerging as responses to the DAS. Although neither of these measures has gained the singular popularity of the DAS, they merit brief discussion. The Marital Satisfaction Inventory (MSI) is a 280 true-false measure which solicits forced choice responses on 11 subscales, including one to gauge the degree of social desirability response bias (Snyder, 1979). These items contain a mix of relationship-level and individual-level target objects. The measure is used as first-order data. Although the full 280-item version has demonstrated adequate reliability and promising concurrent validity (Scheer & Snyder, 1984; Snyder, 1979; Snyder, Wills, & Keiser, 1981), apparently the power of the instrument resides largely in four of the 11 subscales, leading Snyder (Snyder & Regts, 1982) to advance two super-factors entailed in these four sub-scales: disaffection and disharmony. These two super-factors display adequate internal consistency and stability, and they are capable of discriminating normal from clinical couples (Snyder & Regts, 1982). Given that the full 280-item measure is lengthy, the researcher might be better served with the four subscales which assess disaffection and disharmony through 26 items and 18 items, respectively. Although the complete measure was designed for use with marital couples, only slight modification of the disaffection and disharmony items would be necessary for their use with nonmarital romantic couples.

The Index of Marital Satisfaction (IMS) appeared in the published literature at the same time as the DAS (Hudson & Glisson, 1976) but has reappeared in revised form more recently (Cheung & Hudson, 1982). The 25 Likert-type items contain a mix of relationship-level and individual-level target objects and solicit data for first-order interpretation. Apart from the DAS, this is the only other evaluative measure designed for use with both marital and nonmarital couples. The unidimensional scale has demonstrated excellent internal consistency across three different samples (Cheung & Hudson, 1982). The IMS has demonstrated its ability to distinguish among those with and without marital problems and its ability to correlate in theoretically expected ways with several additional variables (Cheung & Hudson, 1982). In short, although the tradition of the IMS is clinical, the measure has demonstrated its psychometric adequacy for research work as well.

To make the simple point that a measure of relationship quality need not be cognitive or affective in nature, the behaviorally-based Spouse Observation Checklist (SOC; Patterson, 1976; Weiss & Perry, 1983) is also included in Table 3, despite its applicability only to the marital relationship. The original SOC is a checklist of 406 pleasing and displeasing behavioral episodes or events in 12 content domains which the spouse/observer typically fills out every 24 hours. Some modified versions of the SOC have recently emerged, as well (Atkinson & McKenzie, 1984; Christensen & Nies, 1980; Weiss & Perry, 1983). Although the mean agreement between spouses does not demonstrate adequate reliability, a given spouse's observations are stable across time (Christensen & Nies, 1980; Jacobson & Moore, 1981; Margolin, 1978). Because the SOC is reviewed elsewhere (Straus & Brown, 1978), a lengthy review of its validation evidence will not be undertaken here. Suffice it to say, however, that individual spouse reports of the frequencies of pleasing and displeasing behaviors correlate with other indices of satisfaction or adjustment (Barnett & Nietzel, 1979; Birchler, Weiss, & Vincent, 1975; Margolin, 1978; Wills, Weiss, & Patterson, 1974). Further, the degree of spouse agreement in their observations also correlates with the couple's adjustment (Jacobson & Moore, 1981; Robinson & Price, 1980).

Conclusion

This chapter provides a selective review of multi-attribute relationship measures, unitary measures of relationship progress and intimacy, and evaluative measures of relationship quality. Collectively, these 21 measures provide personal relationships researchers with measurement options which promise improved psychometric adequacy when compared to the ordinary language operationalization and single-item indicators found in extant literature. However, several recommendations can be advanced about the measures. First, several of them have been validated with the "known groups" method of concurrent validation in which the "known groups" were the ordinary language labels of "acquaintance," "close friend," and so on. Given the problematic nature of ordinary language operationalization discussed in the chapter's introduction, other validation efforts are necessary. At a minimum, the various measures reviewed should be correlated with one another to determine areas of convergence and divergence. Second, several of the measures draw heavily upon individual-level target objects, especially perceptions of the relationship partner, that is, *having* a partner. Measures which focus exclusively on the *relationship* as the target object are still relatively absent. Further, the measures having individual-level target objects generally do not balance *having* a partner against one's perceptions of *being* a partner, yet both elements seem necessary in understanding personal relationships. The third recommendation concerning relationship measures is the need to use them at the second-order. Very few of the measures reviewed here display second-order conceptualizations. As noted above, this is not a validity indictment for the researcher who is theoretically interested in relationships as experienced by the individual. However, if researchers seek to understand the relationship as a unit, these measures should be used to provide second-order data. Although most of these measures have been used only for first-order data, nothing precludes the combination of measurement scores from individual sources to derive a relationship score.

References

Altman, I., & Taylor, D. (1973). *Social penetration: The development of interpersonal relationships.* New York: Holt, Rinehart & Winston.

Antill, J.K., & Cotton, S. (1982). Spanier's Dyadic Adjustment Scale: Some confirmatory analyses. *Australian Psychologist, 17,* 181–189.

Atkinson, B.J., & McKenzie, P.N. (1984). The personalized Spouse Observation Checklist: A computer-generated assessment of marital interaction. *Journal of Marital and Family Therapy, 10,* 427–429.

Bagarozzi, D.A., & Atilano, R.B. (1982). SIDCARB: A clinical tool for rapid assessment of social exchange inequities and relationship barriers. *Journal of Sex and Marital Therapy, 8,* 325–334.

Bagarozzi, D.A., & Pollane, L. (1983). A replication and validation of the Spousal Inventory of Desired Changes and Relationship Barriers (SID-

CARB): Elaborations on diagnostic and clinical utilization. *Journal of Sex and Marital Therapy, 9,* 303–315.

Barnett, L.R., & Nietzel, M.T. (1979). Relationship of instrumental and affectional behaviors and self-esteem to marital satisfaction in distressed and non-distressed couples. *Journal of Consulting and Clinical Psychology, 47,* 946–957.

Baucom, D.H. (1983). Conceptual and psychometric issues in evaluating the effectiveness of behavioral marital therapy. *Advances in family intervention, assessment and theory, 3,* 91–118.

Baxter, L., & Bullis, C. (1985). *A profile of turning points in the development of romantic relationships and their association with relationship satisfaction.* Manuscript submitted for publication.

Birchler, G.R., Weiss, R.L., & Vincent, J.P. (1985). A multimethod analysis of social reinforcement exchange between maritally distressed and non-distressed spouse and stranger dyads. *Journal of Personality and Social Psychology, 31,* 349–360.

Bochner, A.P. (1984). The functions of human communicating in interpersonal bonding. In C.C. Arnold and J.W. Bowers (Eds.), *Handbook of rhetorical and communication theory* (pp. 544–621). Boston: Allyn and Bacon.

Bochner, A.P., Krueger, D.L., & Chmielewski, T.L. (1982). Interpersonal perception and marital adjustment. *Journal of Communication, 32 (3),* 135–147.

Booth, A., Johnson, D., & Edwards, J.N. (1983). Measuring marital instability. *Journal of Marriage and the Family, 45,* 387–393.

Cheung, P.L., & Hudson, W.W. (1982). Assessment of marital discord in social work practice: A revalidation of the Index of Marital Satisfaction. *Journal of Social Service Research, 5,* 101–118.

Christensen, A., & Nies, D.C. (1980). The Spouse Observation Checklist: Empirical analysis and critique. *American Journal of Family Therapy, 8,* 69–79.

Davis, K.E., & Todd, M.J. (1982). Friendship and love relationships. *Advances in descriptive psychology, 2,* 79–122.

Davis, K.E., & Todd, M.J. (1985). Assessing friendship: Prototypes, paradigm cases and relationship description. In S. Duck and D. Perlman (Eds.), *Understanding personal relationships* (pp. 17–37). London: Sage.

Davis, K.E., Todd, M.J., & Denneny, J.B. (1985). *Personal networks, friendships, and love relationships over the life cycle.* Unpublished manuscript, University of South Carolina.

Duck, S. (Ed.) (1982). *Personal relationships 4: Dissolving personal relationships.* New York: Academic Press.

Duck, S. (Ed.) (1984). *Personal relationships 5: Repairing personal relationships.* New York: Academic Press.

Duck, S., & Gilmour, R. (Eds.) (1981a). *Personal relationships 1: Studying personal relationships.* New York: Academic Press.

Duck, S., & Gilmour, R. (Eds.) (1981b). *Personal relationships 2: Developing personal relationships.* New York: Academic Press.

Duck, S., & Gilmour, R. (Eds.) (1981c). *Personal relationships 3: Personal relationships in disorder.* New York: Academic Press.

Duck, S., & Perlman, D. (Eds.) (1985). *Understanding personal relationships: An interdisciplinary approach.* London: Sage.

Edwards, A.L. (1957). *Techniques of attitude and scale construction.* New York: Appleton-Century-Crofts.

Filsinger, E.E., McAvoy, P., & Lewis, R.A. (1982). An empirical typology of dyadic formation. *Family Process, 21,* 321–335.

Fitzpatrick, M.A. (1976). *A typological approach to communication in relationships.* Unpublished doctoral dissertation, Temple University.

Fitzpatrick, M.A. (1977). A typological approach to communication in relationships. *Communication yearbook, 1,* 263–275.

Fitzpatrick, M.A. (1984). A typological approach to marital interaction: Recent theory and research. *Advances in experimental social psychology, 18,* 1–47.

Fitzpatrick, M.A., & Best, P. (1979). Dyadic adjustment in traditional, independent, and separate relationships: A validation study. *Communication Monographs, 46,* 167–178.

Fitzpatrick, M.A., Best, P., Mabry, E., & Indvik, J. (1984). *An integration of two approaches to relational conflict.* Unpublished manuscript, University of Wisconsin-Madison.

Fitzpatrick, M.A., Fallis, S., & Vance, L. (1982). Multifunctional coding of conflict resolution strategies in marital dyads. *Family Relations, 31,* 61–70.

Fitzpatrick, M.A., & Indvik, J. (1982). The instrumental and expressive domains of marital communication. *Human Communication Research, 8,* 195–213.

Fitzpatrick, M.A., Tenney, B., & Witteman, H. (1983). *Compliance-gaining in marital interaction.* Paper presented at the International Communication Association Conference, Dallas.

Fitzpatrick, M.A., Vance, L., & Witteman, H. (in press). Interpersonal communication in the casual interaction of marital partners. *Language and Social Psychology.*

Furman, W. (1984). Some observations on the study of personal relationships. In J.C. Masters and K.L. Yarkin (Eds.), *Boundary areas in psychology: Social and developmental psychology* (pp. 15–42). New York: Academic Press.

Furman, W., & Buhrmester, D. (1985). Children's perceptions of the personal relationships in their social networks. *Developmental Psychology, 21,* 1016–1022.

Hays, R.B. (1984). The development and maintenance of friendship. *Journal of Social and Personal Relationships, 1,* 75–98.

Hays, R.B. (1985). A longitudinal study of friendship development. *Journal of Personality and Social Psychology, 48,* 909–924.

Hudson, W.W., & Glisson, D.H. (1976). Assessment of marital discord in social work practice. *Social Service Review, 50,* 293–311.

Huston, T.L., & Robins, E. (1982). Conceptual and methodological issues in studying close relationships. *Journal of Marriage and the Family, 44,* 901–925.

Jacobson, N.S., & Moore, D. (1981). Spouses as observers of the events in their relationship. *Journal of Consulting and Clinical Psychology, 49,* 269–277.

Kantor, D., & Lehr, W. (1975). *Inside the family.* San Francisco, CA: Jossey-Bass.

Kelley, H.H., Berscheid, E., Christensen, A., Harvey, J.H., Huston, T.L., Levinger, G., McClintock, E., Peplau, L.A., & Peterson, D.R. (1983). *Close relationships.* San Francisco, CA: W.H. Freeman.

Kelley, H.H., & Thibaut, J.W. (1978). *Interpersonal relations: A theory of interdependence.* New York: Wiley.

King, C.E., & Christensen, A. (1983). The Relationship Events Scale: A Guttman scaling of progress in courtship. *Journal of Marriage and the Family, 45,* 671–678.

La Gaipa, J. (1977). Testing a multidimensional approach to friendship. In S. Duck (Ed.), *Theory and practice in interpersonal attraction* (pp. 249–270). New York: Academic Press.

La Gaipa, J. (1979). A developmental study of the meaning of friendship in adolescence. *Journal of Adolescence, 2,* 201–213.

La Gaipa, J. (1981). Children's friendships. In S. Duck and R. Gilmour (Eds.), *Personal relationships 2: Developing personal relationships* (pp. 161–185). New York: Academic Press.

La Gaipa, J., & Wood, H.D. (in press). An Eriksonian approach to conceptions of friendship of aggressive and withdrawn preadolescent girls. *Journal of Early Adolescence.*

Lewis, R. (1973). The Dyadic Formation Inventory: An instrument for measuring heterosexual couple development. *International Journal of Sociology of the Family, 2,* 207–216.

Lively, E. (1969). Toward conceptual clarification: Case of marital interaction. *Journal of Marriage and the Family, 31,* 108–114.

Locke, H., & Wallace, K. (1959). Short marital adjustment and prediction tests: Their reliability and validity. *Marriage and Family Living, 21,* 251–255.

Margolin, G. (1978). Relationships among marital assessment procedures: A correlational study. *Journal of Consulting and Clinical Psychology, 46,* 1556–1558.

Margolin, G., Talovic, S., & Weinstein, C.D. (1983). Areas of Change Questionnaire: A practical approach to marital assessment. *Journal of Consulting and Clinical Psychology, 51,* 920–931.

McCarthy, B. (1981). Studying personal relationships. In S. Duck and R. Gilmour (Eds.), *Personal relationships 1: Studying personal relationships* (pp. 23–46). New York: Academic Press.

Miller, R.S., & Lefcourt, H.M. (1982). The assessment of social intimacy. *Journal of Personality Assessment, 46,* 514–518.

Montgomery, B.M. (1984). Communication in intimate relationships: A research challenge. *Communication Quarterly, 32,* 318–325.

Norton, R. (1983). Measuring marital quality: A critical look at the dependent variable. *Journal of Marriage and the Family, 45,* 141–151.

Norton, R. (1985). *Communicative behaviors in a marriage: Co-oriented and equitable perceptions of males and females.* Manuscript submitted for publication.

Parks, M. (1982). Ideology in interpersonal communication: Off the couch and into the world. *Communication yearbook, 5,* 79–107.

Patterson, G.R. (1976). Some procedures for assessing changes in marital interaction patterns. *Oregon Research Bulletin, 16(7).*

Reddon, J.R., Patton, D., & Waring, E.M. (1985). The item-factor structure of the Waring Intimacy Questionnaire. *Educational and Psychological Measurement, 45,* 233–244.

Roach, A.J., Frazier, L.P., & Bowden, S.R. (1981). The Marital Satisfaction Scale: Development of a measure for intervention research. *Journal of Marriage and the Family, 43,* 537–546.

Robinson, E.A., & Price, M.S. (1980). Pleasurable behavior in marital interaction: An observational study. *Journal of Consulting and Clinical Psychology, 48,* 117–118.

Sabatelli, R.M. (1984). The Marital Comparison Level Index: A measure for assessing outcomes relative to expectations. *Journal of Marriage and the Family, 46,* 651–662.

Schaefer, M.T., & Olson, D.H. (1981). Assessing intimacy: The PAIR Inventory. *Journal of Marital and Family Therapy, 7,* 47–60.

Scheer, N.S., & Snyder, D.K. (1984). Empirical validation of the Marital Satisfaction Inventory in a nonclinical sample. *Journal of Consulting and Clinical Psychology, 52,* 155–164.

Sharpley, C.F. & Cross, D.G. (1982). A psychometric evaluation of the Spanier Dyadic Adjustment Scale. *Journal of Marriage and the Family, 44,* 739–741.

Sharpley, C.F., & Rogers, H.J. (1984). Preliminary validation of the abbreviated Spanier Dyadic Adjustment Scale: Some psychometric data regarding a screening test of marital adjustment. *Educational and Psychological Measurement, 44,* 1045–1049.

Sillars, A.L., Pike, G.R., Redman, K., & Jones, T.S. (1983). Communication and conflict in marriage: One style is not satisfying to all. *Communication yearbook, 7,* 414–429.

Snyder, D.K. (1979). Multidimensional assessment of marital satisfaction. *Journal of Marriage and the Family, 41,* 813–823.

Snyder, D.K., & Regts, J.M. (1982). Factor scales of assessing marital disharmony and disaffection. *Journal of Consulting and Clinical Psychology, 50,* 736–743.

Snyder, D.K., Wills, R.M., & Keiser, T.W. (1981). Empirical validation of the Marital Satisfaction Inventory: An actuarial approach. *Journal of Consulting and Clinical Psychology, 49,* 262–268.

Spanier, G.B. (1976). Measuring dyadic adjustments: New scales for assessing the quality of marriage and similar dyads. *Journal of Marriage and the Family, 38,* 15–28.

Spanier, G.B., & Cole, C.L. (1976). Toward clarification and investigation of marital adjustment. *International Journal of Sociology of the Family, 6,* 121–146.

Spanier, G.B., & Thompson, L. (1982). A confirmatory analysis of the Dyadic Adjustment Scale. *Journal of Marriage and the Family, 44,* 731–738.

Stephen, T.D. (1984a). A symbolic exchange framework for the development of intimate relationships. *Human Relations, 37,* 393–408.

Stephen, T.D. (1984b). Symbolic interdependence and post-break-up distress: A reformulation of the attachment construct. *Journal of Divorce, 8,* 1–16.

Stephen, T.D. (in press). Fixed-sequence and circular-causal models of relationship development: Divergent views on the role of communication in intimacy. *Journal of Marriage and the Family.*

Stephen, T.D., & Markman, H.J. (1983). Assessing the development of relationships: A new measure. *Family Process, 22,* 15–25.

Straus, M.A. (1969). *Family measurement techniques.* Minneapolis, MN: University of Minnesota Press.

Straus, M.A., & Brown, B. (Eds.) (1978). *Family measurement techniques: Abstracts of published instruments, 1935–1974.* Minneapolis, MN: University of Minnesota Press.

Thompson, L., & Walker, A.J. (1982). The dyad as the unit of analysis: Conceptual and methodological issues. *Journal of Marriage and the Family, 44,* 889–900.

Ting-Toomey, S. (1983). Coding conversation between intimates: A validation study of the Intimate Negotiation Coding System (INCS). *Communication Quarterly, 31,* 68–77.

Waring, E.M. (1984). The measurement of marital intimacy. *Journal of Marital and Family Therapy, 10,* 185–192.

Waring, E.M., & Reddon, J.R. (1983). The measurement of intimacy in marriage: The Waring Intimacy Questionnaire. *Journal of Clinical Psychology, 39,* 53–57.

Weiss, R.L., & Cerreto, M.C. (1980). The Marital Status Inventory: Development of a measure of dissolution potential. *American Journal of Family Therapy, 8,* 80–85.

Weiss, R.L., Hops, H., & Patterson, G.R. (1973). A framework for conceptualizing marital conflict, a technology for altering it, some data for evaluating it. In L.A. Hamerlynck, L.C. Hardy, and E.J. Mash (Eds.), *Behavior change: Methodology, concepts, and practice.* Champaign, IL: Research Press.

Weiss, R.L., & Perry, B.A. (1983). The Spouse Observation Checklist: Development and clinical applications. In E.E. Filsinger (Ed.), *Marriage and family assessment.* Beverly Hills, CA: Sage.

Wheeless, L.R. (1976). Self-disclosure and interpersonal solidarity: Measurement, validation, and relationships. *Human Communication Research, 3,* 47–61.

Wheeless, L.R. (1978). A follow-up study of the relationships among trust, disclosure, and interpersonal solidarity. *Human Communication Research*, *4*, 143–157.

Wills, T.A., Weiss, R.L., & Patterson, G.R. (1974). A behavioral analysis of the determinats of marital satisfaction. *Journal of Consulting and Clinical Psychology*, *42*, 802–811.

Wright, P.H. (1969). A model and a technique for studies of friendship. *Journal of Experimental Social Psychology*, *5*, 295–309.

Wright, P.H. (1974). The delineation and measurement of some key variables in the study of friendship. *Representative Research In Social Psychology*, *5*, 93–96.

Wright, P.H. (1985). The Acquaintance Description Form. In S. Duck and D. Perlman (Eds.), *Understanding personal relationships* (pp. 39–62). London: Sage.

Wright, P.H., & Bergloff, P.J. (1984). *The Acquaintance Description Form and the study of relationship differentiation*. Paper presented at the Second International Conference on Personal Relationships, Madison.

Wright, P.H., & Keple, T.W. (1981). Friends and parents of a sample of high school juniors: An exploratory study of relationship intensity and interpersonal rewards. *Journal of Marriage and the Family*, *43*, 559–570.

Yelsma, P. (1984). Functional conflict management in effective marital adjustment. *Communication Quarterly*, *32*, 56–61.

CHAPTER 8

Group Communication Research: Considerations for the Use of Interaction Analysis

Randy Y. Hirokawa

Over the years, a number of small group scholars have called for the systematic observation and analysis of face-to-face interaction (or communication) in small group settings. Authors like Gouran and Fisher (1984), Hackman and Morris (1975), and McGrath and Altman (1966) suggest that the study of group interaction processes can provide us with an understanding of the relationships among various "input" and "output" variables. Others like Bales (1950, 1970), Bales and Cohen (1979), and Poole, Seibold, and McPhee (1985) maintain that the systematic study of group interaction processes can provide important insights regarding the structure and culture of the group, as well as the personality profile of its members.

Traditionally, researchers interested in studying group communication processes have relied on a method of analysis called *interaction analysis.* Based on the pioneering work of Robert F. Bales in the early 1950s (see Bales, 1950), the method has been employed by scores of researchers in a variety of academic disciplines (see, e.g., Amidon & Hough, 1967; Coulthard, 1977). In fact, recent reviews of the small group literature clearly indicate that the vast majority of studies focusing on group communication processes have relied on the method of interaction analysis in assessing the nature of group interaction (see, e.g., Cragan & Wright, 1980; Gouran & Fisher, 1984; Hare, 1976; Hirokawa, 1982).

In recent years, however, the method of interaction analysis has come under increasing criticism by a number of communication scholars. Bochner (1978, p. 183), for example, criticized the method on the grounds that it overly simplifies the complex nature of human communication. Hawes (1978, p. 16) questioned the theoretical foundation of the method and concluded that it produces nothing more than abstractions of the reality of talk. O'Keefe, Delia, and O'Keefe (1980) contend that traditional interaction analysis methods do not allow a researcher to discover the important structural features of group interaction.

While some of the criticisms leveled against the method of interaction analysis reflect legitimate concerns which cannot be easily dismissed, it is important to recognize that such criticisms do *not* necessarily "sound the death knell for the method as a significant tool in the arsenal of the small group researcher" (Fisher, 1978). On the contrary, several recent authors have pointed out that the method, if used prudently and appropriately by researchers, represents a valuable tool for analyzing the nature and structure of group interaction processes (see, e.g., Bales & Cohen, 1979; Coulthard, 1977; Fisher, 1977, 1978; Hewes, 1978; Hirokawa, 1982; Poole & Folger, 1981; Poole & Hirokawa, in press). As Fisher (1978) puts it, the value of interaction analysis as a tool for communication inquiry lies in its "intelligent and sophisticated" use by communication researchers.

The present chapter seeks to facilitate the appropriate and sophisticated use of interaction analysis as a method for studying small group interaction. Its goal is to provide the reader with a systematic understanding of some of the important methodological considerations involved in the practice of interaction analysis. In doing so, the chapter is designed to serve as more than a step-by-step procedural guide for doing interaction analysis; it also seeks to provide the reader with an understanding of the critical issues which must be dealt with by a researcher interested in employing the method to study group communication processes. In short, the chapter seeks to provide the reader with the kinds of information and insights necessary to make sound and sensible decisions regarding the utilization of the method of interaction analysis.

Overview of Interaction Analysis

General Description of Method

Before discussing the important methodological considerations involved in the practice of interaction analysis, it would seem wise to clarify the general nature and purpose of the method. Although interaction analysis procedures display considerable variety across research studies (see, e.g., Ellis, 1979; Fisher, 1970; Hirokawa, 1980a,

1983; Mabry, 1975a,b; Poole, 1981; Scheidel & Crowell, 1964), the general approach involves an attempt to classify objectively the communicative behaviors (or actions) of group members in accordance with a set of carefully defined, pre-established categories. In the typical study, trained observers usually segment the interaction process into discrete units, then classify these units within the categories of a particular coding system. In most cases, the observers are instructed to classify each unit into only one of the available categories, and great care is taken to insure that the behaviors are accurately recorded in the exact order they were produced. Thus, the group interaction process is usually operationalized in terms of a stream (or sequential series) of discrete categorized acts—that is, if A, B, and C are the categories comprising one's coding system, then the interaction process might be depicted as: A-C-B-A-C-B-A-. . . . Once all of the relevant units of interaction have been categorized, various statistical procedures are then employed to search for distributional and/or sequential patterns of interaction (see, e.g., Gouran & Baird, 1972; Hirokawa, 1980a,b; Scheidel & Crowell, 1964).

Purpose of the Analysis

Analysis of group interaction data, using the method of interaction analysis, is designed to obtain quantitative, descriptive information regarding the nature of the interaction process. In particular, the analysis seeks to obtain information regarding (a) the interactive structure of the group; (b) the distributional structure of categorized acts; and (c) the sequential structure among categorized acts.

Interactive structure. One of the principal goals of interaction analysis is to obtain a profile of the interactive structure of the group (see Bales, 1950). Here the researcher is interested in identifying the emergent structure of message exchanges among members. For example, if the group consists of four members (A, B, C, and D), the researcher may be interested in discovering how often A talks to B; A talks to C; A talks to D; B talks to C; B talks to D; and C talks to D during the interaction process. In obtaining such data, the researcher is then able to construct a profile of the emergent network configuration of the group—that is, who tends to interact with whom on a regular basis during the discussion.

Distributional structure. Another common goal of interaction analysis is to obtain profiles of the distributional frequency of categorized acts. That is, the researcher seeks to discover how many units of interaction were coded within each of the available categories. For example, if A, B, and C represent the categories in the coding system, the researcher may wish to discover how many units of A, B, and C were produced during the course of the group discussion by the group as a whole, or by individual members of the group. In some cases, the researcher may also want to partition the interaction process into relatively equal time segments, then obtain frequency distribution profiles for each of those time segments (see, e.g., Fisher, 1970; Hirokawa, 1983).

Sequential structure. One of the central assumptions underlying the method of interaction analysis concerns the interdependence of communicative behaviors (Fisher, 1978). That is, behaviors of group members are assumed to be interdependent such that the behavior of a group member is a function of the previous behaviors of other group members. As such, interaction analysis is often used to obtain information regarding the nature of sequential dependencies (or orderings) among categorized acts. For example, the researcher can use the method to discover whether particular categorized units of interaction (e.g., A, B, and C) tend to follow each other in consistent ways (e.g., A—B or A—B—C) during the interaction process. It is important to recognize here that the identification of sequential patterns often necessitates the use of fairly sophisticated time-series statistical procedures like Markov chain analysis (see, e.g., Ellis, 1979; Ellis & Fisher, 1975; Krueger, 1979) or lag sequential analysis (see, e.g., Hirokawa, 1980a; Putnam, 1983).

Considerations for Doing Interaction Analysis

There are at least three major issues which need to be faced by the practitioner of interaction analysis prior to the use of the method: (a) Appropriateness of method, (b) Selection of unit of analysis, and (c) Selection of category system.

Appropriateness of Method

The first and most important consideration in utilizing the method of interaction analysis is whether the method is an appropriate one. Specifically, the researcher needs to ascertain whether the method will allow him/her to obtain the kind(s) of information s/he seeks. As a number of authors have cautioned, the research value of interaction analysis is contingent on the fact that it is employed to obtain data which *can be obtained* through the use of the method (Fisher, 1977).

In deciding whether to employ the method of interaction analysis, the researcher should remember that the method is designed principally to obtain *descriptive* data regarding the nature and structure of the group interaction process. As Bales (1970, p. 92) notes, it is designed to classify "how group members communicate, that is, who does what to whom in the process of their interaction." The method is *not* designed, however, to obtain such nonobservable, "interpretive" data as the content of messages, the personal meanings of group members, the communicative rules and norms underlying the organization of social interaction, or the psychological effects of messages. Information of that nature clearly necessitates the use of alternative methods like content analysis, discourse analysis, or critical analysis (see, e.g., Bormann, Pratt, & Putnam, 1978; Cheseboro, Cragan, & McCullough, 1973; Geist & Chandler, 1984; O'Keefe et al., 1980; Sigman, 1984). In short, the method of interaction analysis is most appropriate when the researcher seeks to obtain descriptive information regarding *observable* aspects of the group interaction process (Fisher, 1977).

Unit of Analysis

A second consideration facing the practitioner of interaction analysis concerns the selection of the basic *unit of analysis.* The researcher must identify the smallest discriminable segment of interaction which can be coded by an observer using the set of available categories (Bales, 1950). The selection of a unit of analysis is not clear-cut, and is further complicated by the general absence of a standardized unit in the group communication literature (Fisher, 1978). For the most part, researchers have utilized at least four different units of analysis: thought units, themes, time intervals, and speech acts.

Thought units. Several researchers have segmented the group interaction process into "thought units" (see, e.g., Bales, 1950, 1970; Crowell & Scheidel, 1961). In this case, the basic unit of analysis is defined as a verbal or nonverbal act which, in its context, can be taken as a single simple sentence expressing or conveying a complete thought or idea (Bales, 1970). As such, the utterance of a group member may consist of one or more units of analysis. For example, the simple statement, "I think we should choose option X" would be coded as a single unit of interaction because it conveys only one complete thought; but a more complex statement like, "I think we should choose X because it meets all of our evaluation criteria" would be coded as two units of interaction because it consists of two distinguishable thoughts ("I think we should choose X" and "It meets all of our evaluation criteria").

Themes. Other researchers have segmented the interaction process into thematic units (see, e.g., Berg, 1967a, b). Here the basic unit of analysis is defined as a group of sequentially-linked utterances focused on the same topic or subject. In using this unit of analysis, the researcher demarcates the beginning and end of a theme (i.e., the first and last statements comprising the thematic unit), then assigns it to one of the available categories. For example, Berg (1967a) initially classified themes into two general categories—"task" and "non-task"—then further classified them into one of two subdivisions of each major category—"substantive" and "procedural" for task; "irrelevant" and "disruptive" for nontask.

Time intervals. Another unit of analysis involves the segmentation of the interaction process into time units (see, e.g., Amidon & Hough, 1967; Hawes, 1972). In this case, the researcher divides the interaction process into specific time periods (e.g., 15-second intervals), then codes each time period according to the available categories. Hawes (1972), for example, divided the interaction process into 10-second intervals, then had his coders classify each interval into one of 13 categories.

Speech acts. Perhaps the most frequently employed unit of analysis in the group communication literature involves the segmentation of interaction into "speech acts" (see, e.g., Ellis, 1979; Ellis & Fisher, 1975; Fisher, 1970; Gouran & Baird, 1972; Hirokawa, 1980a, 1982; Poole, 1981). In this case, the basic unit is defined as "an uninterrupted utterance of a single group member which is perceived to perform a specific function (or action) within the group interaction process" (Hirokawa, 1980b, p. 63). When employing the "act" as the unit of analysis, each uninterrupted utterance is treated as a single codable unit of interaction and assigned to one of the available categories. In cases where a specific act can conceivably be classified into more than one category, the observer is called upon to utilize a pre-established rule to make the assignment. For example, the coder may be told that if statement "X" can be appropriately classified into more than one category, s/he should assign it to the "most appropriate" one.

The selection of a basic unit of analysis is ultimately dependent on the nature and purpose(s) of the research study—that is, what information is sought; what controls need to be implemented; etc. For example, if the researcher is interested in studying the nature of idea development in group deliberation (see, e.g., Scheidel & Crowell, 1964), then s/he would be well-advised to segment the group interaction process into *thought* units. Alternatively, if the researcher is interested in examining the relationship between certain types of communicative actions and specific group outcomes, e.g., consensus formation (Fisher, 1970; DeStephen, 1983); decision quality (Hirokawa, 1980a, 1982, 1983); conflict resolution (Ellis & Fisher, 1975), speech *acts* would seem to be the most appropriate unit of analysis. The use of *thematic* units appears to be most appropriate when the researcher is interested in the topical shift (or movement) of the interaction process; while *time* units seem most appropriate when the researcher wishes to control for the content of what is being coded (Hawes, 1972).

Selection of Category System

Having decided on an appropriate unit of analysis, the next important consideration facing the practitioner of interaction analysis concerns the selection of a category system. As Fisher (1978, p. 4) points out, "The worth of any investigation which employs interaction analysis is ultimately determined by the categories used to classify interaction categories. . . . As units of interaction are classified and placed within categories, they are only as valuable as the conceptual/empirical value of the category-classes themselves."

As in the case of units of analysis, no standardized category system is evident in the small group literature. Bales' (1950, 1970) Interaction Process Analysis (IPA) system is one of the most widely recognized and employed schemes. However, a number of alternative category systems (far too many to be covered in this chapter) have been developed and employed by small group researchers (see, e.g., Amidon & Hough, 1967; Bales, 1950, 1970; Berg, 1967a,b; Borgatta & Crowther, 1965; Ellis & Fisher, 1975; Ellis 1979; Fisher, 1970; Crowell & Scheidel, 1961; Hirokawa, 1982). In fact, several recent critics have suggested that one of the principal reasons why we currently lack integrated group communication research is because researchers have failed to utilize the same coding systems in analyzing group interaction processes (see, e.g., Gouran & Fisher, 1983; Poole, 1981; Poole & Hirokawa, 1986).

Interaction category systems can generally be distinguished on the basis of two characteristics: (a) the nature of their focus—that is, whether they are designed to categorize "micro" or "macro" aspects of interaction; and (b) the degree of their exclusivity—that is, whether a given unit of interaction can be "legitimately" classified into more than one category.

Nature of focus. Category systems can be distinguished on the basis of their *macro* or *micro* focus. *Macro* systems consist of categories which are designed to classify fairly large (or "molar") aspects of group interaction. Berg's (1967a,b) thematic coding system, for example, employed categories designed to describe whether units of interaction (i.e., themes) were either "task" or "non-task" in nature, as well as whether they were "substantive," "procedural," "irrelevant," or "disruptive" in their orientation. Similarly, Ellis' (1979) relational coding scheme was designed to classify interaction units into such broad categories as "strong relationship dominance," "weak relationship dominance," "relational equivalence," "relational deference," and "relational submission." Other coding schemes developed by Hawes (1972), Hirokawa (1980b), and Mabry (1975b) also seek to classify larger aspects of the group interaction process.

Micro systems, on the other hand, are designed to classify smaller (or "molecular") aspects of group interaction. Bales' IPA system, for example, is designed to classify the specific purpose of individual utterances. Thus it is comprised of such categories as "gives information," "agrees," "disagrees," "asks for information," "asks for opinion," and "asks for suggestion" (Bales, 1970). Similarly, the categories comprising Fisher's (1970) "Decision Proposal System" are designed to describe the specific communicative function of individual utterances. Thus the system contains such categories as "statement of favor," "statement of disfavor," "clarification," "modification," "agreement," and "disagreement."

Degree of exclusivity. Interaction category systems can also be distinguished on the basis of the exclusivity of their categories. Most of the existing coding schemes (e.g., Bales, 1950, 1970; Crowell & Scheidel, 1961; Ellis, 1979; Fisher, 1970; Hirokawa, 1980a,b) are *mutually exclusive* systems. That is, each of the categories comprising the system is treated as an independent classification such that a given unit of interaction can only be classified into one of the available categories of the system.

Several researchers, however, have also developed *non-exclusive* category systems (see, e.g., Borgatta & Crowther, 1965; Leathers, 1971). In these cases, the categories comprising the system are such that a given unit of interaction can be coded simultaneously into more than one of the available categories. In Borgatta & Crowther's (1965) "Behavior Scores System," for example, each category represents a specific behavioral description (e.g., "antagonism," "assertive," "supportive," "dominant"), and a given unit of interaction can be coded into more than one category. Thus, a given utterance could be coded as "antagonism-supportive" or "dominant-assertive."

Obviously, the selection of an interaction category system is not a clear-cut one. Its selection is usually dependent upon four considerations. First and foremost, the selection of a category system is guided by the study's research question(s). The category system employed by a researcher should allow him/her to systematically examine those actions and behaviors which are directly relevant to the research question(s). For example, if the researcher is interested in examining the relationship between group interaction and consensus formation, s/he should employ a category system whose categories are directly relevant and theoretically related to consensus formation. Likewise, if the researcher is interested in examining the relationship between group interaction and decisional outcomes, s/he should select a category system which allows him/her to focus on the behaviors most likely to be related to decisional outcomes (Hirokawa, 1982). As Fisher (1978) succinctly puts it, the "GIGO (Garbage In Garbage Out) principle is fully operative in selecting the categories to be used in interaction analysis." By this he means that unless the categories being employed allow the researcher to focus on important behaviors, s/he is unlikely to obtain useful information from the analysis.

The selection of a category system is also influenced by the theoretical orientation of the researcher. More precisely, the category system employed by a researcher "must be consistent with the explanatory framework or rationale being used to guide the act of inquiry" (Fisher, 1978). For example, if the researcher believes that the impact of group interaction on decision quality is best understood by examining "micro" aspects of the interaction process, then s/he would be well advised to select a category system which focuses on smaller aspects of the interaction process. On the other hand, if the researcher believes that the most important interaction variables to examine are more "macro" in nature, then a category system which focuses on larger aspects of the interaction process should be selected. Likewise, if the researcher believes that an understanding of a particular group outcome necessitates the simultaneous, multiple coding of interaction, then s/he would be well advised to select a nonexclusive coding system. However, if the researcher believes that group interaction behaviors tend to function in only one specific way in a given context, then a mutually exclusive system would appear to be more appropriate.

Third, the selection of an interaction category system is influenced by the analytical procedures employed by the researcher. For one thing, the selection of a category system is dependent on whether the researcher intends to code "live" or taped interactions. If the researcher intends to code "live" interactions (i.e., interactions taking place at the time they are being coded), s/he would be well-advised to select a relatively simple category system—that is, one which possesses few categories, and requires coders to make straightforward decisions in coding interaction. On the other hand, if the researcher is able to code taped interactions, then s/he has the luxury of employing more complicated coding schemes, because coders are now able to review portions of the interactions while they are coding them.

The selection of a category system is also influenced by the statistical analyses that are planned for the coded data. As Hewes (1978) points out, the manner in which one codes social interaction must be consistent with the manner in which one intends to analyze the coded data statistically. He suggests, for example, that nonexclusive systems (i.e., those which allow for simultaneous, multiple coding of interaction) are appropriate if one wishes to obtain distributional frequencies and proportions. However, if one wishes to employ stochastic analysis procedures (e.g., Markov chain analysis; lag sequential analysis) nonexclusive systems would present major problems in the interpretation of the results of the analysis. In such cases, mutually exclusive systems would be more appropriate.

Finally, the selection of a category system must be influenced by the *representational* validity of existing systems (Poole & Folger, 1981). Although the issue of representational validity is a complicated one which requires discussion beyond the scope of this chapter, the central concern here is that the researcher selects a system comprised of categories which are meaningful to the interactors themselves. In other words, the purposes, functions, or constructs identified by the coding system need to be recognizable by the participants in the interaction (Poole & Folger, p. 26). In short, the category system selected by a researcher needs to be such that the participants in an interaction are able to identify examples of each category comprising the system accurately. Unless the categories comprising the system are meaningful to the interactors, the results of an analysis using the system are immediately open to criticism (Poole & Folger, 1981). Unfortunately, most of the existing category systems—with the exception of Bales (1970) "IPA" scheme and Fisher's (1970) "Decision Proposal System"—have not been demonstrated to possess representational validity.

Other Considerations

In addition to the three aforementioned considerations, that is, the appropriateness of the method; the selection of a unit of analysis; and the selection of a category system, the practitioner of interaction analysis needs to address several additional issues and considerations. Unfortunately, most of these considerations require extensive discussion beyond the scope of this chapter and can only be mentioned briefly. These additional considerations include: procedures for coding interaction; procedures for establishing intercoder reliability; and procedures for analyzing coded interaction.

Coding interaction. Quite clearly, an important aspect of any study utilizing the method of interaction analysis concerns the procedures employed in coding interactions. Particularly salient is the question of whether to code the entire interaction process, or only random samples of that process. In most cases, it is probably advisable for the researcher to code the entire interaction process. To be sure, if s/he is interested in obtaining a distributional profile of the entire interaction process, or is interested in identifying sequential patterns of interaction within the interaction process, then it is imperative for coders to classify every unit on an act-by-act basis (Bales & Cohen, 1978). However, in some cases the researcher may wish to partition an interaction stream into a number of time segments, then code only a sample of those segments. This is especially useful if the researcher is (a) working with a limited sample of groups (e.g., three of four groups) and wishes to treat each group discussion as multiple samples to increase his/her sample size (see, e.g., Jackson & Jacobs, 1983); (b) interested in controlling for atypical (or otherwise unusual) actions; or (c) interested in controlling for the influence of discussion content on the coding of interaction (see, e.g., Hawes, 1972).

Establishing intercoder reliability. The issue of reliability concerns the degree of agreement among observers. If two or more coders consistently classify units of interaction into the same categories, then the coding is said to be reliable. Guetzkow (1950) suggests that there are two types of coder reliability—*unitizing reliability,* which concerns intercoder agreement regarding the identification of classifiable units; and *categorizing reliability,* which concerns intercoder agreement regarding the classification of units. In establishing the reliability of one's coding, the researcher is faced with several considerations. Most important, s/he needs to make certain that the observers are properly trained, since inadequate instruction is a principal source of low reliability (Ellis, 1977). In doing so, the researcher needs to insure that the coders (a) fully understand the categories comprising the system, (b) possess appropriate classification rules and guidelines, and (c) are allowed enough practice time (on actual interactions) to master the category system being employed (Bales, 1950, 1970).

In addition to insuring the proper training of one's coders, the researcher also needs to monitor the reliability of the coders. The monitoring of intercoder reliability essentially involves the calculation of coder agreement *beyond chance expectations.* The notion of "beyond chance expectations" is important because many existing reliability coefficients fail in this respect (Ellis, 1977). Simple percentage of agreement, for example, is a poor index of reliability because chance agreements are not accounted for. Similarly, measures of reliability based on the degree of correlation between coder classifications are equally problematic. As Ellis (1977) notes, the existence of a high degree of correlation between coders does not necessarily indicate a high degree of agreement. He points out, for example, that a high degree of correlation may be a consequence of the fact that the coders consistently classify units into opposite (or otherwise different) categories. Appropriate and frequently employed measures of inter-coder reliability include Scott's *pi* (1955), Cohen's *kappa* (1960, 1968), and Guetzkow's (1950) categorizing coefficient. The reader may wish to consult Ellis (1977) for a discussion of the relative advantages and disadvantages of alternative measures of reliability.

Analysis of coded data. A final consideration facing the practitioner of interaction analysis concerns the analysis of coded interaction. As noted earlier, coded interactions are typically presented to the researcher in the form of act-by-act streams of sequences. The task of the researcher is to simplify the behavioral streams so as to obtain information regarding interactive, distributional, and/or sequential structures of interaction. Statistical methods and procedures available to the researcher for such purposes are plentiful and, in fact, may be a source of confusion. In selecting methods of data analysis, the researcher needs to keep two things in mind. First, the researcher needs to remember that in most cases coded interaction represents nominal data and needs to be treated as such. Quite often communication researchers analyze nominal data as if they were interval in nature, and this presents problems for the proper interpretation of findings. Second, the researcher needs to recognize that different information requirements necessitate the use of different statistical procedures. For example, simple tests of frequency (e.g., chi-square analysis) are appropriate when the researcher is interested in analyzing either the interactive or distributional structure of interaction, but more complex stochastic procedures—e.g., nonparametric time series analysis (Gottman, 1979), Markov chain analysis (Anderson & Goodman, 1957), lag sequential analysis (Sackett, 1978)—are required if the research seeks to discover sequential patterns of interaction. In selecting any method of analysis, however, the researcher must be certain that (a) the procedure is appropriate for the question(s) s/he is asking, and (b) s/he fully understands the logic and relevant parameters of the statistic being employed.

Problems With Interaction Analysis

Interaction analysis clearly represents a viable approach to the study of group interaction processes. However, interaction analysis (like any method) is subject to a number of criticisms. Specifically, critics have identified three serious problems with the use of the method: (a) Problem of simplicity, (b) Problem of glossing, and (c) Problem of generalizability.

Problem of simplicity. A common criticism of interaction analysis concerns the nature of categories employed in the analysis. Critics maintain that the classification of interaction units into categories typically ignores the multidimensional and multifunctional nature of talk. For example, an utterance may function in one way for one individual, but in an entirely different way for another individual. Thus, coding an utterance into a single category ignores its other possible functions. Fortunately, recent developments in category systems have begun to address this problem. Hirokawa (1980b), for instance, has developed a multidimensional category system which allows coders to simultaneously classify various "macro" and "micro" functions of utterances. Other recent procedures involve the repeated coding of interaction using different category systems (see, e.g., Bales & Cohen, 1978; DeStephen, 1983; Poole, 1981). While the method of interaction analysis does involve the simplification of group interaction processes, steps can be taken to minimize problematic consequences of doing so.

Problem of glossing. A second problem with the method of interaction analysis also concerns the nature of categories employed in the analysis. Critics suggest that no matter how many categories are included in a category system, some important ones will be absent. As a result, the classification of interaction units necessarily involves a certain amount of "glossing"—that is, the improper classification of units due to the absence of appropriate categories. To illustrate this problem, suppose a coder is asked to classify units into one of three categories—A, B, and C. Suppose further that s/he encounters a particular utterance which is neither an "A," "B," or "C." At this point, the researcher must classify the unit in accordance with what s/he believes to be the *most* appropriate category, and, regardless of the choice made, imprecise classification takes place. Once again, however, recent developments in interaction analysis procedures have begun to deal with this problem. In particular, Poole and Folger (1981) have proposed a workable procedure for insuring that one's coding scheme is sufficiently exhaustive—that is, the vast majority of utterances can be classified precisely into the categories of the system.

Problem of validity. A third problem with the method concerns the question of coding validity—that is, the extent to which the coded unit "represents the 'reality' of the function purportedly performed by that communicative act" (Fisher, 1978, p. 12). Critics suggest that because the classification of interaction units inherently involves subjective judgements and inferences, there always exists the danger that the classification of a unit will *not* reflect its actual nature, purpose, or function. For example, an utterance classified as "seems hostile" by a coder may actually be perceived as a "joke" by the participants involved in the interaction. Fortunately, recent methodological advances, particularly those by Poole and Folger (1981), have also made this problem increasingly tractable.

Conclusion

One simple conclusion emerges from the preceding discussion: the method of interaction analysis represents a useful tool for studying small group communication, provided it is used appropriately. The appropriate use of the method necessitates careful consideration of a number of difficult issues and problems at various stages in the research endeavor. As with any method, interaction analysis does have its limitations, and the reader is well advised to explore alternative approaches like discourse analysis or critical analysis before deciding on the method of interaction analysis. If utilized prudently, however, interaction analysis can yield important and useful information regarding the nature of group interaction processes.

References

Amidon, E.J., & Hough, J.B. (1967). *Interaction analysis: Theory, research, and application.* Reading, MA: Addison-Wesley.

Anderson, T., & Goodman, L. (1957). Statistical inference about Markov chains. *Annals of Mathematical Statistics, 28,* 89–110.

Bales, R.F. (1950). *Interaction process analysis.* Cambridge, MA: Addison-Wesley.

Bales, R.F. (1970). *Personality and interpersonal behavior.* New York: Holt, Rinehart & Winston.

Bales, R.F., & Cohen, S.P. (1979). *SYMLOG: A system for the multilevel observation of groups.* New York: Free Press.

Berg, D.M. (1967a). A thematic approach to the analysis of the task-oriented small group. *Central States Speech Journal, 18,* 285–291.

Berg, D.M. (1967b). A descriptive analysis of the distribution and duration of themes discussed by task-oriented small groups. *Speech Monographs, 34,* 172–175.

Bochner, A.P. (1978). On taking ourselves seriously: An analysis of some persistent problems and promising directions in interpersonal research. *Human Communication Research, 4,* 179–191.

Borgatta, E.F., & Crowther, B. (1965). A workbook for the study of social interaction processes. Chicago: Rand McNally.

Bormann, E.G., Pratt, J., & Putnam, L. (1978). Power, authority, and sex: Male response to female leadership. *Communication Monographs, 45,* 119–155.

Cheseboro, J.W., Cragan, J.F., & McCullough, P. (1973). The small group techniques of the radical revolutionary: A synthetic study of consciousness raising. *Speech Monographs, 40,* 136–146.

Cohen, J.A. (1960). A coefficient of agreement for nominal scales. *Educational and Psychological Measurement, 20,* 37–46.

Cohen, J.A. (1968). Weighted kappa: Nominal scale agreement with provision for scaled disagreement or partial credit. *Psychological Bulletin, 70,* 213–220.

Coulthard, M. (1977). *An introduction to discourse analysis.* London: Longman.

Cragan, J., and Wright, D. (1980). Small group research of the 1970's: A synthesis and critique. *Central States Speech Journal, 31,* 197–213.

Crowell, L., & Scheidel, T.M. (1961). Categories for analysis of idea-development in discussion groups. *Journal of Social Psychology, 54,* 155–168.

DeStephen, R.S. (1983). High and low consensus groups: A content and relational interaction analysis. *Small Group Behavior, 14,* 143–162.

Ellis, D.G. (1977). *Issues in analyzing sequential interaction data: A plea for rigor in matters of observation.* Paper presented at the Speech Communication Association, Washington, D.C.

Ellis, D.G. (1979). Relational control in two group systems. *Communication Monographs, 46,* 153–166.

Ellis, D.G., & Fisher, B.A. (1975). Phases of conflict in small group development: A Markov analysis. *Human Communication Research, 1,* 195–212.

Fisher, B.A. (1970). Decision emergence: Phases in group decision-making. *Speech Monographs, 37,* 53–66.

Fisher, B.A. (1977). *Interaction analysis: An underutilized methodology in communication.* Paper presented at the Western Speech Communication Association, Phoenix, AZ.

Fisher, B.A. (1978). *Current status of interaction analysis research.* Paper presented at the Speech Communication Association, Minneapolis, MN.

Geist, P.R., & Chandler, T.A. (1984). Account analysis of influence in group decision-making. *Communication Monographs, 51,* 67–78.

Gouran, D.S., & Baird, J.E. (1972). An analysis of distributional and sequential structure in problem-solving and informal group discussion. *Speech Monographs, 39,* 16–22.

Gouran, D.S., & Fisher, B.A. (1984). The functions of communication in the formation, maintenance, and performance of small groups. In C.C. Arnold and J.W. Bowers (Eds.), *Handbook of rhetorical and communication theory.* Boston: Allyn & Bacon.

Guetzkow, H. (1950). Unitizing and categorizing problems in coding qualitative data. *Journal of Clinical Psychology, 6,* 47–50.

Hackman, J.R., & Morris, C.G. (1975). Group tasks, group interaction process, and group performance effectiveness: A review and proposed integration. *Advances in experimental social psychology, 8,* 45–99.

Hare, A.P. (1976). Handbook of small group research (2nd ed.). New York: Free Press.

Hawes, L.C. (1972). The effects of interviewer style on patterns of dyadic communication. *Speech Monographs, 39,* 114–123.

Hawes, L.C. (1978). The reflexivity of communication research. *Western Journal of Speech Communication, 42,* 12–20.

Hewes, D.E. (1978). The sequential analysis of social interaction. *Quarterly Journal of Speech, 65,* 56–73.

Hirokawa, R.Y. (1980a). A comparative analysis of communication patterns within effective and ineffective decision-making groups. *Communication Monographs, 47,* 312–321.

Hirokawa, R.Y. (1980b). *A function-oriented analysis of small group interaction within effective and ineffective decision-making groups.* Unpublished dissertation, University of Washington.

Hirokawa, R.Y. (1982). Group communication and problem-solving effectiveness I: A critical review of inconsistent findings. *Communication Quarterly, 30,* 134–141.

Hirokawa, R.Y. (1983). Group communication and problem-solving effectiveness: An investigation of group phases. *Human Communication Research, 9,* 292–305.

Jackson, S., & Jacobs, S. (1983). Generalizing about messages: Suggestions for design and analysis of experiments. *Human Communication Research, 9,* 169–191.

Krueger, D.L. (1979). A stochastic analysis of communication development in self-analytic groups. *Human Communication Research, 5,* 314–324.

Leathers, D.G. (1971). The feedback rating instrument: A new means of evaluating discussion. *Central States Speech Journal, 22,* 32–42.

Mabry, E.A. (1975a). Sequential structure of interaction in encounter groups. *Human Communication Research, 1,* 302–307.

Mabry, E.A. (1975b). Exploratory analysis of a developmental model for task-oriented small groups. *Human Communication Research, 2,* 66–73.

McGrath, J.E., & Altman, I. (1966). *Small group research: A synthesis and critique of the field.* New York: Holt, Rinehart, & Winston.

O'Keefe, B.J., Delia, J.G., & O'Keefe, D.J. (1980). Interaction analysis and the analysis of interaction organization. *Studies of Symbolic Interaction, 3,* 25–57.

Poole, M.S. (1981). Decision development in small groups I: A comparison of two models. *Communication Monographs, 48,* 1–24.

Poole, M.S., & Folger, J.P. (1981). A new method of establishing the representational validity of interaction coding schemes: Do we see what they see? *Human Communication Research, 8,* 26–42.

Poole, M.S., & Hirokawa, R.Y. (1986). Communication and group decision-making: A critical assessment. In R.Y. Hirokawa and M.S. Poole (Eds.), *Communication and group decision-making.* Beverly Hills, CA: Sage.

Poole, M.S., Seibold, D.R., & McPhee, R.D. (1985). Group decision-making as a structurational process. *Quarterly Journal of Speech, 71,* 74–102.

Putnam, L.L. (1983). Small group work climates: A lag-sequential analysis of group interaction. *Small Group Behavior, 14,* 465–494.

Sackett, G.P. (1978). The lag sequential analysis of contingency and cyclicity in behavioral interaction research. In J.D. Osofsky (Ed.), *Handbook of infant development.* New York: Wiley, 1978.

Scheidel, T.M., & Crowell, L. (1964). Idea development in small groups. *Quarterly Journal of Speech, 50,* 140–145.

Scott, W.A. (1955). Reliability of content analysis: The case of nominal scale coding. *Public Opinion Quarterly, 19,* 321–325.

Sigman, S.J. (1984). Talk and interaction strategy in a task-oriented group. *Small Group Behavior, 15,* 33–51.

CHAPTER 9

Group Decision Making: An Approach to Integrative Research

Dennis S. Gouran[1]

Over the past two decades, a number of critiques of small group research have been published (e.g., Bormann, 1970, 1980; Cragan & Wright, 1980; Gouran, 1973b, Hirokawa, 1982b, McGrath & Altman, 1966; Mortensen, 1970). Since research on decision making in groups represents a substantial portion of the total volume of that scholarship, one presumes that criticisms applying to the study of small groups in general also apply to the study of decision-making in particular.

Of all the criticisms advanced, the most frequent has been, in the words of Shaw (1981), "the failure to develop integrative theories" (p. 446). Integrative theories, however, require integrative concepts, and their absence is precisely the problem that has characterized, and continues to characterize, research on small group decision-making. At least, none of the general classes of decisional attributes on which research has focused appears to be adequate to serve the function of an integrative concept.

The purposes of this chapter are to: (a) examine the outcome attributes on which researchers interested in decision-making groups have concentrated, (b) show why none of the classes of variables studied, when taken alone, has the promise of becoming an integrative concept, (c) suggest a variable that does have such promise, (d) sketch an approach to its measurement, and (e) discuss the advantages of viewing group decision-making and related research from the perspective suggested.

---

[1] The author wishes to express his appreciation to Susan R. Chapdelaine and Bruce C. McKinney for their assistance in locating and reviewing research on which this chapter is based.

Decision Attributes

Because of the array of variable names, many of which are interchangeable, and the multiplicity of operational definitions that accompany them, it can easily appear as if there is a virtually limitless reservoir of decisional outcomes and related attributes in which researchers have interest. A more careful examination of their work, however, reveals that the variable set is reducible to a comparatively small number. In general, the characteristics on which those doing research on decision-making in small groups have concentrated fall into four categories: (a) the correctness of decisions, (b) the quality of decisions, (c) the utility of decisions, and (d) the acceptability of decisions.[2]

Correctness of Decisions

Early research in group dynamics relied heavily on tasks involving judgments of attributes for which objective measures of the *correctness* of choice were available.[3] Such tasks included estimating the number of beans in a jar (Jenness, 1932), completing true-false tests (Gurnee, 1937), and solving mathematical puzzles, such as the cannibals and missionaries problem (Shaw, 1932) and the horse-trading problem (Torrance, 1954). These types of tasks still appear in research on decision-making in groups, although less frequently. Janssens and Nuttin (1976) had groups estimate the number of objects on a slide,

---

[2] This classificational scheme appears to exclude a variety of decisional outcomes that have attracted the attention of researchers, for example, shifts to risk and caution, polarization, attitude formation and change, compliance, and interpersonal attraction. Although these phenomena are often studied in decision-making settings, they are not outcomes toward which decisional activity is directed. In other words, one could not infer from the purposes for which groups engage in decision making that their intention is to achieve any of these outcomes. On the other hand, given the nature of decision making—that is, choices among alternatives that serve as answers to particular types of questions—one can infer that the activity is directed toward the outcomes on which the chapter focuses. This is not to imply that the other outcomes mentioned are unimportant in the study of group decision making. Consideration of them is often useful in explaining or assessing the correctness, quality, utility, or acceptability of decisions, for they reflect aspects of social influence processes that most certainly enter into the activity of group decision making. In this sense, they serve as *explicantia* rather than *explicanda*.

[3] Correctness, in the context of decision-making research, refers to matters of accuracy and truth, not propriety. It suggests the discovery of an answer to a question or solution to a problem that, according to specified rules, is the only one possible, or one in a restricted few.

and Kanekar and Rosenbaum (1972) used the number of anagrams a group could correctly construct as an index of effectiveness.

Tasks such as those just described have the obvious advantage of permitting one to say with both accuracy and confidence how closely the members of a group have approached their objective, what they have achieved, and how they compare with other groups and individuals. In the latter regard, these tasks perhaps have proved to have the most convenience. One of the main thrusts in early research was to determine whether groups or individuals were better at certain kinds of judgmental tasks. That concern has persisted in research on creative problem-solving, but the focus has shifted from the correctness of choice to the quality of ideas generated.

Tasks which produce easily measurable and quantifiable evidence of correctness lead some individuals to draw a distinction between problem solving and decision making. So long as a task requires choice among available options, however, the distinction is an artificial one. The more serious issue is whether or not research examining the correctness of choices that either groups or individuals make entails tasks that are typical of problems that decision makers usually address. The answer to that question is almost certainly a negative one. The likelihood of a group's ever having to solve a puzzle, estimate the number of beans in a jar, or the like, outside the context of a laboratory study, is small, but even those relying on these kinds of devices are aware of that. The apparent feeling is that the processes involved generalize to other more common situations.

Groups are frequently asked to resolve issues for which the accuracy or correctness of their decision is a concern, for example, determining the guilt or innocence of someone who has been accused of a crime. In these types of situations, however, a fundamental difference exists. The correctness of a decision often is unverifiable. At least, the logical operations and informational requirements for verifying decisions are not the same. Hence, although the concern may be with making a correct decision or accurate judgment, the concept of correctness, at least as historically studied in research on decision making, is far too restricted. It applies most specifically to the type of task that Steiner (1972) labels "disjunctive," that is, one requiring only that one member of a group know the answer to a question or how to solve a problem for the group as a whole to be correct. Most decisional tasks are not of this type, including those for which correctness of choice is ideally the outcome. Although juries, for instance, are charged with determining innocence or guilt, their actual task is to reach agreement about what is the truth. This qualifies the task as "conjunctive," that is, one in which the successful achievement of an objective is dependent on all the members.

Even if the previously mentioned problems did not exist, correctness does not appear to be a very good candidate to serve as an integrative concept. There are simply too many situations involving decision making in which the correctness of choice or the accuracy of judgment are not relevant considerations. In short, correctness lacks the universality demanded on an integrative concept.

Quality of Decisions

Another attribute of decision outcomes on which inquiry has focused falls under the heading of *quality*. Some researchers use the term *quality* interchangeably with *correctness*. Correctness, of course, can be subsumed under quality, in that a correct choice would logically be viewed as possessing higher quality than an incorrect one. It does not follow, however, that all decisions judged to be of high quality would have a corresponding dimension of correctness. The quality/correctness relationship, when it exists, has quality as the genus and correctness as the species.

Most of those doing research on the quality of decisions view the concept from a subjective perspective. To them, quality is an attribute to be inferred from conformity to criteria that those judging it consider to be important, or are otherwise led to believe are important. This allows considerable freedom in the determination of what constitutes the quality of a decision.

In some instances, quality has been assessed in a seemingly objective manner, as in the case of the familiar survival problems (see, for example, Burleson, Levine & Samter, 1984; Hirokawa, 1982a; Miner, 1984). In studies utilizing such tasks, the approach is to have an expert or group of experts specify the decision or set of choices that should be made under a specified set of circumstances and then to determine the extent to which groups make choices consistent with expert opinion. A variation is to have experts rate decisions in terms of quality after the fact (see Hirokawa, 1980). In either case, the so-called expert's opinion serves as the standard of judgment.

Other scholars have used a more arbitray approach by stipulating on a priori grounds what is the "best" decision among a set of alternatives a group is given. For example, Falk (1981), Hoffman (1959), and Hoffman and Maier (1961) all used a task called the "Change of Work Problem." In dealing with this problem, decision-making groups have the option of endorsing the status quo, a new proposal described in the problem, or an "inventive" solution that combines elements of both. Inventive solutions are presumed to be of higher quality because they are the product of the group members' own thinking. Why any particular combination of elements of the "old" and "new" solutions would be necessarily superior to either is not clear.

Still another approach to assessing the quality of decisions relies on perceptual data. In research using this basis for discriminating among decisions, observer/raters (sometimes trained and sometimes not) are asked to assign numerical evaluations to a set of characteristics that the investigator has chosen in relation to the type of issue being discussed (see, for example, Gouran, Brown, & Henry, 1978; Harper & Askling, 1980; Hirokawa & Pace, 1983; Jablin, 1981; Philipsen, Mulac, & Dietrich, 1979). The assumption underlying this method of determininig the quality of a decision is that consistency among raters necessarily reflects attributes of the decision itself.

A focus on the quality of decisions has permitted scholars to investigate the behavior of groups pursuing tasks that more nearly resemble realistic situations. And, as mentioned above, the concept can subsume correctness. These aspects of the concept of quality, therefore, give it an expanded utility and, hence, appeal as an intergrative concept.

Despite the flexibility that quality as an attribute of decisions gives to researchers in studying decisional processes, a number of problems are associated with its use. Except in those cases in which correctness serves as an index of quality, a highly subjective element in assessing it appears to be inescapable. This is not to suggest that subjectively-based judgments provide inherently poor bases for inferring the presence of an attribute in an object of perception. The problem is that such judgments are susceptible to the influence of numerous uncontrolled factors. This increases the likelihood of wide variation in the placement of decisions on a scale of quality.

Even when variation is small, that is, there is a high degree of interobserver consistency, one still faces the problem of knowing whether all relevant criteria for inferring quality have been identified and whether there are commonly shared rules of inference at play. Often the criteria themselves are nonspecific, as in the case of much of the current scholarship on techniques of "creative problem solving," (see Hogarth, 1980). In research on creative problem solving, there is an effort to determine the number of "good" ideas a group or individual generates, but often against an undefined or ill-defined criterion of innovativeness (see, for example, Jablin, 1981; Osborn, 1957; Philipsen et al., 1979).

Because assessments are so heavily reliant on perceptions, the criteria do not have specific referents in decisions themselves, and the rules of assignment are so difficult to draw, quality appears to be a bit too abstract and nebulous to receive serious consideration as an integrative concept. Among other things, it allows for the kind of extreme operationism that Kaplan (1964) suggests characterized the physical sciences and warns against permitting in the social sciences (pp. 39–42).

So fraught with complications is the concept of quality that Janis and Mann (1977) have gone so far as to suggest that it is impossible to assess except in the most limited circumstances. They contend that the quality of decisions can be judged when the concern is with the achievement of a single objective, or what they refer to as "single-valued" decisions (p. 10). If this is true, then quality suffers from the same sort of restrictedness as the concept of correctness. What Janis and Mann appear to be talking about, however, is not the quality of decisions, but more properly their utility, which is the next class of outcomes to be examined.

Utility of Decisions

Because so many of our decisions involve economic or economic-like consequences, many researchers have settled on the *utility* of choices as the focus of inquiry. From an economic perspective, the utility of a choice is a ratio of the gains and losses or benefits and costs associated with it relative to other available choices. Those who have been interested in utility, by and large, have examined cases of decision making for which the consequences are known and then tried to reconstruct the process responsible for these consequences (see, for example, Gouran, 1976, 1984; Head, Short, & McFarlane, 1978; Henry, 1976; Janis, 1972, 1982; McKinney, 1985; Stein & Tanter, 1980; Sweet, 1975). In each of the situations addressed by these researchers, there was general agreement on what the consequences of the decisions involved were. Hence, it was relatively easy to classify them as beneficial or costly.

On first blush, utility seems to have greater potential for serving as an integrative concept than either correctness or quality. Utility applies to a wider variety of decisional situations than correctness and is relatively free of the ambiguity associated with the concept of quality. Once a decision has been made, its utility can be established in terms of the benefits and costs that accrue. This seems to provide a reasonably clear and objective basis for assessing the degree of utility a decision or set of decisions seems to possess. The task situations in which the utility of decisions has relevance, moreover, are of the sort with which decision-makers find themselves dealing. Finally, the concept of utility can subsume both correctness and quality. If making a correct decision is beneficial, that becomes an index of its utility. Similarly, if the members of a group make choices manifesting other characteristics considered important, then quality, so conceived, is an index of utility.

Its appeal notwithstanding, utility presents difficulties as an integrative concept. First, the consequences of any given decision are not always immediate. In fact, they are often separated from a decision by considerable intervals of time. As a result, utility in many cases is indeterminate. This has led some researchers and theorists to adopt the substitute concept of *expected utility* (see, for example, March & Simon, 1958; Restle, 1961; Steiner, 1980). Expected utility may help explain the basis for a decision, but there is no necessary relationship between expected and actual utility. In addition, because of the separation of many decisions from their consequences, other factors can intervene. The inability to foresee such intervening influences can lead to assessments of utility that are contradicted by the emergence of factors that could not be envisioned at the point of decision. Hence, a group that has chosen as it should have on the basis of available information is later viewed as having made a poor or ineffective decision. Conversely, a group making a decision that should not have been made is credited with a good choice. The frequent indeterminancy of utility is probably sufficient to prevent the concept from serving as an integrative concept. A further limitation is the domain of decisions to which utility applies.

Although to a lesser extent than correctness, the concept of utility also appears to suffer from the problem of restrictedness. When considered as a characteristic of decisions made in response to questions of policy (that is, those involving the determination of what course of action should be taken in a given case), the concept makes a great deal of sense. For other kinds of issues that decision-making groups discuss, however, the assessment of choices in respect to their utility seems somewhat out of place. If, for instance, a group is discussing a question of fact, then how does one determine the utility of alternative answers? The same concern can be raised in relation to questions of conjecture and value. There is, of course, a certain utility to the members of the group in being able to reach a decision on such issues. Furthermore, the answers to questions of fact, conjecture, and value can, and often do, enter into the resolution of policy issues. Still, conceiving of decisions stemming from discussions on questions of fact, conjecture, and value as having benefits and costs or gains and losses in the same sense as policy decisions is difficult. Using utility as a basis for assessing these types of decisions, therefore, appears to be stretching the concept beyond the classes of decisions to which it comfortably applies.

Acceptability of Decisions

The final category of outcomes frequently involved in studies of group decision making has to do with the acceptability of choices that the participants make. Acceptability is typically inferred from the degree of agreement a decision or particular choice elicits from the members of a group (see, for example, DeStephen, 1983; Fisher, 1970; Gouran & Geonetta, 1977; Hill, 1976; Kline, 1972; Knutson & Holdridge, 1975; Pace, 1984) and/or the satisfaction they express with it (see, for example, Alderton & Jurma, 1980; Gouran, 1973a; Hirokawa, 1982a, Jurma, 1978, 1979; Vance & Biddle, 1985).

Agreement with a decision and the level of satisfaction it produces are not perfectly correlated. In fact, sometimes the relationship is rather weak (Guetzkow & Gyr, 1954), yet both are taken as indices of the acceptability of decisions. This poses something of a difficulty in considering acceptability as an integrative concept. If the various indices do not yield consistent estimates, then the value of the concept is questionable. The lack of consistency, however, may be attributable to differences in measurement. In the case of satisfaction, for instance, measures have ranged from single-point scales (see Vance & Biddle, 1985) to rather elaborately constructed questionnaires (see Jurma, 1978). Studies of agreement (consensus) have also varied in terms of how free participants are to choose. Some require consensus, whereas others focus on degree of agreement or distance from consensus (see Knutson & Holdridge, 1975). Finally, most studies involving the acceptability of decisions do not include measures of more than one index. As a result, it is difficult to judge whether acceptability is a stable concept.[4]

A reasonable response to the preceding observations is that acceptability is a multidimensional construct. The fact that the correlations among the dimensions are low, therefore, does not provide

---

[4] Of course, there is no necessary reason for suspecting that agreement and satisfaction with a decision must vary uniformly. There are circumstances in which none of the choices open to a group is especially attractive. Under these conditions, the members may agree to the option that is the "lesser of evils." When this is the case, however, one presumes that agreement and "relative satisfaction," in principle, should be highly correlated. A problem for the consumer of research is that investigators do not report relative satisfaction because the responses to alternatives not chosen are not assessed.

an adequate basis for dismissing it as an integrative concept. A more compelling argument for such rejection involves the concept's limited applicability. If a group interacts only to produce a decision with which the members will agree or which meets with their satisfaction, the acceptability is a perfectly appropriate criterion for judging the merits of the choice. Decision-making groups usually have other purposes, however. They meet to solve problems, discover best answers to questions, reduce uncertainty about how they should think, feel, or behave, recommend or take actions, and the like. Therefore, even if measures of acceptability were to have a high degree of precision, the concept taps only one aspect of decisions, albeit an important one. On these grounds alone, its suitability as an integrative concept is seriously open to question. Acceptability is far less suitable than either the concept of quality or utility and, in fact, could be subsumed by both. Since neither of these concepts has significant integrative potential, the indictment of acceptability is all the more damning.

The Need for a Common Denominator

By now, it is clear that none of the classes of decisional attributes investigated in research on decision-making in groups to date is adequate to serve the function of an integrative concept. Of the four reviewed, correctness is possibly the most precise and amenable to measurement, but it applies to a very limited part of the domain of decisional activity. Quality, a more expansive and encompassing concept, is difficult to assess and far too conducive to idiosyncratic definition.[5] Utility can be assessed in relation to the positive and negative consequences of decisions; however, the consequences are not always specifiable, or even apparent. In addition, the various issues or questions that decision-making groups try to resolve do not lend themselves equally to the cost-benefit analysis the concept of utility implies. In some instances, the only reason for a group's discussing a question is to resolve the issue the members are addressing. Beyond the resolution of the issue, there may be no costs or benefits, especially from the point of view of the decision makers. Finally, while all decisions can be conceived as varying in their acceptability to those

---

[5] Were we somehow able to relate quality more closely to specific features of decisions that serve as its referents and of the process by which decisions are generated, the concept could be integrative. Quality is not limited in the same degree as other classes of variables to specific types of decisions or responses to them. Quality as generally conceived, however, represents a dimension of goodness in relation to some function that a decision serves and is not necessarily a direct consequence of the process.

who produce them, acceptability suffers from its own type of restrictedness. Seldom, if ever, would the production of an agreeable or satisfying decision be the sole, or even principal, aim of a group.

Since none of the classes of variables on which studies of group decision making have focused shows much promise for serving as an integrative concept, those interested in the subject are faced with two choices. They can take the position that different situations require the examination of conceptually different attributes and, thereby, abandon the prospect of our ever being able to develop a comprehensive theory of decision making in groups. Or they can attempt to identify a common denominator that will facilitate synthesis of research findings and, hence, the development of an integrative theory. Given the recurrent concern of critics about the absence of integrative theories in the study of small groups in general, the second course seems preferable. This approach to the problem, of course, depends in large measure on the availability of suitable candidates for the role.

To qualify as a common denominator and, hence, integrative concept, what are the requisites a variable must satisfy? At minimum, there appear to be three. For a concept to be integrative, it must (a) apply to the full range of activities that the term *decision-making* represents, (b) be of use in interpreting existing research data, and (c) be amenable to assessment as a research variable in its own right. An integrative concept, then, must have the properties of generality, centrality, and assessability. *Appropriateness* is a concept that meets these requirements, but one that has never been treated as a research variable nor, to my knowledge, even generally regarded as a characteristic of decisions—with the possible exception of answers to questions of value (see Gouran, 1982, pp. 45–64). Even in this case, appropriateness has been used in much the same sense as acceptability. There is another sense, I shall argue, in which the concept of appropriateness, properly conceived surpasses the others reviewed. The merits of this more refined contender for the role of integrative concept are the subject of the next section.

Appropriateness: A Promising Concept

As one considers the nature of decisions, he or she may find it difficult to conceive of attributes common to every type. Given that decisions are choices made in response to questions and that the type of answer called for is suggested by the question, the reasons for a group's considering the issue, and the related task and informational requirements, all decisions can be viewed as varying in terms of their *appropriateness*. To be specific, a decision is *appropriate* to the extent that it represents the choice a group is obliged to make in light of its purpose, the requirements of the task, and what the analysis of information bearing on the available alternatives establishes as reasons for endorsing and rejecting each. This definition sets the concept apart from the others in an important way. Where relevant, the correctness, quality, utility, or acceptability of a decision can be established—however difficult the process of assessment—independently of the process by which the decision is generated. To be considered appropriate, however, a decision must be the one that certain aspects of procedure, if observed, require the decision maker to reach. Appropriateness, therefore, inextricably ties product to process. The question about appropriateness so conceived that now must be addressed is how well the concept satisfies the requirements for being considered integrative.

Generality

The definition of appropriateness presented suggests that the concept applies to the range of activities and situations that come to mind when one is talking about decision making. To make a convincing case, however, requires a bit more demonstration. In the most fundamental sense, a decision represents the answer to one of four categories of questions: fact, conjecture, value, or policy (Gouran, 1982). A question of fact deals with matters of truth (e.g., "Has the incidence of racial discrimination in the United States decreased since the enactment of the civil rights bill of 1964?"), whereas questions of conjecture refer to matters of likelihood (e.g., "Will the agreements reached in the 1985 Summit Talks slow the nuclear arms race?"). Questions of value pose issues involving the justifiability of certain beliefs, attitudes, practices, and the like (e.g., "Should capital punishment be permitted?") in contrast to questions of policy, which are concerned with the merits of alternative course of action (e.g., "What steps should be taken to reduce the federal deficit?").

Each of these types of questions has its own set of requirements for reaching decisions and different bases for selecting among alternatives. If a group were discussing, say, the question of fact referred to above, three possible conclusions that could be reached: Yes, No, and Cannot Say. If the group were concerned about the answer to the question, the members would have to have information with which they could establish to infer the incidence of racial discrimination prior to and following the enactment of civil rights legislation, apply standards of evidence that permit the separation of reliable from unreliable data, and determine any other inadequacies or deficiencies of their information that potentially affect the choice to be made. On the other hand, a group discussing the sample question of value on capital punishment, while having essentially the same three response options, would be attempting to establish, through the use of pertinent information, the consistency of capital punishment with values not in dispute and to identify the implications of affirmative and negative responses to the question.[6] Although the task requirements and the role that information plays in these two cases differ, in both the group would have chosen appropriately if its decision is consistent with what the analysis of information has revealed about the merits of competing alternatives and with the members' purpose. The same characterization applies to questions of conjecture and policy. As an integrative concept, then, appropriateness seems to satisfy the first requisite.

Centrality

Having relevance as a characteristic of all types of decisions that groups make, although important, is not sufficient for appropriateness to achieve status as an integrative concept. For that to occur, its centrality must be evident. In other words, can the study of decision making in groups be reduced to factors that determine the appropriateness of the choices that participants make? Since not all those who investigate decisional processes are interested in the outcomes groups achieve, the answer to the question appears to be no. Among students of decision making, substantial attention, particularly during the past 20 years, has been paid to the variety of ways in which decisions develop (see, for example, Ellis & Fisher, 1975; Mabry, 1975; Poole, 1983; Poole, McPhee, & Seibold, 1982; Scheidel & Crowell, 1964; Stech, 1970). For this group of scholars, the evolution of decisions is an interesting phenomenon unto itself and important to understanding the process of decision making independently of the outcomes groups achieve. Where outcomes are a matter of concern, which they appear to be in the bulk of research on group decision making, appropriateness can serve as the focal point. At least, it appears to be the common denominator for the classes of decisional attributes that have been investigated. In addition, there is no reason to assume that a concern with process precludes a consideration of outcomes. Knowing that groups characteristically approach decisional

---

[6] As Hempel (1965) has noted, the only way in which to resolve questions of value in a logically defensible manner is to evaluate them in terms of their consistency with other values that are unconditionally accepted.

tasks in particular ways, ultimately, could be of assistance in diagnosing the appropriateness or inappropriateness of their choices.

A significant factor suggesting the centrality of appropriateness in decision making is its substitutability for other attributes. Decisions having the properties of correctness, quality, utility, or acceptability in general, although not uniformly, would be considered appropriate by those who have been historically interested in such characteristics. Conversely, decisions determined to be incorrect, low in quality, lacking in utility, or unacceptable to those generating them, it seems reasonable to believe, usually would be regarded as inappropriate. Appropriateness easily substitutes in many instances for all of the previously mentioned classes of outcomes without affecting the conclusions drawn in related research. With the possible exception of quality, the attributes for which appropriateness is substitutable do not exhibit this property in the same degree. One would not, for example, be inclined to substitute *acceptability* as a criterion of the *correctness* of a decision. Because all of the various attributes studied in research on group decision making so often are indices of appropriateness, but not for each other, the concept is more central to an understanding of the variation in decision outcomes than any of the others for which it can be substituted.

In addition to the comprehensiveness that the substitutability of appropriateness for other characteristics of decisions suggests, its centrality can be established by yet another gauge. Appropriateness applies more easily to multivalued decisions than do other concepts. Group decision making, more often than not, is directed toward the achievement of more than one objective, even though only one decision may be involved. As an illustration, a group might be put in the position of finding a solution to a problem that also accommodates competing vested interests. In this type of situation, both the utility and acceptability of the choice the group makes are of interest. Yet neither concept alone provides a good index of whether the optimum choice has been made. A decision having high utility, that is, a favorable benefit to cost ratio, could conceivably be relatively low in its acceptability. By one index, the decision is a good one, and by the other, it is not. Application of the concept of appropriateness would entail a judgment reflecting both objectives. If the dual objectives were not in conflict—that is, both are achievable—then the outcome portrayed would be considered inappropriate. If the two objectives were necessarily in conflict, then the appropriateness of the choice would be determined by which, from the perspective of the group members, is the more important. In either case, the concept of appropriateness allows for a unitary assessment of decisions.

Perhaps the most convincing argument establishing the centrality of appropriateness in decision making is that it suggests a necessary relationship between the characteristics of an individual's thought processes, or a group's interaction, and the outcome. From a theoretical and research perspective, this relationship has considerable appeal. Because the characteristic in question is not independent of the process in which decisions are reached, understanding the sources of variation in appropriateness is more easily possible than in the case of the other contenders.

Assessability

Since the generality and centrality of a concept can be established largely on semantic grounds, it is important that appropriateness as a potential integrative concept satisfy one additional requisite. Can the appropriateness of a decision be assessed? Or is it likely to suffer from the same difficulties as quality? Because the indices of appropriateness vary from issue to issue, the concept could be so susceptible to idiosyncratic interpretation that it would cease to function as the standard of comparison that makes possible the synthesis of data about group decision making and, by implication, general theories of the process. If researchers remember, however, that the appropriateness of a decision is constrained by the purposes of the group, the logical requirements of the task, and the implications of the information consulted in satisfying those requirements, uniform assessment and interpretation are possible.

It is beyond the scope of this chapter to develop a complete taxonomy of the criteria one would use in assessing the appropriateness of decisions as a function of group objectives and the requirements suggested by the type of issue being addressed. Nevertheless, one can outline general criteria that need to be considered. Three that are derived directly from the definition of appropriateness are: (a) consistency with the group's purposes, (b) conformity to the requirements implied by the task, and (c) conformity to agreed upon standards of evidence.

Consistency with the group's purposes. Application of this criterion begins with the question, "What is the group trying to accomplish?" Most fundamentally, decision-making groups attempt to resolve issues for which the answers are in dispute. If this is the only reason for engaging in decision making, then the act of choice renders a decision appropriate. Most groups have a larger range of purposes. They want to make "good" decisions, achieve agreement, furnish grounds for action, and the like. When these motives suggest additional purposes, they alter the standard by which one determines appropriateness, but the general criterion of consistency with the group's purposes remains the same.

Conformity to requirements implied by the task. Insofar as decisions represent answers to one of four categories of questions, the task of decision making requires that a group make a claim among competing claims about what is true, likely, justifiable, or in need of doing. The mere making of a claim, however, is not the only requirement that the task imposes on the members of a decision-making group. In fact, one could argue that this is the least important of the requirements of a task, in that the final claim is one the participants are presumably obliged to make if they have satisified other requirements of inquiry. For any type of question phrased to elicit an affirmative or negative response, for instance, the task requires that a decision-making group identify the possible reasons for responding both affirmatively and negatively, determine what evidence exists to examine the merits of each reason for responding affirmatively or negatively, and establish which of the sets of reasons has the greatest weight of evidence. In many cases, an issue is not phrased so as to elicit an affirmative or negative response, but that does not appreciably alter the set of requirements just identified. In these instances, a group should try to identify the possible positions that can be taken on the issue. Beyond that, the remaining requirements are the same, except that we might substitute the phrase "reasons for and for not supporting each position" for "reasons for responding affirmatively or negatively."

When the information a group consults gives greater weight to the reasons for taking one position over others, the members, in principle, should choose that position, and the appropriateness of the decision is therefore inferred from the group's conformity to the requirement. One needs to remember, however, that a group cannot satisfy this requirement without having first satisified all of the others. Hence, appropriateness is a function of conformity to all of the requirements implied by a decision-making group's task.

Conformity to agreed upon standards of evidence. The preceding discussion of task requirements was predicated on the assumption that the members of a decision-making group have relevant information and the ability to interpret it in relationship to particular issues. We know, of course, that not all information is equally good and that not all decision makers make enough of an effort to discriminate among the sources of information they consult. If a task requires that the members of a decision-making group choose among alternatives on the basis of what information reveals about the relative merits of competing positions on issues, then the processing of information for use in making decisions is an extremely important consideration. If the information used to establish the merits of reasons for taking different positions does not meet accepted standards of evidence, then one cannot infer that the corresponding task requirements have been satisfied, and as a result, any decision reached is inappropriate. That judgment is warranted even if perchance the choice later appears to be the one the group should have made. Such a happenstance would be accidental rather than a product of informed inquiry.

At minimum, for a decision to be considered appropriate, one should expect to find a group having examined its information in light of the qualifications (or reliability) of the sources, the documentation and support of claims, consistency across sources, possible bias, relevance to the issues being explored, and the like. Attention to these matters will not guarantee that a group is going to make the choice that it ideally should, but it does enable one to determine the extent to which the choice the members do make is warranted.

The Measurement of Appropriateness

Unfortunately, instruments for the assessment of appropriateness do not presently exist. The preceding discussion of assessability, however, suggests that the concept poses no unique problems in measurement. The definition of appropriateness indicates a variable that is both continuous and multidimensional. The criteria of consistency with purpose, conformity to task requirements, and conformity to agreed upon standards of evidence further suggest the dimensions on which to focus—at least, in the initial stages of scale construction. Whether, and if so how, these criteria should be weighted are empirical issues that will require a good deal of exploratory and developmental work before standardized instruments can be constructed.

A more immediate concern is the means by which estimates of consistency with purpose, conformity to task requirements, and conformity to agreed upon standards of evidence can best be made. Ideally, the criteria would be so well operationalized that a researcher could apply them in a purely objective fashion. This ideal is far from the realm of possibility in most instances. Exceptions involve cases when a group's purpose is to make a correct judgment or to produce a decision that has a clearly specified consequence that either occurs or fails to occur. In such instances, consistency with purpose is determinate on objective grounds. In general, however, research will have to rely on subjective estimates of the extent to which group decisions satisfy the criteria.

To minimize unwanted variance in estimates of the properties being recommended and concerns about validity, researchers seeking to measure appropriateness will have to be extremely careful to provide evaluators with the information essential to making informed estimates. To assess the consistency of a decision with a group's purposes, for instance, a judge would have to know what, from the point of view of the participants, their purposes are. In addition, the researcher would have to be able to specify what, in light of the purpose or purposes of the group, the task requires, as well as the standards that evidence must meet to warrant particular conclusions about the issues being addressed. Such specifications, of course, will not yield perfect estimates of how well decisions satisfy the criteria, but they surely will increase the likelihood of uniform, numerical representations and, at the very least, have face validity. Training requirements for the use of instruments constructed along the lines suggested are not unusual, but it would be important to select evaluators who have reasonable familiarity with the phenomena encompassed by the specifications.

Advantages and Limitations

By adopting the concept of appropriateness as the defining attribute of group decisions, not only will scholars abet the cause of developing an integrative theory, they will also be able to determine much more systematically than they previously could whether the same factors have the same weight in the choices that groups make within and across decisional contexts. Heretofore, it has been very difficult to assess the role of particular variables in the process of group decision making because the characteristics of decisions have not been examined within a common frame of reference. Appropriateness offers such a frame of reference. The resulting gain in comparability may bring us closer to understanding what factors are most critical to how and how well groups decide.

In addition, as I suggested earlier, the concept of appropriateness better captures the process/outcome relationship than any of the previously studied classes of variables. The appropriateness of a decision is not separable from the process that leads to it and must be judged in relation to a group's purposes as well as its consistency with task requirements and accepted standards of evidence. It makes no sense to speak of appropriateness apart from the process. In contrast, the correctness, quality, utility, and acceptability of a decision can be separated from the process, or at least judged independently of it. In fact, most previous research has reflected this very separation. The concept of appropriateness, because it must be judged in the context of the process of decision making, is fluid enough to take on different values according to the relative importance of each criterion used to assess it as it applies to particular situations. In this sense, the concept extends from the most trivial of decisional problems to those of profound importance.

Despite its advantages, appropriateness is not without its limitations as a potential integrative concept. Although one can assess it by reasonably objective means, the subjective component in such assessments cannot be completely eliminated. Consequently, some decisions will be misclassified or misjudged as to their appropriateness, no matter how refined the criteria employed or rigorously they are applied. Assessment, moreover, is cumbersome, and the bases for selecting criteria that are relevant to particular situations are not always clear. Nor are the bases for determining their relative importance. Finally, there is the problem of being able to identify a group's purposes and whether the ostensible or apparent purposes are congruent with its actual purposes. Nevertheless, the promise of the concept, until otherwise demonstrated, outweighs the potential difficulties associated with its adoption as an integrative concept. At least, that is the point that this chapter has attempted to make.

References

Alderton, S.M., & Jurma, W.E. (1980). Genderless/gender related task, leader communication, and group satisfaction. *Southern Speech Communication Journal, 46,* 48–60.

Bormann, E.G. (1970). The paradox and promise of small group research. *Speech Monographs, 37,* 211–216.

Bormann, E.G. (1980). The paradox and promise of small group research revisited. *Central States Speech Journal, 31,* 214–220.

Burleson, B.R., Levine, G.J., & Samter, W. (1984). Decision-making procedure and decision quality. *Human Communication Research, 10,* 557–574.

Cragan, J.F., & Wright, D.W. (1980). Small group research of the 1970's: A synthesis and critique. *Central States Speech Journal, 31,* 197–213.

De Stephen, R.S. (1983). High and low consensus groups: A content and relational interaction analysis. *Small Group Behavior, 14,* 143–162.

Ellis, D. G., & Fisher, B.A. (1975). Phases of conflict in small group development: A Markov analysis. *Human Communication Research, 1,* 195–212.

Falk, G. (1981). Unanimity versus majority rule in problem-solving groups:

A challenge to the superiority of unanimity. *Small Group Behavior, 12,* 379–400.

Fisher, B.A. (1970). The process of decision modification in small discussion groups. *Journal of Communication, 20,* 51–64.

Gouran, D.S. (1973a). Correlates of member satisfaction in group decision-making discussions. *Central States Speech Journal, 24,* 91–96.

Gouran, D.S. (1973b). Group communication: Perspectives and priorities for future research. *Quarterly Journal of Speech, 59,* 22–29.

Gouran, D.S. (1976). The Watergate cover-up: Its dynamics and its implications. *Communication Monographs, 43,* 176–186.

Gouran, D.S. (1982). *Making decisions in groups: Choices and consequences.* Glenview, IL: Scott, Foresman & Co.

Gouran, D.S. (1984). Communicative iinfluences in decisions related to the Watergate coverup: The failure of collective judgment. *Central States Speech Journal, 35,* 260–269.

Gouran, D.S., Brown, C., & Henry, D.R. (1978). Behavioral correlates of perceptions of quality in decision-making discussions. *Communication Monographs, 45,* 51–63.

Gouran, D.S., & Geonetta, S.C. (1977). Patterns of interaction in decision-making groups at varying distance from consensus. *Small Group Behavior, 8,* 511–524.

Guetzkow, H., & Gyr, J. (1954). An analysis of conflict in decision-making groups. *Human Relations, 7,* 367–382.

Gurnee, H.A. (1937). A comparison of collective and individual judgments of facts. *Journal of Experimental Psychology, 21,* 106–112.

Harper, N.L., & Askling, L.R. (1980). Group communication and quality of task solution in a media production organization. *Communication Monographs, 47,* 77–100.

Head, R.G., Short, F.W., & McFarlane, R.C. (1978). *Crisis resolution: Presidential decision making in the Mayaquez and Korean confrontations.* Boulder, CO: Westview Press.

Hempel, C.G. (1965). Science and human values. In C.G. Hempel (Ed.), *Aspects of scientific explanation* (pp. 81–98). New York: Free Press.

Henry, D.R. (1976). *Decision-making in the Truman administration.* Unpublished doctoral dissertation, Indiana University, Bloomington, Indiana.

Hill, T.A. (1976). An experimental study of the relationship between opinionated leadership and small group consensus. *Communication Monographs, 43,* 246–257.

Hirokawa, R.Y. (1980). A comparative analysis of communication patterns within effective and ineffective decision-making groups. *Communication Monographs, 47,* 312–321.

Hirokawa, R.Y. (1982a). Consensus group decision-making, quality of decision, and group satisfaction: An attempt to sort "fact" from "fiction." *Central States Speech Journal, 33,* 407–415.

Hirokawa, R.Y. (1982b). Group communication and problem-solving effectiveness I: A critical review of inconsistent findings. *Communication Quarterly, 30,* 134–141.

Hirokawa, R.Y., & Pace, R.C. (1983). A descriptive investigation of the possible communication-based reasons for effective and ineffective group decision making. *Communication Monographs, 50,* 363–379.

Hoffman, L.R. (1959). Homogeneity of member personality and its effect on group problem-solving. *Journal of Abnormal and Social Psychology, 58,* 27–32.

Hoffman, L.R., & Maier, N.R.F. (1961). Quality and acceptance of problem solutions by members of homogenous and heterogeneous groups. *Journal of Abnormal and Social Psychology, 62,* 401–407.

Hogarth, R. (1980). *Judgement and choice.* New York: Wiley.

Jablin, F.M. (1981). Cultivating imagination: Factors that enhance and inhibit creativity in brainstorming groups. *Human Communication Research, 7,* 245–258.

Janis, I.L. (1972). *Victims of groupthink.* Boston: Houghton Mifflin.

Janis, I.L. (1982). *Groupthink* (2nd ed.). Boston: Houghton Mifflin.

Janis, I.L., & Mann, L. (1977). *Decision making.* New York: Free Press.

Janssens, L., & Nuttin, J.R. (1976). Frequency perception of individual and group successes as a function of competition, coaction, and isolation. *Journal of Personality and Social Psychology, 27,* 279–296.

Jenness, A. (1932). The role of discussion in changing opinion regarding a matter of fact. *Journal of Abnormal and Social Psychology, 27,* 279–296.

Jurma, W.E. (1978). An experimental study of the relationship of leadership structuring style and task ambiguity to the resulting satisfaction of group members. *Small Group Behavior, 9,* 124–134.

Jurma, W.E. (1979). Effects of leader structuring style and task-orientation characteristics of group members. *Communication Monographs, 46,* 282–295.

Kanekar, S., & Rosenbaum, M.E. (1972). Group performance on a multiple solution task as a function of available time. *Psychonomic Science, 27,* 331–332.

Kaplan, A. (1964). *The conduct of inquiry.* San Francisco, CA: Chandler.

Kline, J.A. (1972). Orientation and group consensus. *Central States Speech Journal, 23,* 44–47.

Knutson, T.J., & Holdridge, W.E. (1975). Orientation behavior, leadership, and consensus: A possible functional relationship. *Speech Monographs, 42,* 107–114.

Mabry, E.A. (1975). Exploratory analysis of a developmental model for task-oriented small groups. *Human Communication Research, 2,* 66–74.

March, J.G., & Simon, H.A. (1958). *Organizations.* New York: Wiley.

McGrath, J.E., & Altman, I. (1966). *Small group research: A synthesis and critique of the field.* New York: Holt, Rinehart and Winston.

McKinney, B.C. (1985). *Decision-making in the President's Commission on the Assassination of President Kennedy: A descriptive analysis employing Irving Janis' groupthink hypothesis.* Unpublished dissertation, Pennsylvania State University.

Miner, F.C. (1984). Group versus individual decision making: An investigation of performance measures, decision strategies, and process losses/gains. *Organizational Behavior and Human Performance, 33,* 112–124.

Mortensen, C.D. (1970). The status of small group research. *Quarterly Journal of Speech, 36,* 304–309.

Osborn, A.F. (1957). *Applied imagination.* New York: Scribner.

Pace, R.C. (1984). *The role of communication in consensus formation: A descriptive analysis of interaction differences between high and low consensus groups.* Unpublished dissertation, Pennsylvania State University.

Philipsen, G., Mulac, A., & Dietrich, D. (1979). The effects of social interaction on group idea generation. *Communication Monographs, 46,* 119–125.

Poole, M.S. (1983). Decision development in small groups II: A study of multiple sequences in decision making. *Communication Monographs, 50,* 206–232.

Poole, M.S., McPhee, R.D., & Seibold, D.R. (1982). A comparison of normative and interactional explanations of group decision-making: Social decision schemes versus valence. *Communication Monographs, 49,* 1–19.

Restle, F. (1961). *Psychology of judgment and choice.* New York: Wiley.

Scheidel, T.M., & Crowell, L. (1964). Idea development in small discussion groups. *Quarterly Journal of Speech, 50,* 140–145.

Shaw, M.E. (1932). A comparison of individuals and small groups in the rational solution of complex problems. *American Journal of Psychology, 44,* 491–504.

Shaw, M.E. (1981). *Group dynamics: The psychology of small group behavior* (3rd ed.). New York: McGraw-Hill.

Stech, E.L. (1970). An analysis of interaction structure in the discussion of a ranking task. *Speech Monographs, 37,* 249–256.

Stein, J.G., & Tanter, R. (1980). *Rational decision making: Israel's security choices, 1967.* Columbus, OH: Ohio State University Press.

Steiner, I.D. (1972). *Group process and productivity.* New York: Academic Press.

Steiner, I.D. (1980). Attribution of choice. *Progress in Social Psychology, 1,* 1–47.

Sweet, K.F. (1975). *The Eisenhower administration in crisis-decision making.* Unpublished dissertation, Indiana University.

Torrance, E.P. (1954). Some consequences of power differences on decision making in permanent and temporary three-man groups. *Research Studies, Washington State College, 22,* 130–140.

Vance, R.J., & Biddle, T.F. (1985). Task experience and social cues: Interactive effects on attitudinal reactions. *Organizational Behavior and Human Decision Processes, 35,* 252–265.

CHAPTER 10

Interpersonal Evaluations:
Measuring Attraction and Trust

Charles H. Tardy

Theory, research, and experience emphasize the importance of attraction and trust to the formation and development of interpersonal relationships. Both constructs may be considered types of evaluations made of and by persons in relationships. Though other types of evaluations may also be important, this chapter reviews only the methods of measuring these two constructs.

Interpersonal Attraction

Interpersonal attraction refers to "a constellation of sentiments which comprise the evaluative orientation of one person toward another" (Huston, 1974, p. 11). These evaluative sentiments are central components of interpersonal relationships. Perhaps for this reason, attraction has been one of the most popular topics of research for the past 15 years. The computer-based bibliographic search conducted for this review revealed more than 300 studies published in psychology journals alone during the five-year period between 1979 and 1984. Research on this topic is regularly published in a broad spectrum of scholarly journals, though not as frequently as in the 1970s.

Most researchers conceive of the sentiments associated with interpersonal attraction as attitudes. For some, these attitudes consist of cognitive, affective, and behavioral dimensions. Others make no such distinction. For some, attraction is limited to "liking," while for others it includes a wider range of sentiments (cf., Blau, 1962). This paper does not attempt to resolve these conceptual disagreements. Rather, I attempt to describe accurately the major approaches to conceptualizing and measuring this concept.

269

Interpersonal Judgment Scale

Developed by Don Byrne (1971) for use in his paradigmatic research on the relationship between similarity and attraction, the Interpersonal Judgment Scale (IJS) measures one person's liking for another specified person. This scale has been used in more studies than any other measure of attraction. Of the six Thurstone-type items constituting the scale, two are used in calculating the attraction score, and four are used to mask the instrument's purpose. One of the attraction items assesses general feelings of liking, while the other assesses desire to participate in an experiment with the specified person. Many studies have employed only the two key items (e.g., Sunnafrank, 1984). Additional items have been used to measure sexual attraction and dating (Byrne, 1971).

The correlation between responses to the two central items is consistently high, indicating internal reliability. That the scale has been used successfully in many studies is evidence of its reliability and validity. Studies employing multiple measures of attraction have observed that the IJS correlates with many other self-report measures of attraction (Byrne, 1971; Brinberg, Coleman, Hoff, Newman, & Risk, 1980; Gormly, Gormly, & Johnson, 1971) as well as with behaviors indicative of attraction, for example, spatial proximity (Byrne, 1971; Krivonos, 1980). Additionally, Clore and Gormly (1974) observed a positive correlation between the IJS and skin conductance when subjects interacted with an agreeable confederate, but correlated negatively when the confederate was disagreeable. Such evidence strongly supports the validity claims made for this measure of interpersonal attraction.

Though this scale has many appropriate uses, it has some important limitations. First, the IJS does not allow the researcher to distinguish among different types of attraction. As first noted by Tedeschi (1974), in some situations a person can be attracted to a person s/he does not like; for example, when the disliked person can provide help. For this reason, some authors differentiate between social and task attraction (e.g., Grush & Yehl, 1979) and others, physical attraction (e.g., McCroskey & McCain, 1974). Although the two items of the IJS seem to reflect a social and task distinction, there is no evidence to suggest that the individual items constitute adequate measures of these two dimensions. Therefore, other instruments should be used when the research project must distinguish among types of attraction.

A second limitation of the use of the IJS is its narrow focus. This scale assesses only a small part of the range of feelings which constitute attraction between two individuals. Generally, the scale can only be used with people who are vaguely acquainted. The instrument would not be appropriate for measuring the amount of attraction between individuals in more developed relationships, for example, married couples.

In conclusion, the IJS is an exceedingly useful measure. Withstanding the test of time, this measure has repeatedly detected predicted differences in experimental studies. For studies attempting to build on previous research, this scale is particularly appropriate. Its brevity and ease-of-use also make it attractive.

McCroskey and McCain's Measure of Interpersonal Attraction

McCroskey and McCain (1974) designed a measure to assess three dimensions of interpersonal attraction: social, task, and physical. Social attraction corresponds to liking, task to dependability, and physical to appearance. Though the authors originally recommended the use of five Likert-type scales for each of the three dimensions, subsequent studies have obtained acceptable results with only four (Andersen & Coussoule, 1980; Woodall, Burgoon, & Markel, 1980). Nonetheless, McCroskey and Richmond (1979) report a new version of the scale designed to obtain reliability coefficients exceeding .90 (see Appendix 1). The revised instrument consists of 12 items for the social, 12 for the physical, and 14 for the task attraction scales. A 7-interval response continuum is used.

In more than a dozen studies using the first version of the interpersonal attraction scales, reliability coefficients never fell below .60. (DeWine & Pearson, 1985; McCroskey & Richmond, 1979). With the increased number of items, McCroskey and Richmond (1979) reported reliability coefficients exceeding .90 for all three scales in studies with students and teachers as subjects.

Several factor analytic studies of the scale support the dimensionality of the instrument (McCroskey & McCain, 1974), though the three scales should not be considered orthogonal (McCroskey & Richmond, 1979). Additionally, the three measures have been found to be differentially affected by independent variables (Hickson, Powell, Hill, Holt, & Flick, 1979; McCroskey, Richmond, Daly, & Cox, 1975). Several studies using behavioral measures have obtained evidence of predictive validity. In Andersen and Coussoule's (1980) study, subjects interviewing a confederate were more socially attracted to the interviewees who gazed continuously than to those who gazed aversively. Woodall et al. (1980) found that subjects rated confederates higher on all three dimensions of interpersonal attraction when the confederates evidenced positive reinforcement nonverbal behaviors, for example, smiles, in an interaction than when no such cues were given. McCroskey, Hamilton, and Weiner (1974) concluded that task and social attraction were differentially related to behavior in a small group setting. Several studies have observed relationships between interpersonal attraction and other self-report measures (McCroskey & Richmond, 1979). This evidence strongly supports the psychometric integrity and utility of the McCroskey and McCain instrument.

As with the IJS, this measure has been most frequently used in studies of individuals in the initial stage of their relationships. These scales also may be too general to accurately detect differences among individuals who have known each other for a long period of time. In other words, the items may have a ceiling over which increased attraction cannot be measured. Newcomb (1979) makes this argument about the use of both ranking and rating the attraction of one person by others in a social group. Other measures may be more appropriate for this purpose.

The multiple dimensions enable researchers to use the McCroskey and McCain measure for a wider range of purposes than the IJS. However, not all studies of interpersonal attraction distinguish among these dimensions. For research that does, these scales can be used with confidence.

Rubin's Liking and Loving Scales

Noting that social scientists have traditionally avoided the subject, Rubin (1970, 1974a, 1974b) developed a self-report measure to be used for the empirical study of attraction in romantic relationships. Rubin distinguished love from liking and constructed scales to measure both. The concept of love involves three components: attraction, caring, and intimacy. However, these three components are interdependent rather than independent. Love is unidimensional. Rubin contrasts love with liking, a much less intense sentiment. Liking refers to general, favorable evaluations of one person by another. The two are related but not identical concepts.

The scales Rubin (1974b) developed to measure loving and liking consist of statements to which subjects respond along a continuum ranging from "Not at all true; disagree completely" to "Definitely true; agree completely." The items were selected from a series of pretests and initial studies, resulting in a reduction from 70 to 9. A factor analysis of each scale indicated that both were unidimensional (Rubin, 1970). Studies have yielded high estimates of internal reliability.

As expected, the loving and liking scales correlated moderately, but not highly, with each other in a study of dating couples. The loving scale correlated much higher with student subjects' estimates of the probability of marrying their dating partner than did the liking scale (Rubin, 1970). Other evidence indicates that students who score high on the loving scale are more likely to be dating a year later than are couples who score low on the loving scale (Hill, Rubin, & Peplau, 1976). Additional behavioral evidence supports the validity of the loving scale. Couples scoring high on the love scale engaged in more mutual looking than couples scoring low (Rubin, 1970). In other words, couples who are in love gaze longer at each other than couples who are not. Both scales have been used successfully by other researchers (e.g., Fazio, Seligman, & Zanna, 1980; Tesser & Paulhus, 1976). Though there is more evidence for the love than the liking scale, both of Rubin's measures appear reliable and valid.

The primary use of the love scale is to assess the degree of attraction among individuals with romantic intentions, though Rubin also reports its use in a study of same-sex friendships (Rubin & McNeil, 1981). Neither Byrne's IJS or McCroskey and McCain's scales are appropriate for this purpose. Consequently Rubin's scale provides a valuable alternative to developing a new measure. The liking scale, on the other hand, appears to measure the same property as does the IJS: undifferentiated "liking." Rubin's scale should be more reliable and yield a wider range of scores than the IJS since it consists of more items. Additionally, the Rubin scale may be more appropriate than the IJS for studies employing nonstudent subjects. One of Byrne's scales refers to "participating in an experiment," an activity undoubtedly alien to people other than students. Rubin's liking scale contains items related both to task attraction (e.g., "I would vote for this person in a class or group election") and social attraction (e.g., "I think this person and I are quite similar to one another"). However this scale is unidimensional and has not been used to distinguish between these two types of attraction.

Other Measures

A multitude of other scales have been used to measure interpersonal attraction. Many studies use one-item scales (e.g., Newcomb, 1960) while a few others require complex computations (e.g., Dalton & Aijen, 1979). Rarely do authors justify the use of new and untested measures. Few even compare their scale to those used in previous studies such as the IJS. Many do not report reliability and validity evidence. Described below are measures representing alternative methods or specialized purposes which merit attention.

Adjective/trait measures. Perhaps the use of adjectives to describe another person is the most common of the other methods of eliciting reports of attraction. For example, Kerber (1981) asked subjects to check a list of traits which they thought the target person possessed. The traits were assigned a priori numerical values representing the degree of favorableness indicated by the adjective. The mean score computed for each subject was the interpersonal attraction score. A variant of this procedure was used by Dalton and Aijen (1979). These authors asked subjects to: (a) list personality traits of the target person; (b) specify the probability that the person possessed each of the traits; and (c) evaluate the traits on a 7-point scale ranging from "good" to "bad." The subjective probabilities were multiplied by the evaluation rating for each trait listed. Summing across all traits, the authors formulated an attraction measure. It is sobering to note that this measure with its relatively complex computation correlated highly with three other measures of attraction, including the 2-item IJS. Pearson correlation coefficients exceeded .66. Consequently, these measures appear to assess the same property of interpersonal attraction as do other, simpler measures.

Social distance and sociometric measures. Two other types of measures frequently mentioned in the literature on interpersonal attraction, but used infrequently, are based on social distance and sociometric principles. Social distance measures require subjects to specify the types of social activities (e.g., work, share a room) one person would be willing to undertake with another person. In a multitrait-multimethod study, Brinberg et al. (1980) concluded that a social distance measure, when compared to the IJS and an adjective/trait measure, lacked discriminant validity. Newcomb's (1960) classic study of roommates used a sociometric measure of attraction. Each person was asked to place the other roommates into one of three groups: like, neutral, and dislike; and then to rank order the individuals in each category. Later Newcomb (1979) argued that the use of such procedures may be insensitive to changes in feeling of attraction over time. (See Lindzey & Byrne, 1968, for a more thorough discussion of these types of measures.)

Measures for special populations. Measures of interpersonal attraction have been developed or adapted for use in studies of special populations. Hernandez's (1982) study required the use of scales to assess task and social attraction among patrol officers. Kitson (1982) constructed a measure of affiliation between a divorced person and his or her former spouse. Barak and LaCrosse (1975) developed a measure subsequently used in many studies of a client's attraction to a counselor. Reaves and Roberts (1983) describe an interesting measure of interpersonal attraction for second-grade children. Responses to questions were elicited with four squares increasing in size and corresponding to a continuum ranging from "would not like" to "would like a lot." Byrne (1971) also adapted the IJS for children in the fourth through twelfth grades.

Miscellaneous measures. Several authors' measures combine the approaches described above. For example, Berg and Archer (1983) use three adjective/trait items and three social distance items. Evidence indicates this scale is highly reliable. An identical approach was taken by Gormley et al. (1971), who used different adjective/trait and different social items. Their scale correlated .72 with the IJS. Such approaches as taken by these authors evidently yield acceptable results.

Conclusion

The measures reviewed provide several alternatives. However, appropriate selection depends upon knowledge of each measure's strengths and limitations. Depending on the purposes of the research project, one of the three should prove acceptable. If special requirements necessitate the development of a new measure, these instruments should provide a convenient starting point.

Interpersonal Trust

Traditionally, trust has been considered an important element of the communication process (Giffin, 1967). Studies on topics ranging from speaker credibility to self-disclosure have attempted to describe the role of trust in understanding outcomes of communication. This section of the interpersonal evaluations chapter focuses on the assessment of trust as a property of relationships. Reviewed are measures which conceive of trust as an attitude held by one person toward another. Excluded are discussions of generalized trust, a personality variable referring to a person's expectation to be treated fairly by all other human beings (Rotter, 1967, 1971, 1980), and game theory, which conceives of trust as an optional behavior within a constrained system of controlled outcomes (Deutsch, 1962; Lindskold, 1978; Schlenker, Helm, & Tedeschi, 1973). Research has frequently indicated that generalized trust does not accurately assess trust among relationship partners (e.g., McDonald, Kessel, & Fuller, 1972; Wheeless & Grotz, 1977). Though important for other purposes, conflict and game theory studies of trust have little relevance for the measurement of trust as an attitude developed in the context of a specific interpersonal relationship (Pearce, 1974).

As with research on several of the topics reviewed in this book, many studies on interpersonal trust have used one-item scales (e.g., Frost, Stimpson, & Maughan, 1978) or instruments developed solely for a particular study and never used again. One study even used a self-disclosure measure as an indicant of trust (Ellison & Fireston, 1974). However, since 1977, studies assessing four measures of interpersonal trust have been published. I first review the four instruments individually and then compare the scales. A final section describes additional resources for studying trust.

Four Measures of Interpersonal Trust

From speaker credibility scales assessing trust and character, Wheeless and Grotz (1977) selected 15 semantic-differential items, for example, trustworthy-untrustworthy, reliable-unreliable, sincere-insincere, to measure interpersonal trust. Factor analyses in two studies support the unidimensionality of the items (Wheeless, 1978; Wheeless & Grotz, 1977). The initial investigation obtained a split-half reliability of .92. In the first study, trust was associated with self-reported disclosure, while in the second, trust correlated with a self-report measure of interpersonal solidarity, a measure of the closeness or intimacy of the relationship. These studies thus provide evidence of the measure's internal stability and support for its construct validity.

In 1980, Larzelere and Huston published the Dyadic Trust Scale, an instrument designed to assess attributions of benevolence and honesty. Factor analysis and item analysis of a 57-item pool drawn from previous scales measuring various types of trust resulted in a final scale of eight statements, for example, "I feel that I can trust my partner completely." The scale yielded a coefficient *alpha* of .93 with a separate sample of subjects. The scale did not correlate significantly with either social desirability or a measure of generalized trust. The Dyadic Trust Scale, social desirability, and generalized trust were correlated with measures of love and self-disclosure. The Dyadic Trust Scale's correlation coefficients consistently exceeded those of the other two variables, providing evidence of the scale's construct validity. The trust measure also discriminated among types of relationships: individuals who were divorced had lower trust scores than those in dating relationships, who in turn were lower than individuals who were cohabiting or married.

Johnson-George and Swap (1982) report the development of another scale to measure trust in specific persons. Forty-three trust items along with Rubin's loving and liking scales were subjected to factor analysis. Since the loving and liking items formed separate factors, the 43 items were analyzed again separately. Four factors resulted for the male subjects, while three were obtained with females. Items composing reliableness and emotional trust factors were similar for both males and females and thus were retained for further analysis. An additional "overall" trust scale was retained for the male subjects. Coefficient *alphas* ranged from .71 to .83 for the subscales. Two studies provided evidence of the validity of the instrument. In the first, reliableness but not emotional trust varied as a function of the experimental manipulation of reliability. In the second, the emotional subscale was more sensitive to the experimental manipulation of betrayal than reliableness.

A recent study by Rempel, Holmes, and Zanna (1985) provides a fourth scale for measuring interpersonal trust. These authors suggest trust consists of three components: faith, predictability, and dependability. A trust scale is developed consisting of 26 items representing the three components. A seven-point Likert-type response option was provided. Factor analysis and item analysis were used to refine the scale, eliminating nine items. The Cronbach *alpha* was .81 for the overall scale and .80, .72, and .70 for the faith, dependability, and predictability subscales, respectively. Love correlated significantly with faith ($r=.46$) and dependability ($r=.25$), but not predictability. Similar patterns of correlations were obtained with measures of the motivational bases of trust. The authors conclude that faith is the most important aspect of love.

Evidence exists for the acceptability of all four of these measures of interpersonal trust. Which of the alternatives is preferable? Two factors make this question difficult to answer. First, no studies have used multiple measures of trust. Consequently no comparative data exist. Second, authors of the more recent studies fail to discuss the previously published measures. For all practical purposes, the measures were developed independently over an eight-year time span. Hence, rationale for the use of one measure as opposed to another must be inferred from the extant studies.

Examination of the items which comprise these scales indicate that the Wheeless and Grotz and the Larzelere and Huston measures request subjects to make more global assessments of the target person than do the other two measures. Statements about specific situations predominate the measures by Johnson-George and Swap (1982) (e.g., "I would go hiking with __ __ __ __ in unfamiliar territory if __ __ __ __ assured me he/she knew the area", p. 1309) and by Rempel et al. (1985) (e.g., "My partner has proven to be trustworthy and I am willing to let him/her engage in activities which other partners find too threatening," p. 102). The semantic-differential scales of Wheeless and Grotz are not bound by such specificities. Though consisting of statements, the Dyadic Trust Scale is equally general (e.g., "I feel that I can trust my partner completely," Larzelere & Huston, 1980, p. 599).

Interestingly, the two scales composed of general items yielded unidimensional solutions in factor analyses, while the scales containing situation-specific items resulted in multiple factors. In absence of a compelling theoretical rationale for some component of the trust construct, the two general scales would appear to be preferable to the two specific ones. Of the two general instruments, the evidence for the validity of the Dyadic Trust Scale is more persuasive. Additionally the internal reliability and construct validity receive support from additional studies which use the scale (Hansen, 1985; White, 1985).

The two scales which emphasized situation specific items yielded different factor structures but shared two similar factors. The reliableness factor of Johnson-George and Swap is analogous to the dependability factor of Rempel, Holmes, and Zanna. Likewise, the emotional trust of the former scale resembles the faith factor of the latter. Both studies provide evidence of the discriminant validity of subscales based on these factors. However, examination of the individual items can lead a reader to question the interpretation of the factor labels. In other words, the content validity of the subscales deserves additional attention. Given that one study was based on an exceptionally small sample size (n=84) and the other yielded unexpected and inconsistent factors, the integrity of these subscales must be interpreted cautiously. These two studies indicate the potential importance of conceptual and empirical work on the topic of interpersonal trust. However, further research and replication are necessary before these measures should be adopted.

Additional Measures

Several studies have developed measures of trust for specialized populations or contexts. Kegan and Rubenstein (1972) review the availability of scales for studying trust in the organizational context. More recent works by Cook and Wall (1980) and by Scott (1983) provide multi-item measures of trust in superiors and peers in the work setting. Imber (1973) describes an instrument for the measurement of children's trust of parents and teachers. The previously described Counselor Rating Form (Barak & LaCrosse, 1975) contains a subscale for measuring clients' trust in counselors. Though extensive validation efforts have not been performed for most of these measures, these studies provide a starting point for researchers who need more specialized measures than the four discussed in the first part of this chapter.

APPENDIX: 1

Interpersonal Attraction Scale

Items

The items listed below are from McCroskey and Richmond's (1979) revised version of the Interpersonal Attraction Scale. Items to be reverse scored are indicated by "(R)". A seven-interval Likert response continuum is used.

Task Attraction Scales

1. If I wanted to get things done, I could probably depend on her/him.
2. He/she would be a poor problem solver. (R)
3. I couldn't get anything accomplished with her/him. (R)
4. I have confidence in her/his ability to get the job done.
5. He/she is a typical goof-off when assigned a job to do. (R)
6. I would enjoy working on a task with her/him.
7. This person is lazy when it comes to working on a task. (R)
8. This person would be an asset in any task situation.
9. I would recommend her/him as a work partner.
10. I could rely on her/him to get the job done.
11. This person takes her/his work seriously.
12. He/she is an unreliable work partner. (R)
13. I could not count on the person to get the job done. (R)
14. I could not recommend her/him as a work partner. (R)

Social Attraction Items

1. I think he/she could be a friend of mine.
2. I would like to have a friendly chat with her/him.
3. It would be difficult to meet and talk with her/him. (R)
4. We could never establish a personal friendship with each other. (R)

5. He/she just wouldn't fit into my circle of friends. (R)
6. He/she would be pleasant to be with.
7. He/she is sociable with me.
8. I would *not* like to spend time socializing with this person. (R)
9. I could become close friends with her/him.
10. He/she is easy to get along with.
11. He/she is unpleasant to be around. (R)
12. This person is not very friendly. (R)

Physical Attraction Items

1. I think he/she is handsome/pretty.
2. He/she is sexy looking.
3. I don't like the way he/she looks. (R)
4. He/she is ugly. (R)
5. I find her/him attractive physically.
6. He/she is *not* good looking. (R)
7. This person looks appealing.
8. I don't like the way this person looks. (R)
9. He/she is nice looking.
10. He/she has an attractive face.
11. He/she is *not* physically attractive. (R)
12. He/she is good looking.

References

Andersen, P.A., & Coussoule, A.R. (1980). The perceptual world of the communication apprehensive. *Communication Quarterly, 28,* 44–54.

Barak, A., & LaCrosse, M.B. (1975). Multidimensional perceptions of counselor behavior. *Journal of Counseling Psychology, 22,* 471–476.

Berg, J.H., & Archer, R.L. (1983). The disclosure-liking relationship: Effects of self-perception, order of disclosure, and topical similarity. *Human Communication Research, 10,* 269–281.

Blau, P.M. (1962). Patterns of choice in interpersonal relations. *American Sociological Review, 27,* 41–55.

Brinberg, D., Coleman, J., Hoff, H., Newman, G., & Risk, L. (1980). Interpersonal attraction: A multitrait-multimethod analysis. *Representative Research in Social Psychology, 11,* 49–54.

Byrne, D. (1971). *The attraction paradigm.* New York: Academic Press.

Clore, G.L., & Gormly, J.B. (1974). Knowing, feeling, and liking: A psychophysiological study of attraction. *Journal of Research in Personality, 8,* 218–230.

Cook, J., & Wall, T. (1980). New work attitude measures of trust, organizational commitment and personal need non-fulfilment. *Journal of Occupational Psychology, 53,* 39–52.

Dalton, C., & Aijen, I. (1979). Self-disclosure and attraction: Effects of intimacy and desirability on beliefs and attitudes. *Journal of Research in Personality, 13,* 127–138.

Deutsch, M. (1962). Cooperation and trust: Some theoretical notes. *Nebraska Symposium on Motivation, 10,* 275–320.

DeWine, S., & Pearson, J.C. (1985, May). *The most frequently used self-report instruments in communication.* Paper presented at the International Communication Association Convention, Honolulu.

Ellison, C.W., & Fireston, I.J. (1974). Development of interpersonal trust as a function of self-esteem, target status, and target style. *Journal of Personality and Social Psychology, 29,* 655–663.

Fazio, R.H., Seligman, C., & Zanna, M.P. (1980). Effects of salience of extrinsic rewards on liking and loving. *Journal of Personality and Social Psychology, 38,* 453–460.

Frost, T., Stimpson, D.V., & Maughan, M.R. (1978). Some correlates of trust. *Journal of Psychology, 99,* 103–108.

Giffin, K. (1967). The contributions of studies of source credibility to a theory of interpersonal trust in the communication process. *Psychological Bulletin, 68,* 104–120.

Gormly, J., Gormly, A., & Johnson, C. (1971). Interpersonal attraction, competence, motivation, and reinforcement theory. *Journal of Personality and Social Psychology, 19,* 375–380.

Grush, J.E., & Yehl, J.G. (1979). Marital roles, sex differences and interpersonal attraction. *Journal of Personality and Social Psychology, 37,* 116–123.

Hansen, G.L. (1985). Perceived threats and marital jealousy. *Social Psychology Quarterly, 48,* 262–268.

Hernandez, E. (1982). Females in law enforcement: Femininity, competence, attraction, and work acceptance. *Criminal Justice and Behavior, 9,* 13–34.

Hickson, M., Powell, L., Hill, S.R., Holt, G.B., & Flick, H. (1979). Smoking artifacts as indicators of homophily, attraction, and credibility. *Southern Speech Communication Journal, 44,* 191–200.

Hill, C.T., Rubin, Z., & Peplau, L.A. (1976). Breakups before marriage: The end of 103 affairs. *Journal of Social Issues, 32,* 147–168.

Huston, T.L. (1974). A perspective on interpersonal attraction. In T.L. Huston (Ed.), *Foundations of interpersonal attraction* (pp. 3–28). New York: Academic Press.

Imber, S. (1973). Relationship of trust to academic performance. *Journal of Personality and Social Psychology, 28,* 145–150.

Johnson-George, C., & Swap, W.C. (1982). Measurement of specific interpersonal trust: Construction and validation of a scale to assess trust in a specific other. *Journal of Personality and Social Psychology, 43,* 1306–1317.

Kegan, D.L., & Rubenstein, A.H. (1972). Measures of trust and openness. *Comparative Group Studies, 3,* 179–201.

Kerber, K.W. (1981). Perceived physiological activity and interpersonal attraction. *Journal of Social Psychology, 113,* 101–113.

Kitson, G.C. (1982). Attachment to the spouse in divorce: A scale and its application. *Journal of Marriage and the Family, 44,* 379–393.

Krivonos, P.D. (1980). The effects of attitude similarity, spatial relationship, and task difficulty on interpersonal attraction. *Southern Speech Communication Journal, 45,* 240–248.

Larzelere, R.E., & Huston, T.L. (1980). The dyadic trust scale: Toward understanding interpersonal trust in close relationships. *Journal of Marriage and the Family, 42,* 595–604.

Lindskold, S. (1978). Trust development, the grit proposal, and the effects of conciliatory acts on conflict and cooperation. *Psychological Bulletin, 85,* 772–793.

Lindzey, G., & Byrne, D. (1968). Measurement of social choice and interpersonal attractiveness. In G. Lindzey and E. Aronson, (Eds.), *Handbook of social psychology: Vol. II. Research methods* (pp. 452–525). Reading, MA: Addison-Wesley.

McCroskey, J.C., & McCain, T.A. (1974). The measurement of interpersonal attraction. *Speech Monographs, 41,* 261–266.

McCroskey, J.C., & Richmond, V.P. (1979). *The reliability and validity of scales for the measurement of interpersonal attraction and homophily.* Paper presented at the Eastern Communication Association Convention, Philadelphia.

McCroskey, J.C., Hamilton, P.R., & Weiner, A.N. (1974). The effect of interaction behavior on source credibility, homophily, and interpersonal attraction. *Human Communication Research, 1,* 42–52.

McCroskey, J.C., Richmond, V.P., Daly, J.A., & Cox, B.G. (1975). The effects of communication apprehension on interpersonal attraction. *Human Communication Research, 2,* 51–65.

McDonald, A.P., Jr., Kessel, V.S., & Fuller, J.B. (1972). Self-disclosure and two kinds of trust. *Psychological Reports, 30,* 143–148.

Newcomb, T.M. (1960). *The acquaintance process.* New York: Holt, Rinehart & Winston.

Newcomb, T.M. (1979). Reciprocity of interpersonal attraction: A nonconfirmation of a plausible hypothesis. *Social Psychology Quarterly, 42,* 299–306.

Pearce, W.B. (1974). Trust in interpersonal communication. *Speech Monographs, 41,* 236–244.

Reaves, J.Y., & Roberts, A. (1983). The effect of type of information on children's attraction to peers. *Child Development, 54,* 1024–1031.

Rempel, J.K., Holmes, J.G., & Zanna, M.P. (1985). Trust in close relationships. *Journal of Personality and Social Psychology, 49,* 95–112.

Rotter, J.B. (1967). A new scale for the measurement of interpersonal trust. *Journal of Personality, 35,* 651–665.

Rotter, J.B. (1971). Generalized expectancies for interpersonal trust. *American Psychologist, 26,* 443–452.

Rotter, J.B. (1980). Interpersonal trust, trustworthiness, and gullibility. *American Psychologist, 35*, 1–7.

Rubin, Z. (1970). Measurement of romantic love. *Journal of Personality and Social Psychology, 16*, 265–273.

Rubin, Z. (1974a). From liking to loving: Patterns of attraction in dating relationships. In T.L. Huston (Ed.), *Foundations of interpersonal attraction* (pp. 383–402). New York: Academic Press.

Rubin, Z. (1974b). Liking and loving. In Z. Rubin (Ed.), *Doing unto others* (pp. 163–174). Englewood Cliffs, NJ: Prentice-Hall.

Rubin, Z., & McNeil, E.B. (1981). *The psychology of being human* (3rd ed.). New York: Harper & Row.

Schlenker, B.R., Helm, B., & Tedeschi, J.T. (1973). The effects of personality and situational variables on behavioral trust. *Journal of Personality and Social Psychology, 25*, 419–427.

Scott, D. (1983). Trust differences between men and women in superior-subordinate relationships. *Group and Organizational Studies, 8*, 319–336.

Sunnafrank, M. (1984). A communication-based perspective on attitude similarity and interpersonal attraction in early acquaintance. *Communication Monographs, 51*, 372–380.

Tedeschi, J.T. (1974). Attributions, liking, and power. In T.L. Huston (Ed.), *Foundations of interpersonal attraction* (pp. 193–215). New York: Academic Press.

Tesser, A., & Paulhus, D.L. (1976). Toward a causal model of love. *Journal of Personality and Social Psychology, 34*, 1095–1105.

Wheeless, L.R. (1978). A follow-up study of the relationships among trust, disclosure, and interpersonal solidarity. *Human Communication Research, 4*, 143–157.

Wheeless, L.R., & Grotz, J. (1977). The measurement of trust and its relationship to self-disclosure. *Human Communication Research, 3*, 250–257.

White, R.H. (1985). Psychological instrumentality and expressiveness in relation to dyadic trust and dyadic adjustment in married couples. *Dissertation Abstracts International, 45*, 2327B.

Woodall, W.G., Burgoon, J.K., & Markel, N.N. (1980). The effects of facial-head cue combinations on interpersonal evaluations. *Communication Quarterly, 28*, 47–55.

CHAPTER 11

Interpersonal Interaction Coding Systems

Charles H. Tardy

This chapter discusses the coding schemes developed by investigators to describe the observed interaction of members of close or personal relationships. Though some approaches to the study of interpersonal interaction may include examination of the exchange of rewards, punishments, etc., only systems for coding messages are considered here. Additionally, the discussion does not review systems developed primarily for the study of small group interaction, for example, Bales' Interaction Process Analysis coding system (Bales, 1950). The purpose of the chapter is to provide the reader with information necessary for selecting among the available systems for interaction coding. This narrow focus precludes discussion of many methodological issues. For example, statistical techniques which allow researchers to analyze the data provided by interaction analysis are not discussed in any detail. Adequate treatment of this subject may be found in works by Castellan (1979), Gottman and Bakeman (1979), and Sackett (1979). Additionally, this chapter does not propose to provide the level of understanding necessary for implementation of the coding schemes. Rather, it outlines the purposes, assets, and deficits of the alternatives. Once a choice is made, resources for mastering the different systems should be utilized. Where relevant, I have provided references to more extensive discussions of the options and requirements of interaction analysis (see also O'Keefe, Delia, & O'Keefe, 1980). Chapter 8 by Hirokawa discusses issues related to decision-making interaction in the small group setting, while chapter 5 by Street on communicator style includes a discussion of the acquisition and analysis of another type of interaction data.

There are several common concerns with regard to each coding scheme. First, the procedure's purpose is identified. Most schemes purport to describe only interaction, rather than measure internal states or traits of the participants (Markman, Notarius, Stephen, & Smith, 1981). Social interaction observation methods are generally more appropriate for studying "contextual, interpersonal, and developmental processes" (Cairns & Green, 1979, p. 222) than for measuring the underlying traits of the interactants. The intended use, however, has important implications for the assessment of the scheme's validity. Second, the procedures for utilizing the scheme are described. The content categories used by different schemes vary quantitatively and qualitatively. Third, evidence concerning reliability and validity is summarized briefly. Steps necessary for obtaining acceptable psychometric properties are identified. Fourth, general uses and limitations of the coding schemes are discussed. The practical limitations as well as the common applications of a coding scheme should be known.

Marital Interaction Coding System

The Marital Interaction Coding System (hereafter referred to as MICS) was developed by Robert Weiss and colleagues to "capture interaction behaviors germane to problem-solving attempts of couples" (Weiss & Summers, 1983, p. 86). The authors utilized the scheme to develop training programs for improving marital stability. Its use having been reported in more than 35 published articles, this coding scheme has been used far more frequently than any other.

The MICS scheme has been revised twice, resulting in three versions, all requiring basically the same procedures, but varying slightly in terms of content categories utilized. A couple's discussion of a real or hypothetical problem is recorded, usually with videotape, though audio-only recordings also have been used. The taped interaction is then coded by trained observers.

The basic coding unit of MICS is the "behavior unit defined as behavior of homogenous content, irrespective of duration or formal grammatical accuracy, emitted by a single partner" (Weiss & Summers, 1983, p. 87). Trained observers select from 30 codes to characterize each discrete act of a speaker, for example, agree, approve, interrupt, mindread, smile/laugh. Some of the codes may be used in combination. Two additional codes are used only for listeners. To reduce the number of categories, investigators have combined individual categories into summary codes, such as positive verbal, positive nonverbal, negative verbal, and negative nonverbal. Even such broad categories as positive and negative have been used as summary codes.

However, the latest version of MICS suggests seven specific functional categories: problem description, blame, proposal for change, validation, invalidation, facilitation, and irrelevant (Weiss & Summers, 1983).

With extensive training of observers, studies have shown acceptable levels of reliability. The authors recommend that tapes coded with less than 70% interobserver agreement should be rescored. However, Jacobson, Elwood, and Dallas (1981) criticize the MICS because the expected agreement among coders cannot be calculated, and, therefore, no statistical test of reliability can be calculated. Additionally, these authors note that few studies report interobserver agreement for each of the 28–32 categories, thus preventing the identification of problematic categories. However, since summary categories, instead of the individual codes, are frequently used for the data analysis, this criticism does not provide grounds for serious concern. Weider and Weiss (1980) provide evidence of MICS's reliability. In their study, summary codes generalize across coders and coding sessions. That is, different coders rating the same interaction transcript obtain comparable results, and coders obtain comparable results when work is done at different times. This method of reliability assessment was advanced by Cronbach, Glesser, Nanda, and Rajaratnam (1972) and is commonly used by marital interaction researchers.

Evidence that MICS summary codes distinguish between distressed and nondistressed couples and detect pre- and post-counseling differences in couples' interaction provides support for the system's discriminant validity. However, Jacobson, et al. (1981) note that no data validate the use of MICS to measure such concepts as "good communication" or "effective problem solving." Additionally, these authors contend there is little support for the positive and negative labels used for the summary codes. Users of this system should consider collecting supplemental data to support the construct validity of their interpretation of MICS data. Folger, Hewes, and Poole (1984) discuss the issue of construct validity of coding systems in great detail and offer suggestions for dealing with this problem.

Couples Interaction Scoring System

John Gottman (1979) and colleagues' Couples Interaction Scoring System (hereafter referred to as CISS) was derived in part from MICS, as well as from Olson and Ryder's (1970) coding scheme for use with the Inventory of Marital Conflict. Like MICS, CISS's purpose is to describe couples' conflict resolution interactions. The primary difference between this and other coding systems is CISS's separation of the content and the affect dimension of messages, or more generally between the verbal and nonverbal.

CISS delineates three aspects of an interaction. The verbal acts, that is, thought units, of the person speaking are classified into 28 content codes. These basic codes are combined to form eight summary codes: agreement, disagreement, communication talk, mindreading, problem solving and information exchange, summarizing other, summarizing self, and expressing feelings about a problem. Unlike the summary codes of many other systems, Gottman's have been demonstrated empirically to be functionally equivalent. In fact, behavior may be coded on the basis of the summary codes rather than with the more numerous basic codes.

The nonverbal behaviors of both the speaker and the listener which accompany each verbal thought unit are given affect and context codes, respectively. These two represent the second and third aspects of interaction coded by this system. The coding manual specifies face, voice, and body cues which denote three affect categories: positive, negative, and neutral. Separate coders classify the verbal and the nonverbal acts.

Intensive, time-consuming training sessions for coders are recommended. Gottman, however, provides ample evidence that observers can achieve and maintain high levels of reliability if appropriate steps are taken. His reliability study yielded average Cohen *Kappas* of .91 for content codes and .72 for affect and context codes. Additionally, following Cronbach's generalizability theory of reliability (Cronbach et al., 1972), Gottman's study, with multiple observers coding multiple transcripts, provided strong support for the reliability of his training procedures and the coding system. From analysis of both the distribution and sequences of codes, CISS has detected differences between distressed and nondistressed couples that were predicted by Gottman's theory (1979). The coding scheme has proved useful in analyzing tapes of laboratory as well as of home interactions and of discussions of real problems as well as of improvised discussions of hypothetical situations. Acceptable results have been obtained with audio tapes as well as with tapes containing both audio and video. Recordings of interactions made by other investigators have also been reanalyzed using this system (Gottman, 1979). These applications testify not only to CISS's flexibility for use with a variety of data forms but also to its generalizability or reliability.

However, Filsinger (1983a) notes that CISS "has been used to measure positive communication skills" (p. 325). As with the use of MICS, the use of CISS to operationalize concepts such as "effective communication" has little empirical support. Investigators assume responsibility for supporting use and interpretation of the codes.

CISS' major asset is its distinction between content and affect. In fact, some investigators have used the affect component of the coding system exclusively (e.g., Sillars, Pike, Jones, & Murphy, 1984). The eight summary codes combined with the three affect codes yield a total of 24 codes, making CISS a comprehensive system. However, since using 24 codes can be very cumbersome for some statistical analyses, this characteristic is also problematic. The system requires considerable effort for use, as do most content analysis methods. Overall, CISS is an important contribution to the research methods available for studying interaction in close personal relationships and deserves serious consideration for future use.

Relational Coding Systems

Twenty years ago, Watzlawick, Beavin, and Jackson (1967) introduced communication and other scholars to Gregory Bateson's distinction between the report and command aspects of communication. The report dimension refers simply to the denotation of explicit messages, while the command aspect refers to the relationship between or among the people communicating implied by an interchange. For example, the command dimension of an interchange between a person seeking directions and a person providing instruction indicates that the questioner is in a subordinate position vis-a-vis the answerer. The term relational communication is used because the command dimension refers to the relationship among communicators. Coding schemes which focus on the relational component of communication are the subject of this section.

The relational dimension derives not from individual messages but rather from the sequence of message transactions. Edna Rogers (1981), in her informative account of the development of this concept emphasizes that "Relational communication stresses the co-defining nature of relationships, the reciprocally defined rules of interdependence of system members" (p. 233). No one person is responsible for defining the relationship.

Two kinds of interchanges have received the most concern of investigators: symmetrical and complementary. Symmetrical interchanges imply similar relational positions, while complementary interchanges imply different relational positions. Watzlawick et al. (1967) characterize symmetrical and complementary transactions as maximizing and minimizing differences, respectfully. Rogers (1981) explains this distinction well:

> In a complementary transaction the interactor's behaviors are fully differential. The relational control definition offered by one interactor is accepted by the other. In a symmetrical transaction one interactor behaves toward the other, as the other behaves toward him. There is a similarity of control definition between the interactors (p. 239).

Though these two are not the only concepts which describe the relationship implied by the command dimension, complementary, and symmetrical relationships have received the most attention.

Relational communication concepts have been used primarily to describe interaction patterns. These ideas proved especially useful in the study of families with maladjusted members (Watzlawick et al., 1967). Communication patterns evident in the family's conversations were considered central to understanding the etiology of psychological disorder. Communication scholars expanded the study of these concepts to include descriptive investigations of other types of relationships, for example, normal families (Millar & Rogers, 1976), decision-making groups (Fisher, 1979), as well as to include systematic studies of relational outcomes, such as understanding and marital satisfaction (Rogers-Millar & Millar, 1979).

In subsequent sections I review the two primary strategies for measuring the relational dimension of communication: the methods of Rogers and Farace (1975), and those of Ellis (1979). A final section compares the two and suggests how they might be used in the future.

Rogers and Farace Method

The method described by Rogers and Farace (1975) evolved from the prior work of Ericson and Rogers (1973), Mark (1971), and Sluzki and Beavin (1965/1977). With only minor revision, this procedure has been used in numerous subsequent published investigations (e.g., Barbatis, Wong, & Herek, 1983).

The first step in using the Rogers and Farace procedure is to segment a communicative interchange into speaking turns. Units must be identified containing one person's message, bordered by the messages of the prior and subsequent speaker(s). A transcription is the most useful medium with which to work.

Each message is then assigned three codes. The first code identifies the speaker. The second code specifies which of five grammatical types characterize the message: assertion, question, talk-over, non-complete, and other. The third code, called the response code, describes the message's relationship to the one immediately prior and consists of the following categories: support, nonsupport, extension, answer, instruction, order, disconfirmation, topic change, initiates-terminates, and other.

A combination of the grammatical and response categories is used to identify the control codes of "one-up," "one-down," and "one-across" maneuvers. For example, a message with a grammatical classification of assertion and response classification of support is given a "one-down" code, while a message with an assertion and topic change classification is given a "one-up" control code. One-up moves indicate that the speaker views him/herself as in control of the relationship, while one-down moves imply the speaker submits to the other's control. One across maneuvers indicate the speaker is trying to minimize or neutralize control. The three directional maneuvers may be considered bids for dominance, submission, and neutrality, respectively.

Each control code, in conjunction with the temporally subsequent control code, constitutes a transactional code. In other words, each message's control code paired with the following message's control code forms a transactional code. Each of the nine possible combinations of control codes indicates one of three types of relationships: complementary, symmetrical, or transitional. For example, a one-up message followed by a one-down message constitutes a complementary transaction, while a one-up message followed by another one-up message exemplifies a symmetrical transaction.

Since all three relational types usually occur during the many transactions which constitute a conversation, an analytical procedure must be used to interpret or summarize the array of relational data. Rogers and her colleagues have employed several. One procedure, perhaps the simplest, calculates the proportion of transactions in each of the three relational categories. However, a more precise measure of relational control may be derived by computing an intensity measure (Courtright, Millar, & Rogers, 1980; Rogers, Courtright, & Millar, 1980). Rather than being grouped into the three relational types, the control codes can be used to compute an intensity score which reflects a broader spectrum of the underlying continuum. Intensity scores are derived by multiplying each message's preassigned grammatical code score by a score for the response code. The resulting values range from 1 to 50. In addition to average intensity for each directional type, numerous other variables may be computed. In fact, one study (Courtright et al., 1980) utilized a dozen different measures of intensity.

Courtright et al. (1980) also describe a procedure for measuring transactional redundancy, the degree of randomness evident in the transactional configurations. If the communicators use each of the nine different transactional codes equally, all possible combinations of the three control codes, the system would be random or chaotic. If on the other hand, only one of the possible configurations was used, the system would be rigid. A computational procedure allows an investigator to assign a score to each dyad reflecting the degree of redundancy along a continuum between these two extremes.

Additional measures of dominance and domineeringness provide assessments of individual communicative behavior (Courtright, Millar, & Rogers-Millar, 1979; Rogers-Millar & Millar, 1979). Domineeringness refers to the number (or proportion) of one-up attempts one person makes during the course of the conversation, while dominance refers to the number (or proportion) of one-up attempts which are successful, that is, which are followed by one-down codes. The former measure involves the messages of each interactant independent of the other speaker's messages, while the latter measure involves the messages and subsequent responses by another speaker. Several computational procedures have been offered for both measures.

The reliability of this coding scheme is assessed on the basis of the categorization of the individual messages into the appropriate grammatical and response categories. Rogers and her colleagues have published several studies based on two data sets for which intercoder agreement exceeded .85, indicating acceptable reliability. However, none of the published studies contain a detailed account of the data gathering procedure. Other authors who have utilized this system also report comparable intercoder reliability coefficients (Ayers & Miura, 1981; Barbatis et al., 1983; O'Donnell-Trujillo, 1981). Rogers and Farace (1975) report that coders need about five hours of training for acceptable results.

The validity of these measures has been the subject of some controversy. Some critics (Folger & Poole, 1982; Folger & Sillars, 1980) argue that the control codes do not represent the perceptions of the people being observed; that a message labeled one-up by an investigator may not be similarly described by the participant. In response, Rogers and Millar (1982) say the codes reflect properties of the relationship which can be empirically linked to other observable relationship characteristics, for example, marital satisfaction, and, consequently, they disavow the relevance of the correspondence or noncorrespondence between perceptions and actual behavior. The Rogers and Farace procedures should not be used if the researcher's theoretical or explanatory basis is the perception or shared interpretation of individuals. Rather, these procedures are most appropriate when individual motivations are considered less important than other bases for understanding or explaining human behavior.

Ellis' RELCOM

A second procedure utilized to code the relational dimension of interaction was developed by Don Ellis and colleagues (Ellis, Fisher, Drecksel, Hoch, & Werbol, n.d.). Like the Farace and Rogers system, the RELCOM coding scheme follows from the pioneering work of Sluzki and Beavin (1965/1977) but, unlike the Farace and Rogers system, contains no grammatical or response categories. Interpreted as a response to a prior message, each message is coded solely on the basis of the relational control function implied by the interchange.

RELCOM, unlike the Farace and Roger scheme, identifies two types of one-up and one-down messages. "Strong" and "weak" varieties of one-up and one-down categories specify degrees of intensity of relational dominance or submission maneuvers. Ellis et al., like Rogers and Farace, recognize a neutral category representing messages which do not attempt to assert or deny relational control. A five-category system, RELCOM provides a wider range of relational control scores than does the three category Rogers and Farace system. On the other hand, the range of RELCOM scores is much narrower than those resulting from the multiplication of the Rogers and Farace grammatical and response codes.

Though studies generally yield adequate intercoder reliability, coefficients around .80 using the Guetzkow formula, one study comparing several relational control measures (Ayres & Miura, 1981) concluded that RELCOM was less reliable than other procedures for assessing symmetry. Perhaps researchers must monitor coders carefully in order to obtain the most reliable results possible. For example, Fisher and Drecksel (1983) checked reliability before, during, and after coding their taped interactions to ensure the stability of coder judgments.

Many studies have used RELCOM primarily to describe interaction (Ellis, 1979; Fisher & Drecksel, 1983). However, other studies have used the system to differentiate between types of individuals (Ellis, 1978), as well as types of groups. For example, Destephen (1983) compared decision-making groups achieving high or low consensus. Differences emerged between the two types of groups in the first but not last meeting. Ellis and McCallister (1980) observed predicted differences in relational dominance and submissiveness characterized by sex-typed male and female discussion groups. Studies such as these support the construct validity of this coding procedure. However, it is subject to the same content validity criticism that was attributed to the Rogers and Farace system. Consequently, its users also must be aware that RELCOM measures phenomena from the perspective of the researcher, not of the observed.

Whereas Rogers and Farace use the adjacent pairs of message codes to identify complementary, symmetrical, and transitory patterns of relational interaction, most users of RELCOM do not. Rather, most studies employ Markov chain statistical analysis procedures to identify significant sequences of relational control maneuvers. This analytical tool allows investigators to describe the interaction in terms of control sequences which have the highest probability of occurring. However, this statistical technique is not part of the RELCOM procedure and could be used with the data generated by the Farace and Rogers method. Likewise, adjacent RELCOM data codes could be subjected to the procedures used by Rogers and Farace. In fact, one recent study (Williamson & Fitzpatrick, 1985) used both techniques to analyze RELCOM data. Both procedures yield summary information about the relationships among the people being studied, rather than about the characteristics of the individual subjects. In addition measures of individual behavior can be computed.

Recommendations

Investigators seeking an appropriate procedure for measuring the relational dimension have clear though difficult choices. The coding systems of both Ellis et al. and of Rogers and Farace have been used reliably and have been shown to be useful in describing interaction, as well as in predicting relational outcomes. However, there are no compelling reasons to select one alternative over the other. Since the two are not interchangeable (O'Donnell-Trujillo, 1981), the choice cannot be considered inconsequential. More must be known about the properties and empirical correlates of both the Farace and Rogers and RELCOM procedures before generalizations can be made across studies using the two different coding strategies. As Rogers and Millar (1982) suggest, perhaps the most appropriate direction for future research is to assess the "predictive utility of each . . . with cross-contextual and developmental analyses" (p. 253).

In deciding which of the two procedures to use or revise, the two major differences in the coding schemes should be noted. First, the unitizing rules significantly differ. Rogers and Farace require a message to be scored twice if its function as a response to the preceding message differs from its function as a stimulus to the subsequent message. This double coding can result in a significant increase in the number of responses coded, as well as the frequency of various relational patterns (O'Donnell-Trujillo, 1981). The second major difference in the two systems is the use of grammatical and response codes. Whereas Farace and Rogers use both categories, RELCOM does not. The absence of this coding element enhances the relative ease of using the RELCOM system. Since transcripts are not required, the time and effort consumed by coding is reduced significantly. However, the Farace and Rogers procedure of coding these two elements vastly increases the data available to the researcher for analysis. As studies have shown (e.g., Courtright, Millar, & Rogers, 1980), these data provide researchers the opportunity for powerful and complex analysis. Other differences are detailed by O'Donnell-Trujillo (1981).

Unfortunately, few studies have employed both measures. The Rogers and Farace procedure has been used primarily to assess the interaction of husband-wife pairs. However, Barbatis et al's. (1983) study of relationships portrayed in commercial television programs indicates the utility of this system for studying communication in other contexts. The RELCOM procedure, on the other hand, has been used to study a variety of interaction types. In addition to examining zero-history, task-oriented discussion groups (Destephen, 1983), studies have observed consciousness-raising adult groups (Ellis, 1979), military roommates (Fisher & Drecksel, 1983), and married couples (Williamson & Fitzpatrick, 1985). Consequently, RELCOM has been used in more diverse studies than the Rogers and Farace system. Either method is appropriate for a variety of types of interpersonal interaction.

These procedures should not be considred sacrosanct. Concerns over content validity suggest that they could be revised profitably. If revisions are made, several suggestions previously offered may prove useful. Since both systems currently rely primarily on verbal interaction, the inclusion of nonverbal messages in the coding system could increase its precision in detecting degrees of relational control. Additionally, validation efforts should focus on individual acts. Previous studies limit validation to the level of the individual subject or to the relationship. O'Donnell-Trujillo (1981) makes several suggestions for validating relational coding schemes.

Alternative Coding Systems

A variety of additional coding systems have been developed, including Patterson's Family Interaction Coding System (1982), Olson and Ryder's Marital and Family Interaction Coding System (Filsinger, 1983a), and Raush's Coding System for Interpersonal Conflict (Raush, Barry, Hertel, & Swain, 1974). Of these three, Patterson's FICS has received the most use. This scheme was developed for studying families with an antisocial or problem child. As such, the system's codes are designed to describe aversive interaction and, consequently, are most appropriate for that purpose. Olson's system was developed for identifying types of couples who differed in terms of their cohesion and adaptation (Olson, Russell, & Sprenkle, 1979). However, Markman et al. (1981) suggest that Olson and Ryder's MFICS is appropriate for describing nonintimate or nonpersonal interactions, but is not sensitive to highly engaging, personal discussions by couples. As its name implies, Raush's CSIC was designed for describing conflicts and problem-resolving strategies. Based on psychoanalytic theory, Raush's scheme is highly original. However, the system's complexity and abstractness present coding ambiguities and require considerable coder discretion (Filsinger, 1983a).

Filsinger (1983b) developed a machine-aided coding system to reduce the time required for scoring interaction data. His codes are derived primarily from MICS and CISS. Unlike these other systems, Filsinger's Dyadic Interaction Coding System provides procedures for including time or duration information in addition to event information (cf., Hewes, 1979). Sillars' (Sillars, Coletti, Parry, & Rogers, 1982) scheme for coding verbal conflict attempts to identify strategies used by couples for resolving conflict. His 27 codes are subsumed by three main categories: avoidance, distributive (competitive acts), and integrative (cooperative acts). The functions identified by these summary codes differentiate Sillars' systems from MICS and CISS.

Gottman (1979; Gottman, Notarius, Markman, Yoppi, Bank, & Rubin, 1976) devised a procedure for assessing participants' perceptions of messages. The "talk table" is a procedure for recording ratings made by subjects during a controlled interaction. After each person talks, the listener rates the speaker along a 5-point continuum ranging from "super negative" to "super positive." Using a similar procedure, Margolin, Hattem, John, and Yost (1985) noted differences between self-ratings and ratings by trained observers. Markman's (1979, 1981) longitudinal studies indicate that this measure of couples' communicative behavior accurately predicts interaction and satisfaction over a five-and-a-half year time span. Though deciphering only a small portion of the meaning of interaction, this scheme evidently does a good job of measuring affect.

Conclusion

The coding schemes identified above constitute the most promising alternatives for investigators studying interaction in close interpersonal relationships. MICS and CISS, in particular, provide coherent and well-planned systems for describing interaction content. However, the investigator's first priority is to ensure that the aspects of the content identified by the coding system are central to the proposed study. This criterion must be satisfied before the system's reliability and validity become relevant. Researchers are obliged to alter a system or develop new ones when the codes or procedures do not serve an investigator's needs.

References

Ayers, J.E., & Miura, S.Y. (1981). Construct and predictive validity of instruments for coding relational control communication. *Western Journal of Speech Communication, 45,* 159–171.

Bales, R.F. (1950). *Interaction process analysis: A method for the study of small groups.* Cambridge, MA: Addison-Wesley.

Barbatis, S.G., Wong, M.R., & Herek, G.M. (1983). A struggle for dominance: Relational communication patterns in television drama. *Communication Quarterly, 31,* 148–155.

Cairns, R.B., & Green, J.A. (1979). Appendix A: How to assess personality and social patterns. In R.B. Cairns, (Ed.) *The analysis of social interaction* (pp. 209–226). Hillsdale, NJ: Erlbaum.

Castellan, N.J. (1979). The analysis of behavioral sequences. In R.B. Cairns (Ed.), *The analysis of social interaction* (pp. 81–118). Hillsdale, NJ: Erlbaum.

Courtright, J.A., Millar, F.E., & Rogers-Millar, L.E. (1979). Domineeringness and dominance: Replication and expansion. *Communication Monographs, 46,* 179–192.

Courtright, J.A., Millar, F.E., & Rogers, L.E. (1980). Message control intensity as a predictor of transactional redundancy. *Communication Yearbook, 4,* 199–216.

Cronbach, L.J., Gleser, C.C., Nanda, H., & Rajaratnam, N. (1972). *The dependability of behavioral measurements.* New York: Wiley.

Destephen, R.S. (1983). Group interaction differences between high and low consensus groups. *Western Journal of Speech Communication, 47,* 340–363.

Ellis, D.G. (1978). Trait predictors of relational control. *Communication Yearbook, 2,* 184–191.

Ellis, D.G. (1979). Relational control in two group systems. *Communication Monographs, 46,* 153–166.

Ellis, D.G., Fisher, B.A., Drecksel, G., Hoch, D. and Werbel, W.S. (n.d.). *REL/COM: System for analyzing relational communication.* Unpublished manuscript, Department of Communication, University of Utah.

Ellis, D.G., & McCallister, L. (1980). Relational control sequences in sex-typed and androgynous groups. *Western Journal of Speech Communication, 44,* 35–49.

Ericson, P., & Rogers, L.E. (1973). New procedures for analyzing relational communication. *Family Process, 12,* 245–267.

Filsinger, E.E. (1983a). Choices among marital observation coding systems. *Family Process, 22,* 317–335.

Filsinger, E.E. (1983b). A machine-aided marital observation technique. *Journal of Marriage and the Family, 45,* 623–632.

Fisher, B.A. (1979). Content and relational dimensions of communication in decision-making groups. *Communication Quarterly, 27,* 3–11.

Fisher, B.A., & Drecksel, G.L. (1983). A cyclical model of developing relationships: A study of relational control interaction. *Communication Monographs, 50,* 66–78.

Folger, J.P., Hewes, D.E., & Poole, M.S. (1984). Coding social interaction. *Progress in Communication Sciences, 4,* 115–161.

Folger, J.P., & Poole, M.S. (1982). Relational coding schemes: The question of validity. *Communication Yearbook, 5,* 235–247.

Folger, J.P., & Sillars, A.L. (1980). Relational coding and perceptions of dominance. In B.W. Morse and L.A. Phelps (Eds.), *Interpersonal communication: A relational perspective.* (pp. 322–333). Minneapolis, MN: Burgess.

Gottman, J.M. (1979). *Marital interaction: Experimental investigations.* New York: Academic Press.

Gottman, J.M., & Bakeman, R. (1979). The sequential analysis of observational data. In M.E. Lamb, S.J. Suomi, and G.R. Stephenson (Eds.), *Social interaction analysis* (pp. 185–206). Madison, WI: University of Wisconsin Press.

Gottman, J., Notarius, C., Markman, H., Bank, S., Yoppi, B., & Rubin, M.E. (1976). Behavior exchange theory and marital decision making. *Journal of Personality and Social Psychology, 34,* 14–23.

Hewes, D.E. (1979). The sequential analysis of social interaction. *Quarterly Journal of Speech, 65,* 56–73.

Jacobson, N.S., Elwood, R.W., & Dallas, M. (1981). Assessment of marital dysfunction. In D.H. Barlow (Ed.), *Behavioral assessment of adult disorders* (pp. 439–479). New York: Guilford.

Margolin, G., Hattem, D., John, R.S., & Yost, K. (1985). Perceptual agreement between spouses and outside observers when coding themselves and a stranger dyad. *Behavioral Assessment, 7,* 235–247.

Mark, R.A. (1971). Coding communication at the relationship level. *Journal of Communication, 21,* 221–232.

Markman, H.J. (1979). The application of a behavioral model of marriage in predicting relationship satisfaction for couples planning marriage. *Journal of Consulting and Clinical Psychology, 47,* 743–749.

Markman, H.J. (1981). The prediction of marital distress. *Journal of Consulting and Clinical Psychology, 49,* 760–762.

Markman, H.J., Notarius, C.I., Stephen, T., & Smith, R.J. (1981). Behavioral observation systems for couples. In E.E. Filsinger and R.A. Lewis (Eds.), *Assessing marriage* (pp. 234–262). Beverly Hills, CA: Sage.

Millar, F.E., & Rogers, L.E. (1976). A relational approach to interpersonal communication. In G.R. Miller (Ed.), *Explorations in interpersonal communication* (pp. 87–103). Beverly Hills, CA: Sage.

O'Donnell-Trujillo, N. (1981). Relational communication: A comparison of coding systems. *Communication Monographs, 48*, 91–105.

O'Keefe, B.J., Delia, J.G., & O'Keefe, D.J. (1980). Interaction analysis and the analysis of interactional organization. *Studies in Symbolic Interaction, 3*, 25–57.

Olson, D.H., Russell, C.S., & Sprenkle, D.H. (1979). Circumplex model of marital and family systems I. *Family Process, 18*, 3–28.

Olson, D.H., & Ryder, R.G. (1970). The inventory of marital conflicts (IMC): An experimental interaction procedure. *Journal of Marriage and the Family, 32*, 443–448.

Patterson, G.R., (1982). *A social learning approach: Vol. 3. Coercive family processes.* Eugene, OR: Castalia.

Raush, H.L., Barry, W.A., Hertel, R., & Swain, M.A. (1974). *Communication, conflict and marriage.* San Francisco, CA: Jossey-Bass.

Rogers, L.E. (1981). Symmetry and complementarity: Evolution and evaluation of an idea. In C. Wilder-Mott and J.H. Weakland (Eds.), *Rigor and imagination: Essays from the legacy of Gregory Bateson* (pp. 231–252). New York: Praeger.

Rogers, L.E., Courtright, J., & Millar, F.E. (1980). Message control intensity: Rationale and preliminary findings. *Communication Monographs, 47*, 201–219.

Rogers, L.E., & Farace, R.V. (1975). Analysis of relational communication in dyads: New measurement procedures. *Human Communication Research, 1*, 222–239.

Rogers-Millar, L.E., & Millar, F.E. (1979). Domineeringness and dominance: A transactional view. *Human Communication Research, 5*, 238–246.

Rogers, L.E., & Millar, F.E. (1982). The question of validity: A pragmatic answer. *Communication yearbook, 5*, 249–257.

Sackett, G.P. (1979). The lag sequential analysis of contingency and cyclicity in behavioral interaction research. In J.D. Osofsky (Ed.), *Handbook of infancy development* (pp. 623–649). New York: Wiley.

Sillars, A.L., Coletti, S.F., Parry, D., & Rogers, M.A. (1982). Coding verbal conflict tactics: Nonverbal and perceptual correlates of the "avoidance-distributive-integrative" distinction. *Human Communication Research, 9*, 83–95.

Sillars, A.L., Pike, G.R., Jones, T.S., & Murphy, M.A. (1984). Communication and understanding in marriage. *Human Communication Research, 10*, 317–350.

Sluzki, C.E. & Beavin, J. (1965/1977). Symmetry and complementarity: An operational definition and typeology of dyads. In P. Watzlawick and J.H. Weakland (Eds.), *The interaction view* (pp. 71–87). New York: Norton.

Watzlawick, P., Beavin, J.H., & Jackson, D.D. (1967). *Pragmatics of human communication: A study of interactional patterns, pathologies, and paradoxes.* New York: Norton.

Weider, G.B., & Weiss, R.L. (1980). Generalizability theory and the coding of marital interactions. *Journal of Consulting and Clinical Psychology, 48,* 469–477.

Weiss, R.L., & Summers, K.J. (1983). Marital interaction coding systems-III. In M.E. Filsinger (Ed.), *Marriage and family assessment* (pp. 85–115). Beverly Hills, CA: Sage.

Williamson, R., & Fitzpatrick, M.A. (1985). Two approaches to marital interaction: Relational control patterns in marital types. *Communication Monographs, 52,* 236–252.

CHAPTER 12

Language Variables: Conceptual and Methodological Problems of Instantiation

James J. Bradac

In their professional lives, social researchers are sensitive to the fact that language has a variable aspect which carries consequences for them, for research respondents, and for consumers of research. For example, it is a methodological truism that certain types of wordings in questionnaire items will bias responses in one direction, whereas other types will bias them in another (Webb, Campbell, Schwartz, & Sechrest, 1966, pp. 19–20; Eiser & Pancer, 1979). Or, to give a second instance, some technical terms used in a research report, for example, "phoneme," "reticular formation" and "morphogenesis," will be meaningful to a particular audience but completely meaningless to others. In a related case, a given term—the psychological construct "androgeny" is a good example—will have one meaning for the research reporter and another very different meaning for unintended audiences who are nonspecialists, a situation which can produce confusion. These and other facts of professional communication force a certain linguistic sensitivity upon those who collect and report social data.

But, more particularly, some of the above-mentioned social researchers are *primarily,* even *exclusively,* interested in questions of language variation. How do social class and ethnic identification affect language styles? When does experienced anxiety affect verbal behavior? How does a communicator's use of high-intensity language affect audience impressions of his or her credibility? How does nonstandard dialect affect impressions of social attractiveness? There is an ample and rapidly growing body of research on "speech evaluation" which addresses questions of this sort (Giles & Powesland, 1975; Ryan &

301

Giles, 1982). Generally, speech evaluation studies are concerned with the antecedents for and consequences of language variation, especially with the latter.

The focus of this chapter is upon this type of research. An attempt is made initially to conceptualize "language" and "language variation." Following this, detailed analyses of several important language variables are offered, which address, in each case, problems, issues, and procedures which are more or less variable-specific. A final section offers a discussion of general issues which cut across the entire language-variable research domain.

Language and Its Many Varieties

There was a time, not long ago actually, when language was viewed as a collection of verbal behaviors learned by members of a speech community (Skinner, 1957). Different communities had different collections as a result of different learning experiences attributable to different environments. This behaviorist view, which essentially equated the meanings of "language" and "speech," has been, for the most part, replaced by a cognitive perspective which defines language as a rule-governed, hierarchical system with phonological, syntactic, semantic, and pragmatic levels (cf., Bradac, Bowers, & Courtright, 1980). This system resides in language users' minds. Language users choose to engage the system (which results in speech), or they choose to leave it disengaged (which results in nonutterance). Thus, "language" and "speech" are separate but related entities. There are several versions of this cognitive view (for the classic statement, see Chomsky, 1957), and there are some important theorists who reject both the cognitive and behaviorist perspectives, opting instead for the position that language is completely a social construction which changes constantly as social beings negotiate their dissimilar realities (e.g., Rommetveit, 1983). There is also a social-cognitive view, whose proponents argue that language is a cognitive system with social entailments (Berger & Bradac, 1982; Bradac, 1983; Giles & Hewstone, 1982; Roloff & Berger, 1982). From the standpoint of this chapter, an eclectic social-cognitive view seems most functional: (a) Language is a special cognitive system unique to humans (and perhaps acquirable by dolphins [Herman, Richards, & Wolz, 1984; but see Premack, 1985]), which can be performed overtly, as in the case of speech; (b) when performed, it serves social functions and inevitably has a social dimension—even "hard-science" arguments about subatomic particles are directed at audiences; and (c) it is a dynamic system.

The last point merits discussion because it deals with the notion of *variation* which is central to this chapter. Language is dynamic in several particular senses. First, language varies epochally, a fact which researchers in the field of historical linguistics have recognized for many years. There are differences between, say, Restoration English and the English used in this chapter. All of the levels of language are implicated in these differences, that is, phonology, semantics, and so on. *But* the fact that we can understand Restoration comedies suggests that some aspects of language change are smooth and slow (from a human as opposed to a cosmic perspective); historical language variation is typically evolutionary, not revolutionary.

Language also varies within epochs. The notion of "dialect" captures this fact; the English spoken in Iowa differs from the English spoken in Mississippi; some Chicanos speak differently than some Anglos. Language varies as a function of social group membership. In some cases this variation serves to protect precarious group identities (Tajfel, 1974; Giles, 1979), whereas in others it serves to exclude nonmembers (Drake, 1980). One of the interesting questions here, which is currently the focus of much research, is: Which group memberships are important in terms of language variation? Do doctors and dentists talk differently than patients (Treichler, Frankel, Kramerae, Zoppi, & Beckman, 1984)? Do friends talk differently than strangers (Applegate & Delia, 1980)? Why are some group differences implicated in language differences while others are not?

Within groups, language also varies as a function of two primary factors: psychological state and situational context. Regarding the former, the language which one uses when depressed may vary considerably from that used when one is elated (Scherer, 1979). Or the language which one uses when relaxed may differ from that used when one is tense or anxious (Höweler, 1972; Bradac, Konsky, & Elliott, 1976). Independently of psychological state, as the communication situation changes, so too will the communicator's language. The style of a formal lecture is often different from the style used when chatting at a party (Joos, 1967). The topic of contextual influences upon language variation is exceedingly complex; the surface can only be scratched here. For example, what is a context? When are contextual shifts noticed and when not? When is the meaning of a particular context negotiated idiosyncratically by interactants and when is the culturally-mandated meaning accepted? When is language used to create contexts and when do context dictate language form? (For a discussion of these and other related issues see Giles & Hewstone, 1982; I return to the problem of context below).

Finally, it should be noted that language varies within situations.

After talking for a while with Speaker B, Speaker A may shift her style in the direction of A's style for purposes of accommodation. In some cases such style shifting may reflect an unconscious process of response matching while in others it may represent an intentional effort to appear polite and friendly. Once again, all of the levels of language are potentially implicated in this form of language variation; linguistic convergence (and divergence) has been obtained for accent, syntax, and lexical choice (Giles, 1973; Scotton, 1985). Some of the most interesting research on speech evaluation is being conducted on this topic, that is, style shifting within situations (Street & Giles, 1982).

Thus, language is a cognized hierarchical structure, aspects of which vary from epoch to epoch, from group to group, from situation to situation, and from speaker to speaker. One can talk of "dialectal" or "ideolectal" variants of a basic structure, although the term "dialect" has been called into question because of the historical and ideological baggage which it carries. Hudson (1980) has proposed the more neutral term "linguistic item" to refer to any and all clusters of linguistic features which vary with speakers and occasions. This term may not be highly communicative, but Hudson's underlying logic is important: language varies not only as a function of geographical differences (as suggested by the old "dialect" label) but also as a function of a large and largely unspecified group of social psychological factors. *Within speaker* differences may be larger than the differences *between* geographically dispersed *groups* in some cases, for example, schizophrenic speaker at time 1 versus time 2 or nonaphasic speaker at time 1 versus aphasic at time 2 following brain trauma.

Both between-group and within-speaker language variation have been investigated in a large number of empirical studies. Important language variables which have been examined in this research are surveyed in the following section. For each variable, unique and important conceptual and methodological issues are raised. Most of these issues address the topics of measurement and operationalization.

Several Language Variables Scrutinized

Six language variables are discussed here, constituting a broad range of linguistic and paralinguistic features. Each has been investigated extensively and each is currently stimulating empirical research in communication and social psychology.

Accent

This variable is discussed first because it has the longest history in the area of speech evaluation research and because it has generated the largest number of studies. Generally, accent refers to pronunciation and intonation; it is a phonological variable. Typical studies in this area have compared the effect of standard and nonstandard accents upon listeners' judgments of speaker status, intelligence, trustworthiness, and other attributes (e.g., Lambert, Hodgson, Gardner, & Fillenbaum, 1960; Bradac & Wisegarver, 1984). Thus, standard American-accented English has been compared with German-accented English (Ryan & Bulik, 1982) and English spoken with a Welsh accent has been compared with English rendered in the BBC style (usually labeled "received pronunciation" or RP; Giles, Wilson, & Conway, 1981).

In all studies examining the communicative consequences of accent varieties, a minimal requirement is for one group of respondents to render judgments of two types of accent. In a "between-groups" version of this, one group of respondents is exposed to one accent while a second group is exposed to another accent. Researchers comparing the effects of two (or more) accent varieties have several options prior to creating the accent samples which respondents will hear. For example, a researcher could use "real-world" excerpts from radio and television programs exhibiting "natural" variation in speaker accents. In this case, Speaker A talking about topic B with accent type C would be compared with Speaker X talking about topic Y with accent type Z. This use of purloined, "real-world" messages is likely to yield data which are high in external or ecological validity but low in internal validity (Cook & Campbell, 1979; Bradac, 1983, 1986). In fact, low internal validity is inevitable in such a case because of the confounding of speaker and topic differences with differences in accent. Another option exists: The researcher can record Speaker A (with accent C) reading a standard passage and then can record Speaker X (with accent Z) reading the same passage (cf., Buck, 1968). Here topic and other variables, for example, lexical choices, are controlled by the standard passage but various speaker idiosyncracies, for example, modal pitch level, are not. This "elicited-accent" approach is potentially higher in internal validity than the "purloined" accent approach described above, but it is lower in internal validity than the "matched-guise" approach where a single speaker records two versions of the standard passage, in one case using accent C and in the other using accent Z. The "matched-guise" procedure originated in research on the consequences of accent (or more broadly dialect) (Lambert, 1967) but it is now commonly used in research on other language variables (e.g., Giles, Wilson, & Conway, 1981). The primary advantage of this procedure is that nontransitory speaker characteristics, for example, modal pitch level, remain constant across versions while accent varies, although irrelevant and confounding variation in characteristics such as volume and rate may still occur. In a given research progam on the consequences of accent varieties, a researcher would be well advised to vary the level of "naturalness" and control from study to study, in one case using purloined messages, in another elicited messages, and so on.

Apart from the issue of researcher control of stimuli (but related to the issue of "naturalness") is the issue of accent typicality: Does Speaker A's rendering of, say, a Mexican-American accent adequately represent the population of Mexican-American accents in the "real world"? Accents vary in degree or broadness (Ball, Giles, Byrne, & Berechree, 1984; Brennan, Ryan, & Dawson, 1975); some accents are clearly phony whereas others sound authentic. Certainly it would be a mistake to generalize the effects of a broad, phony accent to those of an accent which is subtle and apparently real. There are different ways to approach this problem. In the best of all worlds the researcher would use several speakers each of whom is bilingual or bidialectal; this would yield an array of accents which are by definition authentic. (This assumes that the researcher wants to study authentic accents.) Of course, the major problem with this is securing several such speakers. Also the design of an experiment which includes, say, 10 different speakers becomes factorially complex, costly in terms of number of respondents needed to examine between-speaker differences adequately, and so on. A more practical (and typical) procedure is to employ one bilingual or bidialectal speaker whose accent is certified as "authentic" by language specialists or whose accent is perceived correctly by representatives of the respondent population. Probably the most important validity check for manipulations of accent entails respondent perceptions; that is, if respondents believe that the speaker's accent is Southern American, and, if this is the type of accent which the researcher intends to manipulate, then it may not matter very much if language specialists characterize the accent as Southwestern American or even as Midwestern. It is the perceptions and attributions of naive respondents which are typically of exclusive interest in the study of communicative consequences of accent (cf., Bradac & Wisegarver, 1984; Street & Hopper, 1982). On the other hand, disparity in the linguistic categorizations of specialists and nonspecialists is itself an interesting research topic (Bradac, Martin, Elliott, & Tardy, 1980).

Rate

Speakers vary the speed with which they string words together in connected discourse. Speech rate varies among speakers. Speech rate varies within speakers also as a function of topic, situation, and other variables; for example, as a given speaker's level of anxiety increases, his or her rate of speech may increase as well (Scherer, 1979; Siegmann & Pope, 1972). A number of studies have shown that increases in speaker rate are associated linearly with increases in respondent judgments of speaker competence, intelligence, and so on. On the other hand, rate increases typically have a curvilinear, inverted-"U"-type relationship with ratings of trustworthiness, benevolence, and so on (Brown, 1980; Street & Brady, 1982).

The key question here is: How does the researcher create speech samples which vary with regard to rate? There are two recourses in this case. One can electronically (or even mechanically) alter a standard audiotaped sample of speech; for example, one can "compress" a speech sample by deleting pauses and irrelevant phonetic information. This approach has been used by Brown (1980) and his associates. The major strength of this technique is that speech rates can be varied with high precision. Also, samples produced in this way will vary with regard to rate only; that is, other aspects of speech will remain constant across versions, which conduces to high internal validity. On the other hand, a high level of compression may result in a sample which sounds odd or "unnatural" to most listeners (cf., Brown, Giles, & Thackerar, 1985). The alternative is to have a single speaker record a standard passage using different rates. For example, Street and Brady (1982) had a speaker produce versions of a passage at rates of 140, 197, 253, 324, and 376 syllables per minute. Using a single speaker in this way may prevent the problem of "unnaturalness" attached to compressed speech. On the other hand, it may take a great deal of time and effort to record acceptable versions of the standard passage, especially at extremely fast rates. At fast rates even a highly fluent speaker is likely to produce many speech errors, for example, spoonerisms (Motley, Camden, & Baars, 1979) or intrusive sounds (Scherer, 1979). These errors will be confounded with rate accordingly, that is, not distributed equally across samples varying on this dimension. Errors of this sort represent a potential threat to internal validity.

It is encouraging that both the "compressed speech" and "real rate variation" approaches have produced comparable results in research on rate and social evaluation, for example, the linear effect for competence ratings referred to above. Researchers should continue to use both approaches, and it may be useful also to include in future research "real-world" or naturally occurring speech samples which vary in rate. Relatively few researchers have used naturally occurring samples in experimental research on communicative consequences of rate (Apple, Streeter, & Krauss, 1979).

Language Intensity

Through their use of language, communicators indicate the extent to which they deviate from attitudinal neutrality (Bowers, 1964). This is true regardless of the valence of the attitude; that is, a communicator may be extremely positive or slightly positive, extremely negative, or slightly negative about the attitude object. Some level of intensity necessarily is implied in all discourse, whether written or spoken. Of course, in the case of spoken language, communicators signal their level of intensity through various paralinguistic features, for example, loudness, in addition to lexical and syntactic features. Most of the research on communicative consequences of language intensity has manipulated lexical features exclusively, that is, word choice.

There have been two major approaches to the creation of high- and low-intensity messages in experimental research on this variable, and these can be labeled "contextual" and "a-contextual." In the case of the contextual approach, a basic or "kernal" message is created by the researcher who then creates low- and high-intensity message versions by substituting for various words and phrases "weak" and "strong" forms, respectively. The substituted forms reflect the particular message being used in the experiment, i.e., they are pertinent to the specific message context.

The alternative, "a-contextual" approach uses particular words and phrases which have been prescaled as independent entities along the perceived intensity dimension. Thus, the adjective "extremely" might tend to receive higher intensity ratings than the adjective "rather." In a typical scaling study, the words are rated out of context (Jones & Thurstone, 1955). The assumption that the placing of previously scaled words into a particular linguistic context will not affect their initial scale values is highly questionable. For example, the word "really" might be perceived as a relatively intense adjective when rated out of context but as a low-intensity back channel device in a message exchange where one speaker is signaling his attention to and approval of another speaker's remarks.

But a good researcher can and should check the effect of the overall message containing prescaled words by assessing its impact upon judgments of message intensity (Burgoon, Jones, & Stewart,

1975). If this is done, unexpected and unwanted consequences of a specific linguistic context can be eliminated or minimized by substituting different pre-scaled words for the original ones or by altering this context.

Apart from the "a-contextual/contextual" issue, the issue of "magnitude comparability" can be raised for language intensity (and for the other language variables as well) (cf., Bradac, Bowers, & Courtright, 1980): Just how highly intense is a particular high-intensity message used in one study compared to another one used in another study? It is possible that in some of the previous studies, one researcher's "high-intensity message" was in fact more highly intense than the "low-intensity message" used in his or her experiment but was nevertheless lower in intensity than another researcher's "high-intensity message" or in the extreme case lower in intensity than another researcher's "low-intensity message."

This possibility arises from the fact that researchers have been concerned with certifying within-study differences in intensity exclusively, not with certifying differences (and similarities) across studies. More specifically, researchers have not attempted to specify just where on the low-to-high intensity continuum their particular messages reside. This could be done in two ways:

1. Researchers could specify the ratio of number of high-intensity words to all words contained in a message (or the ratio of low-intensity words to all words). This has been done in some cases (e.g., Bowers, 1964). This would allow ratio comparability across messages and studies. But it could still be the case—indeed is likely to be the case—that messages with identical ratios will produce different perceptions of intensity level as a result of the particular words chosen and the interaction of these words with other message variables, for example, message topic.

2. Researchers could use magnitude estimation techniques to equate the extents or ranges of differences perceived between high- and low-intensity messages across studies, perhaps assuming initially (and testing for) the kind of cube root power function obtained for perceptions of increasing intensity in other modalities, for example, judgments of perceived brightness as a function of objective increases in luminosity (Stevens, 1975). Comparable subjective intervals between or among messages could be used across studies.

In spite of the probable magnitude differences across studies and in spite of dissimilar methods of creating high- and low-intensity messages, the research on language intensity has yielded some viable generalizations (Bradac, Bowers, & Courtright, 1980). One could argue that these generalizations are all the more credible for having survived the investigatory imprecision and methodological pluralism described above (Bradac, 1983).

Verbal Immediacy

Not only do communicators signal the strength of their affect, they signal the direction or valence of this affect as well. That is, without saying so directly, a communicator may "leak" the fact that he or she likes or dislikes the topic or object of utterance. This is done through the use of words and phrases which indicate the extent to which a communicator linguistically approaches or avoids the referents of discourse (Wiener & Mehrabian, 1968). The research on this language variable indicates that both trained and untrained respondents can infer correctly, at a level beyond chance, the extent to which communicators like or dislike what they are talking or writing about, despite the absence of overt evaluation in the communicators' messages. The research also suggests that people who feel negatively about the object of discourse do in fact encode their messages differently than people who feel positively (Bradac, Bowers, & Courtright, 1980; Mehrabian & Wiener, 1966). There is also some evidence of an inverse relationship between the deceptiveness of messages and their level of verbal immediacy (Kuiken, 1981). Most of the studies on this variable have used criteria suggested by Wiener and Mehrabian (1968) in operationalizing high- and low-immediacy messages. For example, based on some of these criteria the sentence "I had to dance at the party with that woman" would be less immediate than "my wife and I danced" which in turn would be marginally less immediate than "we danced."

In their introductory comments on verbal immediacy, Wiener and Mehrabian (1968) invoke the concept of "boundary condition" which refers to "the limiting conditions imposed on the possible forms of a communication" (p. 11). They suggest, reasonably enough, that knowledge of the constraints operating on a communicator encoding a message is important in assessing the message's level of immediacy. For example, if there is a stylistic demand for the passive voice, as in some scientific writing (unfortunately), the use of "I was kissed by Sarah" instead of "Sarah kissed me," may *not* signal relatively negative affect. Similarly, the demand for high lexical diversity (discussed below) in formal discourse may coerce the use of the synonym "she" instead of repetition of the form "my wife." But, rather obviously, this presents a real problem for the objective assesser of the immediacy level of a particular message or group of messages: How can the assessor possibly know the real or imagined constraints operating upon communicators? In some clear cases, specific stylistic or grammatical constraints can probably be inferred reasonably, but many other kinds of cultural or institutional constraints may be very difficult to discover. Perhaps instead of worrying about possible boundary conditions, researchers attempting to assess an individual's affect regarding "X" should gather from this person a variety of messages about "X" and "non-X." If a sufficient number of messages is scrutinized (with the attendent large variety of boundary conditions this implies), and if messages about "X" are consistently lower in immediacy than messages about "non-X," then, perhaps, relatively negative affect can validly be inferred—the negativity has transcended a variety of constraints, some of which would support the use of *high* immediacy language forms. In fact, researchers investigating the causes and consequences of verbal immediacy seem not to have worried very much about boundary conditions and related concerns. In spite of this, the findings allow a degree of generalization across studies (Bradac, Bowers, & Courtright, 1980).

Powerful and Powerless Styles

As a consequence of the kind of language they use, some speakers are perceived by their hearers to be powerful persons, whereas others are perceived to be relatively powerless. In a sense this idea can be traced back to Aristotle's (1932) discussion of the intrinsic determinants of ethos or communicator credibility. But the specific claim that particular linguistic variations are associated with the social power of communicators is much more recent. The author of this claim is the anthropologist William O'Barr (1982), although there are some clear and also contemporary precursors, for example, Basil Bernstein (1971). In his original study, O'Barr and associates examined verbal exchanges in courtrooms. It was discovered that certain linguistic forms tended to be used by persons who were "powerful" in this context, for example, judges and expert witnesses, whereas other forms tended to be used by relatively "powerless" persons, for example, defendants with little formal education. The powerless communicators exhibited many intensifiers ("it was really nice"), hedges ("it was sort of nice"), tag questions ("it was nice, wasn't it?") or declaratives with rising intonation ("it was nice?"), hesitations ("it . . . uh . . . was nice"), deictic phrases ("it was nice over there" [pointing]), and polite forms ("yes sir, it was nice"). Thus, a maximally powerless utterance would look like this: "Yes sir, it was really sort of . . . uh . . . nice over there, wasn't it?" By contrast, the powerful communicators' utterances tended to be fluent, terse, and direct.

These linguistic differences between powerful and powerless speakers are similar to the ones which Lakoff (1975) suggests characterize "male" and "female registers," respectively.

Following this initial descriptive analysis, experiments were conducted which demonstrated that powerless language tends to lower listener's and reader's judgments of communicator credibility and attractiveness (Bradac, Hemphill, & Tardy, 1981; Bradac & Mulac, 1984; Erickson, Lind, Johnson, & O'Barr, 1978). In each of the experiments, the various indicators of powerlessness (hedges, hesitations, etc.) were all used to create globally powerless messages which differed from messages which were relatively powerful. Bradac et al. (1981) suggested that in particular real-world contexts the various indicators of powerlessness may *not* covary directly, for example, hesitations may increase while polite forms decrease, in which case the use of globally powerless messages would be unrepresentative. Further, they suggested that the various indicators may not contribute equally to the creation of receiver impressions of powerlessness. These suggestions formed the basis of a study by Bradac & Mulac (1984), in which the individual effects of six ostensible indicators of powerlessness were compared to the effects of an ostensibly powerful message. Results indicated that contrary to what would be expected on the basis of O'Barr's (1982) and Lakoff's (1975) work, intensifiers and polite forms were judged by respondents to be relatively effective and powerful for both male and female communicators in a hypothetical employment interview, as was the ostensibly powerful message. Deictic phrases were perceived to reside at a neutral point. Hedges, tag questions, and hesitations were judged to be relatively ineffective and powerless. This suggests that the previous experimenters may have inadvertently confounded powerful and powerless linguistic forms in their ostensibly powerless messages, thereby diminishing the differences between these messages and their powerful counterparts. This would be a problem primarily where nonsignificant differences were obtained for the two types of messages (cf., Bradac et al., 1981). In future experimental work on this variable, researchers may be well advised to operationalize powerlessness in terms of hedges, hesitations, and tag questions exclusively (Bradac & Mulac, 1984).

But much more work needs to be done on the individual and combined effects of the various linguistic indicators of power and powerlessness. Are there communication contexts in which polite forms will indeed be seen as indicating low power? In other contexts, can communicators enhance their perceived power by hedging a lot? More radically, for persons who are extremely high in ascribed power, for example, the presidents of large corporations, will the use of ostensibly low-power forms actually enhance their power in the eyes of others? The latter possibility seems plausible in that the violation of linguistic expectations may signal the speaker's freedom, independence, autonomy, and internal control of his or her behaviors (Bradac, Hosman, & Tardy, 1978; Jones & Davis, 1965; Murdock, Bradac, & Bowers, 1984).

Lexical Diversity

Some speakers and writers exhibit a rich vocabulary; they frequently use unusual words, but any particular unusual word is used infrequently. The vocabularies of other communicators seem comparatively impoverished and redundant. Some standardized tests of intelligence and aptitude attempt to measure a respondent's vocabulary knowledge by generalizing from a sample of word-recognition responses to the hypothetical population of words that he or she knows. This is a hazardous enterprise for many reasons, for example, words may be known with different degrees of certainty and accuracy—I may recognize that "fiduciary" has some economic implication, and I may even be able to use it appropriately in a sentence ("Were I wealthy, I would not concern myself with details of the fiduciary status"), without grasping its precise meaning. Much less hazardously, analysts and researchers can make claims about *manifest* vocabulary range. Precise and accurate statements can be made about the level of lexical redundancy in a particular sample of discourse, and redundancy levels can be compared across samples. For example, levels of diversity in samples of speech produced by aphasics can be compared with levels in speech samples from nonaphasics (Wachal & Spreen, 1973).

A common measure of lexical diversity, the one most widely used in communication research, is the type-token ratio (TTR). This is calculated by dividing the number of novel words in a sample (types) over the word total (tokens). Thus, the highest TTR achievable is 1.00, whereas the lowest approaches but never quite reaches zero, as in the case of the broken record. The TTR of the first sentence of this paragraph is .94. An extension of this basic measure is the mean segmental type-token ratio (MSTTR). In this case, a discourse sample is broken down into k n-word subsamples, for example, ten 25-word subsamples in the case of a 250-word chunk of discourse. A TTR is then calculated for each subsample, and, following this, the ratios are summed and then divided by the number of subsamples constituting the discourse. This allows researchers to compare the levels of lexical diversity in samples which differ in total number of words. Were the MSTTR not used to compare discourse samples of dissimilar length, the comparison would most likely be spurious because of the fact that redundancy of language strongly tends to increase as the number of words in a message increases—longer passages will typically have lower diversity levels than will shorter ones.

Several studies have used the MSTTR as a basis for assessing lexical diversity in the language behavior of speakers in everyday communication situations. For example, Bradac, Konsky, & Elliott (1976) found that for 25-word samples of speech, college-student interviewees exhibited an MSTTR of .82 with a standard deviation of .05. Other studies have used the MSTTR as a basis for creating experimental messages differing in diversity level. For example, Bradac, Desmond, & Murdock (1977) found that messages exhibiting an MSTTR of .72 produced low ratings of communicator effectiveness compared to messages exhibiting a .82 MSTTR. Interestingly, messages exhibiting an MSTTR of .92, which is two standard deviations above the mean, did not produce higher ratings of effectiveness than the .82 messages. This indicated that the respondents in the study were sensitive to negative deviations from an average level of lexical diversity but were not sensitive to comparable positive deviations. A frequent finding in experiments on the effects of lexical diversity is that high levels of redundancy are associated with low ratings of intellectual competence and socio-intellectual status (Bradac, Bowers, & Courtright, 1980).

As suggested above, diversity levels can be made quantitatively comparable across messages, studies, and researchers which is a highly positive feature. But little attention has been paid thus far to the specific strategies used to create low or high-diversity messages. That is, diversity level can be reduced by repeating adjacent words ("I . . . I . . . I like you."), by avoiding synonyms when these would be appropriate ("The boy ate the apple and the boy climbed the tree" instead of "The boy ate the apple and he climbed the tree"), by repeating words across clausal units ("I came, I saw, I conquered"), by repeating clauses with other linguistic markers signaling an emphatic purpose ("I hated it; I repeat, I hated it"), and so on. Intuitively, it would seem that some high-redundancy forms would *not* lower ratings of communicator competence, particularly those which appear to reflect planning or intentionality on the part of the speaker. For example, if a message recipient appears not to have heard a remark, most observers would probably view an exact repetition of the remark as both intentional and perfectly appropriate (cf., Crow, 1982). It appears that the effects for low-diversity messages produced in the previous research reflect the use of adjacent repetition and nonsynonymy primarily. What is needed is a theory of types of lexical repetition, which could be tested and, if supported empirically, used as a basis for operationalizing messages in future research on the consequences of high and low levels of lexical diversity (cf., Kuiper, 1982).

Some Issues Cutting Across Particular Language Variables

Although each of the language variables discussed above is attended by unique problems of conceptualization and operationalization, there are some issues which are common to all studies of language variation. Some of these have been implied in the previous discussions of the particular variables. For example, it was suggested that experimental studies of lexical diversity can exploit the MSTTR to achieve a degree of precision and comparability across researches; it was suggested also that studies of language intensity have generally failed to use a specific metric in the operationalization of this variable and have thus failed to achieve precision and comparability. The latter charge can be leveled against research on other language variables as well, for example, power of style. Ideally, future studies of discrete variables, that is, variables which are syntactic or lexical and therefore seg-mentizable, will employ ratios in the construction of messages *and* will employ magnitude estimation (or other) techniques to provide information about *perceived* differences among messages. Future studies of continuous variables will in some cases be able to use both objective/ratio and subjective/estimation approaches, as in the case of speech rate, whereas in other cases, for example, accent, the latter "subjective" approach may have to be used exclusively.

Another issue broached briefly above might be labeled "language variable generalizability." The question here is: to what population of language texts can a sample of texts used in a particular study be generalized? This is a very complicated matter, which cannot be discussed in detail here, but the nature of the problem can be sketched. (For a detailed discussion the reader should see Jackson & Jacobs, 1983; Bradac, 1983, 1986.) Basically, the researcher has three options in language variable research: (a) s/he can select "natural" texts from some domain of texts produced for "real-world" purposes; (b) s/he can elicit textual responses from persons in a special research context, typically a laboratory setting; and (c) s/he can create texts for purposes of experimentation. In the case of "a," important questions are: Can the boundaries of the domain of "real-world" texts be specified? What procedure is used for selecting texts? For "b," important questions include: Are the persons from whom texts are elicited aware of their status as research respondents? What criteria are used to select respondents? And for "c," important questions are: Do the artificially created messages correspond to their "real-world" counterparts in terms of theoretically important attributes? Do idiosyncratic features of the texts, for example, particular phrases and words characteristic of the experimenter, represent serious confoundings? (The last question in various forms is a particularly famous one; cf., Clark, 1973 and Jackson & Jacobs, 1983.) In thinking about the answers to these (and other) questions, researchers are thinking about "language variable generalizability."

A third issue might be labeled the problem of context. Do we as researchers systematically include contextual variables in our studies of language variation, or do we ignore these variables? It should be noted that, perhaps surprisingly, many researches studying the effects of language variation in experiments have tended to ignore contextual variation. There are two major senses of context involved here: situational context and message context. The former pertains to nonmessage variables "surrounding" messages, for example, the role of the communicator, communicator gender, and presentation in a formal versus informal situation. The latter pertains to features of messages which provide a context for other features, that is, particular messages are embedded in other messages and particular message characteristics are embedded in other message characteristics. For example, one speaker's high-diversity message may follow another speaker's message of low diversity; the effects of the former message may differ from those produced by a high-diversity message which is preceded by another high-diversity message (Bradac, Davies, & Courtright, 1977). Or, the effects of standard and nonstandard accents may depend to an extent upon the lexical diversity level of the accented messages (Bradac & Wisegarver, 1984), that is, diversity and accent may interact. The major question here is: How do situational context and message context influence the effects of language variables? It seems likely that the effects of many language variables are *crucially* dependent upon both types of context. Language variation does not occur in a vacuum. Potentially, when we ignore context we impose a severe constraint upon the ecological validity of our results. The empirical search for and theoretical analysis of language variable-context linkages is a very important one.

In language variable experiments, some aspects of situational context can be manipulated with relative ease, for example, the status of communicators can be established with brief written remarks read by respondents prior to exposure to experimental messages (Ryan & Bulik, 1982). Or in experiments using written as opposed to oral messages, communicator gender can be established simply by attributing different names—"John" versus "Susan" (Bradac & Mulac, 1984). Other contextual aspects may be more difficult to manipulate; perceptions of situational formality may be a case in point because the dimensions of formality remain relatively obscure (but see Street & Brady, 1982). Similarly, with regard to message context some features can be manipulated with ease but for others this is not the case. In this regard a methodological suggestion of Street and Hopper (1982) is worth noting, namely, that in message experiments a desideratum is the simultaneous manipulation of three language variables. This is reasonable in a number of respects; for one thing, three-way interactions among language variables will typically be interpretable and informative, whereas this will not be true for four-way or higher order interactions. But the difficulty of creating messages which simultaneously manipulate three variables should be noted. That is, keeping diversity at a particular level and keeping intensity at a particular level while establishing a particular level of immediacy, then keeping diversity and immediacy constant while establishing a second level of intensity, and so on is not without its challenges. Researchers exploring the effects of three simultaneously manipulated language variables should prepare themselves to spend many hours in the creation of experimental messages.

It should be emphasized that when we enter the realm of the combined effects of language variables we are entering virtually uncharted territory. This "holistic" approach is something new in language studies. Intriguing possibilities abound. For example, perhaps a particular variable will produce paradoxical effects in the context of other language variables—in some linguistic contexts low lexical diversity may be associated with judgments of high communicator competence. Or another possibility is that two dissimilar patterns of linguistic features may produce the same effect; there may be many roads to Rome linguistically speaking; the general systems principle of equifinality may extend to the production of language effects (Mulac, Lundell, & Bradac, 1986).

A fourth and final issue to be mentioned here pertains to measurement of the effects of language variation. Given that researchers can operationalize numerous language variables, what effects of these variables should be explored, and how can these effects be operationalized? At one level a nebulous answer is possible: Researchers should examine those effects which promise to be theoretically meaningful and these potentially meaningful effects should be operationalized in a wide variety of ways (Cook & Campbell, 1979). On the other hand, it may be useful to note that a consensus of sorts is beginning to emerge among researchers of the effects of language variation, namely, that there appear to be two primary dimensions which the receivers of messages use when judging communicators and their messages: solidarity and competence. Solidarity embraces perceived sociability, warmth, attractiveness, benevolence, pleasantness, and so on. Competence embraces perceived socio-intellectual status, power, dynamism, influence, and so on (cf., Spitzberg's chapter in this volume). Probably, a great deal of progress can be made through the concerted investigation of these dimensions of judgment (which are variously labeled by researchers). Reliable and potentially valid semantic-differential-type instruments assessing competence and solidarity are at hand (Mulac, 1975, 1976; Zahn & Hopper, 1985). Of course, other dimensions of judgment should be examined as well, and idiosyncratic or group-specific structures of construal should be examined increasingly (Applegate & Delia, 1980; Giles & Hewstone, 1982).

Conclusion

It should be noted in closing that some significant issues were not broached for want of space, for example, the virtues of quantitative versus qualitative approaches to message/language analysis. With regard to this issue, it has been suggested by some theorists that the sort of quantitative bias evidenced in this chapter misses the mark in many important instances, that "structuralist" approaches are often more revealing (Hackett, 1985). This is highly debatable and interesting, but one cannot discuss everything in a single chapter, and the problems which *were* discussed are both important and corrigible.

References

Apple, W., Streeter, L.A., & Krauss, R.M. (1979). Effects of pitch and speech rate on personal attributions. *Journal of Personality and Social Psychology, 5*, 715–727.

Applegate, J.A., & Delia, J.G. (1980). Person-centered speech, psychological development, and the contexts of language usage. In R.N. St. Clair and H. Giles (Eds.), *The social and psychological contexts of language* (pp. 245–282). Hillsdale, NJ: Erlbaum.

Aristotle. (1932). *The rhetoric*, (L. Cooper, Jr.) New York: Appleton.

Ball, P., Giles, H., Byrne, J., & Berechree, P. (1984). Situational constraints on the evaluative significance of speech accommodation: Some Australian data. *International Journal of the Sociology of Language, 46*, 115–129.

Berger, C.R., & Bradac, J.J. (1982). *Language and social knowledge: Uncertainty in interpersonal relations.* London: Edward Arnold.

Bernstein, B. (1971). *Class, codes, and control, v. 1. 2.* London: Routledge & Kegan Paul.

Bowers, J.W. (1964). Some correlates of language intensity. *Quarterly Journal of Speech, 50,* 415–420.

Bradac, J.J. (1983). On generalizing messages, cabbages, kings, and several other things: The virtues of multiplicity. *Human Communication Research, 9,* 181–187.

Bradac, J.J. (1986). Threats to generalization in the use of elicited, purloined, and contrived messages in human communication research. *Communicatin Quarterly, 34,* 55–65.

Bradac, J.J., Bowers, J.W., & Courtright, J.A. (1980). Lexical variations in intensity, immediacy, and diversity: An axiomatic theory and causal model. In R.N. St. Clair and H. Giles (Eds.), *The social and psychological contexts of language* (pp. 193–223). Hillsdale, NJ: Erlbaum.

Bradac, J.J., Davies, R.A., & Courtright, J.A. (1977). The role of prior message context in judgments of high- and low-diversity messages. *Language and Speech, 20,* 295–307.

Bradac, J.J., Desmond, R.J., & Murdock, J.I. (1977). Diversity and density: Lexically determined evaluative and informational consequences of linguistic complexity. *Communication Monographs, 44,* 273–283.

Bradac, J.J., Hemphill, M.R., & Tardy, C.R. (1981). Language style on trial: Effects of 'powerful' and 'powerless' speech upon judgments of victims and villains. *Western Journal of Speech Communication, 45,* 327–341.

Bradac, J.J., Hosman, L.A., & Tardy, C.H. (1978). Reciprocal disclosures and language intensity: Attributional consequences. *Communication Monographs, 45,* 1–17.

Bradac, J.J., Konsky, C.W., & Elliott, N.D. (1976). Verbal behavior of interviewees: The effects of several situational variables on verbal productivity, disfluency, and lexical diversity. *Journal of Communication Disorders, 9,* 211–225.

Bradac, J.J., Martin, L.W., Elliott, N.D., & Tardy, C.H. (1980). On the neglected side of linguistic science. Multivariate studies of sentence judgment. *Linguistics: An Interdisciplinary Journal of the Language Sciences, 18,* 967–995.

Bradac, J.J., & Mulac, A. (1984). A molecular view of powerful and powerless speech styles: The role of specific language features and communicator intentions. *Communication Monographs, 51,* 307–319.

Bradac, J.J., & Wisegarver, R. (1984). Ascribed status, lexical diversity, and accent: Determinants of perceived status, solidarity, and control of speech style. *Journal of Language and Social Psychology, 3,* 239–255.

Brennan, E.M., Ryan, E.B., & Dawson, W.E. (1975). Scaling of apparent accentedness by magnitude estimation and sensory modality matching. *Journal of Psycholinguistic Research, 4,* 27–36.

Brown, B.L. (1980). Effects of speech rate on personality attributions and competency evaluations. In H. Giles, W.P. Robinson, and P. Smith (Eds.), *Language: Social psychological perspectives* (pp. 294–300). Oxford, England: Pergamon.

Brown, B.L., Giles, H., & Thackerar, J.N. (1985). Speaker evaluations as a function of speech rate, accent, and context. *Language & Communication, 5,* 207–220.

Buck, J.F. (1968). The effects of Negro and white dialectal variations upon attitudes of college students. *Speech Monographs, 35,* 181–186.

Burgoon, M., Jones, S.B., & Stewart, D. (1975). Toward a message-centered theory of persuasion: Three empirical investigations of language intensity. *Human Communication Research, 1,* 240–256.

Chomsky, N. (1957). *Syntactic Structures.* The Hague: Mouton.

Clark, H.H. (1973). The language-as-fixed-effect fallacy: A critique of language statistics in psychological research. *Journal of Verbal Learning and Verbal Behavior, 12,* 335–359.

Cook, T.D., & Campbell, D.T. (1979). *Quasi-experimentation: Design and analysis issues for field settings.* Chicago, IL: Rand McNally.

Crow, B.K. (1982). *Conversational pragmatics.* Unpublished Dissertation, Unviersity of Iowa.

Drake, G.F. (1980). The social role of slang. In H. Giles, W.P. Robinson, and P. Smith (Eds.), *Language: Social psychological perspectives* (pp. 63–70). Oxford, England: Pergamon.

Eiser, J.R., & Pancer, S.M. (1979). Attitudinal effects of the use of evaluatively biased language. *European Journal of Social Psychology, 9,* 39–48.

Erickson, B., Lind, A.E., Johnson, B.C., & O'Barr, W. M. (1978). Speech style and impression formation in a court setting: The effects of "powerful" and "powerless" speech. *Journal of Experimental Social Psychology, 14,* 266–279.

Giles, H. (1973). Accent mobility: A model and some data. *Anthropological Linguistics, 15,* 87–105.

Giles, H. (1979). Ethnicity markers in speech. In K. Scherer and H. Giles (Eds.), *Social markers in speech* (pp. 251–289). Cambridge, England: Cambridge University Press.

Giles, H., & Hewstone, M. (1982). Cognitive structures, speech, and social situations: Two integrative models. *Language Sciences, 4,* 187–219.

Giles, H., & Powesland, P. (1975). *Speech style and social evaluation.* London: Academic Press.

Giles, H., Wilson, P., & Conway, A. (1981). Accent and lexical diversity as determinants of impression formation and employment selection. *Language Sciences, 3,* 92–103.

Hackett, R.A. (1985). Decline of a paradigm? Bias and objectivity in news media studies. *Critical Studies in Mass Communication, 1,* 229–259.

Herman, L.M., Richards, D.G., & Wolz, J.P. (1984). Comprehension of sentences by bottlenosed dolphins. *Cognition, 16,* 129–219.

Höweler, M. (1972). Diversity of word usage as a stress indicator in an interview situation. *Journal of Psycholinguistic Research, 1,* 243–247.

Hudson, R.A. (1980). *Sociolinguistics.* Cambridge, England: Cambridge University Press.

Jackson, S., & Jacobs, S. (1983). Generalizing about messages: Suggestions for design and analysis of messages. *Human Communication Research, 9,* 169–181.

Jones, L.V., & Thurstone, L.L. (1955). The psychophysics of semantics. An experimental investigation. *Journal of Applied Psychology, 39,* 31–39.

Jones, E.E., & Davis, K.E. (1965). From acts to dispositions: The attribution process in perception. In L. Berkowitz (Ed.), *Advances in social psychology,* 2 (pp. 219–266). New York and London: Academic Press.

Joos, M. (1967). *The five clocks.* New York: Harcourt, Brace & World.

Kuiken, D. (1981). Nonimmediate language style and inconsistency between private and expressed evaluations. *Journal of Experimental Social Psychology, 17,* 183–196.

Kuiper, K. (1982). Once more with feeling: Modifier repetition as a stylistic rule. *Linguistics: An Interdisciplinary Journal of the Language Sciences, 20,* 493–517.

Lakoff, R. (1975). *Language and women's place.* New York: Harper & Row.

Lambert, W.E. (1967). A social psychology of bilingualism. *Journal of Social Issues, 23,* 91–109.

Lambert, W.E., Hodgson, R., Gardner, R.C., & Fillenbaum, S. (1960). Evaluational reactions to spoken languages. *Journal of Abnormal and Social Psychology, 60,* 44–51.

Mehrabian, A., & Wiener, M. (1966). Non-immediacy between communicator and object of comminication in a verbal message: Application to inference of attitudes. *Journal of Consulting Psychology, 30,* 420–425.

Motley, M.T., Camden, C.T., & Baars, B.J. (1979). Personality and situational influences upon verbal slips: A laboratory test of Freudian and prearticulatory editing hypotheses. *Human Communication Research, 5,* 195–202.

Mulac, A. (1975). Evaluation of the speech dialect attitudinal scale. *Speech Monographs, 42,* 182–189.

Mulac, A. (1976). Assessment and application of the revised speech dialect attitudinal scale. *Communication Monographs, 43,* 238–245.

Mulac, A., Lundell, T., & Bradac, J.J. (1986). Male/female language differences and attributional consequences in a public speaking situation: Toward an explanation of the gender-linked language effect. *Communication Monographs, 53,* 115–129.

Murdock, J.I., Bradac, J.J., & Bowers, J.W. (1984). Effects of power on the perception of explicit and implicit threats, promises, and thomises: A rule-governed perspective. *Western Journal of Speech Communication, 48,* 344–361.

O'Barr, W.M. (1982). *Linguistic evidence: Language, power, and strategy in the courtroom.* New York: Academic Press.

Premack, D. (1985). "Gavagai!" or the future history of the animal language controversy. *Cognition, 19,* 207–296.

Roloff, M., & Berger, C.R. (1982). *Social cognition and communication.* Beverly Hills, CA: Sage.

Rommetveit, R. (1983). Prospective social psychological contributions to a truly interdisciplinary understanding of ordinary language. *Journal of Language and Social Psychology, 2,* 89–104.

Ryan, E.B., & Bulik, C.M. (1982). Evaluations of middle class and lower class speakers. *Journal of Language and Social Psychology, 1,* 51–61.

Ryan, E.B., & Giles, H. (Eds.) (1982). *Attitudes toward language variation: Social and applied contexts.* London: Edward Arnold.

Scherer, K.R. (1979). Personality markers in speech. In K.R. Scherer and H. Giles (Eds.), *Social markers in speech* (pp. 147–209). Cambridge, England: Cambridge University Press.

Scotton, C.M. (1985). What the heck, sir: Style shifting and lexical colouring as features of powerful language. In R.L. Street, Jr. and J.N. Cappella (Eds.), *Sequence and pattern in communicative behavior* (pp. 103–119). London: Edward Arnold.

Siegman, A.W., & Pope, B. (Eds.) (1972). *Studies in dyadic communication.* New York: Pergamon.

Skinner, B.F. (1957). *Verbal behavior.* New York: Appleton-Century-Crofts.

Stevens, S.S. (1975). *Psychophysics: Introduction to its perceptual, neural, and social prospects.* New York: Wiley.

Street, R.L., Jr., & Brady, R.M. (1982). Speech rate acceptance ranges as a function of evaluative domain, listener speech rate, and comunication context. *Communication Monographs, 49,* 290–308.

Street R.L., Jr., & Giles, H. (1982). Speech accommodation theory: A social cognitive approach to language and speech behavior. In M.E. Roloff and C.R. Berger (Eds.), *Social cognition and communication* (pp. 193–226). Beverly Hills, CA: Sage.

Street, R.L., Jr., & Hopper, R. (1982). A model of speech style evaluation. In E.B. Ryan and H. Giles (Eds.), *Attitudes toward language variation: Social and applied contexts* (pp. 175–188). London: Edward Arnold.

Tajfel, H. (1974). Social identity and intergroup behavior. *Social Science Information, 13,* 65–93.

Treichler, P.A., Frankel, R.M., Kramerae, C., Zoppi, & Beckman, H.B. (1984). Problems and problems: Power relationships in a medical encounter. In C. Kramerae, M. Schulz, and W. M. O'Barr (Eds.), *Language and power* (pp. 62–88). Beverly Hills, CA: Sage.

Wachal, R.S., & Spreen, O. (1973). Some measures of lexical diversity in aphasic and normal language performance. *Language and Speech, 16,* 169–181.

Webb, E.J., Campbell, D.T., Schwartz, R.D., & Sechrest, L. (1966). *Unobtrusive measures: Nonreactive research in the social sciences.* Chicago, IL: Rand McNally.

Wiener, M., & Mehrabian, A. (1968). *Language within language: Immediacy, a channel in verbal communication.* New York: Appleton-Century-Crofts.

Zahn, C., & Hopper, R. (1985). Language variety and the assessment of listeners' evaluations of speakers. *Journal of Language and Social Psychology, 4,* 113–123.

CHAPTER 13

Self-Disclosure: Objectives and Methods of Measurement

Charles H. Tardy

Few topics have captured the interest of so many scholars as self-disclosure. Information accumulates rapidly despite an absence of consensus among writers about the general nature of self-disclosure and a corresponding absence of standardized measurement procedures. Self-disclosure has been conceptualized many different ways over the last 20 years. This essay does not attempt to resolve these discrepancies (cf., Fisher, 1984). Rather, it reviews the procedures used to study the various conceptual domains of self-disclosure.

The first studies conceived self-disclosure as an individual trait. Reflecting a concern for social and national issues, as did much of his research, Kurt Lewin (1948) compared Germans' and Americans' openness to strangers. Scholarly interest in the topic did not begin to spread until Sidney Jourard in the late 1950s initiated a series of studies that addressed such questions as, "Is disclosure related to mental health?" and "Do women disclose more than men?" (see Jourard, 1971). After 25 years, these questions are still being investigated (e.g. Fisher, 1984; Derlega, Winstead, Wong, & Hunter, 1985). These, and more recent research topics (e.g., Norton, 1983) conceptualize self-disclosure as a characteristic of individuals.

A second approach to the study of self-disclosure involves the examination of relationships, not individuals. Researchers adopting this perspective are concerned more about the quality and quantity of interconnections among people than about the enduring characteristics of separate individuals. Questions reflecting this orientation include: Do we trust people to whom we disclose intimate information more than people to whom we do not (Wheeless & Grotz, 1976)? Does increased amount of disclosure lead to better understanding orincreased liking of relationship partners? The studies which

323

characterize this approach investigate general patterns of disclosure to particular target persons or in particular relationships, but do not attempt to generalize to all situations.

Perhaps most salient to students of communication is the conceptualization of self-disclosure as a characteristic of observable messages. Some messages reveal personal information while others do not. Authors have investigated aspects of self-disclosing messages, such as message content and sequencing. In these studies, investigators examine messages as they are composed by subjects or as they affect subsequent attitudes and behaviors of subjects. Such studies attempt to identify the factors which inhibit, encourage, and result from self-disclosing messages.

In addition to distinguishing among these approaches, authors have identified numerous facets or dimensions of the concept. Initial research (Jourard & Lasakow, 1958) focused only on the amount of disclosure. A second dimension of self-disclosure is intimacy, sometimes called "depth" (Altman & Taylor, 1973). This concept refers to a quality, as opposed to the quantity, of personal information. More specifically, intimacy refers to the privacy of the information about self. Biographical information is not considered intimate, while sexual desires are. Although intimacy and amount have received the vast majority of researchers' attention, many other components have been suggested. Some authors have investigated the valence of the content of information revealed in self-disclosure (e.g., Gilbert & Hornstein, 1975; Gilbert & Whiteneck, 1976). Positive self-disclosure reflects favorably on a person, for example, "I just won the New York state lottery," while negative ones reflect disfavorably, for example, "I frequently lie to my friends." Numerous other dimensions have been identified and are discussed below. Still other dimensions or components of self-disclosure characteristics may be identified in the future.

The procedures utilized to study self-disclosure have aspired to one of four objectives: (a) measure a person's past self-disclosure behavior; (b) elicit and measure a person's self-disclosure behavior; (c) experimentally manipulate self-disclosure; and (d) measure potential or hypothetical self-disclosure. The subsequent discussion identifies and evaluates specific procedures used to achieve these goals. Their appropriateness for use in studies of the three major perspectives on self-disclosure and for investigating particular dimensions of self-disclosure are also addressed.

Measures of Past Self-Disclosure

For various purposes, many investigations have employed measures of a subject's self-disclosure history. Some have used this type of measure to distinguish individuals who disclose little from those who disclose much self information. Others used such measures to compare the communication characterizing different types of relationships. However, the contradictory results of many self-disclosure studies have been attributed to the inappropriate use of these measures (Archer, 1979; Chelune, 1979). Logically, one cannot assume that a measure of past disclosure to a close friend will predict future disclosure accurately to a stranger. The subsequent discussion identifies measures which research has shown to be useful for assessing individual and relationship characteristics.

Topic-Based Scales

By far the most frequently used measure of self-disclosure, Sidney Jourard's 60-item self-report questionnaire first appeared in 1958 (Jourard & Lasakow) and continues to be used in published research (Lester, Brazill, Ellis, & Guerin, 1984). The scale's instructions ask subjects to report how much they have revealed to a specified person regarding 60 different topics of varying intimacy, 10 for each of six general subject areas. The disclosure recipients included mother, father, male friend, female friend, and spouse. Subsequent researchers have altered the response options (Panyard, 1971) and frequently have specified different disclosure targets (e.g., Halpern, 1977). Jourard also formulated 25- (1961b) and 40-item (1961a) versions of the questionnaire. In all its forms, the Jourard scales have demonstrated acceptable internal and test-retest reliability (Jourard & Richman, 1963; Pearce & Wiebe, 1975; Chelune, 1978).

Numerous critics have charged that Jourard's measures lack predictive validity (e.g., Himelstein & Kimbrough, 1963; Lubin & Harrison, 1964). However, Chelune (1978), after reviewing this research, concluded that "The various validity studies, with their somewhat discrepant findings, suggest that the SD-60 is probably a fairly valid measure of past disclosure to a specified target person" (pp. 288–289). He and Jourard (1971) note that many validity studies have attempted to compare disclosure to specific individuals with disclosure to targets and situations not encompassed by the Jourard measure. Users of the scale should generalize only to the domain of behaviors specified in the scale's instructions.

For what purposes should the JSDQ be used? This instrument should be used to assess past self-disclosure to individuals specified in the instrument's instructions. The JSDQ-60 provides measures of breadth and amount of disclosure, but provides no separate assessment of depth or intimacy of disclosure. The JSDQ-40 contains an equal number of items rated high and low in intimacy, while the JSDQ-21's items have been categorized as high, medium, or low intimacy (Jourard, 1971). Separate scores for low and high intimacy disclosure or an average intimacy disclosure score may be computed.

An asset of the Jourard scales is their applicability to a variety of subject populations. In Jourard's and subsequent studies, these instruments have been completed by adults of various ages, occupations, and marital status.

The JSDQ has been used to define two of the three conceptual approaches to studying self-disclosure described earlier. A measure of self-disclosure as an individual characteristic or trait has been obtained by summing scores of disclosure to the different targets. This index measures individuals' tendencies to self-disclose across topic, recipient, or situation. Using the subscores allows the investigator to assess disclosure as a relationship characteristic. These scores provide descriptions of the subject's behavior toward specified persons. Depending upon the version, Jourard's instruments can provide measures of intimacy, as well as amount of self-disclosure to specified target persons.

Several comparable measures have been developed to measure past disclosure to specific individuals. In order to reduce the time necessary for assessing self-disclosure, Miller, Berg and Archer (1983) authored a 10-item scale of the same form as the Jourard scale. This instrument exhibited high internal reliability (Chronbach's *alpha* exceeded .90), correlated significantly with the JSDQ (Pearson *r*'s ranging from .49 to .74 for male and female subjects with scales targeted to friend and stranger targets), and provided evidence of predictive validity. Subjects who scored higher than the median on the self-disclosure to friend scale were rated higher in past disclosure by close friends (sorority sisters) than subjects who scored below the median.

Rubin and Shenker (1978) developed an instrument similar in form to Jourard's. They sought scale items which were more appropriate to their subject population than those of existing scales. Reports by subjects of disclosure to roommates correlated significantly with the reports by the roommates of disclosure received. Separate scores for each topic were computed, providing measures of amount for each of the four general topics representing levels of intimacy. Since the items were selected for use in a study of college students, they may be inappropriate for certain other populations, for example, married couples. Indeed, some of their items which were highly salient to students in the 1970s may seem irrelevant to today's students. A similar 17-item measure yielded comparable results in a study of dating couples (Rubin, Hill, Peplau, & Dunkel-Schetter, 1980).

Recently, Rosenfeld and Welsh (1985) described the development of an instrument to assess disclosure among married couples. From a list of 197 items which had been randomly selected from the Taylor and Altman (1966) pool and rated for intimacy by Solano (1981), the authors chose 63 which represented each of 7 intimacy intervals equally, and which were not rated differently by men than by women. Subjects report the frequency of discussing each topic on a 7-interval scale ranging from "almost never talk about the topic" to "almost always talk about the topic" (Rosenfeld & Welsh, 1985, p. 258). In addition to amount and intimacy, the authors computed a measure of "breadth" (Altman & Taylor, 1973) which represents the number of topics the subject reported discussing. Though no reliability coefficients are reported, the study provided evidence of discriminant validity. Husbands from dual-career marriages reported significantly more disclosure on all three measures than did husbands from single-career marriages, while wives from single-career marriages reported more disclosure than did wives from dual-career marriages on all three measures.

Instruments for more specialized needs have also been developed. To measure the "gilding" or distortion of self-disclosure, Gitter and Black (1976) "required subjects to estimate the degree of trustworthiness (on a scale of 0 to 100) of items they had revealed or items they would hypothetically reveal to the specific target person" (p. 328). Davidson, Balswick, and Halverson (1983) developed the Affective Self-Disclosure Scale for Couples to assess the communication of emotions by one spouse to the other. West and Zingle (1969; West, 1971) authored a self-report measure to assess amount of disclosure by adolescents, ages 13–19. Evidence of reliability and predictive validity is provided.

An important source for the construction of topic-based measures is the pool of 671 items rated for intimacy and categorized into subject groups by Taylor and Altman (1966). Researchers may select items to represent particular content categories (Hendrick, 1981), intimacy categories (Rosenfeld & Welsh, 1985), or both. Instruments based on these measures have demonstrated reliability and convergent validity. In addition to their use in the development of questionnaires, these items have been used for developing experimental messages and for discussion topics to elicit disclosure from subjects.

Semantic-Based Scales

A second type of instrument asks respondents to describe their behavior or personality with terms synonymous with self-disclosure.
Informational topics are not specified while recipients may or may
not be included.

A multifaceted measure of self-disclosure was developed by Wheeless and Grotz (1976). This self-report instrument contains Likert-
type items which describe disclosure behavior, (e.g., "I intimately
disclose who I really am openly and fully in my conversation," Wheeless, 1976, p. 57). The scale consists of items assessing amount,
intimacy, valence, honesty-accuracy, and intent. Factor analyses and
reliability coefficients have demonstrated the internal stability of this
scale. Concurrent validity has been demonstrated in several studies
(Bradac, Tardy, & Hosman, 1980; Stacks & Stone, 1984; Wheeless,
1978; Wheeless & Grotz, 1977). However, to my knowledge, no studies
have assessed the instrument's correspondence with other measures
of self-disclosure.

A similar scale has been developed by Robert Norton (1978, 1983)
for assessing openness as a style of communication. The open communicator provides personal information that "accurately character-
ize(s) the self" (Norton & Montgomery, 1982, p. 399). Further, open
style "signals that the message is personal" or "that the message
should be taken, filtered, or understood to be representational of the
self . . ." (Norton & Montgomery, 1982, p. 401). Consequently, the
notion of open communication is synonymous with self-disclosure,
rather than a distinctly new concept. Norton's multidimensional scaling
study indicated that open style can be distinguished from other communicator style variables (Norton, 1978). This initial measure of
openness was part of a multi-item self-report instrument assessing 11
communicator style traits. Later Norton and Montgomery (1982)
developed a 19-item scale to assess only open style. Their factor
analysis revealed five dimensions: negative openness, emotional openness, general assessment of openness, direct indications of openness,
and nonverbal indications of openness. In their study, the general
assessment items accounted for the greatest variance in other self-
report measures of openness.

Conclusion

In selecting measures of past disclosure, these two types of measures
offer distinctly different advantages and disadvantages. The topic-
based measures yield assessments limited to particular content items

included in the instrument. The semantic-based measures are not limited by topic. Respondents assess behavior across situations, topics, and, sometimes, targets. Such semantic-based measures assume, first, that subjects understand the specific behaviors being addressed by the questionnaire's broad or general terms, and, second, that they can recall these behaviors. Topic-based scales, however, avoid that ambiguity and should be easily understood by the respondents. Both semantic and topic measures share the recall assumption.

For two reasons the topic-based instruments appear preferable to the semantic-based ones. First, considerable research has demonstrated the utility, as well as the shortcomings, of the topic-based measures. Prior investigators have opted for the topic-based measures much more frequently than for the semantic-based ones. Second, several authors (Chelune, 1978; Rosenfeld, Civikly, & Herron, 1979) suggest that considerable random variance is introduced into measures of self-disclosure by allowing subjects to specify particulars, such as target, topic, and situation. This criterion favors the more specific, though, therefore, limited, topic-based scales.

Of the topic-based measures, all those described here have potentially important uses. When selecting among these, or developing one for a special purpose, several guides should be used. These suggestions should, of course, be considered along with the conceptual and practical requirements of a specific investigation. First, all items should be potentially relevant to the subject population. The more the topics represent the experiences of the subjects, the better. Including a large number of topics helps ensure that the measure is not unduly influenced by the idiosyncracies of particular disclosure subjects or topics. Second, items with known intimacy value allow more precise assessment. Investigators should control this source of variance by including items systematically which reflect the range of intimacy values (e.g., Rosenfeld & Welsh, 1985). Instruments should provide for the assessment of either average intimacy across all items or amount at different levels of intimacy, e.g., low, medium, and high.

Assessment of Observed Disclosure

A second strategy commonly used involves the elicitation and assessment of self-disclosure from the subjects. This strategy has been used for all three types of self-disclosure research described earlier. The subsequent discussion first identifies methods used to obtain samples of disclosure from subjects and, second, describes procedures for assessing the obtained samples. Research procedures discussed last combine elicitation and assessment.

Eliciting Self-Disclosure

Self-descriptions. Perhaps the most common procedure for eliciting self-disclosure is to ask subjects to describe themselves. For example, Rubin (1975a) had investigators ask people in public areas of an airport to provide brief, written self-descriptions. The investigator provided an example, allowing the researchers to manipulate the study's independent variable. Archer and Berg (1978) used a similar procedure in a laboratory investigation. The initial self-descriptions were provided by a videotaped confederate with whom subjects thought they were interreacting over a closed circuit television system. Subject responses were videotaped. Lewis's (1970) instrument first requests subjects to supply 10 answers to the question "Who am I?" and then report if each answer has been discussed with a specified target. Unfortunately, no reliability data were reported. The measure did distinguish between gender and some target groups.

Interviews. More structured procedures were used in many studies (Burhenne & Mirels, 1970; Cash & Soloway, 1975; Davis & Sloan, 1974; Grigsby & Weatherley, 1983; Miller & Lefcourt, 1983; Pedersen & Breglio, 1968; Rappaport, Gross, & Lepper, 1973; Waring & Chelune, 1983). These authors specified questions or topics to which subjects responded in writing or orally. The subject, in effect, discloses to the experimenter in these studies. The instructions used frequently encourage, if not demand, intimate disclosure, for example, Davis and Sloan's (1974) instructions to subjects "to be completely open and honest" (p. 360). Questions or interview topics frequently are drawn from either the general topics or specific items from self-disclosure questionnaires such as Jourard's.

Role play. Highlen in several studies (Highlen & Gillis, 1978; Highlen & Johnston, 1979; Highlen & Voight, 1978) utilized audiotaped scenarios exhibiting various situational characteristics which constituted the independent variable of the experiment. Subject role play responses were audiotaped and later coded. Hecht, Shepherd, and Hall (1979) utilized written scenarios to manipulate intimacy and valence. Subjects were requested to write appropriate and inappropriate responses. Klos and Paddock's (1978) role-play procedure for assessing adolescents' relationships with parents includes scenarios to assess the self-disclosure of risky information. These studies indicate the flexibility provided by the role-play procedure.

Conclusions. Researchers infrequently concern themselves with the representativeness of disclosures elicited by procedures such as those described above. Consequently little can be said about the similarity of these disclosures to those people might reveal in other situations. The interview and questionnaire procedures which require subjects to reveal to an experimenter or interviewer are most appropriate for assessing openness in counseling or therapeutic contexts. Such disclosures are unlikely to occur in normal conversations and, therefore, must not be considered indicative of subjects' behavior in other contexts. Consequently, the use of such measures to assess relationships with other persons or subjects' general communicative behavior is unwarranted. However, these procedures may have some utility for investigating psychological aspects of openness or for studying the counseling process. However, researchers should provide a rationale for the use of procedures which are intentionally so obtrusive.

The use of self-descriptions in studies of initial interactions seems quite appropriate. The procedure attempts to maximize the similarity between the experimental analog and natural conversation. However, until generalizability studies are conducted, this assumption is unproven.

Assessment of Elicited Disclosure

After eliciting disclosures from subjects, investigators must systematically assess the properties exhibited. Content analyses and ratings are the two general procedures which most researchers have utilized for translating the disclosures into quantitative data.

Content analysis. Content analysis refers to the segmentation and categorization of discourse. Each statement, thought unit, speaking turn, or time period is identified as a unit of analysis. Trained coders then categorize the unit according to predefined criteria. This procedure requires much more effort than rating, and, consequently, has been used less frequently.

The coding system developed by Chelune (1975) provides clear and comprehensive guidelines for analyzing communication content for the presence of self-disclosure. The basis of his system is the self-reference, defined operationally "as a verbal response (thought unit) which *describes* the subject in some way, *tells something about* the subject, or *refers to some affect* the subject experiences" (Chelune, 1975, p. 133). The percentage of self-references is the recommended measure of amount of self-disclosure. This is preferable to mere frequency of self-references, which does not take into account the fact that some people talk more about all subjects than other people. Additional measures provided by Chelune's system include intimacy, affective consistency, and rate of self-reference. This system has been used reliably by its author in numerous studies (Chelune, 1975; Chelune, Skiffington, & Williams, 1981; Waring & Chelune, 1983), as well as by others (Dindia, 1983).

Temporal measures, especially speech duration, have also been utilized as a measure of amount (e.g., Vondracek, 1969). Although speech duration is not conceptually equivalent to self-disclosure (Bloch & Goodstein, 1971), several studies observed this measure of amount to correlate with intimacy ratings (e.g., Davis & Sloan, 1974). Chelune (1978) concludes that duration is associated with either increased intimacy or perception of increased intimacy.

Several other coding schemes include self-disclosures as one category among many (Stiles, 1978; Sillars, 1980; Whalen, 1969). Of these, only the latter has been used specifically to study self-disclosure. Although these schemes may be useful for some purposes, researchers who focus on self-disclosure will probably not find it efficient to train coders in the use of these more complex analytic schemes. On the other hand, such coding schemes could very well prove useful for studying the communicative context in which self-disclosures occur.

Rating. Perhaps the most common procedure used in self-disclosure research is to rate the discourse along an interval continuum. Raters have been observers of transcribed, recorded, and live conversations or interviews, as well as participants in the conversations. In some studies raters make a single judgment about the person's self-disclosure, while in others separate judgments are made for each segmented part of the discourse, for example, 30-second interval.

Numerous rating scales exist because investigators have favored developing new scales rather than using ones from prior studies. Some scales are based primarily on semantic labels for the intervals. For example, Miller and Lefcourt's (1983) rating scale ranged from "0 to 5, with 0 assigned to 'no verbalization,' 1 for 'superficial, closed, inhibited, reserved,' 3 for 'moderately personal, somewhat revealing of feelings,' and 5 for 'personal, revealing of feelings, involved, open' " (p. 131). Ratings by two judges in their study correlated .94. Others based their intervals on sample disclosure topics or statements which have been prerated. Sermat and Smyth's (1973) 10-point rating scale was based on examples from Taylor and Altman's (1966) list of intimacy-scaled items. Klos and Loomis (1978) asked subjects to recall intimate disclosures and then selected nine of the disclosures which were rated consistently by judges to represent intervals along an 11-point continuum. The investigator provided the scale to subjects who then rated their own disclosure. The scale detected demographic differences between discloser and target groups.

Many studies have evidenced acceptable reliability and convergent validity with these types of procedures for assessing intimacy (e.g., Davis & Sloan, 1974; Doster, 1972; Chaikin, Derlega, Bayma, & Shaw, 1975; Lakin, Oppenheimer, & Bremer, 1982; Miller, Berg, & Archer, 1983; Miller & Lefcourt, 1983; Sermat & Smyth, 1973). Scales for rating amount have been used by Ribner (1974) and Wilson and Dulany (1983). Some researchers do not distinguish between amount and intimacy and have used general measures of openness, for example, Hurley and Hurley (1969), Montgomery (1980), and Simonson, and Bahr (1974).

Rating scales have also been developed and utilized to study other dimensions of self-disclosure. A distinction between evaluative and descriptive intimacy has been articulated by Morton (1978). Morton's method for rating the two was later used by Berg and Archer (1982). Montgomery's (1981) procedures allow for the assessment of general openness and four additional dimensions: negative (reveals disagreement), nonverbal (gestures, vocal expression, etc.), emotional (feelings, moods), and receptive (willingness to receive disclosures). In addition to amount and intimacy, Perl (1983) rates self-focus and risk taking. The similarity of the subject or topic of self-disclosing messages has been rated by Davis and Sloan (1974) and Berg and Archer (1982). The procedures developed by these authors constitute specialized resources for investigators interested in these aspects of self-disclosure.

One perennial issue faced by investigators is the use of subject self-ratings versus the use of ratings by observers. The research on the comparative validity of the two is, however, contradictory. On the one hand is the conclusion of Ehrlich and Graeven (1971): "Persons are directly aware of the magnitude and intimacy of their self-disclosing behavior in dyadic encounters" (p. 398). On the other, some authors contend that participants' perceptions of their own disclosures are distorted and inaccurate (Cline, 1983b). Perceptual and contextual bases of judgments undoubtedly differ between observers and participants (Archer, Berg, & Runge, 1980). Since evidence on the correspondence of observer and participant judgments is contradictory, a conservative approach is recommended. Investigators are advised to validate the use of subject self-reports with observer ratings.

The unitizing decision is another common issue. Prior studies have rated such varied units as 10-second time intervals, two lines of typed transcription, and an entire conversation. Unfortunately, studies rarely include a rationale for the unit selected. One study which compared ratings of individual statements to ratings of conversation segments concluded that the "two methods tap essentially the same phenomena" (Sermat & Smyth, 1973, p. 343). In the absence of general guides, the selection of a rating unit should be a logical function of the purposes of the investigation and the type of self-disclosure elicited. Hill and Stull (1982) provide suggestions for managing the problems unitizing presents for the measurement of self-disclosure reciprocity.

Simultaneously Eliciting and Rating Self-Disclosure

Perhaps Worthy, Gary, and Kahn (1969) were the first authors to utilize intimacy-rated items to elicit disclosive behavior. The investigators obtained 287 personal questions from a group of students. A second group rated the items on an intimacy scale. From this list the authors selected seven sets of 10 questions, each set containing questions of similar intimacy value. Subjects selected one question from each list of questions and wrote the answer. The investigators assigned the intimacy score of the question selected to the written response. DeForest and Stone (1980) also used this procedure.

Siegman and Reynolds (1983, 1984) used prerated interview questions to elicit high and low intimate disclosure from subjects. Six intimate questions and six impersonal questions were selected from a list rated by judges similar to the subjects. The procedure was validated by the use of post-interview rating forms. Subjects perceived the interview with the prerated intimate questions to be significantly more intimate than the interview with impersonal questions. Additionally, the authors observed expected differences between the intimate and impersonal interviews on several objective measures of speech such as verbal productivity and reaction time. Other studies have used similar procedures (Cline, 1983a; Davis, 1976, 1977).

Several authors (e.g., Bloch & Goodstein, 1971; Chelune, 1978) have criticized this technique for assigning intimacy scores to conversations because the interactants might talk intimately about a low-rated item or disclose nothing while talking about a high-rated item. The limited evidence available indicates the contrary. Walker and Wright (1976) supplied topics drawn from the list scaled by Worthy, Gary, and Kahn (1969) to subjects participating in a dyadic conversation. Subjects were given intimate topics, nonintimate topics, or no topics. Judges rated a sample of the conversations and observed intimate disclosure consumed 70% of the time in the intimate condition and less than 10% in the other two conditions. The Siegman and Reynolds (1983, 1984) studies described above also provide evidence of the validity of this type of procedure. The subjects in their studies perceived the interviews based on highly intimate items to be more personal than those based on nonintimate questions. Though limited, this evidence suggests that prerated questions and discussion topics elicit disclosure comparable to their initial rating.

This procedure provides several advantages to its users. First, investigators exercise considerable control over the discourse elicited from subjects. If highly intimate disclosure from certain subjects are desired, items of known intimacy value can be selected to elicit such responses. Second, the procedure reduces the time and effort required for rating or content analyzing the obtained disclosures. Judges or observers do not have to be trained and monitored. However, investigators might find it beneficial to use raters to validate the procedure, as in the study by Walker and Wright (1976).

Conclusions

Eliciting disclosures from subjects provides investigators an accurate, though not necessarily representative, sample of an individual's behavior. The observed behavior is a function of the experiment's unique setting, target, topic, and recipient. A single observation of the subject's behavior in such an atypical situation is unlikely to measure an individual trait or characteristic accurately. The elicited disclosures may provide some insight into relationships between subjects and disclosure targets. However, the cross-situational representativeness of disclosures elicited by experimental protocols remains to be demonstrated. These procedures are most appropriate for studying the process by which individuals reveal themselves through communication with others. Direct observation is essential to the study of self-disclosure as a characteristic of messages.

Experimental Manipulation of Self-Disclosure

In order to assess the effects of self-disclosure on interpersonal processes, many investigators have manipulated self-disclosure experimentally. The discussion below describes procedures for operationally defining self-disclosure as a message rather than as an individual or relational characteristic.

Studies have provided subjects with written scripts portraying an initial interaction between strangers (Berg & Archer, 1980; Bradac, Hosman, & Tardy, 1978), typescripts of an interview (Remer, Roffey, & Buckholtz, 1983), and descriptions purported to have been composed by other subjects, but actually produced by the investigators (Archer & Berg, 1978). Subjects have acted as observers and participants. The use of a written message as an experimental variable increases the investigator's control over variation in tone, eye contact, and other nonverbal variables which may be systematically or randomly associated with self-disclosure. However, the increased precision is offset by a decrease in the degree to which the experimental manipulation mirrors typical interactions.

Audio and videotape recorded self-disclosures have been used frequently (Chaikin & Derlega, 1974; Jones & Gordon, 1972; McAllister & Bregman, 1983; Town & Harvey, 1981). Using recorded messages increases the similarity of the experimental situation to a face-to-face interchange but decreases the investigator's control over extraneous factors.

Perhaps the most common manipulation of self-disclosure is through the use of confederates, individuals who follow the investigator's directions while pretending to be a peer of the actual subjects (e.g., Caltabiano & Smithson, 1983; Ehrlich & Graeven, 1971; Jones & Archer, 1976; Runge & Archer, 1981). Though the disclosure still occurs in a laboratory setting, the procedure is much more realistic than the use of written and recorded messages. However, the investigator has no control over many factors. The similarity between the confederate's behavior in different conditions or between the behavior of several confederates cannot be assured. The potential for experimental artifact is increased (Tittler, Anchor, & Weitz, 1976). To minimize these potential problems, investigators blind the confederate to the hypotheses and standardize the confederate's behavior. Procedures, such as Berg and Archer's (1982) closed-circuit television set-up, may be designed to balance the need for both control and realism.

A few studies have manipulated self-disclosure in field experiments. Harrell (1978) had confederates reveal their name, or not reveal their name, while seeking directions from strangers. Rubin's (1975a) investigators gave "examples" of writing samples and self-descriptions while eliciting responses from adults at an airport. Several guises for manipulating self-disclosure in field settings are described by Rubin (1975b). His research indicates that the potential for field studies is limited primarily by the investigator's imagination.

The dimension of disclosure most frequently manipulated is probably intimacy. However, many studies do not distinguish between intimacy and amount of self-disclosure. Other aspects of disclosure manipulated experimentally include valence (Jones & Gordon, 1972), the sequencing of disclosures (McAllister & Bregman, 1983), public versus private content (Runge & Archer, 1981), and linguistic intensity (Bradac, Hosman, & Tardy, 1978).

Several suggestions can be made for manipulating self-disclosure in experimental studies. First, the content of the disclosures should be validated prior to their use. Some investigators have drawn upon topics rated for their intimacy value. Others have pretested their experimental messages. Both procedures are preferable to reliance solely on the investigator's intuition. Second, the investigator must decide how much contrast should be exhibited by the disclosures. Though widely contrasting disclosures increase the likelihood of finding effects, the disclosures may not represent normal interchanges. As Chelune (1979) suggested, "If the results of impression studies are to be meaningful and generalizable beyond the experimental conditions, the manipulations of self-disclosure must mirror conditions typically found in first encounters" (pp. 14–15). The use of three or more levels of the experimental variable, rather than the typical two, is one way to help achieve this goal. If prerated intimacy topics are used to construct the experimental messages, items could be selected that are within one standard deviation of the mean.

The varied procedures used to study self-disclosure experimentally complement each other. The different operationalizations of the concept decrease the precision of its assessment and the ability to replicate findings from one study to another. This drawback is inherent to the experimental study of language and not unique to the study of self-disclosure (see chapter 12 by Bradac in this volume). The diversity of experimental procedures reflects the complexity and diversity of the phenomena being studied.

Measures of Potential or Hypothetical Disclosure

The last group of measures discussed assess the potential for self-disclosure. These instruments do not measure past disclosures or ones elicited by the investigator. Instruments which measure the individual's willingness to self-disclose and expectations about self-disclosure are the two primary types reviewed.

Measures of willingness to self-disclose have frequently been utilized (e.g., Baxter, 1979; Chelune, 1976; Plog, 1965; Rickers-Ovsiankina, 1956; Rickers-Ovsiankina & Kusmin, 1958). Investigators, however, generally do not distinguish this type of measure from those assessing past or future behavior. Such a distinction promotes conceptual clarity and is therefore worthwhile. Empirical evidence (Pedersen & Breglio, 1968; Daher & Banikotes, 1976), though not entirely consistent (Miller et al., 1983) also suggests that the distinction is an important one.

Numerous measurement options exist. Instructions for the JSDQ have been altered to assess willingness rather than past self-disclosure

(Daher & Banikotes, 1976; Simonson & Bahr, 1974). Other investigators also have changed the instructions to their self-disclosure measures to assess willingness (Miller et al., 1983). Still others developed new measures (Baxter, 1979; Chelune, 1976; Plog, 1965; Taylor, De Soto, & Lieb, 1979). Of these, Chelune's (1976) Self-Disclosure Situation Survey has been used most frequently (e.g., Berg & Peplau, 1982; Chelune, 1977; Neimeyer, 1983; Neimeyer & Fong, 1983; Tardy & Hosman, 1982). This instrument consists of 5 items specifying different physical settings (library, dinner table, etc.) for each of 4 different disclosure recipients (friend, group of friends, stranger, group of strangers). Subjects report their willingness to disclose openly in the situation described by each item. The investigator may compute either a total willingness to self-disclose score or one to reflect the individual's sensitivity to variations among situations. The latter score measures self-disclosure flexibility. In these studies the scale proved reliable and yielded results consistent with the investigators' predictions. Both willingness and flexibility are individual characteristics.

Similar to the willingness scales are instruments assessing the subject's expectations to disclose to a particular individual or in a specified situation. Wilson and Rappaport (1974) modified the JSDQ's instructions to assess expected disclosure to an unknown interviewer. Montgomery (1980) asked subjects to estimate their expectations of openness as well as the openness expected of their group colleagues. Both studies found significant associations between the subject's expected self-disclosure and the investigator's observation of the subject's self-disclosure. Furnham's (1982) 16-item scale contained a likelihood of communicating response option. Expectation measures have been used to assess both individual and relational characteristics.

Dawson, Schirmer, and Beck (1984) report an impressive series of studies validating their measure of "patient difficulty in disclosing content appropriate to health and/or medical interviews" (p. 145). *Alpha* coefficients for the instrument's subscales of personal problems and feelings, response to health care, and life style ranged from .82 to .93 with an overall *alpha* of .93. Validation efforts included a study which observed that patients rating their doctors higher in empathy reported more disclosure ease for the health care subscale than patients with doctors low in empathy. Another study found subjects scoring high on the overall difficulty scale had higher heart rate changes in response to self-disclosing statements than subjects scoring low on the scale. Though the work on this instrument is interesting, the utility of this "difficulty" scale appears limited to research on doctor-patient relations.

Two instruments have been developed to assess factors encouraging or inhibiting disclosures. Petronio, Martin, and Littlefield (1984) constructed a questionnaire which requests respondents to assess the importance of 24 specific setting, receiver, sender, and relationship characteristics as prerequisites to self-disclosure. The items are completed for each of four different topics or content categories. Though reliabilities were not reported for the 16 resulting scales (four conditions for each of the four topics), the *alpha* coefficients for the scales across topics ranged from .70 to .89. Rosenfeld (1979) constructed an 18-item instrument ascertaining the reasons why people do not self-disclose. Test-retest reliability over a two-week time period ranged from .68 to .83. Both the Rosenfeld and Petronio et al. instruments were used to assess individual differences in self-disclosure.

For what purposes should measures of willingness and expectation be used? The most logical answer is to assess these two psychological constructs. For some targets or situations these types may predict future behavior better than measures of past self-disclosure (Chelune, 1979). However the conditions to which this conclusion is limited cannot be specified. Consequently, willingness and expectation should be considered psychological constructs potentially related to, but not isomorphic with, past or future behavior. The nature and strength of the associations among these concepts is a theoretical rather than methodological issue.

Willingness and expectation to disclose will be affected by individual factors as well as others, such as the target and setting. As such, the measures would be most appropriately used to study the individual's predisposition vis-a-vis particular relationships. Chelune's (1976) measure, however, encompasses a variety of situational factors in order to reflect the individual's general willingness to disclose. Likewise, the use of the JSDQ enables the investigator to assess the subject's willingness to disclose over a variety of topics and targets. The more the instrument's topics, targets, and settings represent the situations encountered by the subjects, the better the instrument as a measure of the individual's trait.

Are willingness and expectation measures identical? Though some authors treat them as such (Chelune, 1979), I know of no study which has empirically examined the relationship between the two. A study by Fantasia and Lombardo (1975) did show that subjects selected more intimate items to discuss with a stranger when instructed to select the topics they were "most willing to discuss" than when instructed to choose items they would "most like to discuss." Until conceptual or empirical research associates the two, there is no reason to assume that willingness to disclose and expected disclosure are identical.

Conclusion

From the preceding discussion one simple conclusion emerges: a phenomenal amount of effort has been expended by investigators developing procedures for assessing self-disclosure. The range and variety of instruments and plans match the complexity and diversity of the self-disclosure concept. This discussion attempted to clarify these methodological alternatives so that future investigators can profit from the ingenuity as well as from the mistakes of prior scholarship.

References

Altman, I., & Taylor, D. (1973). *Social penetration: The development of inter-personal relationships.* New York: Holt, Rinehart and Winston.

Archer, R.L. (1979). Role of personality and the social situation. In G.J. Chelune (Ed.), *Self-disclosure: Origins, patterns, and implications of openness in interpersonal relationships* (pp. 28–58). San Francisco, CA: Jossey-Bass, 1979.

Archer, R.L., & Berg, J.H. (1978). Disclosure reciprocity and its limits: A reactance analysis. *Journal of Experimental Social Psychology, 14,* 527–540.

Archer, R.L., Berg, J.H., & Runge, T.E. (1980). Active and passive observers' attraction to a self-disclosing other. *Journal of Experimental Social Psychology, 16,* 130–145.

Baxter, L.A. (1979). Self-disclosure as a relationship disengagement strategy: An exploratory investigation. *Human Communication Research, 5,* 215–222.

Berg, J.H., & Archer, R.L. (1980). Disclosure or concern: A second look at liking for the norm breaker. *Journal of Personality, 48,* 245–257.

Berg, J.H., & Archer, R.L. (1982). Responses to self-disclosure and interaction goals. *Journal of Experimental Social Psychology, 18,* 501–512.

Berg, J.H., & Peplau, L.A. (1982). Loneliness: The relationship of self-disclosure and androgyny. *Personality and Social Psychology Bulletin, 8,* 624–630.

Bloch, E.L., & Goodstein, L.D. (1971). Comment on "Influence of an interviewer's disclosure on the self-disclosing behavior of interviewees." *Journal of Counseling Psychology, 18,* 595–597.

Bradac, J.J., Hosman, L.A., & Tardy, C.H. (1978). Reciprocal disclosures and language intensity: Attributional consequences. *Communication Monographs, 45,* 1–17.

Bradac, J.J., Tardy, C.H., & Hosman, L.A. (1980). Disclosure styles and a hint at their genesis. *Human Communication Research, 6,* 228–238.

Burhenne, D., & Mirels, H.L. (1970). Self-disclosure in self-descriptive essays. *Journal of Consulting and Clinical Psychology, 35,* 409–413.

Caltabiano, M.L., & Smithson, M. (1983). Variables affecting the perception of self-disclosure appropriateness. *Journal of Social Psychology, 21,* 119–128.

Cash, T.F., & Soloway, D. (1975). Self-disclosure correlates of physical attractiveness. *Psychological Reports, 36,* 579–586.

Chaikin, A.L., & Derlega, V.J. (1974). Liking for the norm-breaker in self-disclosure. *Journal of Personality, 42,* 117–129.

Chaikin, A.L., Derlega, V.J., Bayma, B., & Shaw, J. (1975). Neuroticism and disclosure reciprocity. *Journal of Consulting and Clinical Psychology, 43,* 13–19.

Chelune, G.J. (1975). Studies in behavioral and self-report assessment of self-disclosure. (Doctoral dissertation, University of Nevada, 1975). *Dissertation Abstracts International, 37,* 453b.

Chelune, G.J. (1976). The Self-Disclosure Situations Survey: A new approach to measuring self-disclosure. *JSAS Catalog of Selected Documents in Psychology, 6,* (Ms. no. 1367) 111–112.

Chelune, G.J. (1977). Disclosure flexibility and social-situational perceptions. *Journal of Consulting and Clinical Psychology, 45,* 1139–1143.

Chelune, G.J. (1978). Nature and assessment of self-disclosing behavior. *Advances in Psychological Assessment, 4,* 278–320.

Chelune, G.J. (1979). Measuring openness in interpersonal communication. In G.J. Chelune (Ed.), *Self-disclosure: Origins, patterns, and implications of openness in interpersonal relations* (pp. 1–27). San Francisco, CA: Jossey-Bass.

Chelune, G.J., Skiffington, S., & Williams, C. (1981). Multidimensional analysis of observers' perceptions of self-disclosing behavior. *Journal of Personality and Social Psychology, 41,* 599–606.

Cline, R.J. (1983a). The acquaintance process as relational communication. *Communication Yearbook 7,* 396–413.

Cline, R.J. (1983b, May). *The effects of sex and gender on self-reported and behavioral intimacy and control of self-disclosure.* Paper presented at the International Communication Association, Dallas, TX. (ED 232 222.)

Daher, D.M., & Banikotes, P.G. (1976). Measurement of self-disclosure. *Psychological Reports, 38,* 1255–1256.

Davidson, B., Balswick, J., & Halverson, C. (1983). Affective self-disclosure and marital adjustment. *Journal of Marriage and the Family, 45,* 93–102.

Davis, J.D. (1976). Self-disclosure in an acquaintance exercise: Responsibility for level of intimacy. *Journal of Personality and Social Psychology, 33,* 787–792.

Davis, J.D. (1977). Effects of communication about interpersonal process on the evolution of self-disclosure in dyads. *Journal of Personality and Social Psychology, 35,* 31–37.

Davis, J.D., & Sloan, M. (1974). The basis of interviewee matching of interviewer self-disclosure. *British Journal of Social and Clinical Psychology, 13,* 359–367.

Dawson, C., Schirmer, M., & Beck, L. (1984). A patient self-disclosure instrument. *Research in Nursing and Health, 7,* 135–147.

DeForest, C., & Stone, G.L. (1980). Effects of sex and intimacy level of self-disclosure. *Journal of Counseling Psychology, 27,* 93–96.

Derlega, V.J., Winstead, B.A., Wong, P.T.P., & Hunter, S. (1985). Gender effects in an initial encounter. *Journal of Social and Personal Relationships, 2*, 25–44.

Dindia, K. (1983). Reciprocity of self-disclosure: A sequential analysis. *Communication Yearbook, 6*, 506–528.

Doster, J.A. (1972). Effects of instructions, modeling, and role rehearsal on interview verbal behavior. *Journal of Consulting and Clinical Psychology, 39*, 202–209.

Ehrlich, H.J., & Graeven, D.B. (1971). Reciprocal self-disclosure in dyads. *Journal of Experimental Social Psychology, 7*, 389–400.

Fantasia, S.C., & Lombardo, J.P. (1975). The effects of instructions on self-disclosure. *Journal of Psychology, 91*, 183–186.

Fisher, D.V. (1984). A conceptual analysis of self-disclosure. *Journal for the Theory of Social Behavior, 14*, 277–296.

Furnham, A. (1982). The message, the context and the medium. *Language and Communication, 2*, 33–47.

Gilbert, S.J., & Hornstein, D. (1975). The communication of self-disclosure: Level versus valence. *Human Communication Research, 1*, 316–322.

Gilbert, S.J., & Whiteneck, G.G. (1976). Toward a multidimensional approach to the study of self-disclosure. *Human Communication Research, 2*, 347–355.

Gitter, A.G., & Black, H. (1976). Is self-disclosure self-revealing? *Journal of Counseling Psychology, 23*, 327–332.

Grigsby, J.P., & Weatherley, D. (1983). Gender and sex-role differences in intimacy of self-disclosure. *Psychological Reports, 53*, 891–897.

Halpern, T.P. (1977). Degree of client disclosure as a function of past disclosure, counselor disclosure, and counselor facilitativeness. *Journal of Counseling Psychology, 24*, 41–47.

Harrell, W.A. (1978). Physical attractiveness, self-disclosure and helping behavior. *Journal of Social Psychology, 104*, 15–17.

Hecht, M., Shepherd, T., & Hall, M.J. (1979). Multivariate indicies of the effects of self-disclosure. *Western Journal of Speech Communication, 43*, 235–245.

Hendrick, S.S. (1981). Self-disclosure and marital satisfaction. *Journal of Personality and Social Psychology, 40*, 1150–1159.

Highlen, P.S., & Gillis, S.F. (1978). Effects of situational factors, sex, and attitude on affective self-disclosure and anxiety. *Journal of Counseling Psychology, 25*, 270–276.

Highlen, P.S., & Johnston, B. (1979). Effects of situational variables on affective self-disclosure with acquaintances. *Journal of Counseling Psychology, 26*, 255–258.

Highlen, P.S., & Voight, N.L. (1978). Effects of social modeling, cognitive structuring, and self-management strategies on affective self-disclosure. *Journal of Counseling Psychology, 25*, 21–27.

Hill, C.T., & Stull, D.E. (1982). Disclosure reciprocity: Conceptual and measurement issues. *Social Psychological Quarterly, 45*, 238–244.

Himelstein, P., & Kimbrough, W.W., Jr. (1963). A study of self-disclosure in the classroom. *Journal of Psychology, 55,* 437–440.

Hurley, J.R., & Hurley, S.J. (1969). Toward authenticity in measuring self-disclosure. *Journal of Counseling Psychology, 16,* 271–274.

Jones, E.E., & Archer, R.L. (1976). Are there special effects of personalistic self-disclosure? *Journal of Experimental Social Psychology, 12,* 180–193.

Jones, E.E., & Gordon, E.M. (1972). Timing of self-disclosure and its effects on personal attraction. *Journal of Personality and Social Psychology, 24,* 358–365.

Jourard, S.M. (1961a). Age trends in self-disclosure. *Merrill Palmer Quarterly, 7,* 191–197.

Jourard, S.M. (1961b). Self-disclosure scores and grades in nursing college. *Journal of Applied Psychology, 45,* 244–247.

Jourard, S.M. (1971). *Self-disclosure: An experimental analysis of the transparent self.* New York: Wiley-Interscience.

Jourard, S.M., & Lasakow, P. (1958). Some factors in self-disclosure. *Journal of Abnormal and Social Psychology, 56,* 91–98.

Jourard, S.M., & Richman, P. (1963). Disclosure output and input in college students. *Merrill Palmer Quarterly, 9,* 141–148.

Klos, D.S., & Loomis, D.F. (1978). A rating scale of intimate disclosure between late adolescents and their friends. *Psychological Reports, 42,* 815–820.

Klos, D.S., & Paddock, J.R. (1978). Relationship status: Scales for assessing the vitality of late adolescents' relationships with their parents. *Journal of Youth and Adolesence, 7,* 353–369.

Lakin, M., Oppenheimer, B., & Bremer, J. (1982). A note on old and young in helping groups. *Psychotherapy, 19,* 444–452.

Lester, D., Brazill, N., Ellis, C., & Guerin, T. (1984). Correlates of romantic attitudes toward love. *Psychological Reports, 54,* 554.

Lewin, K. (1948). Social-psychological differences between the United States and Germany. In K. Levin (Ed.), *Resolving social conflicts* (pp. 3–33). New York: Harper & Row.

Lewis, D.M. (1970). A TST based technique for the study of self-disclosure. *Sociological Quarterly, 11,* 556–558.

Lubin, B., & Harrison, R.L. (1964). Predicting small group behavior with the self-disclosure inventory. *Psychological Reports, 15,* 77–78.

McAllister, H.A., & Bregman, N.J. (1983). Self-disclosure and liking: An integration theory approach. *Journal of Personality, 51,* 202–212.

Miller, L.C., Berg, J.H., & Archer, R.L. (1983). Openers: Individuals who elicit intimate self-disclosure. *Journal of Personality and Social Psychology, 44,* 1234–1244.

Miller, R.S., & Lefcourt, H.M. (1983). Social intimacy. *American Journal of Community Psychology, 11,* 127–139.

Montgomery, B.M. (1980). Trait, interactionist, and behavior assessment variables in open communication. *Communication Research, 7,* 479–494.

Montgomery, B.M. (1981). Verbal immediacy as a behavioral indicator of open communication content. *Communication Quarterly, 30,* 28–34.

Morton, T.L. (1978). Intimacy and reciprocity of exchange. *Journal of Personality and Social Psychology, 36,* 72–81.

Neimeyer, G.J. (1983). Flexibility of disclosure by counselors. *Psychological Reports, 52,* 977–978.

Neimeyer, G.J., & Fong, M.L. (1983). Self-disclosure flexibility and counselor effectiveness. *Journal of Counseling Psychology, 30,* 258–261.

Norton, R. (1978). A foundation of a communicator style construct. *Human Communication Research, 4,* 99–112.

Norton, R. (1983). *Communicator style.* Beverly Hills, CA: Sage.

Norton, R., & Montgomery, B.M. (1982). Style, content, and target components of openness. *Communication Research, 9,* 399–431.

Panyard, C.M. (1971). A method to improve the reliability of the Jourard Self-Disclosure Questionnaire. *Journal of Counseling Psychology, 18,* 606.

Pearce, W.B., & Wiebe, B. (1975). Item-analysis of Jourard's Self-Disclosure Questionnaire-21. *Educational and Psychological Measurement, 35,* 115–118.

Pedersen, D.M., & Breglio, V.J. (1968). The correlation of two self-disclosure inventories with actual self-disclosure. *Journal of Psychology, 68,* 291–298.

Perl, M.B. (1983). Self-disclosure: Structure and measurement. *Dissertation Abstracts International, 43,* 2351B.

Petronio, S., Martin, J., & Littlefield, R. (1984). Prerequisite conditions for self-disclosing: A gender issue. *Communication Monographs, 51,* 268–273.

Plog, S.C. (1965). The disclosure of self in the United States and Germany. *Journal of Social Psychology, 65,* 193–203.

Rappaport, J., Gross, T., & Lepper, C. (1973). Modeling, sensitivity training and instructions. *Journal of Consulting and Clinical Psychology, 40,* 99–107.

Remer, P., Roffey, B.H., & Buckholtz, A. (1983). Differential effects of positive versus negative self-involving counselor responses. *Journal of Counseling Psychology, 30,* 121–125.

Ribner, N.G. (1974). Effects of an explicit group contract on self-disclosure and group cohesiveness. *Journal of Counseling Psychology, 21,* 116–120.

Rickers-Ovsiankina, M.A. (1956). Social accessibility in three age groups. *Psychological Reports, 2,* 283–294.

Rickers-Ovsiankina, M.A., & Kusmin, A.A. (1958). Individual differences in social accessibility. *Psychological Reports, 4,* 391–406.

Rosenfeld, L.B. (1979). Self-disclosure avoidance: Why am I afraid to tell you who I am? *Communication Monographs, 46,* 63–74.

Rosenfeld, L.B., Civikly, J.M., & Herron, J.R. (1979). Anatomical and psychological sex differences. In G.J. Chelune (Ed.), *Self-disclosure: Origins, patterns, and implications of openness in interpersonal relationships* (pp. 80–109). San Francisco, CA: Jossey-Bass.

Rosenfeld, L.B., & Welsh, S.M. (1985). Differences in self-disclosure in dual-career marriages. *Communication Monographs, 52,* 253–263.

Rubin, Z. (1975a). Disclosing oneself to a stranger: Reciprocity and its limits. *Journal of Experimental Social Psychology, 11,* 233–260.

Rubin, Z. (1975b). Naturalistic studies of self-disclosure. *Personality and Social Psychology Bulletin, 2*, 260–263.

Rubin, Z., Hill, C.T., Peplau, L.A., & Dunkel-Schetter, C. (1980). Self-disclosure in dating couples: Sex roles and the ethic of openness. *Journal of Marriage and the Family, 42*, 305–317.

Rubin, Z. & Shenker, S.S. (1978). Friendship, proximity, and self-disclosure. *Journal of Personality, 46*, 1–22.

Runge, T.E., & Archer, R.L. (1981). Reactions to the disclosure of public and private self-information. *Social Psychology Quarterly, 44*, 357–362.

Sermat, V., & Smyth, M. (1973). Content analysis of verbal communication in the development of a relationship: Conditions influencing self-disclosure. *Journal of Personality and Social Psychology, 26*, 332–346.

Siegman, A.W., & Reynolds, M.A. (1983). Speaking without seeing, or the effect of interviewer absence on interviewee disclosure time. *Journal of Psycholinguistic Research, 12*, 595–602.

Siegman, A.W., & Reynolds, M. (1984). The facilitating effects of interviewer rapport and the paralinguistics of intimate communication. *Journal of Social and Clinical Psychology, 2*, 71–88.

Sillars, A.L. (1980). Attribution and communication in roommate conflicts. *Communication Monographs, 47*, 180–200.

Simonson, N.R., & Bahr, S. (1974). Self-disclosure by the professional and paraprofessional therapist. *Journal of Consulting and Clinical Psychology, 42*, 359–363.

Solano, C.H. (1981). Sex differences and the Taylor-Altman disclosure stimuli. *Journal of Social Psychology, 115*, 287–288.

Stacks, D.W., & Stone, J.D. (1984). An examination of the effect of basic speech courses, self-concept, and self-disclosure on communication apprehension. *Communication Education, 33*, 317–331.

Stiles, W.B. (1978). Verbal response modes and dimensions of interpersonal roles: A method of discourse analysis. *Journal of Personality and Social Psychology, 36*, 693–703.

Tardy, C.H., & Hosman, L.A. (1982). Self-monitoring and self-disclosure flexibility. *Western Journal of Speech Communication, 46*, 92–97.

Taylor, D.A., & Altman, I. (1966). Intimacy-scaled stimuli for use in studies of interpersonal relations. *Psychological Reports, 19*, 729–730.

Taylor, R.B., De Soto, C.B., & Lieb, R. (1979). Sharing secrets: Disclosure and discretion in dyads and triads. *Journal of Personality and Social Psychology, 37*, 1196–1203.

Tittler, B.I., Anchor, K.N., & Weitz, L.J. (1976). Measuring change in openness: Behavioral assessment techniques and the problem of the examiner. *Journal of Counseling Psychology, 23*, 473–478.

Town, J.P., & Harvey, J.H. (1981). Self-disclosure, attribution, and social interaction. *Social Psychology Quarterly, 44*, 291–300.

Vondracek, F.W. (1969). Behavioral measurement of self-disclosure. *Psychological Reports, 25*, 914.

Walker, L.S., & Wright, P.H. (1976). Self-disclosure in friendship. *Perceptual and Motor Skills, 42,* 735–742.

Waring, E.M., & Chelune, G.J. (1983). Marital intimacy and self-disclosure. *Journal of Clinical Psychology, 39,* 183–190.

West, L.W. (1971). A study of the validity of the self-disclosure inventory for adolescents. *Perceptual and Motor Skills, 33,* 91–100.

West, L.W., & Zingle, H.W. (1969). A self-disclosure inventory for adolescents. *Psychological Reports, 24,* 439–445.

Whalen, C. (1969). Effects of a model and instructions on group verbal behaviors. *Journal of Consulting and Clinical Psychology, 33,* 509–521.

Wheeless, L.R. (1976). Self-disclosure and interpersonal solidarity: Measurement, validation, and relationships. *Human Communication Research, 3,* 47–61.

Wheeless, L.R. (1978). A follow-up study of the relationships among trust, disclosure, and interpersonal solidarity. *Human Communication Research, 4,* 143–157.

Wheeless, L.R., & Grotz, J. (1976). Conceptualization and measurement of reported self-disclosure. *Human Communication Research, 2,* 338–346.

Wheeless, L.R., & Grotz, J. (1977). The measurement of trust and its relationship to self-disclosure. *Human Communication Research, 3,* 250–258.

Wilson, M.N., & Dulany, D.E. (1983). An analysis of cognitive control of self-disclosure in a clinical analogue. *Cognitive Therapy and Research, 7,* 297–314.

Wilson, M.N., & Rappaport, J. (1974). Personal self-disclosure. *Journal of Consulting and Clinical Psychology, 42,* 901–908.

Worthy, M., Gary, A.L., & Kahn, G.M. (1969). Self-disclosure as an exchange process. *Journal of Personality and Social Psychology, 13,* 59–63.

CHAPTER 14

Social Support: Conceptual Clarification and Measurement Options[1]

Charles H. Tardy

Evidence of mankind's desire to affiliate abounds. Clubs, churches, bridge parties, car pools, and thousands of other types of formal and informal groups attest to this social fact. Only recently, however, have the positive physical and mental outcomes of such affiliations received attention (Cassel, 1976; Heller, 1979; Kaplan, Cassel, & Gore, 1977). Nonetheless, current research on the topic of social support is accumulating at an astounding rate. In addition to the now normal spate of journal articles and book chapters, 1985 saw the publication of two journal special issues (Brownell & Shumaker, 1984; Shumaker & Brownell, 1985) and several books (Cohen & Syme, 1985; Lin, Dean, & Ensel, 1985; Hobfoll, 1985; Sarason & Sarason, 1985) devoted to this topic.

From the abundance of recently published research there would appear to be no barriers to progress in the study of social support. However, the lack of agreement concerning its conceptualization and measurement impedes the production of valid generalizations about the development and functioning of social support (Sandler & Barrera, 1984; Thoits, 1982). As Leavy (1983) stated in a review of the literature on psychological disorder and social support, "Most support questionnaires are ad hoc measures with questionable reliability and unknown validity" (p. 16). Wilcox (1981) phrased this problem less diplomatically when he said "the concept of social support has been operationalized in a somewhat bewildering assortment of ways" (p. 98). Of the few rigorous studies of the measurement properties of

---

[1] An earlier version of this chapter appeared in the *Ameircan Journal of Community Psychology*, 1985, *13*, 178–202.

347

social support instruments, most do not attempt to build systematically on previous methodologies. Rather, authors frequently appear to start the development process anew, a practice which is costly and inefficient. Though increasingly discussed (Bruhn & Phillips, 1984; Depner & Wethington, 1984; Reis, 1984; Singer & Lord, 1984), little consensus exists on appropriate strategies for measuring social support. Consequently, few studies use identical procedures.

This chapter attempts to resolve these problems by providing a review of the currently available measures of social support. Readers are informed of available methodological options. A description of issues related to the conceptualization of social support precedes a discussion of strategies utilized in previous noteworthy studies.

Conceptual Issues

The varied operational definitions of social support appearing in the literature are symptomatic of the multiple interpretations of the meaning of social support. Unfortunately, the differences too frequently go unnoticed, contributing to misunderstandings and inaccurate generalizations. Cohen and Wills' (1985) recent review of research on the "buffering hypothesis" convincingly demonstrates the necessity of distinguishing among various measurement approaches. The solution to this problem, however, is not to obtain consensus on a single definition. Rather, the solution is to recognize and discuss the issues associated with conceptual and operational definitions. This paper describes five such issues to clarify the decisions facing researchers and to organize the differences among the approaches taken by various authors (cf., Cobb & Jones, 1984; Rook, 1984).

1. *Direction.* Social support is both given and received. The distinction between these two directions in which social support occurs is clear and fundamental. Though research overwhelmingly focuses on the receipt of social support, some authors also attribute importance to the conveyance of support (Cohen & Sokolovsky, 1979; Fischer, 1982; McFarlane, Neale, Norman, Roy, & Streiner, 1981; Miller & Ingham, 1976; Tolsdorf, 1976). Researchers must decide to investigate one or both.

2. *Disposition.* Some studies examine the availability of support (e.g., Barrera, 1981; Sarason, Levine, Basham, & Sarason, 1983) while others examine its enactment (e.g., Barrera, Sandler, & Ramsay, 1981; Burke, 1978; Carveth & Gottlieb, 1979; Dunkel-Schetter, 1984; Shumaker & Brownell, 1984). Support availability refers to the quantity or quality of support to which people have access. The actual utilization of these

support resources is referred to as enacted support. Eckenrode (1983) called these two types potential support and support mobilization.

3. *Description/Evaluation.* Evaluation and description constitute two distinct facets of the social support concept. Illustrating evaluation are studies of people's satisfaction with their social support (e.g., Cauce, Felner, & Primavera, 1982). Other studies propose only to describe social support (e.g., Barrera, Sandler, & Ramsay, 1981; Hammer, 1981). The concept of support evaluation and description correspond to Cohen and Wills' (1985) distinction between functional and structural measures.

4. *Content.* From situation to situation the content of support varies greatly. Loaning someone money involves different commitments and processes than patting someone on the back, though both acts may be supportive. Perhaps the most useful typology of support content eminates from the discussion by House (1981), which distinguishes among four types: emotional, instrumental, informational, and appraisal. Emotional support involves such affects as caring, trust, love, and empathy. Helping behaviors, such as loaning money or giving one's time and skill, are examples of instrumental support. Informational support refers to advice, while appraisal support refers to evaluative feedback, for example, "you're doing a great job!" Although accounting for most types of support content, this category system may not be exhaustive. Several authors (Fiore, Becker, & Coppel, 1983; Cohen & McKay, 1984; Gottlieb, 1978; Walker, MacBride, & Vachon, 1977) suggest alternatives. Content categories may be examined individually or in combination.

5. *Network.* The social dimension of support constitutes the fourth issue. The term "network" was selected because the more common term "source" entails a specific direction of support. Some studies are concerned with the mere existence of the network, while others consider the characteristics of the people in the support network. Some authors even consider the neighborhood and other environmental features as sources of support (e.g., Lin, Dean, & Ensel, 1981).

Though not exhaustive, these five issues encompass the primary elements of social support. All research on this topic makes assumptions about the direction, disposition, description/evaluation, content, and network of support. Additionally, these issues are interdependent. Operational definitions of social support make assumptions about each one.

Appropriate selections among alternative measurement strategies necessitate decisions on these conceptual issues.

Measurement Devices

While a systematic search for studies containing measures of social support was made through computerized services of *Psychological Abstracts* and *Sociological Abstracts,* examination of journal volumes and articles' references provided most citations. More than 100 relevant studies were located. Literally dozens of different measures have been utilized in published research. In selecting instruments for discussion in this chapter, three criteria were used. Instruments which clearly measure some aspect of social support were chosen over those that did not distinguish among the five aspects discussed above. Instruments which measure supportive components of social relations were chosen over those that focused on other aspects such as social participation, integration, or contact. Instruments demonstrating reliability and validity were chosen over those for which no data were available.

Measures Emphasizing Support Network

Measures which elicit members of the support network from subjects utilize methods common to network analysis. In fact, several authors argue that the entire social network should be examined, rather than only the network segment which provides support (Hammer, 1981; Hirsch, 1981; Wellman, 1981). These advocates say social network analysis allows the examination of the larger interpersonal context in which support is embedded and avoids the positive bias inherent in the examination of only contacts which are supportive. However, the topic of social network analysis exceeds the scope of this paper. See Mitchell and Trickett (1980) for a review of the conceptual issues and operational definitions associated with this approach to the study of social support, and chapter 4 by Monge and Contractor for a discussion of network research methods.

Arizona social support interview. Manuel Barrera (1980, 1981) reports the development of an instrument to measure support networks as well as several other aspects of social support. An interviewer first asks the subject to give the names or initials of the people who provide support, for example, "Who would you go to if a situation came up when you needed advice?" (Barrera, 1981, p. 91). The response indicates social support available to the subject. Following each of six such questions, three further questions phrased to be consistent with each topic are asked: (a) Did the person actually give support in the past month? (b) Would you have liked more support? (c) Did you get the support you needed? The answer to the first question describes the enactment of support, while the answers to the second and third evaluate the enacted support. The author includes a question about conflicts or unpleasant interactions and a series of questions requesting descriptions of the individuals named by the respondent. From these data Barrera reported calculating the following measures: (a) total network size; (b) conflicted network size; (c) unconflicted network size; (d) support satisfaction; and (e) support need.

With a sample of 45 college students, the total size measure yielded a test-retest correlation coefficient of .88 over a period of two or more days. Seventy percent of the individuals named appeared on both administrations of the interview. The size of the conflicted network resulted in a lower test-retest correlation coefficient of .54 but was statistically significant. The internal reliabilities of the size measures are not reported. The coefficient *alphas* for the satisfaction and need measures were low, .33 and .52, respectively. The two measures' test-retest correlations were .61 and .80. Together these analyses suggest that the need and satisfaction measures vary considerably with the type of support content but remain relatively stable over time at the aggregate level. In a study of pregnant adolescents, the measures of conflicted network size, need, and satisfaction correlated significantly with several measures of maladjustment-depression, anxiety, and somatization, while unconflicted network size, need, and satisfaction correlated significantly with a measure of negative life events. In another study with college student subjects (Sandler & Barrera, 1984), only support satisfaction and conflicted network size correlated with the three types of psychological maladjustment. Numerous differences between demographic (age and sex) and psychological (Type A and Type B personality) groups were obtained on the various subscales of this instrument in a recent study (Strube, Berry, Goza, & Fennimore, 1985).

This instrument has the advantage of measuring several aspects of social support. In addition to the ones described above, the user could calculate support content and source measures from these data. Consequently, almost all of the aspects of social support can be measured. The negative interaction question may also prove useful for some investigators (Sandler & Barrera, 1984).

Perceived social support from family and friends. Procidano and Heller (1983) report a series of studies assessing measures of perceived social support from family (PSS-Fa) and from friends (PSS-Fr). The two 20-item self-report measures require a simple "yes," "no," or "don't know" response. Some statements are reworded to be used in both scales. The 20-items for friends yielded a coefficient *alpha* of .88, while the family items yielded .90. Factor analysis of each instrument resulted in a single factor solution, further indicating the internal consistency of the items. A pretest indicated a high test-retest reliability ($r=.83$). In a series of studies, both the friend and family scales correlated with measures of psychopathology and distress. In a study of conversational behavior, students who were higher in perceived social support from friends talked more and possessed lower trait anxiety than subjects scoring lower on this measure. Subjects low in perceived social support from family evidenced marked verbal inhibition when talking with a sibling, as compared to subjects with high scores. This study also observed a correlation between negative mood states and perceived social support from friends, but not with perceived social support from family. Neither social support measures correlated with a positive mood state. This finding indicates a potentially significant problem: individuals' reports of social support may be a function of how individuals feel when they complete the instrument. This possibility must be considered by all researchers using self-report measures. The behavioral evidence reported by Procidano and Heller, however, is quite impressive and leads to the conclusions that self-reports can predict behaviors associated with social support.

The scale includes items related to social support provision and receipt. Both enactment and availability are specified by some items. This instrument is a general measure of social support which does not differentiate among the dimensions of direction, disposition, or content. However, since the receipt items overwhelmingly outnumber the provision items, the scale should be interpreted primarily as a measure of support receipt. Likewise, since most of the items appear to assess emotional support, the scale should be considered to measure primarily this type of support content. Though these imprecisions reduce the utility of the instrument, Procidano and Heller's work on the assessment of their measure warrants examination.

Related measures. Several other instruments have used the network elicitation procedure. Claude Fischer and his colleagues (Jones & Fischer, 1978; Phillips & Fischer, 1981) developed a measure of individuals' exchange and support networks to be used in the Northern California Community Survey (Fischer, 1982). Ten questions were included which elicited the names of people who provided support. Eight questions covered three types of social support content: counseling, companionship, and practical help. These three correspond to appraisal, emotional, and instrumental support. Unfortunately, the author reports no reliability estimates of these subscales. Some of the questions refer to support availability, while others refer to enacted support.

McFarlane et al.'s (1981) Social Relationship Questionnaire (SRQ) encompasses both description and evaluation. The authors append a question concerning helpfulness to each of six items which elicit the names of individuals from whom he or she receives support. Another appended item allows the subject to indicate his or her potential for providing support to the persons listed. However, McFarlane, Norman, and Streiner's (1983) failure to find a main or interactive effect on illness has been cited as evidence of this instrument's deficient construct validity (Cohen & Wills, 1985).

Similar procedures were developed by Hirsch (1979) and later were used in several investigations (Kazak & Wilcox, 1984; Potasznik & Nelson, 1984). The Norbeck Social Support Questionnaire (Norbeck, Lindsey, & Carrieri, 1981) also is based on the network listing instructions. Among the additional items included in this instrument are two for each of three types of support content: affect, affirmation, and aid. Vaux's (1982) Social Support Resources measure elicits the names of up to 10 individuals who provide five types of support: emotional, socializing, practical assistance, financial assistance, and advice/guidance. Six follow-up questions assess the nature of the relationship with the persons listed. Vaux and Harrison (1985) noted that scales derived from this measure correlated with other measures of social support. Though only limited evidence is available, this measure appears to be very promising.

Another measure used to assess support from particular segments of the social network is the Moos Family Relationship Index (FRI) and Work Relationship Index (WRI) (Holahan & Moos, 1983, 1985). The FRI assesses the quality of family relationships and consists of three subscales: cohesion, expressiveness, and conflict. The WRI measures quality of relationships in the work setting and consists of three subscales: peer cohesion, staff support, and work involvement. Both the FRI and WRI are derived from a larger set of scales to measure family and work social environments. Though both evidence high internal reliability, the two measures appear to combine aspects of relationships such as intimacy, self-disclosure, and commitment with support. In several studies, the overall scale (Holahan & Moos, 1985) or selected subscales (Kobasa & Puccetti, 1983) have detected a stress-buffering effect of social support on illness. Given the multifaceted nature of these instruments, however, the findings can be attributed only cautiously to social support.

Conclusion. Excepting the measures which specify the support network, these instruments have much in common. Each has been shown to yield acceptable measures of support networks. All provide considerable flexibility for describing network characteristics. None are especially strong for measuring the evaluative aspects of social support. When selecting among these alternatives, prime consideration should be given to the questions which indicate the type of support content assessed by the questionnaires. Naturally the instruments differ in the specific items for assessing support. Only two of these scales include multiple items for separate content types. Vaux's Social Support Resources measure, however, includes a detailed description of each of the types of support content. The others assess generalized support without reference to different types of support content. McFarlane et al.'s (1981) questions refer to "discussion" of topics and may, therefore, elicit names of some people who do not provide support. All else being equal, researchers should choose the instrument whose content is most relevant to the support processes being studied.

Measures Emphasizing Support Content

Interpersonal support evaluation list. The ISEL is one of the few measures to focus on the different types of support content. A version for college students (Cohen & Hoberman, 1983) consists of 48 items while the general population version (Cohen, Mermelstein, Kamarck, & Hoberman, 1985) includes only 40. The scales contain self-statements, equally divided among four content categories: tangible, belonging, appraisal, and self-esteem. Subjects respond by answering "probably true" or "probably false." Strong and consistent evidence of the scales' reliability and validity is provided in Cohen et al.'s (1985) discussion of seven studies with the student version and four studies with the general population version.

In several studies, the ISEL scales correlated with psychological and physical symptomatology. The total score correlated significantly ($r=.46$) with Barrera's Inventory of Socially Supportive Behaviors in a study with student subjects. One cross sectional (Cohen & Hoberman, 1983) and one prospective study (Cohen, McGowan, Fooskas, & Rose, 1984) observed that the ISEL buffered the effects of stress on psychological disorder. The Cohen and Hoberman (1983) study also provided evidence of the independent contributions of the subscales in buffering the effects of stressful life events on both psychological and physical symptomatology. Further evidence of the importance of the subscales derives from a study (Cohen et al., 1985) which observed that the relationship between social support and smoking cessation was attributed primarily to the appraisal dimension. The evidence from these studies strongly supports the discriminant validity of the ISEL.

The ISEL constitutes an important resource for describing the availability of different types of support content. In addition to possessing sound psychometric properties, the instrument is available for both student and general populations. The ISEL, however, provides no information about the support network. The sources of the support are left for speculation.

Several other published measures also provide for separate assessments of different types of support content (Norbeck, Lindsey, & Carrieri, 1981; Norbeck & Tilden, 1983; Schaefer, Coyne, & Lazarus, 1981). However these studies do not inspire confidence in the use of their respective scales for assessing the specific content types (Cohen & Wills, 1985). Additionally, some scales reviewed elsewhere in this chapter, for example, Fischer's (1982) Social Support Network Interview, provide for the assessment of different types of support content.

Measures Emphasizing Support Description/Evaluation

Most of the measures reviewed elsewhere in this chapter clearly distinguish between description and evaluation. Many of the instruments reviewed in the support networks section provide for both the description of the support providers and the evaluation of the support provided. The measures described in this section place greater emphasis on these two aspects.

Social support questionnaire. Sarason et al. (1983) report a series of studies which assess a self-report questionnaire to describe and evaluate the availability of social support. Respondents supply the names or initials of supporters for each of 27 problems or subjects, for example, "Whom can you really count on to listen to you when you need to talk?" and then rate the level of satisfaction with the total support for that issue along a six-point continuum from very satisfied to very dissatisfied. The authors calculate a measure which describes availability, by dividing the number of people providing support by the number of items (SSQN), and the satisfaction with available support, by dividing the summed score by the number of items (SSQS). The availability description score yielded a test-retest correlation of .90 over a period of 4 weeks with a sample of 107 college students. The satisfaction score was slightly less stable with a correlation of .83. Both measures correlated significantly and negatively with depression scores in another study of students. A third study, also with college students, observed a positive relationship between support availability and the occurrence of positive life events, the perceived effect of those events, the extent to which the events were expected, and the degree to which the subjects felt they had control over the occurrence of those events. The satisfaction measure was associated negatively with negative life events and control over those events. An additional experimental study found that subjects classified as externals on a locus of control scale persisted longer and evidenced less cognitive interference during a stressful task when the subjects had more, as opposed to less than the average number of supporters.

A more recent study by Sarason, Sarason, Hacker, and Basham (1985) provides additional evidence of the validity of this questionnaire. Subjects scoring in the top and bottom quintile of the SSQN were observed in structured and unstructured dyadic interactions. Self-reports, experimenter ratings, and partner reports converge to indicate that subjects high in social support were more socially competent than subjects low in social support. Additionally, individuals high in social support gave responses to a story completion task which were rated more competent. Though not reported in detail, comparable results were obtained when subjects were grouped according to scores on the satisfaction scale of the SSQ. This accumulation of evidence strongly supports the viability of this measure of social support.

In addition to the two procedures described above for scoring the instrument, other alternatives exist. Sarason et al. (1983) also calculated several measures of network characteristics, for example, number of family supporters. However, the results indicated that such measures are highly intercorrelated with the SSQN score and, therefore, are of little value. Nonetheless, the data gathered with the SSQ are amenable to multiple scoring procedures. Consequently, studies which focus on the support network might be able to use this instrument.

Before using this questionnaire, the content of the items should be carefully examined. Sullivan and Reardon (1985) selected 16 of the items most relevant to cancer patients. This modification did not jeopardize the scale's reliability or its ability to detect a relationship between social support and coping styles. Most of the SSQ questions specify emotional support, for example, "Who accepts you totally, including both your worst and best points?" Items representing other types of support are in the minority.

Social support appraisals. A second important measure of this aspect of social support, the Social Support Appraisals scale (SS:A) has been developed by Vaux (Vaux & Harrison, 1985; Vaux, Phillips, Holly, Thomson, Williams, & Stewart, 1986). Following Cobb's (1976) conceptualization of social support, this instrument measures the subjective appraisal of social support. More specifically, the measure focuses on feelings of love, esteem, and belonging that result from social interaction. The scale consists of 23 items to which subjects respond on a 4-point agree-disagree continuum. Eight of the items refer to family, seven to friends, and eight to "others." In a series of studies employing five student and five community samples, average *alpha* coefficients were approximately .80, .84, and .90 for the family, friend, and total scales. Family and friend subscales correlated at approximately $r=.51$. All three correlated moderately ($r=.30$ to .40) with the support network satisfaction measure derived from the SS:R. The scales related in predictable ways to Procidano and Heller's (1983) PSS-Fr and PSS-Fa. Low but significant correlations were obtained with measures of social support network availability, a behavior based measure of support availability, and with a measure of depressed mood. Overall, the evidence strongly supports the internal reliability and construct validity of the SS:P.

Revised Kaplan Scale. An interesting procedure to evaluate social support has been used by Turner (1981). Originally designed by Kaplan (1977), the instrument consists of a series of vignettes which describe people who vary systematically in social support. Subjects compare themselves to the persons described in the vignette.

Turner (1981) reports four studies utilizing nine vignettes to measure social support. With samples of normal parents, maladaptive parents, mentally ill adults, and hearing-impaired adults, internal reliability of the scale ranged from .79 to .83 using the coefficient *alpha*. In factor analyses with three other sets of variables, the social support items loaded together. And, perhaps most important, the social support measure consistently related to measures of psychological well-being. Turner (1983) reports that the Revised Kaplan Scale was the most powerful predictor of parenting problems and psychological distress in studies of new mothers and adults losing their hearing. Turner and Noh (1983) observed that the relationship between social support and distress varied with class and with type of life events experienced by mothers following childbirth.

The scale does not distinguish among sources of social support. A later version of this instrument includes subscales for three types of support. A study by Vaux (n.d.) reports *alpha* coefficients for the three subscales: network, .66; love, .58; and esteem, .51. Consequently, Turner's measure does not appear to be a strong measure of the separate content types. However, vignettes could be composed which embody different characteristics of support. The reliability and validity data from Turner's studies indicate the potential utility of this strategy. In a contrary opinion, Cohen and Wills (1985) suggest that the measure lacks construct validity because Turner's (1981) study did not support a buffering hypothesis. They contend that the Kaplan scale merely assesses social competence or some related personality trait.

Measures Emphasizing Support Disposition

The measures described elsewhere in this chapter specify enactment or availability, and sometimes both, but do not focus primarily on the disposition of social support. One instrument that does emphasize enactment is reviewed below. With the possible exception of the SSQN, none of the measures reviewed place central importance on availability.

Inventory of socially supportive behaviors. Manuel Barrera's ISSB focuses strictly on the receipt of behaviors providing support (Barrera, 1981; Barrera et al., 1981). Subjects report the frequency of occurrence during the past month of such behaviors as being given a ride to see a doctor or being loaned $25. The self-report measure consists of 40 such statements describing the enactment of various content types of support. The scale requests no information about the support network.

As a univariate measure, the scale has shown a high degree of internal consistency as indicated by a coefficient *alpha* of .93 with college students and .92 with pregnant adolescents. Cohen and Hoberman (1983) obtained an *alpha* coefficient of .92 with a sample of college students. A test-retest correlation of .88 was obtained over at least 2 days (Barrera, 1981). The ISSB correlated significantly with a measure of negative life events in two studies (Barrera, 1981) but not in a third (Sandler & Barrera, 1984). Stokes and Wilson (1984) report that social network characteristics of men but not women predicted ISSB scores.

Two studies factor analyzed the ISSB, both reporting similar but not identical factor solutions (Barrera & Ainlay, 1983; Stokes & Wilson, 1984). In one study reliability coefficients of .85, .71., .83, and .77 were obtained for the emotional support, tangible assistance, cognitive information, and directive guidance dimensions, respectively (Stokes & Wilson, 1984). Additionally, a measure composed of emotional support items significantly differentiated men from women, providing tentative evidence of the discriminant validity of content measures derived from the ISSB. The other factor analytic study did not report internal reliability coefficients or form scales from the four factors.

The primary purpose of the instrument is to describe the enactment of supportive behaviors. The goal is achieved by noting such acts which occurred in the past month. This strategy allows for the identification of recent events though neglecting prior ones. If desired, the time frame could be altered.

The ISSB specifies no source for the support. However, the instructional set could be altered to specify support from a specific source. In pretesting the instrument, Barrera observed that the instrument with a family instructional set correlated significantly with the Moos family environment questionnaire (Barrera et al., 1981). Additionally, the instructional set might be altered to assess the provision instead of the receipt of support. Naturally, the previously reported reliability and validity evidence would not apply to the instrument if such changes were made. Nonetheless, altering this instrument would be more efficient than designing a completely new one.

Cohen and Wills (1985) argue that the ISSB confounds availability and recent need for social support, a need perhaps resulting from recent stressful events, and is, therefore, inappropriate for studying the stress buffering effects of social support. This problem applies to any measure of enacted support and is limited to studies assessing stress. This criticism delimits the appropriate use of the ISSB but does not diminish the psychometric soundness of the ISSB.

Measures Emphasizing Direction

The assumption that only received social support is important predominates in the literature. Consequently no measures emphasize the provision of social support. McFarlane et al.'s (1981) Social Relationship Scale includes an item to indicate if subjects have given support. Procidano and Heller's (1983) scales include a few "support provided" items along with the mostly "received" ones. Perhaps recent interest (Shumaker & Brownell, 1984) in the provision and reciprocity of support will lead to the development of measures which place greater emphasis on this aspect of social support.

Conclusion

Considerable improvements in the measurement of social support have been made in the last five years. Researchers no longer need to utilize ad hoc scales. In fact, for many purposes researchers need to develop no instruments at all, as perfectly good ones exist. Certainly there is room for improvement. Clear patterns of strengths and weaknesses exist (Tardy, 1985). Undoubtedly new measures will be constructed and the present ones revised. Awareness of the capabilities as well as the limitations of current instruments should promote efficient and rational progress in the study of social support.

References

Barrera, M. (1980). A method for the assessment of social support networks in community survey research. *Connections, 3*(3), 8–13.

Barrera, M. (1981). Social support in the adjustment of pregnant adolescents: Assessment issues. In B.H. Gottlieb (Ed.), *Social networks and social support* (pp. 69–96). Beverly Hills, CA: Sage.

Barrera, M., & Ainlay, S.L. (1983). The structure of social support: A conceptual and empirical analysis. *Journal of Community Psychology, 11,* 133–143.

Barrera, M., Sandler, I.N., & Ramsay, T.B. (1981). Preliminary development of a scale of social support: Studies on college students. *Journal of Community Psychology, 9,* 435–447.

Brownell, A., & Shumaker, S.A. (Eds.). (1984). Social support: New perspectives in theory, research, and intervention, Part I. Theory and research. *Journal of Social Issues, 40*(4), 1–137.

Bruhn, J.G., & Phillips, B.U. (1984). Measuring social support: A synthesis of current approaches. *Journal of Behavioral Medicine, 7,* 151–169.

Burke, R.J. (1978). Sex differences in adolescent life stress, social support, and well-being. *Journal of Psychology, 98,* 277–288.

Carveth, W.B., & Gottlieb, B.H. (1979). The measurement of social support and its relation to stress. *Canadian Journal of Behavioral Science, 11,* 111–116.

Cassel, J. (1976). The contribution of the social environment to host resistance. *American Journal of Epidemiology, 102,* 107–123.

Cauce, A.M., Felner, R.D., & Primavera, J. (1982). Social support in high-risk adolescents. *American Journal of Community Psychology, 10,* 417–428.

Cobb, S. (1976). Social support as a moderator of life stress. *Psychosomatic Medicine, 38,* 300–314.

Cobb, S., & Jones, J.M. (1984). Social support, support groups and marital relationships. In S. Duck (Ed.), *Personal relationships: 5. Repairing personal relationships* (pp. 47–66). London: Academic Press.

Cohen, C.I., & Sokolovsky, J. (1979). Health-seeking behavior and social networks of the aged living in single-room occupancy hotels. *Journal of the American Geriatrics Society, 27,* 270–278.

Cohen, L.H., McGowan, J., Fooskas, S., & Rose, S. (1984). Positive life events and social support and the relationship between life stress and psychological disorder. *American Journal of Community Psychology, 12,* 567–587.

Cohen, S., & Hoberman, H.M. (1983). Positive events and social supports as buffers of life change stress. *Journal of Applied Social Psychology, 13,* 99–125.

Cohen, S., & McKay, G. (1984). Social support, stress and the buffering hypothesis: A theoretical analysis. In A. Baum, S.E. Taylor, & J.E. Singer (Eds.), *Handbook of psychology and health. Vol. 4: Social psychological aspects of health* (pp. 253–267). Hillsdale, NJ: Erlbaum.

Cohen, S., Mermelstein, R., Kamarck, T., & Hoberman, H.M. (1985). Measuring the functional components of social support. In I.G. Sarason and B.R. Sarason (Eds.), *Social support: Theory, research and applications* (pp. 73–94). Dordrecht: Martinus Nijhoff.

Cohen, S., & Syme, S.L. (Eds.), (1985). *Social support and health.* New York: Academic Press.

Cohen, S., & Wills, T.A. (1985). Stress, social support, and the buffering hypothesis. *Psychological Bulletin, 98,* 310–357.

Depner, C.E., & Wethington, E. (1984). Social support: Methodological issues in design and measurement. *Journal of Social Issues, 40,* 37–54.

Dunkel-Schetter, C. (1984). Social support and cancer: Findings based on patient interviews and their implications. *Journal of Social Issues, 40,* 77–98.

Eckenrode, S. (1983). The mobilization of social supports: Some individual constraints. *American Journal of Community Psychology, 11,* 509–520.

Fiore, J., Becker, J., & Coppel, D.B. (1983). Social network interactions: A buffer or a stress. *American Journal of Community Psychology, 11,* 423–439.

Fischer, C.S. (1982). *To dwell among friends: Personal networks in town and city.* Chicago, IL: University of Chicago Press.

Gottlieb, B.H. (1978). The development and application of a classification scheme of informal helping behaviours. *Canadian Journal of Behavioral Science, 10,* 105–115.

Hammer, M. (1981). Social supports, social networks and schizophrenia. *Schizophrenia Bulletin, 7,* 45–56.

Heller, K. (1979). The effects of social support: Prevention and treatment implications. In A.P. Goldstein and F.H. Kanfer (Eds.), *Maximizing treatment gains* (pp. 353–382). New York: Academic Press.

Hirsch, B.J. (1979). Psychological dimensions of social networks: A multi-method analysis. *American Journal of Community Psychology, 7,* 263–277.

Hirsch, B.J. (1981). Social networks and the coping process: Creating personal communities. In B.H. Gottlieb (Ed.), *Social networks and social support* (pp. 149–170). Beverly Hills, CA: Sage.

Hobfoll, S.E. (Ed.). (1985). *Stress, social support, and women.* Washington, DC: Hemisphere.

Holahan, C.J., & Moos, R.H. (1983). The quality of social support: Measures of family and work relationships. *British Journal of Clinical Psychology, 22,* 157–162.

Holahan, C.J., & Moos, R.H. (1985). Life stress and health: Personality, coping, and family support in stress resistance. *Journal of Personality and Social Psychology, 49,* 739–747.

House, J.S. (1981). *Work stress and social support.* Reading, MA: Addison-Wesley.

Jones, L., & Fischer, C.S. (1978). A procedure for surveying personal networks. *Sociological Methods and Research, 7,* 131–148.

Kaplan, A. (1977). *Social support: The construct and its measurement.* Unpublished bachelor's thesis, Brown University, Providence, RI.

Kaplan, B.H., Cassel, J.C., & Gore, S. (1977). Social support and health. *Medical Care, 25*(Suppl.), 47–58.

Kazak, A.E., & Wilcox, B.L. (1984). The structure and function of social support networks in families with handicapped children. *American Journal of Community Psychology, 12,* 645–661.

Kobasa, S.C., & Puccetti, M.C. (1983). Personality and social resources in stress resistance. *Journal of Personality and Social Psychology, 45,* 839–850.

Leavy, R.L. (1983). Social support and psychological disorder: A review. *Journal of Community Psychology, 11,* 3–21.

Lin, N., Dean, A., & Ensel, W.M. (1981). *Social support scales. Schizophrenia Bulletin, 7,* 73–89.

Lin, N., Dean, A., & Ensel, W.M. (1985). *Social support, life events, and depression.* New York: Academic Press.

McFarlane, A.H., Neale, K.A., Norman, G.R., Roy, R.G., & Streiner, D.L. (1981). Methodological issues in developing a scale to measure social support. *Schizophrenia Bulletin, 7,* 90–100.

McFarlane, A.H., Norman, G.R., & Streiner, D.L. (1983). The process of social stress: Stable, reciprocal, and mediating relationships. *Journal of Health and Social Behavior, 24,* 160–173.

Miller, P., & Ingham, J. (1976). Friends, confidants, and symptoms. *Social Psychiatry, 11,* 51–58.

Mitchell, R.E., & Trickett, E.J. (1980). Task force report: Social networks as moderators of social support. *Community Mental Health Journal, 16,* 27–44.

Norbeck, J.S., Lindsey, A.M., and Carrieri, V.L. (1981). The development of an instrument to measure social support. *Nursing Research, 30,* 264–269.

Norbeck, J.S., & Tilden, V.P. (1983). Life stress, social support and emotional disequilibrium in complications of pregnancy: A prospective multivariate study. *Journal of Health and Social Behavior, 24,* 30–46.

Phillips, S.L., & Fischer, C.S. (1981). Measuring social support networks in general populations. In B.S. Dohrenwend and B.P. Dohrenwend (Eds.), *Stressful life events and their contexts* (pp. 223–233). New York: Prodist.

Potasznik, H., & Nelson, G. (1984). Stress and social support: The burden experienced by the family of a mentally ill person. *American Journal of Community Psychology, 12,* 589–607.

Procidano, M.E., & Heller, K. (1983). Measures of perceived social support from friends and from family: Three validation studies. *American Journal of Community Psychology, 11,* 1–24.

Reis, H.T. (1984). Social interaction and well-being. In S. Duck (Ed.), *Personal relationships: 5. Repairing personal relationships* (pp. 21–45). London: Academic Press.

Rook, K.S. (1984). Research on social support, loneliness, and social isolation: Toward an integration. In P. Shaver (Ed.), *Annual review of personality and social psychology: 5. Emotions, relationships, and health* (pp. 239–264). Beverly Hills, CA: Sage.

Sandler, I.N., & Barrera, M. (1984). Towards a multimethod approach to assessing the effects of social support. *American Journal of Community Psychology, 12,* 37–52.

Sarason, I.G., Levine, H.M., Basham, R.B., & Sarason, B.R. (1983). Assessing social support: The social support questionnaire. *Journal of Personality and Social Psychology, 44,* 127–139.

Sarason, I.G., & Sarason, B.R. (Eds.). (1985). Social support: Theory, research, and application. Dordrecht: Martinus Nijhof.

Sarason, B.R., Sarason, I.G., Hacker, T.A., & Basham, R.B. (1985). Concomitants of social support: Social skills, physical attractiveness, and gender. *Journal of Personality and Social Psychology, 49,* 469–480.

Schaefer, C., Coyne, J.C., & Lazarus, R. (1981). The health related functions of social support. *Journal of Behavioral Medicine, 4,* 381–406.

Shumaker, S.A., & Brownell, A. (1984). Toward a theory of social support: Closing of conceptual gaps. *Journal of Social Issues, 40,* 11–36.

Shumaker, S.A., & Brownell, A. (Ed). (1985). Social support: New perspectives in theory, research, and intervention, Part II. Interventions and policy. *Journal of Social Issues, 41*(1), 1–125.

Singer, J.E., & Lord, D. (1984). The role of social support in coping with chronic or life-threatening illness. In A. Baum, S.E. Taylor, and J.E. Singer (Eds.), *Handbook of psychology and health: Vol. 4. Social psychological aspects of health* (pp. 269–277). Hillsdale, NJ: Erlbaum.

Stokes, J.P., & Wilson, D.G. (1984). The inventory of socially supportive behaviors: Dimensionality, prediction, and gender differences. *American Journal of Community Psychology, 12,* 53–69.

Strube, M.J., Berry, J.M., Goza, B.K., & Fennimore, D. (1985). Type A behavior, age and psychological well-being. *Journal of Personality and Social Psychology, 49,* 203–218.

Sullivan, C.F., & Reardon, K.K. (1985, May). *Social support satisfaction and health locus of control as discriminators of breast cancer patient coping style preferences.* Paper presented at the International Communication Association, Honolulu, HA.

Tardy, C.H. (1985). Social support measurement. *American Journal of Community Psychology, 13,* 178–202.

Thoits, P.A. (1982). Conceptual, methodological, and theoretical problems in studying social support as a buffer against life stress. *Journal of Health and Social Behavior, 10,* 341–362.

Tolsdorf, C.C. (1976). Social networks, support and coping. *Family Process, 15,* 407–418.

Turner, R.J. (1981). Social support as a contingency in psychological well-being. *Journal of Health and Social Behavior, 22,* 357–367.

Turner, R.J. (1983). Direct, indirect, and moderating effects of social support upon psychological distress and associated conditions. In H.B. Kaplan (Ed.), *Psychological stress: Trends in theory and research* (pp. 105–155). New York: Academic Press.

Turner, R.J., & Noh, S. (1983). Class and psychological vulnerability among women: The significance of social support and personal control. *Journal of Health and Social Behavior, 24,* 2–15.

Vaux, A. (n.d.) *Appraisals of social support: Love, respect and involvement.* Manuscript submitted for publication, Southern Illinois University.

Vaux, A. (1982). *Measures of three levels of social support: Resources, behaviors, and feelings.* Unpublished manuscript, Southern Illinois University.

Vaux, A., & Harrison, D. (1985). Support network characterstics associated with support satisfaction and perceived support. *American Journal of Community Psychology, 13,* 245–268.

Vaux, A., Phillips, J., Holly, L., Thomson, B., Williams, D., & Stewart, D. (1986). The social support appraisals (SS:A) scale: Studies of reliability and validity. *American Journal of Community Psychology, 14,* 195–219.

Walker, K.N., MacBride, A., & Vachon, M.L.S. (1977). Social support networks and the crisis of bereavement. *Social Science and Medicine, 11,* 35–41.

Wellman, B. (1981). Applying network analysis to the study of support. In B.H. Gottlieb (Ed.), *Social networks and social support* (pp. 171–200). Beverly Hills, CA: Sage.

Wilcox, B.L. (1981). Social support in adjusting to marital disruption. In B.H. Gottlieb (Ed.), *Social networks and social support* (pp. 97–115). Beverly Hills, CA: Sage.

CHAPTER 15

Socially-Based Anxiety: A Review of Measures

Mark R. Leary

Although social anxieties have been discussed in the scientific literature at least since Darwin (1872/1955), topics such as shyness, communication apprehension, dating anxiety, and embarrassment have received widespread research attention only recently (for reviews, see Buss, 1980; Daly & McCroskey, 1984; Jones, Cheek, & Briggs, 1986; Leary, 1982a; 1983a). As interest in socially-based anxieties has grown, researchers have developed increasingly refined ways of measuring both the immediate experience of anxiety in interpersonal contexts and the predisposition to feel socially anxious.

The objective of this chapter is to review and critique commonly used methods of assessing social anxiety, as well as to introduce the reader to new approaches that seem to have promise. Consistent with this volume's focus, I will restrict my coverage to measures that are applicable to the study of anxiety in interpersonal encounters, such as conversations, in which true person-to-person *inter*action occurs. Measures of anxiety experienced specifically when one is speaking or performing before others (such as speech and audience anxiety) will not be discussed; the tendency to become nervous when speaking or performing before audiences is conceptually and empirically distinguishable from the tendency to experience anxiety in "contingent" social interactions (see Leary, 1983a, 1983c). Further, although measures exist that assess anxiety in specific types of encounters (such as in interactions with members of the other sex; Rehm & Marston, 1968), the instruments discussed here are applicable to the study of anxiety in social interactions of all kinds.

Conceptual Issues

"Anxiety" refers to a response characterized by apprehension regarding a potentially negative outcome, physiological arousal (i.e., activation of the sympathetic nervous system), and a subjective feeling of tension or nervousness. As such, anxiety involves three interrelated components; cognitive, physiological, and affective. *Social* anxiety is anxiety that is precipitated by interactions with other people, specifically out of concerns with how one is perceived and evaluated by others (Schlenker & Leary, 1982).

Confusion has been generated by including certain behaviors—such as inhibition, avoidance, or reticence—in some definitions and measures of social anxiety. As I have discussed elsewhere (Leary, 1982b; 1983b), defining anxiety in terms of overt behavior not only creates conceptual confusion, but confounds the measurement of social anxiety and its behavioral correlates. Feeling anxious or fearful is conceptually distinguishable from fleeing or avoiding the feared situation. Although the occurrance of these behaviors correlates with social anxiety, there is not a one-to-one relationship between anxiety and such behaviors. The importance of maintaining the distinction between anxiety and behavior becomes clear as we proceed.

Spielberger (1966) first introduced the distinction between "state" and "trait" anxiety, a distinction relevant to this chapter. State anxiety refers to the actual and immediate experience of anxiety in a particular setting at a particular time. A person who is currently anxious would be said to be experiencing state anxiety. Trait anxiety, on the other hand, refers to the dispostion or tendency to experience anxiety across situations and time. Some individuals experience anxiety more frequently than others and are therefore considered high in dispositional or trait anxiety.

Most studies of social anxiety in communication and psychology have focused on trait social anxiety or social *anxiousness.* I will review four measures of general trait social anxiousness in detail, then briefly mention three related scales. Having done so, I will turn to affective, cognitive, and physiological measures of state social anxiety.

I selected instruments and techniques for inclusion in this chapter on the basis of two criteria. Some were chosen because of their widespread use and unquestionable validity as measures of state or trait social anxiety. However, because social anxiety has become a popular topic for investigation only recently, several potentially important measures have not yet received extensive use. From this group I discuss those measures that show strong evidence of reliability and validity and that, in my judgment, have the most promise for future research in the area. I have excluded from consideration scales that have been used in a single study and those for which psychometric data are not available.

Measures of "Trait" Social Anxiety

Social Avoidance and Distress Scale

The growth of scholarly interest in socially-based anxiety during the last 15 years can be traced, in part, to the publication of the Social Avoidance and Distress Scale (SAD) by Watson and Friend in 1969. The SAD Scale has been used in hundreds of studies to identify subjects with varying degrees of social anxiety (e.g., Smith, Ingram, & Brehm, 1983; Steffen & Redden, 1977), to examine cognitive, emotional, and behavioral correlates of social anxiousness (e.g., Goldfried & Sobocinski, 1975; Natale, Entin, & Jaffe, 1979), and to assess the effectiveness of interventions designed to reduce high levels of chronic social anxiety (e.g., Christensen & Arkowitz, 1974; Haemmerlie & Montgomery, 1982).

The SAD Scale consists of 28 statements, balanced equally with positively and negatively worded items. Although the original scale used a true-false response format, much recent research has used 5-point Likert scales on which respondents indicate the degree to which each statement is characteristic or true of themselves. Interitem reliability (Cornbach's alpha or KR-20) of the 28 items is approximately .90 on both true-false and Likert versions of the scale (Leary, Knight, & Johnson, 1987; Watson & Friend, 1969), and test-retest reliability falls around .75 (Girodo, Dotzenroth, & Stein, 1981; Watson & Friend, 1969). The correlation with social desirability is −.25 (Watson & Friend, 1969).

Evidence of construct and criterion validity is quite strong. Scores on the SAD correlate highly (r's > .50) with other measures of social anxiousness, including shyness, interaction anxiousness, fear of negative evaluation, and audience anxiety (Jones, Briggs, & Smith, 1986; Leary, 1983c; Watson & Friend, 1969). In real face-to-face interactions, high scorers on the SAD spontaneously generate more negative self-thoughts about their social performances (Cacioppo, Glass, & Merluzzi, 1979), underestimate the positivity of their social behaviors and others' reactions to them (Clark & Arkowitz, 1975), demonstrate greater concern with others' evaluations (Smith et al., 1983), report feeling more nervous and less relaxed (Clark & Arkowitz, 1975; Leary, 1980; Leary, Knight, & Johnson, 1987), and are judged as being more anxious and "shy" by others (Clark & Arkowitz, 1975; Leary, 1980). Higher scorers also have higher needs for social approval (Goldfried & Sobocinski, 1975) and are more likely to remember negative feedback from others than are low scorers (O'Banion & Arkowitz, 1977).

Although Watson and Friend (1969) alluded to distinct avoidance and distress subscales and factor analyses have obtained separate avoidance and anxiety factors (Patterson & Strauss, 1972), virtually all research has summed all 28 items rather than used the subscale scores. However, for reasons discussed above, the separate use of the two subscales is strongly advised for most research purposes in order not to confound the measurement of social anxiety with the measurement of avoidance (Leary, 1983b). Both subscales have adequate alpha coefficients (> .80) and they correlate .75 with one another (Jennings, 1985; Leary, Knight, & Johnson, 1987; Watson & Friend, 1969). Unfortunately, few studies have examined the validity of the subscales, but existing research supports their utility (see Jennings, 1985; Leary, Atherton, Hill, & Hur, 1986; Leary, Knight, & Johnson, 1987).

Shyness

Shyness is an affective-behavioral syndrome characterized by social anxiety *and* inhibition (Leary, 1986a). Although shyness includes an anxiety component, "shyness" is not synonymous with social anxiety.

Whereas the SAD Scale assesses social anxiety and avoidance, the Shyness Scale (Cheek & Buss, 1981) assesses social anxiety and inhibition. The original Shyness Scale consists of nine items that tap both the affective (anxiety) and behavioral components of shyness (such as inhibition, awkward behavior, and gaze aversion). The scale was designed to measure shyness independently of the simple preference for being alone, thereby avoiding contamination with sociability (the preference for being with others rather than alone) and avoidance. Indeed, the correlation with sociability is low ($r = -.31$), and two factors emerge on factor analyses of shyness and sociability items (Cheek & Buss, 1981). Cronbach's alpha coefficient for the scale generally exceeds .80. Cheek (1983) has revised the scale, dropping one item and adding five others. The revised 13-item scale has an alpha coefficient of .90 and a 45-day test-retest reliability of .88. Both the original and revised versions are provided in Appendix 1.[1]

Research supports the validity of both versions of the Shyness Scale.

---

[1] I have reprinted scales in this chapter only when they currently are not widely available from another source.

Shyness correlates positively with a variety of measures of social anxiousness and shyness, public self-consciousness (the tendency to think about the public aspects of oneself and others' reactions to them), fearfulness, and feelings of inhibition in real encounters (Cheek & Buss, 1981; Cheek, Carpentieri, Smith, Rierdan, & Koff, 1986; Cheek & Melchoir, 1985; Jones, Briggs, & Smith, 1986). Further, shy individuals initiate interactions with others less frequently (Miller, Berg, & Archer, 1983), talk less during laboratory conversations (Cheek, 1983; Cheek & Buss, 1981), and have more difficulty overcoming feelings of loneliness in new situations (Cheek & Busch, 1981).

Both versions of the Shyness Scale appear quite adequate as measures of shyness. Although the revised version is probably the better of the two, fewer studies have used it to date and there is no empirical evidence that it actually predicts affect or behavior better than the original scale. Whichever measure is used, researchers should keep in mind that scores on the Shyness Scale reflect a combined measure of social anxiety *and* inhibition, and should not be used when a measure of social anxiousness per se is desired.

Interaction Anxiousness

Observing that most scales measure both the tendency to experience social anxiety *and* the tendency to behave in an inhibited, awkward, reticent, and/or avoidant fashion, I developed the Interaction Anxiousness Scale (Leary, 1983c). Actually, two subscales were developed—one for anxiety experienced in contingent, conversational settings and one for anxiety experienced when speaking or performing before audiences. However, only the first concerns us here.

The Interaction Anxiousness Scale (IAS) consists of 15 items that are answered on 5-point Likert scales (ranging from "not at all" to "extremely characteristic or true of me"). The scale assesses self-reported anxiousness in a variety of social settings (job interviews, cross-sexed encounters, telephone conversations, interactions with authority figures), but does *not* include any items dealing with overt behaviors. Cronbach's alpha for the IAS is very high (around .90; Jennings, 1985; Leary, 1983c) and eight-week test-retest reliability is .80 (Leary, 1983c).

Evidence of construct validity is very good. For example, scores on the IAS correlate positively with other measures of social anxiety, shyness, public self-consciousness, and speech anxiety. Further, the scale correlates −.63 with social self-efficacy (the expectation that one is socially effective), and .69 with the avoidance subscale of the SAD. IAS scores also correlate significantly with self-reported nervousness in laboratory conversations and with people's concerns about how they are being perceived by others (Leary, 1986b; Leary, Atherton, Hill, & Hur, 1986). The IAS is recommended when a pure measure of the tendency to experience social anxiety, unconfounded by its behavioral correlates, is desired.

Personal Report of Communication Apprehension

The three scales described above have received their greatest use among researchers in psychology. Among researchers in communication, McCroskey's (1970, 1976, 1977, 1982a) Personal Report of Communication Apprehension (PRCA) has been the most commonly used measure of socially-based anxiety. As defined by McCroskey (1977, p. 78), communication apprehension is social anxiety aroused by "real or imagined communications with another person or persons." McCroskey (1977) originally developed four versions of the PRCA— one for college students, 10th graders, 7th graders, and preliterate children (McCroskey, 1976). However, only the college version has received wide use.[2]

The PRCA-college possesses high interitem reliability (alpha coefficients in excess of .90 in most studies) and strong evidence of criterion validity. However, because the items on this version of the PRCA deal chiefly with anxiety experienced in public speaking situations, McCroskey (1982a,b) developed a new 24-item scale that includes four 6-item subscales that assess anxiety in public speaking situations, dyadic conversations, meetings/classes, and group discussions. The new, PRCA-24 is presented in Appendix 2.

The PRCA-24 demonstrates high interitem reliability (alpha > .90), as does its four constituent subscales (alphas > .85). Scores on the PRCA-24 correlate highly with self-reported state anxiety experienced in real communicative encounters (McCroskey & Beatty, 1984)

---

[2] Although the terms are sometimes used interchangably, communication apprehension and social anxiety are not synonymous. Rather, social anxiety is a broader term that refers to anxiety resulting from the prospect or presence of interpersonal evaluation (Schlenker & Leary, 1982). Strictly speaking, an individual may feel socially anxious without communicating or even interacting with another person, as when one feels uncomfortable appearing in one's swimsuit—untanned and out-of-shape—at the beginning of the summer (and the individual may feel socially anxious even among strangers with whom he or she has no intention of interacting). Communication apprehension, on the other hand, refers to social anxiety that emerges from people's concerns about communicating with others (McCroskey, 1977). A comparison of the Interaction Anxiousness Scale and the PRCA-24 (Appendix 2) will show that items on the PCRA-24 tap anxiety that is explicitly aroused by interpersonal communication, whereas items on the IAS are more general.

and with people's willingness to communicate with others in the four contexts tapped by the scale (McCroskey, Beatty, Kearney, & Plax, 1985). Although criterion validity is excellent, construct validity—examining the relationship between the PRCA-24 and relevant constructs to establish convergent and discriminant validity—is lacking at present.

However, McCroskey and his colleagues have done a good job of demonstrating the applicability of the PRCA and PRCA-24 to real life settings. For example, their studies have examined the role of communication apprehension in the professional lives of chiropractors (Allen, Richmond, & McCroskey, 1984) and pharmacists (Berger, Baldwin, McCroskey, & Richmond, 1983). Further, an unusual amount of cross-cultural data exists regarding the PRCA (e.g., Fayer, McCroskey, & Richmond, 1984).

Even so, the PRCA has its critics. Porter (1979), for example, challenged the usefulness of both the construct of communication apprehension and the PRCA. Although he raises some important issues that all researchers interested in social anxiety must address, much of his case is based upon an erroneous attempt to validate a measure of anxiousness with behavioral criteria. Because the relationship between anxiety and behavior is indirect and meager, (Leary, 1983b, 1986a; Leary & Atherton, 1986), it makes little sense to insist that a measure of social anxiousness correlate strongly with specific overt behaviors. I return to this point below.

Additional Measures

Social anxiety. The social anxiety subscale of the Self-Consciousness Scale (Fenigstein, Scheier, & Buss, 1975) has brevity to recommend it in situations in which a longer scale would be problematic. This scale consists of only six items with an alpha coefficient of .80 and a test-retest reliability of .73. Available data support its validity as a measure of social anxiety (e.g., Buss, 1980; Greenberg, Pyszczynski, & Stine, 1985). There are two potential drawbacks to this measure, however: it includes items dealing with anxiety in both conversational and public speaking situations, and two of the items tap specific behaviors rather than anxiousness per se.

Social reticence scale. The Social Reticence Scale (Jones & Russell, 1982) takes a somewhat broader view of shyness than the Cheek and Buss measure, including items that assess social anxiety, inhibition, loneliness, isolation, concerns with being perceived as unfriendly, and cognitive distraction. Because all items on the original SRS were worded such that endorsement indicates high anxiety, Jones and Briggs (1986) recently revised it.

The SRSII consists of 20 items, has an alpha coefficient of .91, and a test-retest correlation of .87 over eight weeks. The SRSII correlates highly with other measures of shyness and social anxiety (r's > .70), and moderately with assertiveness, extraversion, fearfulness, and loneliness. Validity data shows that respondents who score high on the SRSII are rated as more anxious and shy by others. Although the SRSII has not yet been widely used, the scale is useful when a broad measure of shyness and related difficulties is desired. However, because the scale includes items that tap several different yet related constructs, the total scale score is difficult to interpret.

Fear of negative evaluation. Most researchers concur that the essential ingredient in social anxiety is a concern for how one is perceived and evaluated by others (see Schlenker & Leary, 1982, 1985; Zimbardo, 1977). Thus, a construct that is conceptually related to social anxiousness is Fear of Negative Evaluation (FNE; Watson & Friend, 1969). The original FNE scale consists of 30 true-false items, has a KR-20 reliability coefficient of .94, and displays strong evidence of construct and criterion validity (Watson & Friend, 1969). However, because many of the items are redundant, straining both the time and patience of research subjects, I developed a brief, 12-item version of the FNE that has a reliability coefficient comparable to the original (alpha = .88), with which it correlates .96 (Leary, 1983d). Both the long and brief versions possess good psychometric properties and correlate moderately with more direct measures of social anxiousness, such as SAD, Interaction Anxiousness, shyness, and audience anxiety scales (Jennings, 1985; Jones, Briggs, & Smith, 1986; Leary, 1983d; Watson & Friend, 1969). Compared to people who score low on the scale, high scorers are more concerned with being evaluated, report being more bothered by performing poorly, and are more motivated to perform well (Leary, Barnes, & Griebel, 1986). Although not a measure of social anxiousness per se, the FNE scale is often used to identify individuals who are most prone to feelings of social anxiety.

Embarrassability. Embarrassment is social anxiety that occurs in response to a self-presentational predicament—a situation in which events have undesirable implications for the impressions one wishes to make on others (Buss, 1980; Miller, 1986). Modigliani (1968) constructed an Embarrassability Scale that measures people's tendency to become embarrassed. This measure lists 26 potentially embarrassing situations, such as falling down in a public place, forgetting another person's name, or walking in on someone in the bath. Respondents indicate how embarrassed they would feel in each situation. The scale has an alpha coefficient of .88 (Modigliani, 1968).

Unfortunately, this fascinating measure has received only minimal use. However, available data show that scores on the scale correlate positively with fear of negative evaluation, shyness, social anxiety, audience anxiety, public self-consciousness, and feelings of inadequacy (Miller, 1985; Modigliani, 1968).

Measures of "State" Social Anxiety

Comparatively little attention has been devoted to the development of measures of "state" social anxiety, partly because researchers have been less interested in the immediate experience of social anxiety than in the disposition to feel socially anxious and partly because research on state anxiety is often more difficult and time-consuming in that it requires subjects to actually interact with one another. Even so, previous work offers a number of suggestions (and warnings) for those interested in studying state social anxiety.

Affective Measures

As noted above, anxiety may be regarded as having affective, cognitive, and physiological components. Affective measures of state anxiety consist chiefly of self-reports. If we want to know how anxious an individual *feels*, the most straightforward approach is to ask him or her directly.

In many instances, this may be done with a single question that asks the subject something akin to "How nervous did you feel during the interaction?" to which the subject responds on a Likert-type scale that ranges from "not at all" to "extremely." This technique is quite useful as long as the researcher keeps two potential problems in mind.

The first is that subjects may be unwilling to admit the extent of their anxiety. Words such as "nervous" and "anxious" carry negative connotations that imply' maladjustment or inappropriate insecurity. Thus, social desirability motives may create a "ceiling" effect on responses. This problem may be minimized, in part, by telling the subject in advance that virtually everyone feels nervous in such situations, thereby reducing the stigma associated with appearing nervous.

The second problem regards the *wording* of the question. Should the question be phrased in terms of anxiety, nervousness, worry, tension, discomfort, or uncertainty, or should their opposites be used (e.g., calm, relaxed, comfortable)? Not only are naive subjects likely to interpret and define these terms differently than the researcher, but I've found that subjects often respond differently to terms that, from my perspective, are roughly synonymous (such as anxious and nervous)!

One solution is to ask subjects to rate how they felt on *several* anxiety-relevant adjectives. If this technique is used, some adjectives should be worded in the direction of anxiety (e.g., tense, worried) and some worded in the direction of the absence of anxiety (e.g., relaxed, calm) to control for response biases. Zuckerman's (1960) Affect Anxiety Check List provides a list of 21 such adjectives, although a few (such as "happy" and "loving") are less directly relevant to anxiety than others. The internal consistency of Zuckerman's list of adjectives is .85.

Cognitive Measures

If people are anxious in a particular social setting, we should be able to ascertain the extent of their apprehension by examining their thoughts. The cognitive component of anxiety involves thoughts regarding the negative event or outcome that the individual is facing, his or her attempts to deal with the threat, and thoughts regarding his or her ability to do so. Unfortunately, like feelings, thoughts are not open to direct inspection, and we must rely on subjects' self-reports. Although getting subjects to divulge their thoughts may sound like an approach fraught with insurmountable problems, recent work on cognitive response suggests otherwise.

The thought-listing procedure. One of the best ways to measure subjects' thoughts is the "thought-listing procedure." Although there are several variations of this approach (see Cacioppo & Petty, 1981 for a detailed discussion), one method relevant to the measurement of social anxiety is as follows. Before or after subjects' participation in an interaction, they are told that the researcher is interested in people's thoughts while they interact. Subjects are given a sheet of paper with 12 five-inch lines on it and are told to list any and all thoughts they had during the conversation (or, if assessed beforehand, while waiting to interact). They are instructed simply to write down the first thought they had on the first line, the second thought on the second line, and so on, ignoring grammar, spelling, and punctuation, and while being as concise as possible. Further, subjects are told not to try to fill every space, but just to write down the thoughts they had, being as accurate and as honest as possible (see Cacioppo & Petty, 1981; Petty & Cacioppo, 1977, for examples in other domains).

Later, trained judges can rate the thoughts for the degree of apprehensiveness expressed in each statement. I have used a 4-point scale (0 to 3), rating each thought as reflecting no apprehension, minimal apprehension, moderate apprehension, or high apprehension. In order to eliminate contextual cues, judges should either rate the thoughts in a random order or one judge should rate each subjects' thoughts from beginning to end while the other rates them from end to beginning. Considerable training and practice may be needed to achieve acceptable levels of interrater reliability. Even so, when summed across thoughts for a subject, we've obtained interrater reliability coefficients as high as .85 in two studies. In lieu of training judges, some researchers ask *subjects* to score their own thoughts for apprehension. One study shows that results obtained with this method are virtually identical to those resulting from the use of trained judges (Tarico, Van Velzen, & Altmaier, 1984).

At least four meaningful indices of cognitive apprehension may be obtained from ratings of subjects' thoughts: a total apprehension score per subject, an average apprehension score per thought (total apprehension score divided by number of thoughts per subject), and the number and proportion of apprehensive thoughts (thoughts with a non-zero rating). Of course, subjects' thoughts may also be content analyzed in various ways.

Only a few studies of social anxiety have used the thought-listing procedure, but their results provide evidence for the validity of the technique. For example, Cacioppo, Glass, and Merluzzi (1979) used this procedure to study males' cognitions during an interaction with an unfamiliar female. Subjects' self-statements were coded as positive, negative, or neutral. Results showed that highly socially anxious men spontaneously generated more negative cognitions. In our research on evaluation apprehension (Leary, Barnes, & Griebel, 1986), the thought-listing data were quite sensitive to experimental manipulations designed to raise and lower subjects' anxiety over possible losses of self- and social esteem.

Questionnaire methods. Glass, Merluzzi, Biever, and Larsen (1982) developed an alternative method of assessing thoughts relevant to social anxiety. Their Social Interaction Self-Statement Test consists of a list of 30 positive and negative thoughts an individual might have in an interaction with a member of the other sex. Subjects who have interacted with a person of the other sex in a laboratory conversation are asked to rate how often they had each thought before, during, and after the interaction, and responses are summed to provide a cognitive apprehension score. Split-half reliability coefficients are .73 for positive and .86 for negative self-statements. Scores on this scale correlated positively with self-reported anxiety (r's = .4 − .8) but, curiously, the correlation between this measure and scores obtained using an open-ended thought-listing procedure were only weak to moderate. A factor analysis of this measure suggests that anxiety-relevant thoughts may take several distinct forms. Factors were obtained that reflected self-deprecation, positive and negative anticipation, fear of negative evaluation, and coping thoughts. Although not yet widely used, this measure offers a new direction in the assessment of anxiety-relevant cognitions. Similar questionnaires could be developed to assess apprehensive cognitions in other domains.

Space does not permit a more detailed discussion of cognitive approaches to the measurement of state social anxiety. The interested reader is referred to Glass and Merluzzi (1981), Davison, Robins, and Johnson (1983), and Cacioppo and Petty (1981) for fuller treatments.

Physiological Measures

Despite the fact that anxiety always involves some degree of physiological arousal, physiological measures have not been widely used in research on social anxiety. This may be due to the complexity of physiological indices, questions regarding the best indicators of various states, the obtrusiveness of most measures of this type, and issues regarding appropriate ways of analyzing physiological data.

For example, there is considerable disagreement regarding which physiological modality is the best indicant of anxiety (heart rate, GSR, blood pressure, muscle tension, brain temperature, etc.; see Beatty, 1984; Martin, 1961). Surprisingly, these various indices of arousal do not correlate well with one another. Further, although there is agreement that physiological changes that occur in response to experimental factors should be adjusted on the basis of baseline data, there is no universally accepted method of doing this. For example, should simple differences between baseline and experimental conditions be used, or should these differences be adjusted to control for the magnitude of the baseline, creating a proportion of change over the baseline (Lacey, 1956; Porter, 1979; Wilder, 1957)?

To complicate matters, correlations between physiological indices and self-reported anxiety are notoriously weak. For example, some studies have obtained *no* correlation between heart rate and self-reports of social anxiety, even though heart rate was affected by other factors as predicted (Borkovec, Stone, O'Brien, & Kaloupek, 1974; Leary, 1986b; Miller & Arkowitz, 1977)! Other studies have found a moderate correlation between arousal and self-reports (see Beatty, 1984).

Although physiological measures of social anxiety are strongly encouraged, researchers who wish to use them should become expert in the use of these techniques. The interested reader is referred to Martin (1961), Izard and Hyson (1986), and Beatty (1984) for introductions to the physiological measurement of anxiety.

Behavioral Measures

Many researchers use "behavioral" measures of social anxiety, such as low eye contact, figiting, reticence, inhibition, and speech disfluencies. Although these sorts of behaviors do correlate with social anxiety, their use as *measures* of anxiety is ill-advised. Not only does this obscure the meaning of "anxiety," but more importantly, *behavior is not a valid indicator of social anxiety* (Leary, 1983b).

To use an analogy, confronting an angry bear at close range in the woods would make virtually everyone afraid. However, individuals' reactions in such a situation differ greatly. Some may run away in panic, some may calmly and slowly walk away, some may throw rocks, some may be immobilized by fear, whereas still others, though frightened, may try to appear unconcerned for the benefit of onlookers. Although all are afraid, they react differently, and we would have difficulty determining the extent of each person's anxiety simply by observing his or her behavior. In the same way, in an interpersonal context, many individuals interact fully and competently in spite of subjective social anxiety, whereas others appear quiet, flustered, and inept, even though they are not in the least bit anxious. As a result, the correlation between subjective social anxiety and specific behaviors is only weak to moderate.

I should not be interpreted as discouraging the use of behavioral measures in social anxiety research. On the contrary, the nature of the relationship between social anxiety and overt behavior is of considerable importance. However, whether behavior and anxiety are related in any particular setting is an empirical question, and behavioral indices should never be used as measures of social anxiety per se.

Conclusions

Researchers interested in social anxiety and related phenomena have a number of options regarding how to measure the target constructs. Not only must decisions be made regarding whether trait or state measures are most appropriate, but choices made regarding whether to examine affective, cognitive, or physiological aspects of anxiety. In an ideal situation, one would want to measure all three components, but in practice, doing so often requires greater time and effort on the part of subjects than can be justified or else the procedures interfere with other aspects of the research project. In light of this, researchers should carefully consider the nature of their hypotheses and choose judiciously the kinds of measures that will best answer their research questions.

APPENDIX 1

Cheek and Buss Shyness Scale

INSTRUCTIONS: Please read each item carefully and decide to what extent it is characteristic of your feelings and behavior. Fill in the blank next to each item by choosing a number from the scale printed below.

1 = very uncharacteristic or untrue, strongly disagree
2 = uncharacteristic
3 = neutral
4 = characteristic
5 = very characteristic or true, strongly agree

1. I feel tense when I'm with people I don't know well.*
2. I am socially somewhat awkward.*
3. I do not find it difficult to ask other people for information. (R)
4. I am often uncomfortable at parties and other social functions.*
5. When in a group of people, I have trouble thinking of the right things to talk about.
6. It does not take me long to overcome my shyness in new situations. (R)
7. It is hard for me to act natural when I am meeting new people.
8. I feel nervous when speaking to someone in authority.*
9. I have no doubts about my social competence. (R)
10. I have trouble looking someone right in the eye.*
11. I feel inhibited in social situations.*
12. I don't find it hard to talk to strangers.* (R)
13. I am more shy with members of the opposite sex.*
14. When conversing I worry about saying something dumb.*

Note. Items from the original Cheek and Buss (1981) Shyness Scale are indicated by an asterisk (*). The revised scale (Cheek, 1983) consists only of items 1 through 13.

(R) indicates that the item is reverse-scored before summing.

APPENDIX 2

Personal Report of Communication Apprehension–24

Directions: This instrument is composed of 24 statements concerning your feelings about communication with other people. Please indicate in the space provided the degree to which each statement applies to you by marking whether you (1) Strongly Agree, (2) Agree, (3) Are Undecided, (4) Disagree, or (5) Strongly Disagree with each statement. There are no right or wrong answers. Many of the statements are similar to other statements. Do not be concerned about this. Work quickly, just record your first impression.

1. I dislike participating in group discussions.
2. Generally, I am comfortable while participating in group discussions.
3. I am tense and nervous while participating in group discussions.
4. I like to get involved in group discussions.
5. Engaging in a group discussion with new people makes me tense and nervous.
6. I am calm and relaxed while participating in group discussions.
7. Generally, I am nervous when I have to participate in a meeting.
8. Usually I am calm and relaxed while participating in meetings.
9. I am very calm and relaxed when I am called upon to express an opinion at a meeting.
10. I am afraid to express myself at meetings.
11. Communicating at meetings usually makes me uncomfortable.
12. I am very relaxed when answering questions at a meeting.
13. While participating in a conversation with a new acquaintance, I feel very nervous.
14. I have no fear of speaking up in conversations.
15. Ordinarily I am very tense and nervous in conversations.
16. Ordinarily I am very calm and relaxed in conversations.
17. While conversing with a new acquaintance, I feel very relaxed.
18. I'm afraid to speak up in conversations.
19. I have no fear of giving a speech.
20. Certain parts of my body feel very tense and rigid while giving a speech.

21. I feel relaxed while giving a speech.
22. My thoughts become confused and jumbled when I am giving a speech.
23. I face the prospect of giving a speech with confidence.
24. While giving a speech I get so nervous, I forget facts I really know.

Note. Four subscale scores and a total apprehension score are calculated as follows:
Group = 18 − (1) + (2) − (3) + (4) − (5) + (6)
Meeting = 18 − (7) = (8) + (9) − (10) − (11) + (12)
Dyadic = 18 − (13) + (14) − (15) + (16) + (17) − (18)
Public = 18 + (19) − (20) + (21) − (22) + (23) − (24)
Overall CA = Group + Meeting + Dyadic + Public
Source: McCroskey (1982a)

References

Allen, J., Richmond, V.P., & McCroskey, J.C. (1984). Communication and the chiropractic profession, Part I. *Journal of Chiropractic, 21,* 25–30.

Beatty, M. (1984). Physiological assessment. In J.A. Daly and J.C. McCroskey (Eds.), *Avoiding communication* (pp. 81–94). Beverly Hills, CA: Sage.

Berger, B.A., Baldwin, H.J., McCroskey, J.C., & Richmond, V.P. (1983). Communication apprehension in pharmacy students: A national study. *American Journal of Pharmaceutical Education, 47,* 95–102.

Borkovec, T.D., Stone, N.M., O'Brien, G.T., & Kaloupek, D.G. (1974). Evaluation of a clinically relevant target behavior for analog outcome research. *Behavior Therapy, 5,* 503–513.

Buss, A. H. (1980). *Self-consciousness and social anxiety.* San Francisco, CA: Freeman.

Cacioppo, J.T., Glass, C.R., & Merluzzi, T.V. (1979). Self-statements and self-evaluations: A cognitive-response analysis of heterosocial anxiety. *Cognitive Therapy and Research, 3,* 249–262.

Cacioppo, J.T., & Petty, R.E. (1981). Social psychological procedures for cognitive response assessment: The thought-listing technique. In T.V. Merluzzi, C.R. Glass, and M. Genest (Eds.), *Cognitive assessment* (pp. 309–42). New York: Guilford.

Cheek, J.M. (1983). *The revised Cheek and Buss shyness scale.* Unpublished manuscript, Wellesley College.

Cheek, J.M., & Busch, C.M. (1981). The influence of shyness on loneliness in a new situation. *Personality and Social Psychology Bulletin, 7,* 572–577.

Cheek, J.M., & Buss, A.H. (1981). Shyness and sociability. *Journal of Personality and Social Psychology, 41,* 330–339.

Cheek, J.M., Carpentieri, A.M., Smith, T.G., Rierdan, J., & Koff, E. (1986).

Adolescent shyness. In W.H. Jones, J.M. Cheek, and S.R. Briggs (Eds.), *Shyness: Perspectives on research and treatment.* New York: Plenum.

Cheek, J.M., & Melchoir, L.A. (1985). *Are shy people narcissistic?* Paper presented at the American Psychological Association, Los Angeles.

Christensen, A., & Arkowitz, H. (1974). Preliminary report on practice dating and feedback as a treatment for college dating problems. *Journal of Counseling Psychology, 21,* 92–95.

Clark, J.V., & Arkowitz, H. (1975). Social anxiety and self-evaluation of interpersonal performance. *Psychological Reports, 36,* 211–221.

Daly, J.A., & McCroskey, J.C. (1984). *Avoiding communication.* Beverly Hills, CA: Sage.

Darwin, C. (1872/1955). *The expression of emotion in man and animals.* New York: Philosophical Library.

Davison, G.C., Robins, C., & Johnson, M.K. (1983). Articulated thoughts during simulated situations: A paradigm for studying cognition in emotion and behavior. *Cognitive Therapy and Research, 7,* 17–40.

Fayer, J.M., McCroskey, J.C., & Richmond, V.P. (1984). Communication apprehension in Puerto Rico and the United States I: Initial comparisons. *Communication, 13,* 49–66.

Fenigstein, A., Scheier, M., & Buss, A.H. (1975). Public and private self-consciousness: Assessment and theory. *Journal of Consulting and Clinical Psychology, 43,* 522–527.

Girodo, M., Dotzenroth, S.E., & Stein, S.J. (1981). Causal attribution bias in shy males. *Cognitive Therapy and Research, 5,* 325–338.

Glass, C.R., & Merluzzi, T.V. (1981). Cognitive assessment of cognitive-evaluative anxiety. In T.V. Merluzzi, C. R. Glass, and M. Genest (Eds.), *Cognitive assessment* (pp. 388–438). New York: Guilford.

Glass, C.R., Merluzzi, T.V., Biever, J.L., & Larsen, K.H. (1982). Cognitive assessment of social anxiety: Development and validation of a self-statement questionnaire. *Cognitive Therapy and Research, 6,* 37–56.

Goldfried, M.R., & Sobocinski, D. (1975). Effect of irrational beliefs on emotional arousal. *Journal of Consulting and Clinical Psychology, 43,* 504–510.

Greenberg, J., Pyszczynski, T., & Stine, P. (1985). Social anxiety and expectation of future interaction as determinants of favorability of self-presentation. *Journal of Research in Personality, 19,* 1–11.

Haemmerlie, F.D., & Montgomery, R.L. (1982). Self-perception theory and unobtrusively biased interactions: A treatment for heterosocial anxiety. *Journal of Counseling Psychology, 29,* 362–370.

Izard, C., & Hyson, M.C. (1986). Shyness as a discrete emotion, In W.H. Jones, J.M. Cheek, and S.R. Briggs (Eds.), *Shyness: Perspectives on research and treatment.* New York: Plenum.

Jennings, S.R. (1985). *The relationship of personality factors to social anxiety and disaffiliation.* Unpublished doctoral dissertation, University of Texas.

Jones, W.H., & Briggs, S.R. (1986). *Manual for the Social Reticence Scale.* Palo Alto, CA: Consulting Psychologists Press.

Jones, W.H., Briggs, S.R., & Smith, T.G. (1986). Shyness: Conceptualization and measurement. *Journal of Personality and Social Psychology, 51,* 629–639.

Jones, W.H., Cheek, J.M., & Briggs, S.R. (Eds.) (1986). *Shyness: Perspectives on research and treatment.* New York: Plenum.

Jones, W.H., & Russell, D. (1982). The social reticence scale: An objective measure of shyness. *Journal of Personality Assessment, 46,* 629–631.

Lacey, J.L. (1956). The evaluation of autonomic responses: Toward a general solution. *Annals of the New York Academy of Sciences, 67,* 125–164.

Leary, M.R. (1980). *The social psychology of shyness: Testing a self-presentational model.* Unpublished doctoral dissertation, University of Florida.

Leary, M.R. (1982a). Social anxiety. In L. Wheeler (Ed.), *Review of personality and social psychology* (Vol. 3). Beverly Hills, CA: Sage.

Leary, M.R. (1982b). *Problems with the construct and measurement of social anxiety.* In M. Leary (Chair), Recent advances in social anxiety. Symposium presented at the American Psychological Association, Washington, D.C.

Leary, M.R. (1983a). *Understanding social anxiety: Social, personality, and clinical perspectives.* Beverly Hills, CA: Sage.

Leary, M.R. (1983b). The conceptual distinctions are important: Another look at communication apprehension and related constructs. *Human Communication Research, 10,* 305–312.

Leary, M.R. (1983c). Social anxiousness: The construct and its measurement. *Journal of Personality Assessment, 47,* 66–75.

Leary, M.R. (1983d). A brief version of the Fear of Negative Evaluation Scale. *Personality and Social Psychology Bulletin, 9,* 371–376.

Leary, M.R. (1986a). Affective and behavioral components of shyness: Implications for theory, measurement, and research. In W.H. Jones, J.M. Cheek, and S.R. Briggs (Eds.), *Shyness: Perspectives on research and treatment.* New York: Plenum.

Leary, M.R. (1986b). The impact of interactional impediments on social anxiety and self-presentation. *Journal of Experimental Social Psychology, 22,* 122–135.

Leary, M.R., & Atherton, S.C. (1986). Self-efficacy, anxiety, and inhibition in interpersonal encounters. *Journal of Social and Clinical Psychology, 4,* 256–267.

Leary, M.R., Atherton, S.C., Hill, S., & Hur, C. (1986). Attributional mediators of social inhibition and avoidance. *Journal of Personality, 54,* 188–200.

Leary, M.R., Barnes, B.D., & Griebel, C. (1986). Cognitive, affective, and attributional effects of potential threats to self-esteem. *Journal of Social and Clinical Psychology, 4,* 461–474.

Leary, M.R., Knight, P.D., & Johnson, D.A. (1987). Social anxiety and dyadic conversation: A verbal response analysis. *Journal of Social and Clinical Psychology, 5,* 34–50.

Martin, B. (1961). The assessment of anxiety by physiological behavioral measures. *Psychological Bulletin, 58,* 234–255.

McCroskey, J.C. (1970). Measures of communication-bound anxiety. *Speech Monographs, 37,* 269–277.

McCroskey, J.C. (1976). *Alternative measures of communication apprehension.* Unpublished manuscript, West Virginia University.

McCroskey, J.C. (1977). Oral communication apprehension: A summary of recent theory and research. *Human Communication Research, 4,* 78–96.

McCroskey, J.C. (1982a). *An introduction to rhetorical communication* (4th ed.). Englewood Cliffs, NJ: Prentice-Hall.

McCroskey, J.C. (1982b). Oral communication apprehension: A reconceptualization. *Communication Yearbook, 6,* 136–170.

McCroskey, J.C., & Beatty, M.J. (1984). Communication apprehension and accumulated communication state anxiety experiences: A research note. *Communication Monographs, 51,* 79–84.

McCroskey, J.C., Beatty, M.J., Kearney, P., & Plax, T.G. (1985). The content validity of the PRCA-24 as a measure of communication apprehension across communication contexts. *Communication Quarterly, 33,* 165–173.

Miller, L.C., Berg, J.H., & Archer, R.L. (1983). Openers: Individuals who elicit intimate self-disclosure. *Journal of Personality and Social Psychology, 44,* 1234–1244.

Miller, R.S. (1985). *The nature of embarrassability: Correlates and sex differences.* Paper presented at the American Psychological Association, Los Angeles.

Miller, R.S. (1986). Embarrassment: Causes and consequences. In W.H. Jones, J.M. Cheek, and S.R. Briggs (Eds.), *Shyness: Perspectives on research and treatment.* New York: Plenum.

Miller, W.R., & Arkowitz, H. (1977). Anxiety and perceived causation in social success and failure experiences: Disconfirmation of an attribution hypothesis. *Journal of Abnormal Psychology, 36,* 665–668.

Modigliani, A. (1968). Embarrassment and embarrassability, *Sociometry, 31,* 313–326.

Natale, M., Entin, E., & Jaffe, J. (1979). Vocal interruptions in dyadic conversation as a function of speech and social anxiety. *Journal of Personality and Social Psychology, 37,* 865–878.

O'Banion, K., & Arkowitz, H. (1977). Social anxiety and selective memory for affective information about the self. *Social Behavior and Personality, 5,* 321–328.

Patterson, M.L., & Strauss, M.E. (1972). An examination of the discriminant validity of the social avoidance and distress scale. *Journal of Consulting and Clinical Psychology, 39,* 1969.

Petty, R.E., & Cacioppo, J.T. (1977). Forewarning, cognitive responding, and resistance to persuasion. *Journal of Personality and Social Psychology, 35,* 645–655.

Porter, D.T. (1979). Communication apprehension: Communication's latest artifact? *Communication Yearbook, 3,* 241–259.

Rehm, L.P., & Marston, A.R. (1968). Reduction of social anxiety through modification of self-reinforcement. *Journal of Consulting and Clinical Psychology, 32,* 565–574.

Schlenker, B.R., & Leary, M.R. (1982). Social anxiety and self-presentation: A conceptualization and model. *Psychological Bulletin, 92,* 641–669.

Schlenker, B.R., & Leary, M.R. (1985). Social anxiety and communication about the self. *Journal of Language and Social Psychology, 4,* 171–192.

Smith, T.W., Ingram, R.E., & Brehm, S.S. (1983). Social anxiety, anxious self-preoccupation, and recall of self-relevant information. *Journal of Personality and Social Psychology, 44,* 1276–1283.

Spielberger, C.D. (Ed.) (1966). *Anxiety and behavior.* New York: Academic Press.

Steffen, J.J., & Redden, J. (1977). Assessment of social competence in an evaluation-interaction analogue. *Human Communication Research, 4,* 30–37.

Tarico, V.S., Van Velzen, D.R., & Altmaier, E.M. (1984). *A comparison of thought-listing rating methods.* Unpublished manuscript, University of Iowa.

Watson, D., & Friend, R. (1969). Measurement of social-evaluative anxiety. *Journal of Consulting and Clinical Psychology, 33,* 448–457.

Wilder, J. (1957). The law of initial value in neurology and psychiatry: Facts and problems. *Journal of Nervous and Mental Disorders, 125,* 73–86.

Zimbardo, P.G. (1977). *Shyness.* New York: Jove.

Zuckerman, M. (1960). The development of an Affect Anxiety Check List for the measurement of anxiety. *Journal of Consulting Psychology, 24,* 457–462.

Author Index

Subject Index

/